Sex Trafficking in the United States

Sex Trafficking in the United States

Theory, Research, Policy, and Practice

ANDREA J. NICHOLS

Columbia University Press   *New York*

Columbia University Press
Publishers Since 1893
New York   Chichester, West Sussex
cup.columbia.edu
Copyright © 2016 Columbia University Press

Library of Congress Cataloging-in-Publication Data
Names: Nichols, Andrea J., author.
Title: Sex trafficking in the United States : theory, research, policy,
and practice / Andrea J. Nichols.
Description: New York : Columbia University Press, [2016] |
Includes bibliographical references and index.
Identifiers: LCCN 2016006295 | ISBN 9780231172622 (cloth : alk. paper) |
ISBN 9780231172639 (pbk. : alk. paper) | ISBN 9780231542364 (e-book)
Subjects: LCSH: Human trafficking—United States. | Prostitution—United States. |
Sex crimes—United States.
Classification: LCC HQ281 .N526 2016 | DDC 306.3/620973—dc23
LC record available at http://lccn.loc.gov/2016006295

Columbia University Press books are printed on permanent
and durable acid-free paper.
Printed in the United States of America

Cover design: Jordan Wannemacher

Contents

vii

Contents

Sex Trafficking in the United States

Part I

Contemporary Debates of Theory, Research, and Policy

Sex Trafficking

An Introduction

In 2012 Larry Stinson was found guilty of trafficking three women on the website *Kansas City Escort*. Police uncovered the case in a sting operation by searching through suspicious ads posted on the website. One of the trafficked women reported to law enforcement that she first met Stinson on Facebook and soon formed an intimate relationship with him. Within weeks of their newly formed relationship, Stinson said that he would provide her with food, clothing, and shelter if she worked for him selling sex. She indicated that soon after Stinson attempted to strike this bargain, she was forced to sell sex while Stinson kept her earnings, beat her when she tried to run away, and was physically abusive to her and the other young women under his control. She reported that he psychologically intimidated her as well by routinely displaying firearms, and stated that Stinson even beat one of the other women into unconsciousness. Upon further investigation it was found that Stinson had recruited multiple women into his prostitution ring through Facebook. Another woman had known Stinson in high school and came into contact with him on Facebook, where she disclosed that she was in serious financial straits. Stinson told her that he knew of a job opportunity where she could make a lot of money quickly. She agreed to meet with him and was soon exploited, as he confiscated the money he initially enticed her with. As the investigation of Stinson progressed, yet another woman was found to be under Stinson's control. She was first involved in a romantic relationship with Stinson and then began selling sex for him. At first she split her earnings with him, but the business arrangement quickly turned coercive. She reported that she was forced to sell sex even when she complained of pain, and that he held a gun to her head when she tried to run away. She described being beaten, taken across state lines, and coerced into recruiting others on Facebook for Stinson's prostitution ring. "He said his goal was to have the entire front page of an escort section of a webpage with 'his girls.'"[1] Stinson pled guilty to a federal sex trafficking charge and was sentenced to 120 months in federal prison.

Cases like this are all too familiar to social service providers across the United States, including those who work with sex trafficking survivors, commercially sexually exploited youth, or sex workers seeking assistance. Such cases are also becoming more familiar to the public. In recent years sex trafficking has gained visibility in the United States through increased media coverage, political support, legislative accomplishments, expansion of social services for sex trafficking survivors, and the increased number of community antitrafficking activist organizations. Sex trafficking is not a new phenomenon, but the process of redefining sex trafficking through key legislation has helped bring this problem to heightened public and political attention.

Defining Sex Trafficking: Key Legislation

According to the UN Protocol to Prevent, Suppress, and Punish Trafficking in Persons, commonly referred to as the Palermo Protocol, Article 3, paragraph (a), trafficking is defined as

> the recruitment, transportation, transfer, harbouring or receipt of persons, by means of the threat or use of force or other forms of coercion, of abduction, of fraud, of deception, of the abuse of power or of a position of vulnerability or of the giving or receiving of payments or benefits to achieve the consent of a person having control over another person, for the purpose of exploitation. Exploitation shall include, at a minimum, the exploitation of the prostitution of others or other forms of sexual exploitation, forced labour or services, slavery or practices similar to slavery, servitude or the removal of organs.
>
> (United Nations 2004, 42)

The Palermo Protocol was first developed in 2000, in part due to renewed interest in combating violence against women in the international arena and in part based on efforts to address organized crime. Sex trafficking, as a form of both organized crime and violence against women, is included within the UN definition of human trafficking. The definition maintains a wide scope in its use of general and neutral language, conceptualizing human trafficking as inclusive of male, female, adult, or child trafficking victims, among others. This definition also includes a variety of forms of trafficking as well, such as sex trafficking, labor trafficking, servitude, and organ trafficking. The United States and Argentina were largely responsible for drafting the protocol, which became voluntary international law in 2000 (Stolz 2005). Rather than a law or set of laws that all nations are required to adhere to, voluntary international law lays the foundation for nations to develop their own laws. Accordingly, following the debut of the Palermo Protocol, various nations then partnered as signatories, and many ratified this legislation and drafted their own national legislation.

Drawing from the Palermo Protocol, the United States developed federal legislation, the Trafficking Victims Protection Act (TVPA), the same year. According to the TVPA, a severe form of trafficking is currently defined as

a) A commercial sex act induced by force, fraud, or coercion, or in which the person induced to perform such act has not attained 18 years of age; or

b) the recruitment, harboring, transportation, provision, or obtaining of a person for labor or services, through the use of force, fraud, or coercion for the purpose of subjection to involuntary servitude, peonage, debt bondage, or slavery.[2]

The TVPA largely aimed to address both labor and sex trafficking in the United States. Section 8a primarily addresses sex trafficking, whereas section 8b is mainly used to address labor trafficking. Like the Palermo Protocol, the definition of trafficking is intentionally broad in outlining who could be considered a potential victim. Sex trafficked people in the United States can be noncitizens or U.S. citizens, adults or minors, women or men, boys or girls, or those of any gender identity. However, the bulk of the research suggests that the majority of sex trafficked people identified in the United States are women and girls, and are U.S. citizens (Farrell et al. 2012; Hepburn and Simon 2013; Martin et al. 2014; Raphael, Reichert, and

Powers 2010; Reid 2011; Smith, Vardaman, and Snow 2009). While prostitution of minors and sexual exploitation of adults through coercive means has existed throughout history, the TVPA redefined them as sex trafficking. This new definition indicates that the United States views sexual commerce under these circumstances as crimes and takes them seriously. The TVPA is U.S. federal legislation, yet the definition that it provides is interpreted and implemented differently in various sites. Every state has now criminalized trafficking and created its own sex trafficking laws and policing protocols; however, the majority of sex trafficking cases are referred to federal prosecutors and are investigated and prosecuted on a federal level (Clawson, Dutch, and Cummings 2006; Clawson et al. 2008; Farrell et al. 2012). International, federal, and state antitrafficking legislation as well as prosecution, sentencing, and law enforcement are discussed in depth in chapter 9.

Defining Sex Trafficking: Common Misconceptions

Smuggling, Migration, and Sex Trafficking

Despite the fifteen-year-old legal definition provided in the TVPA, there remain some common misconceptions about the way sex trafficking is defined by researchers, law enforcement, social service providers, and the general public. First, one common misconception is that sex trafficking, smuggling, and migration for the purposes of sex work are synonymous. Sex trafficking is distinct from both smuggling and migration. Sex trafficking is by law viewed as a crime against an individual in which a commercial sex act is prompted through the use of force, fraud, or coercion, or in which the individual involved in the sex act is a minor. In terms of consent, there is either coerced consent or no consent to commercial sex acts or, if the survivor is a minor, the individual cannot legally consent to sex acts. Sex trafficked persons, under federal law, are labeled as victims.

In contrast, smuggling is legally viewed as a "crime" against the United States. Smuggling can be defined as the facilitated "illegal" entry of an individual from one country into another. Essentially, smuggling is an unauthorized border crossing. In terms of consent, there is no coercion in a smuggling case; the individual willingly consented to illegally enter the country with the assistance of the "smuggler" and so is not a victim in the eyes of the law. While smuggling is distinct from trafficking, it is important to note that a smuggling situation can develop into a sex trafficking situation. Accordingly, there is some overlap between smuggling and trafficking cases in such circumstances. For example, individuals may agree to be smuggled into another country because they are seeking a better life and expecting to gain employment in domestic work, nail salons, restaurants, bars, agricultural labor, or massage parlors but may then experience subsequent exploitation through forced or coerced commercial sex acts.

Migration is also distinct from smuggling and trafficking. Migration simply refers to movement from one region to another. Migration can be legal and voluntary, or illegal and voluntary (smuggling), or illegal and involuntary (such as in a trafficking situation). A majority of trafficking survivors in the United States who are originally from other nations first migrate to the United States legally with work visas, often with false promises of legitimate employment, and are exploited after their arrival (Hepburn and Simon 2013). For example, Alex "Cowboy" Campbell was convicted of trafficking four women from Belarus and Ukraine who legally entered the United States but did not yet have legal status as U.S. citizens.[3] Campbell recruited the women to work in his spa in Mount Prospect, Illinois, and they were subsequently forced into Campbell's sex trafficking ring. Campbell used "bait and switch" tactics—prosecutors contend that Campbell recruited the women with massage parlor jobs and offered them a place to live and assistance with the immigration process. Campbell then confiscated their passports, immigration papers, and other identification documents, regularly beat and raped them, forced them into the commercial sex industry, and kept most of their earnings. He was found to have victimized twenty other women under similar circumstances. Campbell is perhaps best known for being one of the few traffickers to receive a life sentence. According to the judge, this stringent sentence was delivered largely because Campbell branded the trafficked women with tattoos that marked their obedience to him.

Sex trafficked people originating from outside of the United States may more frequently come from Mexico, Honduras, Guatemala, and other neighboring middle-income and low-income nations as well as Southeast Asia and Eastern Europe (Heil 2012; Smith, Vardaman, and Snow 2009; U.S. Department of State 2014). They seek better job opportunities in wealthier nations, like the United States, as willing migrants or as those who are voluntarily smuggled into the country but may then find themselves involved in a sex trafficking situation. Or survivors may be trafficked first within another nation, and then retrafficked into the United States (Kara 2010). According to Interpol, victims are trafficked internationally into the United States by plane, boat, or unidentified means. Interpol reported evidence in the early 2000s that some survivors traveled first to South Africa, acquired false identification documents, and then entered into the United States through international airports. Interpol also reported that individuals have been trafficked into the United States by ships crossing the Pacific Ocean to the United States. Canadian authorities found cargo vessels trafficking victims from Southeast Asia who attempted to enter the United States by way of Vancouver, British Columbia (Richard 2000). There is recent evidence of Somali women and Vietnamese women and children who have been trafficked through the Canadian border into Minnesota.[4] Primary countries of origin reported by the U.S. Department of State in 2010 were the Dominican Republic, El Salvador, Haiti, Honduras, India, Mexico, the Philippines, and Thailand, although this data does not differentiate between labor and sex trafficking. The U.S. Department of State (2014) reported that those who were internationally trafficked in 2013 most frequently came from Mexico, the Philippines, Thailand, India, Honduras, Guatemala, and El Salvador. The U.S. Department of State (2012) reported that people trafficked internationally are arriving from Central or South America and are entering the United States through the Mexican border.[5] Yet the concept of sex trafficked people as only those from other countries trafficked into the United States is problematic because it ignores the fact that sex trafficked persons can also be, and more frequently are, U.S. citizens.[6]

Importantly, crossing national boundaries or state lines is a not necessary criterion for a situation to be labeled as sex trafficking. Research shows that U.S. citizens compose the majority of sex trafficked people in the United States (Farrell et al. 2012; Martin et al. 2014; Polaris Project 2014a; Smith, Vardaman, and Snow 2009; U.S. Department of State 2014).[7] In reviewing prosecuted cases of sex trafficking across the districts with the highest prosecution rates, Amy Farrell and colleagues (2012) found 81% of sex trafficking survivors were U.S. citizens. Similarly, the Polaris Project found in an analysis of sex trafficking cases from 2007 to 2012 that traffickers were most frequently male U.S. citizens working as pimps with young adult and minor females, and 60% of sex trafficking cases involved U.S. citizens (Polaris Project 2013). Smuggling involves transportation, and trafficking involves exploitation based upon the use of force, fraud, coercion, or situations involving minors (Hepburn and Simon 2013). Sex trafficking is not only an issue of nationality, and movement is not required. Trafficking of U.S. citizens is referred to as domestic trafficking. In cases involving minors, the term "domestic minor sex trafficking," or DMST, is commonly used.

Physical Restraint

A second common misconception of sex trafficking is that sex trafficking victims must experience physical restraint. While restricted physical movement may be present, it is not a necessary criterion. Most sex trafficked people do have freedom of physical movement. Their bondage to their trafficker most often involves psychological abuses, exploitation of vulnerability, and other elements of coercive control, as discussed in depth in chapter 5. The international and national discourse on sex trafficking often uses the terminology of modern-day slavery, and awareness campaigns will frequently include images of women and girls in chains. While the chains are largely intended to be symbolic, and while there are cases that do involve chains or other forms of physical restraint, these images invoke physical restraint as typical in sex trafficking cases (Heil and Nichols 2015; Hoyle, Bosworth, and Dempsey 2011). For example, the well-publicized case of Ariel Castro involved the kidnapping and routine rape of three young women who were held captive in Castro's home in Ohio for more than a decade and were often physically restrained. This is a case that could be framed as sex trafficking because it meets the criteria of section 103b of the TVPA—the individuals were obtained for sexual services through the use of force and coercion and for the purpose of involuntary subjection to involuntary sexual servitude or sexual slavery. Yet the majority of sex trafficked individuals are not physically restrained (Heil and Nichols 2015; Hoyle, Bosworth, and Dempsey 2011). Even in the Castro case, the women were not under physical restraint at all times; rather, it was the fear of physical violence and elements of coercive control that kept these women captive for so long.

In more typical cases of sex trafficking in the United States, sex trafficked girls are psychologically attached to their traffickers through intimate relationships (Lloyd 2012; Heil and Nichols 2015; Martin et al. 2014; Polaris Project 2014a; Smith, Vardaman, and Snow 2009).[8] In such cases, this emotional bond is the intended result of a pimp's initial professions of love and affection. Pimps first pose as a boyfriend to gain the trust and love of usually younger girls and then talk the girls into selling sex for them. Jody Raphael and Brenda Myers-Powell (2010) found in their study of trafficked women and girls in Chicago that the majority were pimped by such "boyfriends," and forced or coerced prostitution was one element of abuse among a variety of physical and psychological abuses. In addition, Joan A. Reid (2010) stated that trafficked girls maintain trauma bonds with their traffickers, and it is primarily this psychological bond that keeps girls attached to their pimps. In other cases psychological controls go beyond the coercive control typical in cases of co-occurring intimate partner violence and sex trafficking. In a case in Florida, a girl from Guatemala was kept captive not by locks and chains but by her cultural and religious belief that her trafficker owned her soul, as he possessed a necklace with a lock of her hair encapsulated in it (Heil 2012). Another common type of sex trafficking is survival sex, in which a minor is engaged in the commercial sex industry due to lack of choices and a need for survival—physical restraints are not present. Accordingly, while some survivors of sex trafficking do experience physical restraint, it is not typical nor is it a requirement for classification as sex trafficking.

Prostitution and Choice

A third misconception of sex trafficking is that if minors "choose" involvement in the commercial sex industry, they are consequently not considered sex trafficking victims. Under the United States TVPA, all minors involved in any form of commercial sex are considered victims, as an individual under the age of 18 cannot legally consent to sex acts. Anyone who purchases sex acts involving a minor is engaging in statutory rape and, in some jurisdictions, may also be viewed as a sex trafficker. Similarly, any individual who "pimps" a minor is legally considered a sex trafficker. Minors, according to the TVPA, are automatically considered victims of a crime whether they "agreed" to a commercial sex act or not. By definition, a commercial sex act includes things other than prostitution, including stripping, pornography, escort, and other sexual services that may not involve sexual intercourse (Heil and Nichols 2015; Hepburn and Simon 2013; Kotrla 2010). As discussed in detail in chapter 9, while the federal law appears to protect minors, in some states minors are still considered criminals for engaging in commercial sex due to state laws or the way sex trafficking laws may be misinterpreted or improperly enforced (Boxill and Richardson 2007; Farrell et al. 2012; Kalergis 2009; Lloyd 2012; Nichols and Heil, 2014).

In addition, adults can also be sex trafficked, yet adults engaged in commercial sex are often labeled as willing sex workers out of the perception that adults "choose" to sell sex (Heil 2012). While some adult women and men choose sex work as an occupation, others are sex trafficked (Dempsey 2011; Weitzer 2010). In any case, when an adult engages in a commercial sex act involving force, fraud, or coercion, the situation fits the legal definition of sex trafficking.

Sex Trafficking Prevalence

The prevalence of sex trafficking in the United States remains unclear and is the subject of heated debate. Research examining sex trafficking prevalence largely draws from cases reported to or uncovered by law enforcement, prosecuted cases, and reports from social service agencies (Banks and Kyckelhahn 2011; Clawson, Dutch, and Cummings 2006; Clawson et al. 2008; Farrell et al. 2012). In terms of reported cases, about 1,000 survivors a year are officially detected and recognized in the United States justice system. The Department of Justice reported that 2,515 suspected incidents of human trafficking were investigated between January 2008 and June 2010, of which 80% were identified as sex trafficking cases (Banks and Kyckelhahn 2011). Similarly, between 2007 and 2008 the Human Trafficking Reporting System indicated 1,020 cases of sex trafficking in the United States (Kyckelhahn et al. 2009). Likewise, in 2009 the National Human Trafficking Resource Center (NHTRC) showed 986 reported cases of trafficking, and about 60% of these were sex trafficking cases. In 2014 the NHTRC and BeFree Textline, both national hotlines monitored by the Polaris Project, reported 1,611 potential sex trafficking situations and 292 direct calls from survivors.

In terms of prosecuted cases, in 2000, a year following TVPA, only four cases of human trafficking were federally prosecuted. This was expected, as the legislation had just been introduced, and the new definition of sex trafficking resulted in a "new" charge. Such cases had previously been prosecuted under other charges, and the low number suggests prosecutors continued to charge sex trafficking as other crimes, such as rape, pimping, pandering, enticement of a minor into prostitution, child pornography, or, infrequently, under the Mann Act. However, over time federal prosecutors began using the sex trafficking charge under the TVPA. In 2005, 35 sex trafficking cases were federally prosecuted (Clawson et al. 2008). In 2010 there were 71 successfully prosecuted sex trafficking cases (Hepburn and Simon 2013). In 2011 the Department of Justice reported a total of 105 prosecuted sex trafficking cases. Farrell and colleagues (2012) maintained that in 2012 federal prosecutors prosecuted 162 defendants in sex trafficking cases. Most recently the U.S. Department of State (2014) reported initiating 161 trafficking cases with 222 defendants engaged in sex trafficking, securing 113 sex trafficking convictions. These figures represent federal prosecutions, but sex trafficking can also be prosecuted on a state level.

Importantly, in the recent past, states did not have to report state sex trafficking convictions to the federal government. State sex trafficking convictions were first reported in 2013 under stipulations of the 2008 TVPA reauthorization act, but the hard data is not yet available. Researchers report that state-level prosecutions are relatively low but rising (Farrell et al. 2012). Like federal prosecutors in the time immediately following the TVPA, state prosecutors continue to prosecute sex trafficking cases as other crimes that they are more familiar with prosecuting, such as rape, conspiracy to prostitute a minor, or enticement of a child into prostitution (Clawson et al. 2008; Farrell et al. 2012). Farrell and colleagues noted that in 2011 the number of convictions under state-trafficking laws was in the dozens, at least as reported to the federal government. By 2014 this number was "in the hundreds," indicating increased development and use of state law (U.S. Department of State 2014).

In sum, with shifts in legislation and the way sex trafficking is defined, more cases are coming forward for prosecution (Hopper 2004).[9] However, estimating sex trafficking prevalence based on prosecuted cases is problematic, and prosecution rates remain low for a variety of reasons. In particular, researchers note that many cases are not prosecuted or are prosecuted as other crimes. Prosecutors will prosecute a case under a charge that they feel they can win (Clawson et al. 2008; Farrell et al. 2012; Nichols and Heil 2014). If a federal prosecutor believes the case will be difficult to win, the case is then kicked back to the state level and will likely be prosecuted as another crime. Prosecutors are reluctant to take cases in which there is insufficient evidence or when the survivor does not want to testify (Farrell et al. 2012; Nichols and Heil 2014).

Further, sex trafficking is often unreported, misreported, or is simply not identified. A wide body of research reveals the many barriers and challenges to identifying and reporting sex trafficking cases (Goodey 2008; Heil 2012; Kara 2010; Kotrla 2010; Nichols and Heil 2014). Traffickers take great measures to assure nondetection through the use of hidden venues or venues within insular communities (Nichols and Heil 2014). They use interstate circuits and constant movement paired with psychological and physical abuse of their victims (Nichols and Heil 2014; Smith, Vardaman, and Snow 2009; Williamson and Prior 2009). Police may misidentify and misreport the crime as prostitution, a sex offense, domestic violence, or illegal immigration (Heil 2012; Hopper 2004; Nichols and Heil 2014; Raphael and Myers-Powell 2010). Survivors may not want to report their victimization. Sex trafficked people from other countries may fear deportation and law enforcement in a foreign country and may also fear their own arrest for undocumented immigration or involvement in a crime (Heil 2012; Hopper 2004). Domestically and internationally trafficked people may fear traffickers' reprisals—they or their family members may be threatened with violence. Domestically trafficked women and girls, in particular, may not want to report their victimization because of trauma bonds and love for their trafficker (Lloyd 2012; Reid 2010). Moreover, domestically trafficked survivors may have a history of negative interactions with law enforcement or a record of prostitution. They may consequently fear arrest and charges of prostitution and so avoid contact with the justice system. In sum, due to underreporting, underprosecution, and underdetection of sex trafficking, its prevalence remains difficult to estimate (Farrell et al. 2012; Goodey 2008; Hepburn and Simon 2010; Hopper 2004; Kotrla 2010; Reid 2010).

As a result, researchers have attempted to estimate sex trafficking prevalence while considering barriers to identification, prosecution, and reporting. The U.S. Department of State estimated there were 15,000–18,000 sex trafficking victims in 2012. Yet the Central Intelligence Agency estimates 50,000 victims are trafficked for the purposes of commercial sexual exploitation in the United States annually (Hepburn and Simon 2013). Average estimates from social service providers suggest 100,000–300,000 each year (Polaris Project 2014b).[10] According to End Child Prostitution Child Pornography and Trafficking of Children for Sexual Purposes (ECPAT), as many as 300,000 children may be at risk of sexual exploitation in the

United States annually. Some government reports and advocacy organizations offer no explanation of how such estimates were conceived. In other instances researchers have drawn estimates from economic modeling, meta-analysis, regionally based estimates, or surveys of police, prosecutors, and victim service providers (Estes and Weiner 2001; Curtis et al. 2008; Farrell et al. 2010; Martin et al. 2014). The consensus among experts is that a valid estimate is impossible to attain due to the methodological challenges associated with identifying a hidden and vulnerable population, lack of accurate reporting, and lack of knowledge among survey respondents, such as police, in studies examining sex trafficking (Curtis et al. 2008; Nichols and Heil 2014).

One could form a conservative estimate by using data from social service provider organizations. In a study of Kansas City, reports from social services provider Veronica's Voice identified 140 child sex trafficking survivors that the organization served between 2000 and 2009 (Wade 2008). This averages out to 15.5 DMST survivors a year. At an extremely conservative estimate of child sex trafficking, one could multiply 15.5 by the number of major U.S. cities (which would not include small cities or rural areas—large tracts of geographic territory). At the time of this writing, there were thirty-eight cities with populations over a quarter million. This averages out to 589 child sex trafficking victims a year in an admittedly unreliably low estimate, as it does not account for the likelihood of higher rates of sex trafficking in cities larger than Kansas City, nor does it include cities smaller than 250,000. This number also only includes child victims. Trafficking of adults is harder to estimate because their exposure to force, fraud, or coercion is often unknown, but minors' victimization is inherent in the definition of the TVPA. Yet this number could easily be doubled, as identified adult survivors compose 55% of sex trafficking survivors (U.S. Department of State, 2013). Also note that this is just one organization in one city. For perspective, an organization in Nevada, WestCare Nevada, reported providing services to 400 child sex trafficking survivors in 2007 (Kennedy and Pucci 2007). Multiplying this number by the number of major cities yields an estimate of 15,200 child sex trafficking survivors, similar to the estimate currently claimed by the U.S. Department of State. Yet there are currently thirty cities with populations even larger than Las Vegas. Also, note this estimate only includes child survivors and is only based on identified cases reported to one organization in the city. Consequently, estimates of sex trafficking that account for adults, unreported cases, cases reported to other organizations, cities with populations under a quarter million, and potentially larger numbers of trafficking victims in larger cities would be inarguably, definitively higher. Such estimates indicate that the Department of State estimate of 15,000 a year is conservative. The prevalence of sex trafficking remains unclear, and any estimate should be regarded with caution. The growth rate is difficult to measure as well.

The growth rate of sex trafficking in the United States is unknown, with some researchers indicating that the growth rate is "relatively flat" in North America more generally (Kara 2010, 17), while others suggest it is a rapidly increasing crime. Those who argue that the growth rate is flat typically use the number of recently reported or prosecuted cases to draw such conclusions. Analyzing growth based on the number of reported or prosecuted cases is problematic because there are a number of factors that influence prosecution and reporting rates, as previously discussed. Still other researchers point to the increased number of hotline calls as an indicator of sex trafficking as a growing crime. The NHTRC reported a 259% increase in hotline calls between 2008 and 2012. Some of these calls are unrelated to reporting cases or accessing services, such as individuals requesting information about human trafficking. Yet social service providers also report growing demand for services (Polaris Project 2014b). These factors may be an artifact of growing awareness and better identification of sex trafficking or could indeed represent sex trafficking as an increasingly occurring crime.

In sum, it is difficult to estimate both the number of sex trafficking survivors and the relative growth of the problem. However, multiple studies show that social service providers, police, and prosecutors report the number of sex trafficked people in need of services, particularly safe shelter, exceeds the number of available services (Clawson et al. 2008; Farrell et al. 2012). As Linda Smith, Samantha Healy Vardaman, and Melissa A. Snow (2009, 11) state, based on a study of DMST in ten U.S. cities, "the numbers demonstrate with certainty that domestic minor sex trafficking is occurring and in sufficiently sizable numbers to merit the public's and the community leadership's prioritization in fighting the crime of domestic minor sex trafficking." The importance of establishing prevalence is largely based upon whether the number of victims/survivors justifies available funding streams. The prevalence of intimate partner violence was unknown at the beginnings of the 1970s battered women's movement because it was also a hidden problem relegated to the private sphere (Nichols 2014a). Similar to sex trafficking, the demand for services exceeded the availability. Because of the high demand for services, increased funding streams expanded the availability of services, moving from a handful of shelters in the 1970s to more than 800 in the 1980s (Nichols 2014a). Ostensibly, if it is known that the demand for services far exceeds the availability of services, this should serve as a baseline justification for funding and expanding services available to sex trafficked and commercially sexually exploited people (Heil and Nichols 2015).

Supply, Demand, and Profitability

Some researchers contend that market forces guide sex trafficking prevalence (Hughes 2007; Kara 2010; Smith, Vardaman, and Snow 2009) and that the roots of sex trafficking can be understood in economic terms of supply, demand, and profitability (Kara 2010; Kotrla 2010; Smith, Vardaman, and Snow 2009). Traffickers are motivated by profits, and consumers are motivated by demand for prostitution. Many researchers argue that sex trafficking would not exist without demand (Ekberg 2004; Hughes 2007; Kara 2010; Kotrla 2010; Smith, Vardaman, and Snow 2009; Martin et al. 2014). About 10–20% of men in the United States have purchased sex in their lifetime, indicating a demand for prostitution (Shively et al. 2012). Traffickers work to recruit or otherwise coerce survivors into the trade (supply) and then profit by the exchange. The United Nations estimates sex trafficking to be a $15 billion a year business globally. One researcher maintains that sex trafficking yields a 70% net profit on average (Kara 2010). Compared to illegal drugs and arms trafficking, sex trafficking is considered more profitable: sex trafficking produces continuous profits (sex trafficked people can repeatedly sell sex, or be sold and resold, both to clients and other traffickers), whereas arms and drugs are sold and profited from in a single transaction. Additionally, there is less risk involved. A federal prosecutor who took part in an interview-based research study stated, "One of the pimps said he got out of drugs and into prostitution because you could make more money and wouldn't get as much time in jail" (Busch-Armendariz, Nsonwu, and Heffron 2009, 8). Researchers report that serious barriers to identification and prosecution produce a system with relatively little risk for traffickers, despite relatively stringent punishments (Farrell et al. 2012; Heil and Nichols 2014; Hepburn and Simon 2013).

Sex traffickers can receive life sentences in particularly heinous cases, and a mandatory minimum sentence of 10 years can be received for trafficking a minor, 15 years if the child is under the age of 14 (Hepburn and Simon 2013). Yet traffickers take great measures to avoid detection (see chapter 7). For example, to ensure that a transaction cannot be traced to them directly, traffickers coerce survivors into reserving hotel rooms in the survivor's name and on her credit card, and survivors often post their own online ads or ads for the other girls (Farrell et al. 2012; Heil and Nichols 2014). In addition, as discussed previously, such cases are also often reported, charged, and prosecuted as other crimes with a lower sentence.

Trafficking does not entail a regular or predicted salary; a trafficker's annual income depends on the number of survivors engaged in the trafficking enterprise, what their quota is—if they have a quota, and even the operation's location within the United States. The Polaris Project (2014a), a Washington, D.C.–based nonprofit working with survivors of human trafficking conducted an analysis of quotas based on direct client accounts and reported a range of $500–$1,500 per night. One teenage girl was forced to meet quotas of $500/night, seven days a week, and forced to give the money to her trafficker each night. This particular pimp also controlled three other women. Based on these numbers, Polaris Project estimates that "the pimp made $632,000 in one year from four young women and girls" (Polaris Project 2014a). Another study conducted in Chicago found that pimps earned between $150,000 and $500,000 annually, depending on the scale of the operation (Raphael and Myers-Powell 2010). While the "salary" of a trafficker varies, this research suggests the profitability typically exceeds by far the median annual salary of workers, about $26,000, in the United States (Raphael and Myers-Powell 2010; Polaris Project 2014a).

Chapter Summary

This chapter provides an overview of basic dynamics of sex trafficking in the United States. First, the legal definition of sex trafficking in the United States is derived from the Trafficking Victims Protection Act (TVPA). The TVPA draws from the Palermo Protocol, the international antitrafficking legislation drafted in 2000. The TVPA stresses that any sex act induced by force, fraud, or coercion, or which involves a minor, is sex trafficking. This can include domestic victims or victims who are internationally trafficked, adults or minors, and those of any sex or gender identity. The definition of trafficking does not require movement or crossing national, state, or other regional boundaries. Physical restraint is also not a condition required to label a case as sex trafficking. The majority of survivors are tied to their traffickers through psychological elements of coercive control. Second, sex trafficking prevalence is difficult to estimate because many cases go undetected. Survivors may not wish to report their victimization because they anticipate negative responses from law enforcement or their traffickers. Survivors may also be bound to their traffickers psychologically and may not wish to report their trafficker for a variety of related reasons. Reported cases are also limited by the ability of law enforcement to identify sex trafficking cases. Prosecution rates are limited by prosecuting under another charge, nonreporting of state prosecutions, and lack of sufficient evidence and victim cooperation. Due to these issues with prosecution, misreporting, and victim reporting, the prevalence of sex trafficking remains unclear. Finally, sex trafficking is a profitable business, with net earnings that may exceed profits from drug or arms trafficking, depending on the scale of the operation. Sex trafficking is driven by such profits as well as the demand of clients.

Chapter Overviews

The book is organized into three main parts: contemporary debates of theory, research, and policy; dynamics of sex trafficking in the United States; and responses to sex trafficking. Chapter 1 describes "the basics" of sex trafficking in the United States, including legal definitions, common misconceptions, prevalence, and profitability. Chapter 2 examines the politics of sex trafficking from feminist, political, sociological, and criminological perspectives. The feminist theoretical perspectives of sex trafficking examined in this book include radical feminism, liberal feminism, and intersectional feminism. Political perspectives of sex trafficking include the competing neoliberal and abolitionist perspectives. Drawing from the field of criminology, deterrence theory and displacement theory are also described and applied to various aspects of sex trafficking. Sociological perspectives emphasize the role of weak social institutions, weak social safety nets, and identity-based oppression. Pornography, prostitution, legislation related to prostitution, and their relationship to sex trafficking are examined through these theoretical lenses in chapters 3 and 4.

Chapter 5 synthesizes the growing body of work examining sex trafficking survivors in the United States. The chapter emphasizes vulnerabilities to sex trafficking using the intersectional theory highlighted in chapter 2, including race, class, age, sex, gender identity, sexual orientation, immigrant status, and intellectual disability. The role of weak social institutions in facilitating sex trafficking/commercial sexual exploitation (CSE) is detailed as well, such as education systems, family systems, and economic systems. How such factors work in tandem with weak social safety nets to produce increased risk of sex trafficking is then highlighted. Pathways into sex trafficking/CSE and barriers to leaving are also presented.

Chapter 6 begins by investigating the characteristics and backgrounds of pimps and traffickers and the social-environmental influences on trafficking involvement. A typology of trafficking is also offered, delineating the types of sex trafficking present in the United States. This includes various types of pimp-controlled trafficking, international trafficking, familial trafficking, and buyers-as-traffickers. The chapter details the formation of "love" relationships, specifically examining sex trafficking as an extension of intimate partner violence, particularly in cases of DMST. Abduction and fraud are also illustrated as types of trafficking. Survival sex of minors, in which buyers are viewed as traffickers, is examined. Familial trafficking, cases in which parents traffic their children, is also detailed. The chapter concludes with a discussion of the glorification of pimp culture in the United States and its relationship to sex trafficking victimization.

Chapter 7 specifically examines sex trafficking operations. The chapter investigates venues for trafficking such as hotels, truck stops, private parties, the Internet, the streets, escort agencies, and massage parlors as well as the use of interstate circuits in various parts of the United States and international flows that include the Canadian and Mexican borders. The role of technology and trafficking is specifically examined in terms of both recruitment and solicitation. In addition, other trafficking techniques to avoid detection, such as exploitation of the "bottom girl," use of throwaway phones, and other methods are described. The role of organized crime rings, small-scale operations, and individual "entrepreneurs" is also detailed.

Chapter 8 explores the buyers of sex and the relationship between demand, prostitution, and sex trafficking. Characteristics of buyers are examined as well as their motivations to buy sex. The prevalence of purchased sex in the United States and debates about the role of clients implicated in sex trafficking victimization are also detailed. An examination of the benefits and challenges of demand reduction responses concludes the chapter.

In chapter 9 the background and development of federal anti–sex trafficking legislation is described, including a detailed account of the 2000 TVPA and the key components of its reauthorizations in 2003, 2005, 2008, and 2013. In addition, the chapter examines state laws and the ways the laws themselves vary as well as their implementation, related challenges, and relationship to the TVPA. Further, the ways sex trafficking cases are prosecuted, including federal prosecution, state prosecution, and the challenges associated with each are explained in depth. Current challenges to law enforcement are examined as well, including key issues with identification, investigation and reporting, and implementation of the law.

Chapter 10 specifically investigates the practices of those who work with or may come into contact with sex trafficking survivors in the social services sector. The organizations examined include the health care industry, rape and sexual assault services, domestic violence services, child protective services, juvenile facilities, and organizations that explicitly work with sex trafficked and commercially sexually exploited people. Professional practices with survivors, such as trauma informed care, survivor-defined advocacy, survivor-led programs, cultural competency, the stages of change model, and motivational interviewing are explored, along with cognitive processing therapy, eye movement desensitization and reprocessing, and transformational relationships.

Chapter 11 examines grassroots activism and the anti–sex trafficking movement in the United States. Specifically, the chapter delineates antitrafficking activism in the following subsections: grassroots organizations, political activism, media activism, and the activism of international organizations operating in the United States. The chapter begins by describing antitrafficking activism, including the work of survivors, professionals in the legal and social services, and their political and community partners. In addition, the chapter examines the work of other grassroots organizations that emphasize awareness and training for identification, such as in truck stops, travel plazas, train stations, bus stops, airlines, and hotels. The chapter then explores activism in the political arena and the development of legislative accomplishments on the federal and state levels to protect and prevent revictimization of trafficking victims. The presence of international antitrafficking organizations and their impact on antitrafficking efforts in the United States are also described. Last, media organizations who have lent their support to antitrafficking activism, providing news coverage, documentaries, and exposure of antitrafficking activists' efforts, are examined.

Chapter 12 describes the Green Dot initiative, with a "what can you do?" approach. This bystander intervention, first developed to respond to sexual assault and violence against women on college campuses, is applied to sex trafficking and provides responses that the average person can engage in. The chapter also sums up key areas of concern in the previous chapters, providing recommendations for policy and practice regarding social services and the justice system as well as community awareness, outreach and prevention, and suggestions for cultural and societal change.

Use of Terms

There are debates within the academic and practitioner-based communities regarding use of language in the sex trafficking discourse. One point of contention in the antitrafficking movement lies in the use of the labels "victim" or "survivor." In part, the preferred use of certain terms is a manifestation of one's background. Social workers and others in the social services arena typically prefer use of the term "survivor" because it respects the agency, resilience, strength, and survival of trafficked and exploited people. Survivors manage to survive various forms of abuses and trauma, and that resilience should be honored. Survivors also overcome a multitude of barriers to engage in various forms of help-seeking (Curtis et al. 2008).[11] Even though there is victimization, resistance and agency are also important characteristics of survival and of trafficking experiences. In contrast, various members of the justice system including police, prosecutors, detectives, and attorneys tend to prefer the term "victim" because the term "victim" highlights the serious nature of the multiple forms of abuses that are experienced, including various forms of coercive control, and sexual, physical, economic, and psychological abuses. "Victim" is also the language used in the justice system, such as in police and court reports and dispatching. Girls Education and Mentoring Services in New York, one of the best-known programs providing services for young women and girls who have experienced sex trafficking/CSE, illustrates a trajectory from victim to survivor to survivor-leader in their Victim, Survivor, Leader program.[12] Similarly, in this book both terms are used—survivors themselves use both terms, and the audience for this book will likely include a broad spectrum of readers, including those of social and legal services backgrounds.

In addition, outside of the discussion of the definitions of sex trafficking that various ideological groups hold in chapters 2–4, the term "sex trafficking" is used in the rest of the book to refer to the legal definition provided by the TVPA (described earlier) because this is the definition that, in part, shapes the work of social service providers and law enforcement as well as the experiences of survivors. In addition, the term "commercial sexual exploitation" is used to encompass experiences that do not neatly fit into the legal definition. Sex trafficking can take the form of survival sex, which refers to an individual who sells sex for basic necessities such as food, clothing, and shelter. Survival sex is often referred to as a form of CSE because individuals who sell sex to have their basic needs met tend to have few other alternatives, and they are more likely to be easily exploited by pimps and buyers. Exploitation involves taking advantage of a vulnerability, like the lack of basic survival needs, homelessness, addiction, poverty, or disability. In such situations involving a minor, CSE/survival sex is sex trafficking. In the case of adults, force, fraud, or coercion must also be present to be legally termed "sex trafficking." Accordingly, the categorization of CSE is used to describe adults whose vulnerabilities are exploited in commercial sex, with the understanding that similar trauma experiences are present regardless of legal definitions and age designations. At times the book uses a combination of terms, sex trafficking/CSE, because of the overlapping experiences and related psychological and health effects involved in CSE (see chapter 11). The term "sex workers" is used to describe adults who willingly sell or trade sex without force, fraud, coercion, or exploitation present.

Last, the term "buyer" is used to describe those who purchase sex. The terms "client," "customer," "trick," or "John" are commonly used in the extant research. "Buyer" was chosen, somewhat arbitrarily to maintain consistency throughout. In discussing service provision to survivors, such as in chapter 10, survivors are often referred to as "clients" of the social services program. To avoid confusion, the term "buyer" is used for those who purchase sex, instead of "client."

Discussion Questions

1. What are the distinctions between smuggling, migration, and trafficking? In what ways may they be interrelated? Include dynamics of consent, legality, and movement.

2. Where do we get our information about sex trafficking? What are some challenges to estimating sex trafficking prevalence based upon these sources?

3. Is the information in this chapter consistent with what you thought you knew about sex trafficking? Why or why not?

Theoretical Perspectives and the Politics of Sex Trafficking

Theoretical perspectives are often described as general statements about reality or ways of looking at the world. They can also be viewed as "explanations" for social phenomena—they attempt to explain why certain conditions of society exist. In examining social problems like sex trafficking and commercial sexual exploitation, such explanations can be used to guide targeted change, as the explanations may work to uncover the roots of the problem. A long history of theoretical and political debates sets the stage for contemporary antitrafficking efforts. These perspectives on sex trafficking have become highly politicized and continue to guide policy, public perception, and funding streams. This chapter examines the feminist, political, sociological, and criminological perspectives represented in the academic, political, and public discourse, which provide background and context for various aspects of this book. Specifically, the first part of this chapter describes the competing feminist and political perspectives of sexual commerce. Following, sociological and criminological perspectives are explained, illustrating societal and cultural influences of, and responses to, sexual commerce. Sex trafficking is not condoned by any of these ideological groups, but some groups wish to abolish all forms of sexual commerce as a means to eradicate sex trafficking, whereas others wish to preserve sexual commerce while criminalizing sex trafficking. The theoretical and political arguments implicated in these plans of action are detailed below.

Feminist Perspectives

Feminists are those who recognize aspects of sex and gender inequality and work to change them, with the overall aim of equal power, opportunity, and status afforded to women and men (Baumgardner and Richards 2010; Nichols 2014a). While feminists generally share in this aim, various types of feminists may differ in their conceptualizations of sex/gender inequality and ways of eradicating it (Baumgardner and Richards 2010; hooks 2014; Singh 2011). The result has been fragmentation within the feminist movement and theoretical divisions into various types of feminism. Radical feminism, liberal feminism, and intersectional feminism are examined here, all of which vary considerably in their applications to sexual commerce.

Liberal Feminist Perspectives

The liberal feminist perspective explains sex/gender inequality in the context of the conditions that limit or oppress the individual choices of women and girls (Jaggar 1988; Nichols 2014a; Singh 2011; Donovan 2012). Liberal feminism is sometimes referred to as "choice" feminism because its core tenet highlights the individual rights and choices of women (Rich 2010). Consequently, liberal feminism often focuses on the micro level, taking a "bottom-up" approach to eradicating sex/gender inequality with the initial focal point centering on examining individual choice and its relationship to oppression (Singh 2011). Liberal feminists maintain that the social phenomena that restrict individual choices of women should be removed as a measure for eliminating sex/gender inequality.

As liberal feminist perspectives largely center on the individual freedom of women and equality of choice, such perspectives hold that the choice to participate in sexual labor should be present and used if individuals choose. Moreover, liberal feminists maintain that sexual labor-by-choice can be empowering and financially lucrative (Weitzer 2010; Doezema 2001; Liu 2012). Liberal feminists also indicate that the right to engage in sexual commerce challenges notions of oppressive traditional femininity, such as suppressed sexuality of women, and contests traditional notions of monogamy and archaic connotations of the sexual "purity" of women. Because women make up the majority of those in prostitution, state control of prostitution equates state control of women's bodies. The state is generally patriarchal in its disproportionate male representation, so anti-prostitution legislation reflects male domination of women's sexuality and reinforces traditional sexism in women's disempowered sexuality. Liberal feminist perspectives maintain that when the choice to engage in sexual labor is not there, the result is gender inequality by the suppression of a woman's right to do what she wishes with her own body. Because sexual commerce is regarded as a form of labor, liberal feminists prefer the term "sex work" over "prostitution" to describe those who willingly choose to work in the commercial sex industry.

The term "agency" is used in various facets of the social sciences to describe free will. Agency is consequently viewed by liberal feminists primarily in the context of individual choice; individuals express agency when they choose to engage in sex work and are denied agency when they are forced or coerced into sex work. Liberal feminists also view state-imposed restrictions on those who choose to engage in sex work as denying agency because it limits or otherwise oppresses the choices of individuals. In terms of victimization, liberal feminists maintain that victimization occurs when agency is removed and choices are absent. Liberal feminists also note victimization and agency can occur simultaneously; willing sex workers can be victimized by others in the course of their occupation. Agency does not preclude victimization, and victimization does not preclude agency. Sex trafficking is viewed as distinct from sex work, with the former involving force, fraud, coercion, or minors and the latter involving free choice. Liberal feminists tend to support criminalization of sex trafficking but decriminalization or legalization of prostitution and public support for sex workers. Liberal feminists support agency on an individual level, viewing the role of sex workers in society as disconnected from the role of women and girls more generally—the agency of individuals involved in sex work does not have a broader negative impact on the agency of women and girls in society. This is in direct opposition to the views of radical feminists.

Radical Feminist Perspectives

The radical feminist perspective works to explain sex/gender inequality in the context of the patriarchal conditions embedded in broader social structures that subordinate all women and girls (Jaggar 1988; Dempsey 2011; Nichols 2014a; Singh 2011). Radical feminism is at times referred to as "essentialist" feminism because it homogenizes and focuses on the common experiences of women and girls. Radical feminism may also be viewed as "greater good" feminism because it emphasizes the changes needed in society to benefit the majority of women and girls in broader macrostructural perspective (Dempsey 2007). Radical feminist perspectives generally take a "top-down" approach, emphasizing the societal level changes necessary for shifts in a gender biased culture and society as a means to ameliorate sex/gender inequality (Baumgardner and Richards 2010; Jaggar 1988).

This "greater good for all women" perspective maintains that the way women are involved in sexual labor provides a blueprint for the way all women are viewed in society. The radical feminist view of sexual commerce holds that phenomena like pornography and prostitution reflect and reproduce social environments in which women are viewed largely as sexual objects of subordinate status, interfering with how they are viewed in various aspects of society, including the workplace, political arena, and interpersonal relationships. Such perspectives indicate that gender equality can never exist in societies where men view women as sexual commodities; sexual commerce is consequently viewed as an affront to gender equality (Ekberg 2004; Dempsey 2011). Various forms of sexual commerce are viewed as indistinct; sex trafficking, prostitution, and pornography are inherently intertwined in the radical feminist perspective. Radical feminists tend to prefer the terms "sex trafficking," "commercial sexual exploitation," or "prostituted people" as opposed to "sex work."

In terms of agency, radical feminists view the agency of all women and girls in society as reduced through the sexual objectification of women in sexual commerce. The perspective holds that the state denies agency to all women and girls when sexual labor is condoned. State sanctioning of the commodification of women's bodies reduces and legitimizes the status of women and girls to that of sex objects rather than equal partners, creating an environment conducive to sex trafficking. All in the commercial sex industry are viewed as victims, denied of their agency by patriarchal oppression. Radical feminists note victimization as inherent to sexual commerce, for the women involved in it as well as all women in society (Dempsey 2011). Radical feminists typically wish to abolish all forms of sexual commerce as a means of eradicating sex trafficking. While this perspective focuses on the common experiences of all women, or what is perceived to benefit the greater number of women and girls, intersectional feminism focuses on the unique experiences of individuals within the overarching dynamics of sex/gender inequality.

Intersectional Perspectives

Intersectional feminism explains sex/gender inequality as resulting from patriarchy but simultaneously holds that patriarchy manifests in different ways based upon social identities. Intersectional feminism holds that sex/ gender inequality is not experienced in a vacuum, and other social identities, such as race, class, religion, ethnicity, immigrant status, and lesbian, gay, bisexual, transgender, queer/questioning* (LGBTQ*) identities (*indicates any additional nonbinary, gender-fluid, or sexual minority groups), impact one's experiences with sex/gender inequality. Such identities intersect to inform one's experiences, hence the term "intersectional feminism" (Crenshaw 1991). For example, intersectional feminists note that black women do not experience sex/gender inequality in the same way white women do, lesbian women do not experience such inequality in the same way heterosexual women do, and lower-class women experience inequality differently from upper-class women. Intersectional feminism may also explore gender more broadly, going beyond examining the ways gender impacts women, to include the ways gender identity and expression impact men, transgender, and nonbinary or genderqueer people. Intersectional feminism aims to bring a nuanced view to understandings of sex/gender inequality within the context of intersecting identities. In turn, eradicating sex/gender inequality is intertwined with eradicating multiple forms of inequality, such as racism, classism, and heterosexism (Eisenstein 1983; hooks 2014). Intersectional feminists note the importance of examining multiple identities simultaneously to better understand the multiplicity of roots of inequality and to consequently improve the identification of sources of oppression in order to better eradicate them. Importantly, intersectional feminists note that broadly eradicating the inequality that all women experience will likely only address inequalities experienced by majority groups, such as white, heterosexual, cisgender (nontransgender), and middle/upper-class women (Eisenstein 1983; hooks 2014; Rubin 1975). The needs of all women are not met equally in essentialist approaches. Decades of feminist discourse, debate, and research show this to be true (Baumgardner and Richards 2010; Crenshaw 1991; hooks 2014; Collins 2008; Renzetti, Curran, and Maier 2012).

Intersectional feminist perspectives are not as commonly used to examine sexual commerce, at least in the United States. However, synthesizing various forms of research shows that the choice to engage in sexual commerce is impacted by various identities, particularly identities cor-related with inequality (Heil and Nichols 2015; Hughes 2005; Martin et al. 2014; Curtis et al. 2008; Raphael and Myers-Powell 2010; Banks and Kyckelhahn 2011). In the United States, women and girls as well as those of marginalized races, lower classes, undocumented, or LGBTQ* status may be more likely to engage in sexual commerce due to lack of options in a society that marginalizes these identities; that is, sex work can be used as a survival strategy, and marginalized people are at heightened risk of sex trafficking (see chapter 5). For example, African American women and girls compose 40% of sex trafficking victims in federally prosecuted cases while composing only 13% of the population, and African Americans com-pose 55% of juvenile prostitution arrests, which is a form of sex trafficking, according to the U.S. TVPA.[1] Transgender people may be more likely to engage in sexual commerce due to workplace discrimination and reduced access to transgender-related health care (Mock 2014). Similarly, barriers to exiting prostitution may be heightened for those of marginalized identities. Research finds that sex trafficked LGBTQ* youth are exposed to discrimi-nation by some social service providers in child protective services and otherwise have fewer choices in accessing services (Heil and Nichols 2015). Oppression can consequently be viewed not only as sex/gender inequal-ity but also within the context of heightened vulnerability related to social identities. At the same time, sex work can be viewed as a survival strategy for some. Essentialist solutions that remove this survival strategy without offering an alternative serve only to further marginalize and problematize the lives of those who are disproportionately vulnerable while providing benefit to those who have privileged identities.

In intersectional feminist perspective, agency is viewed as being impacted by lack of choices, barriers, or marginalization related to one's combined identities. Agency is also expressed in actively resisting oppres-sion and surviving multiple forms of oppression; it may be seen in the con-text of using sex work as a survival strategy, an enjoyable occupation, or a way to otherwise enhance one's position in society. Similarly, victimization is also uniquely experienced based on social identities and may be height-ened for those with vulnerable identities. The emphasis on identity-based oppression makes intersectional feminist perspectives distinct from liberal or radical feminist perspectives. Such oppression leads to increased risk of sex trafficking and exploitation. In addition, intersectional feminism rejects essentialist feminism, noting that there is no single common experience of all women, and that "greater good" feminism basically amounts to the greater good for people of nonmarginalized identities by not acknowledging, including, or addressing intersecting inequalities (Crenshaw 1991; hooks 2014).

The various forms of feminist theoretical perspectives overlap in their common interest of examining and eradicating sex/gender inequality, but the focus is different, and each consequently holds different ideas about how to ameliorate sex/gender inequality. Notably, as described earlier, radical feminism, liberal feminism, and intersectional feminism are broad theoretical models. These theoretical models have been applied to all types of social phenomena, such as wage inequality, choice of occupation, intimate partner violence, reproductive rights, rape and sexual assault, and more. These perspectives differ in their tenets, particularly related to agency, victimization, the role of the state, marginalized identities versus common experience, and focal points of analysis. Yet they overlap in their grounding in feminist principles, specifically, the focus on sex/gender inequality and the work needed to eliminate it. Because feminists are not a monolithic group and do not hold a single universal feminist perspective, heated feminist debates have arisen in a variety of areas, including sexual commerce. While these perspectives overlap with each other in complex and competing ways, importantly, feminist perspectives of sexual commerce also overlap considerably with the political perspectives of liberalism, conservativism, neoliberalism, and abolitionism.

Political Perspectives

Neoliberalism can be described as a political perspective that views government involvement in commerce as intrusive. Neoliberalism is a spin-off of liberalism, a political philosophy that emphasizes the advancement of freedom through progressive or ameliorative social changes (Klein 2008). This is quite distinct from radical or reactionary philosophies that call for revolution and a more complete overhaul of the existing order, or from conservative philosophies that view change as threatening to the stability and social order of society. Liberalism posits that the existing order is basically just but can be improved through modest adjustment or limited reforms. Neoliberalism, by comparison, focuses explicitly on freedom from the constraints of the state. Like liberalism, the philosophy holds that the basic social order is not bad; rather, the constraints that the state imposes that limit the freedom of individuals are viewed negatively and are consequently the targets of limited reforms. Most expressions of neoliberalism have been focused on removing any barriers or restrictions on capital in the form of deregulation, emphasizing individual consumer choice as an expression of freedom, advancing the narrative of the free market as the ultimate public commons and removing the state as an actor in social life via privatization. This is ironically almost identical to traditional conservative laissez-faire philosophies of commerce. The perspectives are distinct in that conservatives do not support privatization or nonstate involvement in issues viewed as undermining traditional morality, such as sexual commerce. For neoliberals, this limiting of government involvement does not exclude sexual commerce.

Neoliberal Perspectives

Researchers have applied neoliberalism to sexual commerce, developing what is widely known as the neoliberal perspective of sex work (Dempsey 2011; Outshoorn 2005; Weitzer 2010). Neoliberalism largely centers upon deregulation of sex markets, putting the choices in the hands of consumers and sellers and removing them from the constraints of the state, suggesting instead that the state should support free-market sexual commerce as a legitimate form of production of capital. Neoliberal political perspectives suggest that individuals should have a right to sell various aspects of their sexuality if they choose. Individual agency is central to the neoliberal perspective of sexual commerce, conceptualizing men and women as active agents in control of their own individual decision making. Within this perspective, people are only viewed as victims if they are victimized in the course of their occupation, if they are minors, or if they are forced, defrauded, or coerced to engage in sexual commerce. Otherwise, sexual labor is viewed as a form of sexual freedom or financial opportunity; criminalization of sex work is a denial of agency. Like liberal feminists, neoliberals are more likely to prefer the term "sex work" to describe commercial sex or sex acts, legitimizing sexual labor as a viable occupation. Neoliberals often describe antitrafficking activism as a "moral crusade" that grossly misrepresents the issue as an unwarranted excuse to eradicate all forms of sexual commerce (Weitzer 2010; Schaeffer-Grabiel 2010; Oselin 2014;

Doezema 1999). Such researchers highlight the inflation of the magnitude of the problem, the use of horror stories to gain public support, the non-acknowledgment of willing sex workers, and the anti-immigration sentiments tied in to antitrafficking efforts to abolish sexual commerce (Weitzer 2010; Schaeffer-Grabiel 2010; Oselin 2014; Doezema 2005). This perspective is juxtaposed to that of abolitionism.

Abolitionist Political Perspectives

Abolitionism generally refers to the movement to end slavery and has been widely applied to sexual commerce, becoming what is known as the abolitionist perspective of sexual commerce (Ekberg 2004; Dempsey 2011; Outshoorn 2005). Abolitionism, in this context, aims to eradicate all forms of sexual labor, maintaining that all forms of sexual commerce depict women as commodities, as secondary to men, or as sexual outlets for men. In abolitionist terms, those engaging in sexual commerce are referred to as sex slaves. Allowing individual sex workers agency is viewed as denying the agency of all women and girls; the state provides agency to all women and girls by denying agency of willing sex workers. All women engaging in sexual labor are viewed as victims of sexual slavery due to limited opportunities, lack of better alternatives, or forced entrance into sexual commerce. Abolitionists tend to prefer the terms "survivors," "slaves," "victims," or "prostituted people" to describe those involved in the commercial sex industry (Bales and Soodalter 2009; Dempsey 2011). The language of modern-day slavery is commonly used to describe sex trafficking and any form of sexual commerce; sex trafficking and sexual commerce are viewed as indistinct. Forms of sexual commerce, such as pornography and prostitution, are regarded as types of sex trafficking and modern-day slavery.

Overlapping Feminist and Political Perspectives

As the reader may have surmised at this point, feminist and political perspectives overlap considerably. Liberal feminists and neoliberals tend to support one's right to engage in sex work, whereas radical feminists and abolitionists wish to eliminate all forms of sexual commerce.

Importantly, radical feminism does not equal abolitionism; rather, it is the larger perspective that informs the abolitionist model of sexual commerce. Abolitionism in this context literally means abolishing all forms of sexual commerce—including prostitution, pornography, and sex trafficking. Yet there are some abolitionists who wish to abolish sexual commerce but who are not feminist and do not subscribe to feminist principles. Religious conservatives who want to eradicate sexual commerce for religious moral reasons as opposed to reasons of sex/gender inequality would be one example. Although radical feminists developed the abolitionist model on feminist principles, the model can be engaged by those who do not identify with feminism.

Similarly, liberal feminism does not equal neoliberalism. They overlap in the context of sexual commerce in that they share the focus on supporting agency through individual choices. However, there are neoliberals who do not subscribe to feminism at all. They simply believe everyone should have the choice to engage in sex work if they choose to; they are not necessarily focusing on women's rights per se (some neoliberals do, others do not). Similarly, liberal feminists may not oppose state involvement in commerce in other sociopolitical contexts, but they overlap with neoliberalists in agreement of the right to engage in sex work. While these nuances are important, it is absolutely true that radical feminists generally support abolitionism and liberal feminists tend to support neoliberalism in the context of sexual commerce.

Importantly, longstanding and enduring political and feminist debates impact contemporary sex trafficking discourse and policy. Among the arguments predating and most central to the academic and public sex trafficking dialogue are those focused on pornography and prostitution, the subject matter of chapters 3 and 4. Such debates emphasize contention between political liberals and conservatives, radical and liberal feminists, and related neoliberal and abolitionist responses, and are intertwined with sex trafficking–related policy, activism, and backlash. Before closing this chapter and entering into these debates in applied contexts, the following is a review of the sociological and criminological perspectives of sexual commerce and sex trafficking. While not commonly taking center stage in the antitrafficking discourse, these perspectives hold serious implications for preventing and responding to sex trafficking and commercial sexual exploitation.

Sociological Perspectives

Sociological perspectives broadly examine and attempt to explain various conditions of society. Perspectives within sociology that are particularly relevant to the study of sex trafficking include those focused on social institutions, inequality, and various aspects of culture. An examination of social conditions that perpetuate or ameliorate sex trafficking are included throughout this book. Perspectives focused on social institutions or macrostructural approaches literally examine the role of social institutions in perpetuating social problems, including sex trafficking. In particular, as Erin Heil and Andrea Nichols (2015) note, exposure to weak social institutions increases one's risk of sex trafficking or exploitation. The weak social institutions examined in this book include education systems, economic systems, the criminal justice system, and the family. Heil and Nichols (2015) found that weak education systems, with high rates of student and teacher turnover, high drop-out rates, and high truancy rates, are associated with sex trafficking victimization. Unsurprisingly, a mass of research implicates economic drive as a motivation for selling sex. Accordingly, the economy as a weak social institution and related dynamics of social stratification such as poverty and a low minimum wage, combined with a lack of social safety nets, are implicated in sex trafficking victimization and commercial sexual exploitation (Heil and Nichols 2015; Oselin 2014; Kara 2010). While some sex workers do not want to do other work, research suggests that a vast majority of those who sell sex do (Curtis et al. 2008; Dank et al. 2015). For example, Dank and colleagues (2015) reported 93% did not want to be engaged in the commercial sex industry; they were involved for an economic or survival strategy. Ineffective criminal justice interventions that make it difficult to exit involvement in the commercial sex industry are associated with continued sex trafficking and exploitation, evidenced by high recidivism rates. In addition, the family serves as a weak social institution facilitating sex trafficking under conditions of sexual abuse, intergenerational transmission of commercial sex involvement, neglect, domestic violence, substance abuse, or even sex trafficking their own children or relatives (Heil and Nichols 2015; Kotrla 2010; Oselin 2014; Raphael and Myers-Powell 2010). Sociological perspectives focused on societal inequality, such as race, class, sex, gender, and sexual orientation–based inequality, are nearly identical to the intersectional feminist perspective described earlier. The difference is that intersectional feminism situates these identities within sexed and gendered contexts, whereas the sociological perspective focuses more broadly on advantaged and disadvantaged groups in society, their self-interests, and the power of advantaged groups to maintain their power through structural and cultural privilege. Further, aspects of culture that devalue some identities compared to others are implicated in sex trafficking and exploitation as well. Sociological perspectives largely work to target the root of sex trafficking, suggesting that aspects of the social environment are connected, whereas criminological perspectives largely work to explain interventions and responses to sex trafficking crimes.

Criminological Perspectives

Criminological perspectives are born from the field of sociology but focus exclusively on various aspects of law making, law breaking, and the responses to crime (Sutherland and Cressey 2006; Vito and Maahs 2012; Akers and Sellers 2009). There are key aspects of criminological theorizing that are important to antitrafficking efforts, including deterrence and rehabilitation. The feminist and political perspectives described earlier largely work to analyze the question "what should constitute a crime?," and the sociological perspectives work to answer the question "what causes crime?" However, the discourse examining criminological perspectives largely works to analyze the question "what is the most effective way to respond to crime?" There is a massive body of literature examining deterrence and rehabilitation in a variety of substantive areas, including substance abuse, homicide, sex offenses, property crimes, and more. This work can be applied to various aspects of sex trafficking and exploitation.

Deterrence

Deterrence theory largely relies on the assumption that if the punishment for a crime is severe enough, people will be less likely to commit a crime, thereby deterring or preventing the crime. Centuries of criminological research examining deterrence theory produces mixed results, finding deterrence is largely unsuccessful unless it is swift, certain, and its ramifications outweigh the crime's benefits (Akers and Sellers 2009; Vito and Maahs 2012). The United States largely engages in deterrence-based policy regarding sex trafficking and prostitution through criminalization (see chapter 4). Research suggests that criminalization of prostitution and sex trafficking, at least in its current form, does not offer support for deterrence (see chapters 4 and 9). While deterrence theory revolves around punishment, rehabilitation attempts to prevent future crime by "fixing" current offenders of the law, and prevention efforts work to ameliorate the root causes or risks associated with the problem.

Rehabilitation and Prevention

Rehabilitation is a response to crime that works to facilitate the offender's reform so that a person can become a functional member of society free from the committal of crime. In contrast, prevention works to provide resources to at-risk people to prevent future crime or victimization. A rather large body of work finds that, in general, programs and policies addressing risk factors at early ages prevents future crime and victimization (Hawkins et al. 2005, 2007; Corrigan, Lonsck, and Videka 2007; Lipsey 2009; Lundahl, Nimer, and Parsons 2006; Stoltzfus and Lynch 2009). This includes involving at-risk children in after-school activities and social development programs and engaging their parents in education and training related prevention programs. Prevention work in the area of sex trafficking is limited and largely in its early stages (outside of education and awareness campaigns). Groups like My Life, My Choice in Boston; the Polaris Project in Washington D.C.; and YouthSpark in Atlanta have developed prevention curriculum.

The criminological research related to rehabilitation is mixed, finding success in some areas and ineffectiveness in others. Regarding sex trafficking or prostitution, direct rehabilitation of sex traffickers is not generally known to be practiced. Limited efforts focus on restorative justice, which involves accountability determined in collaboration with the trafficker and the survivor (Gomez and Going 2015). Rehabilitation is offered in limited ways to survivors of sex trafficking in the form of services for trafficking survivors and organizations serving those exiting the sex industry (chapter 11). In some areas there is a pipeline from the courts directly into rehabilitation style programs that works to assist girls and women exiting prostitution and sex trafficking. The best programs have nearly a 75% success rate (Oselin 2014).[2] Rehabilitation for buyers is also available in limited form and with mixed success rates. "John schools" are described in chapter 8. The response to sex trafficking is largely deterrence oriented rather than rehabilitation oriented, as evidenced by the arrest, fine, and incarceration of those who sell sex, lack of available services, and relative lack of focus on prevention and rehabilitation (Heil and Nichols 2015; Oselin 2014).

Chapter Summary

This chapter examined the feminist, political, sociological, and criminological perspectives of sexual commerce and their relationships to sex trafficking. Feminist perspectives all emphasize sex/gender inequality but vary in their perspectives of sexual commerce in relationship to sex trafficking. Liberal feminists focus on agency, supporting individual rights to engage in sex work and sexual empowerment while condemning forced or coerced prostitution or prostitution of minors. Radical feminists focus on patriarchal social structures that reproduce oppression of women and girls, viewing all sexual commerce as sex trafficking. Intersectional feminists recognize the role of intersecting identities and increased susceptibility to sex trafficking/commercial sexual exploitation due to lack of better alternatives as well as the use of sex work as a survival strategy for marginalized groups. Political perspectives of sexual commerce include conservative, liberal, neoliberal, and abolitionist views. Conservative views largely emphasize morality, depicting sexual commerce as opposing traditional morality. Liberal views emphasize freedom of sexual expression, with neoliberalism focusing more exclusively on freedom from state constraints on sexual commerce. Abolitionism aims to eradicate all forms of sexual commerce, viewed as forms of modern-day slavery that victimize those working in the commercial sex industry. In addition, sociological perspectives emphasize the role of social institutions, inequality, and culture in producing, preventing, and addressing sex trafficking. Lastly, criminological perspectives highlight responses to sex trafficking, such as deterrence, prevention, and rehabilitation-based policy. Such perspectives guide antitrafficking activism as well as policy designed to address sex trafficking. The next two chapters delineate the ways in which these feminist, criminological, and political ideological camps have responded to the issues of pornography and prostitution, and the relationship of these issues to sex trafficking–related policy.

Discussion Questions

1. Describe the dynamics of agency and victimization in liberal, intersectional, and radical feminist perspectives.

2. Describe the distinctions between conservative, liberal, neoliberal, and abolitionist perspectives of sexual commerce.

3. How might a sociological perspective be used to guide prevention of sex trafficking?

[3]

Pornography

In December 2011 detectives in Boise, Idaho, began investigating Andrew Millas, who had posted videos on a website known for distributing child pornography. The undercover detectives began online chats with Millas and were able to convince him to send them photos and images. Millas not only sent the undercover officers images he had produced, but he even sent a live broadcast of a sex act with a minor recorded with a web camera. Boise Police collaborated with police in Fairview Heights, Illinois, a suburban community just outside of St. Louis where Millas was living at the time, and the Fairview Heights police quickly made an arrest. Investigators for the FBI found nearly 15,000 files and nearly a million images in Millas's possession.[1] Some of the recovered files showed 43-year-old Millas himself having sex with a teen and films of other minors engaged in sex acts. In 2012 Andrew Millas was sentenced to 35 years in prison for producing and transporting child pornography. When people trade pornographic videos with one another through online sites, they are trading something of value—this constitutes commercialized sex. When pornography involves a minor, it fits the legal framework of sex trafficking indicated in the Trafficking Victims Protection Act (TVPA). While cases of child pornography like the case of Andrew Millas are directly linked to sex trafficking, debates surrounding the relationship between pornography and sex trafficking are much broader.

There are more than 45 years of theoretical and political debates that impact the academic and public discourse surrounding sex trafficking today. Among the arguments predating and most central to this discourse are those focused on pornography and prostitution (prostitution is the subject of chapter 4). Recognizing sex trafficking situated within these ongoing historical debates is essential because such perspectives are highly politicized and directly inform sex trafficking–related policy. Central points of contention relate to censorship and the role of pornography in facilitating a cultural environment conducive to violence against women, the general degradation of women, and the demand for sex trafficking. Known as "the Porn Wars," the feminist and political debates of pornography and the relationship of pornography to modern-day sex trafficking discourse are examined in this chapter.

The Politics of Pornography

Early Political Perspectives of Pornography

The pornography industry is a profitable business, growing in distribution, sales, and profitability, particularly since the advent of the Internet. Conservative estimates place the current annual profitability of the pornography industry in the United States at around $12 billion (Bridges et al. 2010). The pornography industry largely developed and widely expanded in the United States in the 1950s. From this time until the 1970s, the public discourse involving pornography generally centered upon sociopolitical debates between those with liberal or conservative political perspectives. Conservatives were opposed to pornography for moral reasons. Social conservatives maintained that pornography undermined traditional values, the sanctity of marriage, religious morals, and the stability of society (Bridges and Jensen 2011; Nichols 2014b; Weitzer 2011). Such groups upheld the traditional mores of society by declaring that sexuality should be relegated to the private realm and should only be expressed between a man and a woman in a monogamous marriage. In contrast, social liberals supported freedom of sexual expression. They held that individuals have the right to express themselves in the way they choose, including free expression of sexuality. Liberals generally maintained that individuals have the right to participate in, profit from, and view pornography (Bridges and Jensen 2011; Nichols 2014b; Weitzer 2011).

While liberal/conservative political arguments dominated prior to the 1970s, the advent of second wave feminism shifted the public and academic discourse from political debates to feminist debates. In what became known as the Porn Wars of the 1980s, debates within the feminist community added a layer of complexity to the seemingly dichotomous liberal/conservative social and political debates. Radical feminists typically opposed pornography while liberal feminists were more likely to support it. Radical feminist arguments would later become central to abolitionist sex trafficking discourse and policy development, whereas liberal feminist arguments would continue to counter them.

Radical Feminist and Abolitionist Perspectives of Pornography

As indicated in chapter 2, radical feminists and abolitionists generally view sex trafficking, pornography, and prostitution as synonymous because they all objectify and commodify women's bodies. Well-known radical feminist law professor Catharine A. MacKinnon (2005) suggests that pornography is no different from prostitution in that a sex act takes place for commercial gain, but the act of sex is not delivered in person, rather, through photos, digital images, and recorded or live videos. All prostitution is viewed as sex trafficking in radical feminist perspective. Because all pornography is viewed as a form of prostitution, pornography is therefore viewed as sex trafficking. In this sense, these three forms of sexual commerce are viewed as indistinct.

As a result, radical feminists generally wish to abolish pornography, prostitution, and sex trafficking simultaneously. Radical feminist perspectives hold that they are interrelated largely for the following reasons: (1) demand for prostitution is the root cause of sex trafficking, and pornography drives demand; and (2) pornography fuels sex trafficking by creating a cultural environment where degradation, objectification, commodification, and violence against women are normalized (Dines 2010; Dworkin 1981; MacKinnon 2005).

Theoretical criticisms of radical feminist views of pornography contend that the perspective denies the agency of individuals choosing to engage in pornography and renders invisible those who enjoy performing as well as the financial rewards (Weitzer 2011). The perspective is also criticized for being essentialist in that it homogenizes the experiences of all women in pornography. Further, such arguments erase the existence of same-sex oriented individuals and those of nonbinary identities in creating, producing, and consuming pornography by framing all pornography as violence against women. This perspective also ignores pornography made by women for women and forms of pornography that depict equal initiation and enjoyment of sexuality between men and women. These critiques coincide with liberal feminist or neoliberal views of pornography (Tucker 1990; Weitzer 2011; Duggan and Hunter 2006).

Liberal Feminist and Neoliberal Perspectives of Pornography

In contrast to radical/abolitionist ideologies of pornography, neoliberals and anticensorship liberal feminists indicate that women should have the right to do whatever they want to with their bodies, including making and profiting from pornographic videos. Anticensorship liberal feminists maintain that rights to engage in pornography give women agency by allowing free choice to sell their sexual labor. Well-known anticensorship liberal feminists Lisa Duggan and Nan Hunter (2006) note in their classic book *Sex Wars* that antipornography activism oppressed women's rights and worked to preserve traditional and hegemonic sexuality.

In direct opposition to radical feminist views, many liberal feminists continued to maintain anticensorship activism and upheld ideologies of free sexuality. Liberal feminists pointed out that there were many forms of pornography, and some forms of pornography involve actors who mutually provide and receive pleasure and appear to maintain equal power of their sexuality. Liberal feminists opposed forms of pornography depicting violence against women but did not agree with radical feminist perspectives that maintained all pornography reflected violence against women or was otherwise detrimental to women in society (Bakehorn 2010; Duggan and Hunter 2006; Weitzer 2011). Such groups also maintain that the relationship of pornography consumption to demand for prostitution is unclear at best (Weitzer 2011).

Neoliberals and liberal feminists disentangle pornography from sex trafficking. Neoliberals suggest that they are distinct, and pornography can only be labeled as sex trafficking when force, fraud, or coercion are involved, or when the actor(s) are under 18. Neoliberals and liberal feminists maintain that all pornography is not inherently implicated in sex trafficking. Accordingly, they also disagree with radical feminists, stating that abolition of pornography is not necessary to end sex trafficking, as the two are distinct. Neoliberals believe this restriction would unjustly deny the agency of individuals who choose to create, sell, and act in pornography as well as limit the free choice of buyers. If participants are consenting adults, then neoliberals and liberal feminists suggest that pornography is unrelated to sex trafficking; child pornography and forced pornography are already punishable by law, so eradicating pornography is unnecessary (Weitzer 2011).

Theoretical criticisms of this perspective include that it is a microlevel perspective that ignores the broader context and impact on women as a subordinate group more generally. Further, it ignores the gender and sex dynamics of pornography production and consumption because pornography disproportionately benefits male producers and men are the primary consumers. Critics also maintain that liberal feminists ignore the link between pornography and violence against women, of which sex trafficking is viewed as another form. This is a hotly contested field of study (Bakehorn 2010; Bridges et al. 2010; Dines 2010; McKee 2005; Loftus 2002; Weitzer 2011).

The following sections tease out the direct and indirect ways pornography has been linked to sex trafficking victimization. Direct ways include child pornography. Indirect ways include contribution to an environment sexually objectifying and devaluing women and girls. The discussion of indirect influence begins by examining the debates relating pornography to demand for prostitution, violence against women, and the general degradation of women situated within the feminist and political frameworks described earlier.

Key Areas of Pornography Debates and Sex Trafficking

Demand

The topic of demand is a cornerstone of abolitionism—if there were no demand for sexual commerce, then sex trafficking would not exist. Abolitionists argue that pornography facilitates demand. Radical feminist MacKinnon (2005, 3) states:

> As a form of prostitution, pornography creates demand for women and children to be supplied for sexual use to make it, many of whom are trafficked to fill that demand . . . [and] consuming pornography is an

experience of bought sex, of sexually using a woman or a girl or a boy as an object who has been purchased. As such, it stimulates demand for buying women and girls and boys as sexual objects in the flesh in the same way it stimulates the viewer to act out on other live women and girls and boys the specific acts that are sexualized and consumed in the pornography.

The available research suggests that the relationship between pornography, demand for prostitution, and consequent sex trafficking is unclear. The number of men who view pornography is much greater than the number of men who buy sex. If pornography truly fueled demand, then the number of men buying sex would be inarguably greater. Rates of men in the U.S. who have ever purchased sex have remained relatively constant and have even slightly declined (see chapter 8). Moreover, LGBTQ* and dominatrix pornography are not addressed in these arguments, nor is the fact that women also view pornography, albeit in smaller numbers (Duggan and Hunter 2006; Weitzer 2011). Does this similarly increase the demand of women for male or female sex workers, or the demand for LGBTQ* sex workers? This relationship has not been examined in the research literature. Further, the radical feminist/abolitionist argument typically uses a definition of sex trafficking that conflates all sexual commerce with sex trafficking, not acknowledging that working in pornography can be a legitimate career choice for those who are adults, who freely consent, and who enjoy their work and the financial benefits. In neoliberal/liberal feminist perspective, demand for pornography involving adults does not equal demand for sex trafficked people to make it because many actors in pornography, particularly in regulated markets in the United States, are adult free agents (Weitzer 2010, 2011). At the same time, demand for child pornography inherently entails sex trafficking in its creation, thus demand in this case does lead to sex trafficking. In addition to demand, violence against women is another key area of contention regarding pornography and sex trafficking.

Violence Against Women

Another debated issue is whether there is a correlation between pornography and acts of violence against women in society and whether pornography itself is a form of violence against women. Radical feminists principally emphasize the role of pornography in relationship to violence against women and relate it to sexual objectification of women. For example, well-known antipornography activist Andrea Dworkin (1981) and profeminist activist John Stoltenberg (1999) maintain that objectification of women is an inherent part of pornography in which a woman is reduced to her body parts. Dworkin indicated that objectification is associated with dehumanization; it is easier to commit an act of violence directed toward an object rather than a person. John Stoltenberg later elaborated on this perspective:

> There is a perceptible sense in which every act of sexual objectifying occurs on a continuum of dehumanization that promises male sexual violence at its far end. The depersonalization that begins in sexual objectification is what makes violence possible; for once you have made a person out to be a thing, you can do anything to it you want.

> (1999, 45)

Radical feminists/abolitionists suggest that it is this objectification that allows for sex trafficking to occur (MacKinnon 2005). Essentially, this argument indicates that pornography is inherently objectifying, which creates the social environment conducive to sex trafficking in which women are viewed as objects to be purchased and sexual outlets for entitled men.

One area of debate under the overarching theme of violence against women is the depiction of particularly heinous or physically violent pornography. Neoliberals criticize radical feminists for highlighting atrocious cases of violence against women depicted in pornography (Weitzer 2011). This includes rape camps, torture, mutilation, children forced to perform in live Internet sex shows, bestiality, and even death (Dines 2010; Hodge 2008; Hodge and Lietz 2007). The purpose of the "worst-case" tactic is to draw attention to the matter, to emphasize that such portrayals do exist in pornography, and to provide justification for eradicating it (Dines 2010; Hodge and Lietz 2007). Such arguments are used to support abolition of pornography, suggesting that it is inherently linked to sex trafficking in making these forms of pornography because they contain coercion, violence, or minors.

Neoliberal and liberal feminist critics argue that abolition of pornography as a whole is unnecessary because pornography containing such acts of violence already violates the law. In such cases these depictions could be used as evidence in criminal court proceedings, and problematic forms of pornography could be addressed through already existing laws rather than complete abolition (Weitzer 2011). Pornographers could face charges of kidnapping, rape, assault, and even murder in response to worst-case scenarios (Tucker 1990; Weitzer 2011). Neoliberals and anticensorship liberal feminists further critique the extant research in this area on the grounds that such research only examines worst-case scenarios and generalizes those worst-case scenarios to all forms of pornography (Hartley 2005). Research conducted within the last 15 years finds that extreme violence in pornography such as rape, torture, death, or use of weapons occurs infrequently (Barron and Kimmel 2000; Bridges et al. 2010). Contemporary analyses are limited; consequently, the extent of violent or demeaning pornography is unclear, particularly with the advent of the Internet and widespread accessibility of unregulated images. Moreover, images and videos offered online but based in other countries depicting worst-case scenarios would be difficult to address through U.S. legal systems, aside from possession charges (Hughes 2007; MacKinnon 2005).

While the vast majority of pornography does not involve worst-case scenarios of rape, torture, mutilation, or death, other forms of aggression are present. Frequency of violence in pornography, depending on how it is measured, ranges from 1.9% (McKee 2005) to 70% (Bridges et al. 2010), with other estimates indicating about 25% contain aggression (Barron and Kimmell 2000; Cowan et al. 1988). What accounts for this wide range of violence and aggression uncovered in pornography research? It is the way aggression and violence are defined. Ana J. Bridges and colleagues point out that prior work on pornography, such as in McKee (2005), does not define acts as violent if the woman appears to enjoy it. They believe that this operationalization of violence in pornography is problematic because the actors in pornography are generally required and paid to appear to enjoy the sex acts that are a part of the script. "Notably, McKee coded violence only when an act was clearly intended to cause harm *and* was met with resistance by the target of aggression. Therefore, acts where the target appeared to enjoy the harm or aggression, or where there was no active attempt to avoid the harm, were not coded as 'violent'" (Bridges et al. 2010, 1068). On the opposite end of the spectrum, Bridges and colleagues defined aggression much more broadly, which could also be viewed as methodologically challenging. For example, spanking was labeled as an act of physical violence, yet light spanking may not be perceived as physically harmful but as enjoyable and intended to facilitate orgasm.

Bridges and colleagues (2010) found in an analysis of 304 scenes from a random sample of the top-selling pornography videos (N = 50) that there were high levels of physical aggression. Some form of physical aggression, which the researchers defined as including spanking, gagging, choking, hair pulling and slapping, was depicted in 88% of the scenes.

> Women were spanked on 953 occasions, visibly gagged 756 times, experienced an open-hand slap 361 times, had their hair pulled or yanked on 267 separate occasions, and were choked 180 times. Men, however, were spanked only 26 times, experienced an open-hand slap in 47 instances, and for all other aggressive acts, were aggressed against fewer than 10 times.
>
> (Bridges et al. 2010, 1076–77)

In such cases, females typically responded to these things with pleasure or neutrality. Bridges and colleagues found that males were the aggressor in about 70% of cases and females were in 30% of cases, but in both instances 94% of scenes had female targets of aggression regardless of whether the aggressor was male or female. Accordingly, there is some research support that there is at least some level of inequality in spanking, gagging, and slapping in top-selling pornography videos in the United States.

Some radical feminists have indicated that pornography is like an addiction in which men need a "harder hit" each time, increasing their likelihood of seeking out harder-core pornography, including increasingly violent pornography or younger actors (Dines 2010). There is no reliable research evidence that this is the case. In contrast, David Loftus (2002) found in researching men who viewed pornography that, counter to the idea that men need a "harder hit" of pornography, the majority did not initially or increasingly seek out violent or fetishized pornography. Multiple studies show men are consistent with their pornography interests; that is, their consumption is static (see also Klein 2008; McKee 2006; Weitzer 2011). Moreover, Ronald Weitzer (2011) notes that in comparing two studies conducted over ten years apart (Barron and Kimmel 2000; Bridges et al. 2010), the levels of serious aggression were identical, indicating that pornography is not increasingly violent, refuting the "harder hit" arguments. At the same time, the documentary *The Price of Pleasure* (Picker and Sun 2008) indicated that, while men may not be seeking out increasingly fetishized pornography, the pornography industry does alter their offerings to include new and different forms of sex, evidenced by the advent and increased popularity of ass-to-mouth penetration and multiple orifice penetration in pornography.

Research that examines pornography distribution and rates of violence against women is inconclusive—in some sites with higher rates of pornography distribution there are higher rates of violence against women, and in other sites there are lower rates of violence against women. The research is problematized in its inability to control for other contextual dynamics in the cities under examination that impact crime rates. Lab studies are also methodologically challenged and show inconclusive results (Weitzer 2011). There is also a significant body of research that examines the relationship between rape-myth mentalities and pornography. Rape myths are beliefs about rape that typically blame the woman who is raped while the offenders are viewed as innocent. Newer research does not find support for one rape myth, at least in that scenes in contemporary pornography do not show an unwilling participant who resists sex who eventually enjoys it, which was a recognized problem with pornography prior to the 2000s (Bridges et al. 2010). Yet research does find some forms of pornography support rape-myth mentalities as well as harassing behaviors directed toward women (Bridges et al. 2010; Hall, Hirschman, and Oliver 1994; Mulac, Jansma, and Linz 2002; Zillmann 1989; Zillmann and Bryant 1982).

Inequality and Relative Degradation

In addition to violence against women, inequality and relative degradation are other points of contention. Such dynamics include inequality between men and women in giving and receiving sexual pleasure, in playing the dominant or subordinate role in sex, and in unequally conducting or receiving acts of degradation, and even conflict over what qualifies as degradation. Degrading acts under debate include derogatory name calling, ass-to-mouth penetration, and ejaculation on the face.

First, pornographic videos do display inequality in that they are more likely to portray women giving rather than receiving oral sex (Bridges et al. 2010; McKee 2005). Bridges and colleagues found in an analysis of 304 scenes from 50 videos selected from a random sample of the top-selling videos that women performed oral sex on men in 90% of scenes, and men did so in 53% of scenes. Men were also more likely to play a dominant role, controlling the dynamics of the oral sex in both scenarios (Bridges et al. 2010). All of this indicates that pornography is largely for male pleasure (androcentric) rather than for female pleasure (gynocentric).

In addition, men's ejaculation on the faces of women is common in pornography and may be viewed as a degrading act, although Bridges found this in only 3% of scenes, whereas 58% involved ejaculating in the woman's mouth (Bridges et al. 2010; Schauer and Wheaton 2006). Further acts of degradation may include ass-to-mouth scenes, in which a male actor engages in anal sex with the female, then receives oral sex from her. Bridges found this in 41% of scenes of top-selling pornographic videos. Double penetration, where two male actors simultaneously penetrate one woman both anally and vaginally, or orally and anal/vaginally, occurred in 19% of scenes. Verbal aggression may be viewed as another form of degradation, including name calling, most commonly, "bitch," "whore," or "slut." Bridges found nearly half of scenes involved derogatory language, overwhelmingly directed at women by men. "Aggregately speaking across the sample spectrum, women were verbally insulted or referred to in derogatory terms 534 times, whereas men experienced similar verbal assaults in only 65 instances" (Bridges et al. 2010, 1076).

Contemporary pornography does depict women enjoying and showing pleasure at a variety of acts that may be labeled as degrading. This may support a different type of myth distinct from rape myths in that such acts are normalized as desirable by both men and women in pornography (Bridges et al. 2010). The question then remains—do women generally enjoy ejaculate in their mouths and on their faces; being called "slut," "bitch," or "whore" during sex; having their hair pulled; or getting spanked, slapped, gagged, or choked? Some would call this inherently degrading and relate it to a form of violence against women (Dines 2010). Radical feminists absolutely take this position. Yet others have suggested this is homogenizing and subjective, that fantasy is distinct from reality, and if there is consent, then degradation arguments are irrelevant. For example, in a critique of Dines (2010), who represents the degradation viewpoint of pornography, Weitzer (2011, 670) states:

She does give examples of acts that she considers inherently degrading; these include anal sex, ejaculation on a woman's body, two or more men having sex with one woman, and multiorifice intercourse. Whether these acts are indeed perceived as degrading by viewers and actors does not figure into Dines's argument. They are simply defined as perverted by fiat.

Some interpret degradation to be a subjective issue, while others determine degradation to be inherent to particular acts. Radical feminists and abolitionists maintain that degradation leads to a cultural environment that devalues and objectifies women, and is consequently conducive to sex trafficking victimization. Neoliberals maintain that the way women are portrayed in pornography is subjectively defined, and unrelated to sex trafficking.

Culture and Advertising

Gail Dines (2010) argues that aspects of pornography seep into our mainstream advertising under the adage "sex sells." Such images sexualize both women and men. Sexualization can be empowering or disempowering. Using a definition of power equating high status, respect, control, authority, strength, or dominance, certain images of empowering sexuality in advertising are present. Yet such images of women are relatively few compared to women who are not portrayed in a sexually empowering way. Further, the ways women and men are sexually objectified in mainstream advertising is distinct. Men are more often portrayed in positions of strength, with muscular bodies and positioned in ways representing power. In contrast, women are more typically positioned in positions of vulnerability, in terms of extreme thinness, and positioned either sexually or in positions of helplessness. Men and women are both sexually objectified, albeit in different ways. Advertising showing women with their mouths open and tongues out depicting oral sex, or with the addition of some phallic object, such as a liquor bottle, lollipop, finger, flower, or pen is common. Ostensibly, men also engage in oral sex, yet mainstream advertising does not include erotic images of men's mouths or tongues to sell a product. Similarly, women lying on the ground with their rear ends in the air, or crouching on the floor are also not uncommon, modeling the image of sexual positioning. In contrast, men are rarely depicted in a way emulating sexual positioning in mainstream advertising. This represents both heteronormativity and androcentrism in its unequal depictions. Perhaps women, bi people, gay men, and others would be more likely to buy a product if an advertisement of a man seductively licking a lollipop, or with his mouth suggestively on a peach, or beer bottle was present. There is a difference in the ways men and women are sexualized.

In addition, the woman-as-accessory is also common in mainstream advertising. Take the Dos Equis commercial in which a man in his 60s who is well dressed and is described as "the most interesting man in the world" has the company of three young beautiful women who do not speak at all during the commercial; rather, they laugh and hang on his every word with sultry glances. Another example is the infamous Coors Light commercial where, ostensibly, if you drink Coors, you can have sex with twins. Each twin sits on either arm of the lucky man who gets their attention. In contrast, one rarely sees a powerful older wealthy woman, "the most interesting woman in the world," or any woman with an attractive sexualized young man or twins on each arm in mainstream advertising. Using the definition of sexual empowerment described earlier, who has the status, dominance, respect, and authority in these scenarios? Sexualized images used to sell products for mass consumption serve to sexually objectify women in distinct ways that indicate both their vulnerability and that their presence is as an accessory or for male pleasure. This also reinforces binary sex/gender systems and heteronormativity.

None of this directly relates to sex trafficking victimization, but, in radical feminist perspective, it does fuel a culture that views and sexualizes men and women in different ways, reflecting and reproducing a power imbalance and normalizing sexual objectification of women. To rectify this, equal sexualization of men; broader frameworks for the sexualization of men, women, and nonbinary or transgender people; or sexualizing women in a way representing power and status as opposed to weakness and reduced status may be called for. In addition to distinctions in mainstream advertising, there are various aspects of cultural support for male sexual desire of young female bodies.

Cultural Support for Domestic Minor Sex Trafficking

There is a culture of pornography that emphasizes teen porn, Lolita, and the schoolgirl fetish, which lends cultural support for domestic minor sex trafficking. Such forms of pornography fetishize the adolescent female form and normalize male desire for teen girls, facilitating demand for teen female bodies in part through culture. In the United States in 2013, the number two and number three pornography search terms were "teen" and "college," respectively (Feinberg 2013). "Teen" was ranked as the number one pornography-related search term in Texas, Florida, Wisconsin, Michigan, South Carolina, Mississippi, Missouri, and Oregon. Traditional college-age girls typically range from 17 to 21 years old. While blurring the lines between minors and adults in this age block, certainly these young women still represent a promotion of desire for teen or nearly teen women. In addition, *Girls Gone Wild* is also a popular video series that depicts young women, typically 17–20 years old, topless, and highly sexualized as "jailbait" and "barely legal" (Picker and Sun 2008).

"Lolita" is a character in a novel in which an adult male character lives with Lolita's mother. Lolita is 11 years old. The novel is written from the perspective of the adult male character, who expresses insatiable desire for Lolita. He eventually drugs and rapes her, finally satisfying the desire that steadily builds throughout the novel. The novel reached critical acclaim for the ability of the author, Vladimir Nabokov, to so convincingly express and intensify from start to finish the pedophilic desire of the adult male for Lolita. However, culturally, the content of the book is forgotten, while Lolita is currently projected as a young adolescent seductress who willingly tempts and teases men. Lolita is related to the "schoolgirl fetish," which is more or less normalized in U.S. culture. This fetish usually depicts girls in short pleated skirts, white socks, and black Mary Jane shoes, the typical school uniform for Catholic middle and high school girls. Teen porn, Lolita, and the schoolgirl fetish have become popularized in mainstream pornography, helping to normalize male desire for young females.

Similarly, younger looking girls with lollipops—a candy almost exclusively consumed by children—are also present on the covers of mainstream pornographic films (Bridges et al. 2010). Bridges and colleagues (2010) found in a random sample of fifty of the top-selling pornographic videos that 12% bore titles indicating that the female actors were young, underage, or teens, including *Teen Fuck Holes, Teenage Spermaholics, Anal Teen Tryouts, Cum Craving Teens*, and *Barely Legal*. Further, such films held both visual cues and scripted language indicating adolescent or otherwise childlike pornography. Visual cues included schoolgirl uniforms, pigtails, and braces on their teeth as well as babysitter characters (babysitters are typically adolescents). Moreover, scripted lines depicted childlike status, such as "I'm doing homework" or "I can't smoke" (Bridges et al. 2010).

While the argument can be made that the actors in such films must legally be 18 years of age and that the films only represents fantasy, it cannot be ignored that the fantasy that is supported is for a girl under 18, or just above, indicated by the titles, content, and appearance of the actors. Further, what does it mean to support a fantasy of teens and schoolgirls? While such videos may not involve sex trafficking, it supports a cultural environment conducive to and normalizing male sexual desire for school-girls and teens, or at least youthful bodies. Blurring the lines between minors and adults through words such as "barely legal" or "jailbait" or "just turned 18" is problematic for the same reason in that the line only exists in the context of punishment for sex with minors or child pornography and does not address the reason for this line. What does it mean when the pornography industry legally portrays adult women as adolescent objects of male sexual desire? Sex or sex acts with a minor legally constitute sex trafficking.

Advertising and television depicting the sexualization of youthful bod-ies is also related. For example, American Apparel ads notoriously use very young looking models posing in sexualized ways. The models might be 18, but they look much younger. Similarly, TLC show *Toddlers and Tiaras* depicts child beauty pageants for young beauty queens as young as 3 years old. The show has come under controversy multiple times. In one instance, a mother was noted for sexualizing 4-year-old Maddy Jackson by padding her chest to look like Dolly Parton. Her mother stated, "When she wears the fake boobs and the fake butt it's just an added extra bonus" (Canning and Pereira 2011). *Toddlers and Tiaras* also came under controversy when 3-year-old Paisley wore a costume emulating Julia Roberts's character in *Pretty Woman*, including black thigh-high boots, a midriff-baring top, and short tight skirt. Roberts played a sex worker in this film, and the child imitating her was referred to as a "prosti-tot." The girls are also known for sexualized dancing in the talent portion of the competition. Six-year-old Eden wore a showgirl costume, and her mother told a reporter that the cos-tumes were what judges noticed (Canning and Pereira 2011). Perhaps most overt was the show in which a little girl, 8-year-old Laci, actually wore strips of meat, essentially attempting to perform in a meat bikini (Lester 2012). Madonna's gold cone bra was also imitated. The series ended in 2013, with three spin-off series starring children from the original show. Reruns of the show still play on TLC and the TLC website, and on other popular Internet sites. The comedy film *Jackass Presents: Bad Grandpa* (Tremaine, 2013), cre-ated, written, produced, and acted by those of *Jackass* movie fame, included a scene with a little boy dressed up like the girls from *Toddlers and Tiaras* as he participated in a beauty pageant in which he used a stripper pole.

The intent was to overtly mock *Toddlers and Tiaras*. In the film, it was viewed as inappropriate and unacceptable for the boy to do it, yet similar actions are celebrated and normalized on *Toddlers and Tiaras* when performed by girls.

From advertisements depicting women engaged in pseudo-sex acts, to women as sexual accessories, to sexualized ads of youthful bodies, to beauty pageants of sexualized girls, our culture is somewhat tolerant and conditioned to view these things as normal. This book asks "What does that have to do with sex trafficking?" Sociologists emphasize the social environment and the impact this holds on the perspectives and views of those in society, including the ways that culture shapes desire. Radical feminist and abolitionist perspectives hold that a culture that sexually objectifies, degrades women and girls, and to some extent normalizes these things is a culture ripe for sex trafficking. Neoliberals and liberal feminists draw distinctions by age and choice, paying particular attention to children and the role of coercion. The research described above supports and refutes particular claims on both sides and can be subjectively interpreted. While such arguments are indirect and somewhat abstract, forms of pornography that are directly linked to sex trafficking are detailed in the following section.

Child Pornography as Sex Trafficking

According to the TVPA, any commercial sex act involving a minor is sex trafficking. Commercial sex acts take a variety of different forms, including pornography (Kotrla 2010; MacKinnon 2005). Those who possess, produce, sell, distribute, or trade child pornography for something of value could be viewed as sex traffickers. Moreover, some argue that possession, distribution, and production of child pornography is related to the issue of demand for both child pornography and prostitution of minors, which is central to the current sex trafficking discourse among researchers, academics, practitioners, and justice system initiatives (Smith, Vardaman, and Snow 2009; MacKinnon 2005). Possession of child pornography is not widely considered an act of sex trafficking, but possession of child pornography is related to sex trafficking both directly and indirectly. First, possession is directly related in terms of demand. An individual possesses child pornography because they have a demand for the content. This demand creates a market for the production of pornography, where inherently, children are sex trafficked to create it. Second, although the relationship is presently unclear, if an individual possesses such items, ostensibly, this indicates a potential demand for sex trafficking in the form of prostituted minors as well. It is unknown the proportion of those viewing child pornography and those who buy sex from minors. The following subsections examine possession, production, and distribution of child pornography in relationship to sex trafficking.

Possessing Child Pornography

There have been some high-profile federal child pornography possession cases in the Eastern District of Missouri. For example, in 2013 St. Louis priest Father William Vatterott was sentenced to just over 3 years in prison for possession of child pornography.[2] The Archdiocese of St. Louis was involved in cooperating with federal investigators, and the case became controversial due to the involvement of the Catholic priest. Similarly, a student at the Roman Catholic Kenrick-Glennon Seminary in St. Louis, Nickolas Eugene Pinkston, pled guilty to charges of trying to receive child pornography through the mail in 2012. The case garnered controversy not only because of his religious status but because he led confirmation classes in St. Louis for seventh and eighth graders at St. Ambrose Catholic Elementary School and was perceived afterward as an unknown or silent threat to the community. The U.S. Postal Service first became aware of Pinkston's affinity for child pornography when U.S. postal inspectors noted that Pinkston received mail in 2010 from an Ohio-based Internet site that allowed access to images of naked prepubescent and pubescent minors. Because of this he was flagged as a potential possessor of child pornography. Inspectors then sent advertisements for pornography DVDs to Pinkston's home under the cover of a fake distributor as part of an undercover operation. Pinkston proceeded to request the videos *Young Teen Girls (13–16)*, *Pre-Teen Girls*, and *Children's Sex Orgy*, which had 9- to 11-year-olds participating in various sex acts.[3] He was arrested when he picked up *Children's Sex Orgy* at the post office. Upon searching Pinkston's residence, inspectors found more pornography. Some of his pornography collection involved Pinkston apparently filming and photographing a nude preteen girl in India. Yet another film, titled *Jr. Beauty Pageant* involved images of nude minor girls. Pinkston also possessed multiple child pornography images on his computer. Pinkston will likely be sentenced to five years in prison without parole for possession of child pornography.[4] These two examples of possession illustrate a demand for sex trafficked children as children are sex trafficked to make the pornography. Buyers of child pornography could be viewed similarly to buyers of trafficked minors, who have been charged with sex trafficking in some jurisdictions (MacKinnon 2005; Smith, Vardaman, and Snow 2009). Increasingly, cases related to trafficked minors have involved successful prosecutions of the buyers as sex traffickers (chapter 8). Currently, those possessing child pornography are not charged with sex trafficking.

Producing Child Pornography

While possession of child pornography is not generally conceived of as a direct act of sex trafficking, producing child pornography directly fits the legal definition because it involves a commercial sex act involving a minor.[5] Like possession of child pornography, cases involving production of pornography are still generally prosecuted under previously existing laws. For example, in 2013 Poplar Bluff, Missouri, resident David Cathey was sentenced to 30 years in prison for two federal charges of producing child pornography. Cathey photographed two minor girls whom he caused to enact sexually explicit behaviors. The children were under 12 years old at the time the photos were taken. Cathey was caught when he sold his computer and forgot to take out a disc with the sexually explicit images of the girls.[6]

In 2013 Samuel Gonzales, also of Poplar Bluff, Missouri, was sentenced to 50 years in prison for recording himself performing sexual acts on a 9-year-old girl and for attempting to receive child pornography— he asked a 13-year-old girl to send him naked pictures of herself over the phone. In yet another case in Poplar Bluff, Missouri, in 2013, Jeffrey Shelton received a 120-year sentence on three felony charges, "including attempted production of child pornography, production of child pornography and possession of child pornography."[7] In 2012 neighbors called the police upon witnessing Shelton abusing his girlfriend. Shelton had abducted a 5-year-old girl just hours earlier. Shelton left the residence after hitting his girlfriend and also left his phone behind, which held sexually explicit content of the 5-year-old girl as well as separate images of a 10-year-old girl. It was later found that Shelton threatened physical harm toward the children. Shelton had more than two hundred images of child pornography on his computer. Pornographic images of children are typically sold or traded for other images among consumers and producers of pornography alike; through these transactions, child pornography becomes a commercial sex act involving a minor, fitting the legal definition of sex trafficking provided in the TVPA.

Girls are not the only victims of child-pornographers-as-sex-traffickers. In 2013 Matthew Hansen received a 20-year sentence for eight felony counts of attempted production of child pornography as he enticed minor boys to perform sexually for his videos over a five-year period in the St. Charles County area. The Fort Zumwalt School District elementary school teacher, volunteer fireman, and camp counselor recorded more than seventy-five preteen boys undressing for their showers at camp. In another case in 2013, 20-year-old martial arts instructor Chris Horton was indicted on five counts of sexual exploitation of a minor and one count of attempted sexual exploitation of a minor. The martial arts instructor from Belleville, Illinois, video-recorded himself sexually abusing martial arts students. Two were age 6, one was age 10, and he attempted to recruit another minor, aged 7, for the same purpose. Investigators found fifty-seven videos depicting child pornography on Horton's iPhone, created over the course of about a year. He was sentenced to 90 years for producing child pornography.[8] The sex acts involving minors were recorded, producing something of value to the perpetrator, as he could view the materials over and over. Such production of child pornography technically qualifies as sex trafficking (MacKinnon 2005). In other cases the commercial aspect of the sexual exchange is even more direct; a case in Salt Lake City, Utah, involved parents forcing their children to watch and then enact pornography. The parents charged a fee to observers, who paid in cash or with drugs (Smith, Vardaman, and Snow 2009).

The examples in this section represent only a handful of federally prosecuted cases; there are also those prosecuted at the state and county levels and many others that remain unidentified. Some of the cases were discovered by a chance mistake of a perpetrator, others by discovery and reporting by someone else, and still others through purposeful investigation or chance identification by law enforcement. There are likely many more unidentified cases of child pornography possession, production, and distribution. These examples show that there is some level of demand for sex acts with children. People would not possess, produce, or distribute child pornography if there was no demand for such acts. Any commercial exchange of sex acts or acts that result in producing something of value involving minors is a form of sex trafficking, regardless of what charge it is prosecuted under. Gender plays a role, in that the vast majority of the perpetrators involved with federal child pornography charges are men, whether possessing, producing, or distributing it. Typically, white men of all ages, classes, and regions are the perpetrators. The victims are both boys and girls, although more cases involve girls.

Chapter Summary

Political and feminist perspectives of pornography are general reflections of ideologies interrelated with sex trafficking discourse and debate. Neoliberals and their liberal feminist allies maintain that pornography and sex trafficking are distinct, and only pornography involving minors or those forced, defrauded, or coerced into producing pornography entails sex trafficking. Further, neoliberals and many liberal feminists maintain that the way women are portrayed in pornography is distinct from the way women and girls are viewed more generally in society. They also note that pornography rarely involves severe violence against women, and notions of degradation are subjective. Neoliberals maintain that the direct relationship between sex trafficking and violence against women to pornography is unclear or typically not present. As a result, such groups do not believe pornography should be abolished and maintain anticensorship principles. In contrast, radical feminists and abolitionists believe that sex trafficking and pornography are inherently intertwined because pornography is viewed as creating demand for sex trafficking and for the people who are trafficked to create it as well as demand for prostitution. Radical feminists maintain that pornography creates a social environment that normalizes degradation and subordination of women. Through this devaluation, women are seen as commodities for sexual purchase and objects for violence. Radical feminists/abolitionists view pornography and prostitution as forms of sex trafficking and consequently believe that all three should be abolished. These groups all agree that pornography involving children is sex trafficking. The TVPA maintains that any commercial sex act involving children is sex trafficking. Buyers, distributors, and producers of child pornography may consequently be labeled as sex traffickers. Cultural factors that promote normalized sexual desire for youthful bodies may be implicated in sex trafficking in the form of pornography, such as pornography labeled "teen," which is legal if the actors are 18 or older; the Lolita/schoolgirl fetish; and sexualized child beauty pageants. The U.S. Supreme Court upholds liberal/neoliberal/liberal feminist tenets of pornography, censoring only pornography involving children or subjectively determined and rarely enforced obscenity violations solidifying pornography as a form of free speech.

Discussion Questions

1. Describe at least three key radical feminist arguments used to justify eradication of pornography, and summarize the research supporting and refuting these arguments.

2. What is the Supreme Court's determination about pornography and censorship? Do you agree or disagree, and why?

3. In what ways do some types of pornography contribute to cultural desire for young adult female bodies?

[4]

Prostitution

In November 2012 a teenager went to her high school counselor to get help coping with a sexual assault. Daniel Onodera was arrested for the assault and was also alleged to be the leader of a prostitution ring involving minors in Colorado. The subsequent investigation identified three teen girls, one of them 13 years old and the others 16, as survivors/victims. The girls did not know each other but shared common characteristics in that they had each run away from home, were truant from school, and had substance abuse problems facilitated by Onodera. The girls were provided with methamphetamine, Xanax, and cocaine and were then expected to have sex with members of Onodera's prostitution ring as well as strangers in exchange for drugs. The seven perpetrators ranged in age from 20 to 57; Onodera was 42. The charges included trafficking of a child, pimping of a child, sexual assault of a child, solicitation of a child for prostitution, pandering, keeping a place of child prostitution, child prostitution-induce-ment, contributing to the delinquency of a minor, and two violent crime counts.[1] Onodera was sentenced to 120 years to life in 2015.

Cases like this are not typically viewed as controversial because it is the likely consensus that Onodera's actions should be acknowledged as criminal because children were involved. Yet prostitution that does not involve children has been the subject of policy debate among political ideologues, sex workers, sex trafficked people, and feminists for decades. Such debates primarily revolve around the relative agency and victimization of those who sell sex as well as the societal impact of prostitution policy. Currently and for the last 15 years, discussion about the relationship of prostitution to sex trafficking has been the centerpiece of these debates as those who are victimized in sex trafficking are victimized within the larger context of prostitution. Accordingly, this chapter examines the political and feminist discourse surrounding prostitution. Further, the chapter describes the benefits and challenges of competing models of prostitution policy—explicitly, the prohibitionist, abolitionist, decriminalization, and legalization models informed by these competing feminist and political debates as well as criminological theories of deterrence and displacement—in association to sex trafficking.

Feminist Perspectives of Prostitution

Liberal Feminist Perspectives of Prostitution

Because liberal feminism generally supports and places priority on women's individual choices, many liberal feminists view prostitution as an expression of agency in that individuals may choose sex work as an occupation. The emphasis is on choice—if individuals choose to sell sex, then they are expressing agency in adopting this choice. In such cases, when those who sell sex have control over the choice to sell sex, the choice in buyers, and the choice in contraception and have control over their own earnings, liberal feminists use the term "sex work."

At the same time, liberal feminists, or "choice" feminists may point out that it is often women's reduced opportunities and choices that make them more likely to engage in the commercial sex industry, and they simultaneously emphasize that women should have the choice to do what they want with their bodies. Sex work may be a rational choice for survival or earning a living, or for sexual empowerment or autonomy. Liberal feminism may overlap with intersectional and transnational feminism, which point out that, in a global context, it is typically women who migrate from or are trafficked from poor nations to high-income nations to provide sexual services, or those in marginalized or vulnerable positions in society who are sex workers. This illustrates the role of global power dynamics and social stratification in selling sex as both a viable survival strategy and as an indicator of exploitation of economic vulnerability (Outshoorn 2005).

Some liberal and transnational feminists suggest that antiprostitution efforts are rooted in Western feminism and coincide with conservative mores of sexuality.

> Many women in the sex industry in the rich industrialized countries are little different than those women migrants working in domestic labor or the entertainment business as waitresses, barmaids, or dancers. Only if one sees sexual contact as utterly different from other kinds of body contact can one isolate sex work from other types of services providing care for the body, such as hairdressing, nursing, or massage.
>
> (Outshoorn 2005, 147–48)

Liberal feminists as a whole are more likely to draw a clear line between sex trafficking and sex work, with sex trafficking involving force, fraud, coercion of minors, and sex work involving consenting adults.

A group called Call Off Your Old Tired Ethics (COYOTE), a sex workers' union, can be used to illustrate the liberal feminist perspective of prostitution. COYOTE began in 1973 and aimed to improve the working conditions of sex workers in San Francisco by decriminalizing prostitution and eradicating the associated social stigma (Shaver 2005). The group prefers the term "sex work" as opposed to "prostitution," which validates the practice as a viable job alternative and simply another form of labor. The group acknowledges the agency of sex workers as those who willingly choose sex work as a career. While acknowledging agency, COYOTE simultaneously acknowledged victimization but maintained that such victimization is largely due to the illegality of sex work, not the sex work itself, which forces sex workers into unsafe working conditions and exposes them to further harm in arrest, fines, and jail time. Pointedly, sex workers themselves have created unions and the Sex Workers' Rights Movement to improve their working conditions and to reduce victimization. At the same time COYOTE has also worked to provide services for thousands of sex workers, primarily women, who need assistance with various legal and social services as well as crisis counseling and support groups (Shaver 2005). COYOTE illustrates that regardless of agency and choice, many individuals are still victimized through prostitution (Dempsey 2011). Yet the existence of willing sex workers cannot be denied as their visibility is present in organizations, unions, antitrafficking efforts, and the United Nations (Lutnick and Cohan 2009; Outshoorn 2005; Dempsey 2011; Doezema 2005; Shaver 2005). Moreover, such groups argue that it is the illegality of prostitution that facilitates their victimization.

Radical Feminist Perspectives of Prostitution

In contrast, radical feminists describe all prostitution as sex trafficking and a form of violence against women (Ekberg 2004; Farley 2004; MacKinnon 2005; Dempsey 2011). Gunilla Ekberg suggests that the legalization of prostitution is an expression of patriarchy: "Legalization of prostitution means that the state imposes regulations with which they can control one class of women as prostituted" (2004, 1190). Radical feminists largely hold the perspective that prostitution is paid rape, regardless if an individual consents to it or not. Radical feminists maintain that the much larger number of women and girls involved in prostitution reflects a patriarchal society that commodifies women's bodies. Accordingly, radical feminists see all people who sell sex as victims of this system. Radical feminists reject the idea that prostitution can be a completely voluntary free choice and note that prostitution violates human rights. Catharine MacKinnon (2005) maintains that it is a false dichotomy "to distinguish trafficking from prostitution, as if trafficking by definition is forced and prostitution by definition is free." Accordingly, radical feminists view sex trafficking and prostitution as synonymous.

The organization Breaking Free, which serves survivors of sex trafficking/ prostitution in the Minneapolis–St. Paul area, is a representation of the radical feminist perspective of prostitution. Women Hurt in Systems of Prostitution Engaged in Revolt (WHISPER), the precursor to Breaking Free, was founded by a group of women who were sexually exploited in prostitution. The group's aim was to raise awareness about the victimization of prostituted people as well as the need for available services. This group maintained that prostitution inherently involves sexual exploitation and that those in the commercial sex industry are victims of pimps, buyers, and members of the community. They pointed out the disproportionate victimization of prostituted people in the context of physical violence, rape, sexual assault, and serial killing. When WHISPER lost support in the 1990s, Venita Carter, the executive director of WHISPER and a survivor of prostitution, formed Breaking Free "as an Afro-Centric non-profit agency helping women and girls escape systems of prostitution and sexual exploitation through advocacy, direct services, housing, and education."[2] Carter writes on the Breaking Free website: "Prostitution is not the world's oldest profession. It is the world's oldest oppression." The organization uses the term "sex trafficking/prostitution," not "sex work," grouping the words together purposefully to indicate that they are viewed as one and the same. To highlight the harms encountered in prostitution, Breaking Free notes, "we must first recognize sex trafficking/prostitution as a form of violence against women." Commercial sexual exploitation is further described as "a practice by which a person achieves sexual gratification, financial gain, or advancement through the abuse or exploitation of a person's sexuality by abrogating that person's human right to dignity, equality, autonomy, and physical and mental well-being."[3]

Each of these perspectives of prostitution has informed various models of prostitution policy practiced around the globe. Although the focus of this book centers on the United States, it is important to understand these global models and their outcomes as they have the potential to guide prostitution and sex trafficking policy in the United States—and to some extent already have. As is discussed in chapter 2, radical feminists and abolitionists have traditionally supported abolitionist models of prostitution policy, and liberal feminists and neoliberals are more likely to support legalization or decriminalization models. Importantly, the type of system with the worst outcomes for sex workers and sex trafficked/exploited people is the prohibitionist system practiced in the United States. The following sections go beyond feminist and political theoretical debates to include criminological theory and research applied in the area of prostitution policy models and the relationship to sex trafficking.

Models of Prostitution Policy

Deterrence Model

In the deterrence model, also referred to as the prohibitionist model or criminalization model, prostitution is criminalized, including the sale and purchase of sex. The prohibitionist approach to prostitution centers on ideologies of deterrence through criminalization. As described in chapter 2, the deterrence model is based on the assumption that punishment deters undesirable behaviors or crimes. Sex-for-sale is viewed as a criminal act on the part of anyone involved—sex workers, buyers, and any third parties, such as "managers," "pimps," "madams," or "traffickers." Those who sell sex are viewed as expressing agency in making the choice to sell sex. In prohibitionist systems, those who sell sex are largely viewed by the legal system as criminals who knowingly violate the law and not as victims, with the exception of those who are recognized as meeting legal definitions of sex trafficking. The United States currently follows the prohibitionist model, with a few exceptions in the state of Nevada, regarding prostitution policy, as do China, Cambodia, Jamaica, Malta, Philippines, Romania, Slovenia, Sri Lanka, Tanzania, Uganda, Vietnam, and others.

There are several problems associated with prohibitionist models of prostitution policy. First, sex workers have limited legal rights to defend themselves if they are victimized in the course of their involvement in the commercial sex industry. If those who sell sex or are trafficked seek assistance from law enforcement, they may be putting themselves at risk for their own arrest because prostitution is labeled as a criminal activity (Lutnick and Cohan 2009; Dank et al. 2015). Sex trafficked people, including minors, are often misidentified as criminals. Moreover, if a buyer did not pay for services rendered, or the buyer robbed the sex worker, the sex worker would be unlikely to seek assistance from law enforcement because the engagement in illegal activity would have to be disclosed in creating a police report. This is also the case for those who sell sex and are raped, beaten, or otherwise injured during the course of their occupation. While they have the legal right to seek police assistance for this type of victimization, disclosing their illegal occupation, dealing with the negative social stigma, and risking arrest deters many sex workers/prostituted people from disclosing victimization to law enforcement. Law enforcement is not typically viewed as an ally, nor are police departments seen as safe spaces, because of the illegality of sex-for-sale and the related arrest, fines, and jail time. Similarly, researchers find in prohibitionist systems that when sex workers/prostituted people do ask law enforcement for assistance, they may be rejected, victimized by law enforcement, or arrested for outstanding warrants (Lutnick and Cohan 2009; Nichols 2010). Research finds reports of sex workers who are victimized when asking for help and who may even be coerced into sexual activity with officers as a "bargain" to avoid arrest and fines (Lutnick and Cohan 2009; Nichols 2010; Curtis et al. 2008). In addition, researchers find that those who sell sex are disproportionately arrested, charged, and fined compared to buyers or pimps. Violence against those in the commercial sex industry is rampant by police, buyers, pimps/traffickers, and community members in prohibitionist systems. One study found that about 30% of sex workers were threatened with arrest by police unless they had sex with them, were arrested after sex with police, or were arrested after refusing sex with police (Lutnick and Cohan 2009). Contrary to law enforcement and advocacy efforts to reduce the harm to individuals as well as general society, sex workers in fact indicated an increased risk to their own health as well as the public health in that they were less likely to use condoms because officers would use them as evidence of intent to commit prostitution (Lutnick and Cohan 2009).

Aspects of harm reduction are also limited in prohibitionist models. Harm reduction works to literally reduce the harm to the individual—in this case, the individual selling sex. Harm reduction typically includes street outreach, safe shelter, social services to assist with exiting prostitution, substance abuse services, health screenings, and access to condoms and dental dams to prevent sexually transmitted infections (STI) as well as various forms of contraception. In the United States, harm-reduction efforts are limited or nonexistent depending on the region. Harm reduction is largely restricted to the largest cities, and services are extremely limited.

In addition, the assumption that criminalization acts as a deterrent is not supported by the extant research. The recidivism rate for prostitution is very high; accordingly, the idea that arrest and charges directed at those who sell sex helps prevent prostitution is simply not borne out by the research. As one sex trafficking survivor who was coerced to engage in prostitution pointed out, when sex workers are arrested and fined, they have no way to pay the fine, so they sell sex to pay off the fine (Heil and Nichols 2015). As a result, the cycle of prostitution is perpetuated by arrest-and-fine tactics rather than deterred. Criminalization also prevents exiting prostitution because it is more difficult to get a job with a prostitution record (Heil and Nichols 2015). Those who exit sex trafficking may be channeled back into the commercial sex industry due to lack of options. Importantly, prostitution occurs in areas where it is criminalized—just because something is illegal does not mean it goes away. Evidence suggests deterrence-based prostitution policy is ineffective and too simplistic in its current form and is damaging to sex workers and trafficking survivors alike.

In addition to lack of support for deterrence, displacement may also occur. Displacement theory is related to deterrence theory and criminalization of prostitution. The basic idea of displacement theory is that when a particular act is criminalized in one place, it simply moves to another. For example, if a friend says on New Year's Eve that there is a road block on a particular street where law enforcement is checking for drinking and driving, does that stop everyone from having a glass of champagne at midnight and driving home? Or would they simply go another way? Within the specific context of prostitution and sex trafficking, there is evidence to suggest that displacement is the result of deterrence-based policy. Some researchers suggest that profitability combined with low risk makes displacement more likely in cases of prostitution and sex trafficking (Heil and Nichols 2014).

For example, Ric Curtis and colleagues (2008) noted displacement in New York City with tougher restrictions on sex work intended to deter prostitution. They noted that under the Giuliani administration (1994–2001) there was a crackdown on the sex industry in New York City. Stores selling pornographic magazines, books, and videos as well as strip clubs and peep shows were restricted by location; they were required to be 500 feet from each other as well as 500 feet from churches, schools, and residential areas and some commercial and manufacturing areas as well. This changed the face of establishments around Times Square and was known to reduce the number of street-level sex workers in Midtown as a result (see Sviridoff et al. 2000). However, prostitution rose in the surrounding boroughs. So while sex work decreased in one area, it was displaced to another. This "squeezing the balloon" effect did little to reduce the amount of sex work overall. Similarly, in 2002 the Bloomberg administration worked to eradicate sex workers from the streets of New York by increasing punishments, such as increased arrests of both sex sellers and buyers as well as increased undercover stings. The result was the diversification of the sex industry, which moved increasingly underground, largely involving online solicitation or solicitation through the use of phones and meeting in private residences or hotels. Consequently, prostitution was displaced from the street to the indoors, making sex trafficking even more difficult to identify (Curtis et al. 2008).

In sum, deterrence models are found to be lacking, at least as currently implemented. They do little to deter sex workers and their buyers or sex traffickers. Further, the deterrence model is currently the worst model for sex workers, who lack legal recourse, are disproportionately victimized and arrested, and experience the revolving door back into prostitution as a result of misguided criminal justice policy. This model may also make sex trafficking more difficult to identify due to mistrust of police, fear of arrest, and movement to more hidden venues. Moreover, aspects of harm reduction are limited, such as street outreach, passing out free condoms, and the availability of social services for those exiting prostitution. In order for this model to improve, decriminalizing the sale of sex, increasing harm-reduction efforts, and providing additional resources for those who sell sex are called for. Essentially, this would mean moving toward a different model of prostitution policy—namely, abolitionist, decriminalization, or legalization models.

Decriminalization and Legalization Models

Decriminalization and legalization models are in some ways similar, yet they are distinct. Decriminalization relates to eliminating laws that prevent the sale or purchase of sex and consequently removes law enforcement interventions involved in prohibiting sexual commerce. Legalization also eliminates laws preventing sexual commerce, but the state is still involved in regulating the sex industry, including setting the locations or "zones" where prostitution is allowed and determining the circumstances under which individuals are allowed to buy and sell sex. In the legalization model, sex workers typically pay taxes on their income and receive benefits from the state. They may also be required to procure a license and maintain periodic health screenings and, for females, gynecological exams. Ideologically, the goal of both models is to legitimize sex work as a respected occupation and to offer increased protections to sex workers. Sex workers are seen as expressing agency, as those who willingly engage in sexual commerce. Legalization and decriminalization models criminalize sex trafficking—or selling sex induced by force, fraud coercion, or when minors are involved—but not the sex work. Buyers are also not criminalized and are viewed as purchasers of a legitimate service. Neoliberals and liberal feminists who see sexual commerce as a legitimate occupation engaged in by those expressing agency and free choice (described in chapter 2) tend to support legalization or decriminalization models. Organizations such as the Sex Workers Project and partners of the Global Alliance Against Traffic in Women support such models as well (see chapter 11).

A benefit of decriminalization and legalization models is that sex workers as well as sex trafficked people have recourse for their victimization. If they are victimized by buyers, traffickers, pimps, managers, or members of the community, they can go to law enforcement for assistance without fear of arrest, fine, or other punishment. Such models are consequently known to improve working conditions. In addition, harm reduction is typically included in such models, although the quality varies depending on the resources of the nation. Legalization models in high-income countries are generally regarded as offering the most extensive harm-reduction benefits to sex workers. Harm reduction works to offer social services and health services to sex workers. Sex workers may also get assistance with substance abuse issues, exiting prostitution, and access to medical care and condoms. Legalization may involve regulations such as mandatory health screenings, obtaining licensing and registration as a sex worker, and designated zones in which sex work can take place. Ideologically, legalization attempts to regulate sexual commerce with the aim of protecting public order and public health, and improving working conditions for those who willingly engage in sex-for-sale. The Netherlands, Germany, Switzerland, Austria, Hungary, Denmark, Greece, Turkey, Senegal, and Victoria, Queensland, and the Northern Territory in Australia, are examples of some nations who offer harm reduction as part of their legalization model.

While there are some benefits to legalization models, some challenges exist as well. For example, while sex workers are screened for STIs, the human immunodeficiency virus (HIV), and other communicable infections, their buyers generally are not, with some exceptions. As a result, buyers' health is protected, but sex workers' health is not protected. The frequent blood tests and gynecological exams and filling out paperwork were also described as laborious by sex workers in one study, with sex workers preferring decriminalization to legalization/regulation models to avoid weekly health exams (Lutnick and Cohan 2009). Moreover, sex workers continue to be disproportionately victimized compared to the general population in legalization/decriminalization nations (Dempsey 2011). Further, while ideologically the shift to legitimate employment was supposed to destigmatize sex work, research bears out that sex workers have not yet attained the status of respected service providers in legalization/decriminalization models. At the same time, the stigma is notably the worst in nations with the most restrictions on prostitution, namely, in prohibitionist nations (Lutnick and Cohan 2009).

Ideologically, while sex workers have legal recourse for victimization, some nations practicing legalization models report ongoing abuses and harassment by police. For example, The Association, a sex workers' rights organization in Hungary, reported that police routinely harass sex workers. Police facilitate eviction of sex workers from their apartments for conducting sex work outside of legal zones. Social service providers and sex workers from The Association note that officers are known to stop sex workers and ask them to come to their cars, forcing them to step just outside of a legal zone, and then the sex workers are fined. If they do not comply, they can be fined for resisting an officer. Police also impose littering fines in the same way, throwing trash at sex workers, then arresting or fining the sex worker for littering (Hungarian Civil Liberties Union 2013).

In contrast, decriminalization does not involve extensive regulations on zoning, licensing, and mandatory health screenings like the legalization model. Existing regulations are the same as those covering other areas of employment. Like legalization models, decriminalization also aims to improve working conditions for sex workers through harm reduction but poses fewer legal challenges to sex workers such as harassment related to legal/illegal zones and fees for licensing or to work in legal zones. New South Wales in Australia and New Zealand exercise the decriminalization model. Even in these locales, there is some evidence of regulation. Brothel owners in New Zealand are required to get brothel licensing, and in New South Wales street prostitution is not legal. Research indicates that health, safety, and working conditions of willing sex workers are best in legalization/decriminalization models (Lutnick and Cohan 2009). Sex workers in San Francisco, where prostitution is criminalized, report favoring decriminalization, in order to improve their lives (Lutnick and Cohan 2009).

Some researchers indicate that legalization of sex work increases sex trafficking, but the research in this area is limited and findings are complex. If all prostitution is labeled as sex trafficking, then overall this is true. If sex trafficking is viewed as distinct in respect to sex work, then the research is unclear. Ideologically, the legalization model is intended to reduce sex trafficking because willing sex workers could legitimately practice their occupation, quashing a need for sex trafficking (Outshoorn 2005; Segrave 2009; Limoncelli 2010; Cho, Dreher, and Neumayer 2013). The "substitution effect" is the term used to describe this dynamic, that trafficked people would literally be substituted with willing sex workers. In contrast, the "scale effect" is the term used to describe the dynamic that holds that legalization expands prostitution markets, drawing in more local customers as well as sex tourists, which in turn increases trafficking to meet the demand of expanded markets (Cho, Dreher, and Neumayer 2013; Limoncelli 2009). In an analysis of 150 countries, Cho and colleagues (2013) found that the scale effect had more of an impact than the substitution effect, that legalization increased sex trafficking overall. Niklas Jakobsson and Andreas Kotsadam (2011) also found increased sex trafficking in legalized markets in an examination of 31 European nations.

In some nations practicing the legalization model, there is evidence of higher rates of sex trafficking, such as in the Netherlands and Germany (Cho, Dreher, and Neumayer 2013). Germany, for example, has a legalization model and has one of the largest markets for prostitution in Europe; it also has higher rates of sex trafficking compared to abolitionist nations in Europe. A two-tier legal and illegal system may develop, and is characteristic of some nations practicing the legalization model (Cho, Dreher, and Neumayer 2013; Shared Hope International 2011; Kara 2010). The illegal system arises alongside the legal system as participants attempt to avoid licensing fees, rigorous health screenings, or harassment or deportation related to immigration, or attempt to avoid operating in the more expensive approved zones or to capitalize on the markets drawn in through legalization.

Yet, in some nations with legalization/decriminalization models, a low rate of sex trafficking and reduced victimization of sex workers is found, such as in locales in Australia and in New Zealand. This may be due to regional and cultural factors, including the cost and ease of travel/migration from those in low-income countries who are vulnerable to exploitation and can easily be trafficked into higher income locations. Trafficked people in Western, Northern, and Southern Europe are predominately those from low-income nations (Cho, Dreher, and Neumayer 2013; Kara 2010; Limoncelli 2009; Shared Hope International 2011). In the Netherlands there are a comparatively larger number of illegal immigrants who are particularly vulnerable to exploitation due to undocumented status and consequent fear of the legal system and deportation. In contrast, Victoria, Australia, with a relatively low number of illegal immigrants, has a similar model to the Netherlands but shows no increase in sex trafficking and reduced victimization of those in the sex industry. Thus, regional contextual dynamics are implicated in distinctions between countries using the same model (Cho, Dreher, and Neumayer 2013). The majority of sex trafficking occurs intraregionally, indicating that regional dynamics are important to consider as well as the push and pull factors within a particular region in terms of the outcomes of legalization (Stolz 2005). Overall, high-income countries with a legalization model that have larger populations and larger numbers of migrants who are susceptible to exploitation experience increased sex trafficking based on current data and compared to similar nations with alternate models (Cho, Dreher, and Neumayer 2013). Randall Akee and colleagues (2010) found in a global cross-sectional dyad country sample that overall, regardless of the prostitution policy model, there was no difference in trafficking. Low-income countries have a lack of resources for enforcing criminalization and supporting harm reduction or regulation (Kara 2010). Accordingly, the policy at hand will have little effect (Cho, Dreher, and Neumayer 2013).

In sum, overall benefits of both decriminalization and legalization models include increased access to harm reduction, legal recourse for victimization, and low sex trafficking and victimization of sex workers in some locations. Challenges to legalization models include ongoing police harassment, development of the two-tier legal/illegal system in some locations, increased sex trafficking in some sites, and heightened risk of exploitation of undocumented immigrants in some locations. The relationship between the legalization model and sex trafficking depends upon regional contextual dynamics. In order for the legalization model to improve, addressing police harassment and providing citizenship, increased resources, and services to immigrants is recommended.

Abolitionist Model

Recall from chapter 2 that abolitionism literally refers to eradicating slavery. In the context of commercial sex, abolitionists view sexual commerce as a form of modern-day slavery. Consequently, one aim of abolitionism is to eradicate prostitution, which is viewed as a form of sex trafficking. The abolitionist model is a unique blend of criminalization and decriminalization. Simply put, it is illegal for anyone to be involved in prostitution except the prostituted person; buying sex is criminalized, selling sex is decriminalized. Buyers as well as third parties, such as pimps, managers, madams, or traffickers, are criminalized. The abolitionist model is commonly referred to as the "Swedish model," as it originated in this Nordic country in 1999. The abolitionist model also includes various aspects of harm reduction, such as social welfare policies that assist people in exiting and avoiding prostitution/sex trafficking. In addition, the Swedish model includes public education campaigns to raise awareness of the harms experienced by prostituted people, with the aim of changing social norms that support sex trafficking/prostitution (Ekberg 2004; Dempsey 2011). The model supports the radical feminist view of sexual commerce and works to change the social environment to one where women are seen as equal partners, not as sexual commodities (Ekberg 2004; Dempsey 2011; Outshoorn 2005). Iceland, Norway, and Sweden all follow the abolitionist model. Many antitrafficking organizations in the United States support the abolitionist model, such as the Coalition Against Trafficking in Women as well as organizations directly serving survivors of sex trafficking, commercial sexual exploitation, and those choosing to exit prostitution (see chapter 11). A central tenet of the abolitionist model is that prostitution fuels demand, and sex trafficking occurs to meet that demand for the purpose of profit. Thus, buyers are targeted by law enforcement as well as awareness campaigns because demand by buyers is seen as the root cause of the problem.

The outcomes of the Swedish policy include a decline in street prostitution as well as the number of men who have purchased sex (County Administrative Board of Stockholm 2014; Crouch 2015; Ministry of Health and Social Issues 2010). The County Administrative Board of Stockholm (2014) reports that street prostitution has declined 50% following the implementation of the policy, based on data collected by the Prostitution Units, or Mikamottagningarna, in Stockholm, Gothenburg, and Malmö. Similarly, when Norway adopted the Swedish model in 2009, a sizable reduction in street prostitution also occurred (Ministry of Health and Social Issues 2010). Moreover, the number of men who reported buying sex in Sweden declined by 40% between 1995 and 2009 (County Administrative Board of Stockholm 2014). Presently 7.5% of Swedish men between the ages of 18 and 65 indicate having ever bought sex, and no Swedish women indicate having bought sex. Another 2010 report from the Swedish Ministry of Health and Social Issues held similar findings, reflecting changed attitudes about prostitution as well as a decline in street prostitution. The Swedish model is often framed as a utopian model of successful policy in reducing and working to eliminate sex trafficking. Yet there are some important challenges associated with the policy.

Critiques of the abolitionist model largely center on agency and individual freedoms. Those who view sex trafficking as distinct from sex work view this model as restricting individuals' freedom to engage in sexual commerce. Because sex trafficking and prostitution are viewed as indistinct, research tends to examine and report findings of prostitution as a whole and measures the success of the policy accordingly. Other critiques suggest that criminal displacement occurred as a result of the policy, that prostitution itself was simply moved rather than deterred. Specifically, the illegality of buying sex pushed prostitution underground or to other countries. For example, following the 1999 implementation of the policy in Sweden, prostitution increased in Denmark and Norway, where selling sex was legal (Norway adopted the Swedish model in 2009) (Ekberg 2004; Ministry of Health and Social Issues 2010). Swedish men may simply travel to neighboring nations to buy sex where prostitution is legal, such as Denmark or the Netherlands, which are easy to access. Similarly, while street prostitution markedly declined, indoor prostitution and solicitation online may have increased (Levy and Jakobsson 2014). A report from the Swedish Association for Sexuality Education indicated that the decline in street prostitution may not reflect an overall decline in prostitution; rather, increased use of cell phones and the Internet to arrange transactions may have simply moved street solicitation indoors (Crouch 2015). The research in this area is unclear, with some reports suggesting a large increase in online ads soliciting sex-for-sale, indicating criminal displacement. The County Administrative Board of Stockholm (2014) reported that the number of online ads targeting men seeking sex from women increased from 304 to 6,965 in an eight-year period. The same report found the number of ads targeting men seeking sex from men increased from 190 to 702 in the same study period. Yet the report found that single individuals were responsible for multiple ads and duplicate ads, traced through repeated phone numbers used in the solicitations, suggesting that this increase in prostitution facilitated online was not as high as it appeared. However, the report did not include how many were repeat or multiple ads by the same individuals. In comparative analysis, street prostitution and Internet solicitation were three times higher in neighboring countries Norway and Denmark in 2008, whereas only online solicitations showed any signs of increase in Sweden (Ministry of Health and Social Issues 2010). Taken together, the research suggests an overall decline in prostitution in Sweden since the policy was established but with some level of displacement to other neighboring countries and moving indoors with solicitation occurring through use of technology. Some researchers report the number of individuals selling sex online in Sweden is currently relatively static, as is selling sex overall, after street prostitution reportedly dropped 50% following implementation of the Swedish model (County Administrative Board of Stockholm 2014; Crouch 2015; Ministry of Health and Social Issues 2010).

While some research indicates that prostitution is down considerably in Sweden, the proportion of women selling sex from low-income nations, such as Romania, Bulgaria, and Nigeria, have increased since the 1990s (County Administrative Board of Stockholm 2014; Crouch 2015). Of street-level sex workers and those advertising escort prostitution online in Sweden, 80% are not Swedish (County Administrative Board of Stockholm 2014). This indicates that women in Sweden are less likely to be willing to engage in sex work, probably because other opportunities are available. Gay men are thought to compose the majority of domestic prostitution in Sweden (County Administrative Board of Stockholm 2014). In neighboring nations, the same pattern is also present—the majority of sex workers and sex trafficked people are primarily women coming from low-income nations, who are either trafficked or seeking work or survival opportunities. There are some researchers who suggest that antitrafficking efforts are really about anti-immigration efforts. Further, abolitionism is viewed by some as a white, middle-class, Western women's movement attempting to oppress the job opportunities of poor women of color or women from low-income nations (Outshoorn 2005). Some transnational feminists decry the idea that these women need to be "taken care of" or "protected" (Doezema 1999, 2001; Outshoorn 2005).

Importantly, the Swedish policy has been criticized for increasing the risk of victimization of prostituted people, particularly street-level prostitution, because sex workers must make quick decisions about buyers to avoid getting caught by police (Levy and Jakobsson 2014). While those who sell sex would not be arrested if the transaction was uncovered by police, the buyer would, thus interfering with profitability of the sex worker. Since the livelihood of those engaged in selling sex depends on the buyer, the assessment of risk is sacrificed in order to secure the buyer. Unfortunately, this may pose increased violence directed toward those who sell sex compared to situations in which they would have time to do a surface-level risk assessment without fear of losing a buyer due to law enforcement involvement (Levy and Jakobsson 2014).

The model has also been criticized for not including some of the benefits of the harm-reduction model, particularly initiatives created to make selling sex safer, such as passing out free condoms through street outreach or through drop-in clinics. In order to get services, individuals must essentially agree not to sell sex, which is antithetical to harm-reduction models (Crouch 2015). In addition, those who sell sex remain highly stigmatized in Sweden, serving as a barrier to accessing services, "making it difficult for women to get help from social services and the police, and stoking their fear of eviction or loss of custody of their children" (Crouch 2015).

The number of Swedes supporting criminalization of selling sex has increased, essentially supporting the deterrence model, which poses the worst outcomes for sex workers and trafficked people (Crouch 2015; County Administrative Board of Stockholm 2014). About half of women and more than a third of men in Sweden support criminalization (County Administrative Board of Stockholm 2014). This indicates that concern for the well-being of those who sold sex or were otherwise prostituted, originally a central tenet of the abolitionist model, has lost some cultural support to those in favor of criminalization.

In sum, the research indicates the Swedish model is associated with an overall reduction of prostitution in Sweden. Yet a proportion of this decline involves displacement to hidden venues within Sweden or pushes it to neighboring nations. Sex trafficking is reportedly lower in Sweden compared to other neighboring nations with legalization models, but it is similar to locales in Australia and New Zealand that have legalization or decriminalization models (Cho, Dreher, and Neumayer 2013). In order for the policy to be more successful, it would need to be widely adopted to avoid criminal displacement. Moreover, nations practicing this model would need to bridge gaps between those who sell sex and law enforcement. In addition, it is imperative that the model include nonconditional elements of harm reduction—client-centered services, assistance with substance abuse and exiting prostitution, access to health screenings, and free condoms and other forms of contraception as well as increased resources to migrants.

How Do These Debates Relate to Sex Trafficking in the United States?

Simply put, there is no perfect model of prostitution policy. Which is the best policy? This depends on what the goal is. If the goal is to improve the working conditions and safety of sex workers, then decriminalization or legalization models with extensive harm-reduction efforts are best. If the goal is to reduce prostitution, then the abolitionist model is the best model. If the goal is to reduce sex trafficking, then the research suggests that location and regional contextual factors are key. In some areas, abolitionism is best; in other areas, decriminalization/legalization may work just as well. Generally speaking, the deterrence model is the most harmful for those who willingly engage in sexual commerce as well as sex trafficked people who are criminalized as sex workers. Despite the hotly contested political and feminist debates about prostitution, there is general agreement that sex trafficking, in which prostitution is induced by force, fraud, or coercion, or involves minors, is disempowering and criminal (Kempadoo and Doezema 1998; Dempsey 2011; Weitzer 2010). However, these groups disagree on the model of prostitution policy that would best prevent and address sex trafficking victimization.

These debates directly relate to policy, both historically and presently, specifically on whether to distinguish sex trafficking from sex work. The international Convention for the Suppression of the Traffic in Persons of 1949, which was both antitrafficking as well as antiprostitution, was the first attempt toward abolitionism.[4] Many states did not ratify it because it conflated sex trafficking and prostitution and viewed them as inherently interrelated. Many European nations have adopted legalization policy. In the international political arena, the UN Vienna Declaration (1993) worked to address violence against women; condemned trafficking, not prostitution; and again marked a clear distinction between the two.[5] The focus was on consent and nonconsent to engage in sex work (Outshoorn 2005). Similar dynamics exist in the present-day responses to trafficking. In part due to these ongoing heated debates on both trafficking and prostitution, the United Nations again moved away from abolitionism in the drafting of the 2000 Palermo Protocol, international legislation drafted to address human trafficking (see chapter 9).[6] Consequently, historically and presently, there is a clear line drawn between sex trafficking and sex work in the definitions provided by the international community. Nations develop their own prostitution policies; the United States adopted language similar to the Palermo Protocol, delineating a distinction between sex trafficking and prostitution, among contentious political and feminist debates (see Stolz 2005). At the same time, recent changes in the United States indicate a movement toward abolitionism, although not completely or uniformly, and have also resulted in heated policy debates. Shifts include a renewed focus on enforcing the criminalization of buyers (see chapter 8) and reducing criminal punishments of trafficked people, particularly minors (see chapter 9).

Incorporating the voices of survivors of sexual exploitation/sex trafficking as well as those who otherwise sell sex is important in developing or changing models of prostitution policy as these groups are the most affected. Ignoring or marginalizing the existence of any of these groups is damaging to their safety and autonomy. Drawing from their experiences and recommendations is important because they can be used to shape both policy and practice. Ostensibly, those who sell sex know best about what measures can facilitate their safety (Lutnick and Cohan 2009). Similarly, sex trafficked or commercially sexually exploited people can provide important insights into their lived experience to shape policy (Lloyd 2012). The existence of sex-workers-by-choice cannot be ignored; they are present regardless of ideologies that oppose them. While such choices are often socially conditioned choices, sex workers who enjoy their work are present. There are international organizations of sex workers working for sex workers' rights worldwide. Counterarguments to this ideology point out that, while recognizing the presence of sex-workers-by-choice, the harms of prostitution outweigh the benefits, as evidenced by the higher rates of victimization (Dempsey 2011). This calls for increased opportunities and better-available choices through education and training for work that is less risky and more rewarding. Including the voices of both trafficked people and willing sex workers is important in drafting models of prostitution policy in order to produce the best outcomes for all groups affected by such policies.

Chapter Summary

Various models of prostitution policy show benefits and challenges. Challenges to the deterrence model, currently used in the United States, include lack of recourse for sex trafficked/exploited people and sex workers for their victimization, revictimization through criminalization, lack of harm-reduction efforts, decreased safety, and barriers to exiting prostitution. Benefits to legalization and decriminalization models include increased harm-reduction efforts, increased safety, reduced sex trafficking in some sites, and reduced revictimization in the justice system. Challenges to the legalization model include the development of the two-tiered legal/illegal system and increased sex trafficking in some sites, continued stigma and police harassment, and difficulty complying with strict regulations. Outcomes of the abolitionist model include decreased prostitution and reduced sex trafficking. Challenges include limited or conditional harm-reduction efforts, continued stigma of willing sex workers, and reduced safety. Debates remain between radical feminists/abolitionists and liberal feminists/neoliberals in the United States. Areas of agreement generally revolve around decriminalizing the sale of sex and criminalizing buyers of minors. Areas of contention include the criminalization of buyers. Neoliberals and many liberal feminists maintain that willing sex workers as well as buyers should be free from the constraints of the state. Sex trafficking should be criminalized; sex work should not. In contrast, abolitionists and radical feminists indicate that buyers should be duly targeted by law enforcement to reduce demand and consequent sex trafficking. The United States appears to be shifting policy somewhat. The U.S. Trafficking Victims Protection Act draws a clean line between sex work and sex trafficking that is consistent with neoliberal and liberal feminist perspectives. The implementation of decriminalization of minors selling sex as well as a renewed focus on criminalizing buyers is consistent with abolitionist and radical feminist perspectives.

Discussion Questions

1. Describe the benefits and challenges of various models of prostitution policy.
2. If you were to design a model of prostitution policy, what would it look like and why?
3. Why is harm reduction so important, regardless of the prostitution policy at hand?

Part II

The Dynamics of Sex Trafficking in the United States

[5]

Survivors

Like most teens, fifteen-year-old "Johlyn" met and became involved with a sixteen-year-old boy, who she believed to be her boyfriend. Then he convinced her to come away with him for a weekend, and she found that he was not a boyfriend at all but was a pimp who had deceived her. Johlyn indicated that once her so-called boyfriend had her in the car, he took her to a house with other girls involved in the sex trade. Johlyn said she was drugged and forced to have sex for money in different hotels over a five-day period. In the meantime, her parents were searching for her in multiple cities and had filed a missing person's report. Johlyn was finally able to contact her dad by phone to ask for help, telling him the hotel and room number where she was being kept in San Luis Obispo, California. Her father contacted the police, who arrested the teen boy who had posed as her "boyfriend," along with two adults. Charges included human trafficking, false imprisonment, and conspiracy to kidnapping (Shaddox 2015).

Cases of abduction such as this are not as common as other forms of sex trafficking (chapter 6), but they are not unknown. Trafficking more commonly involves survival sex of minors and "boyfriend" pimps. The reader may wonder how survivors get involved in sex trafficking situations. While anyone is at risk, and while those of different social classes, races, sexes, and gender identities have been trafficked, various factors heighten one's likelihood of becoming exploited or trafficked. This chapter describes such vulnerabilities using sociological and intersectional perspectives. Risk factors include age, sex, gender identity, sexual orientation, poverty, racial marginalization, intellectual disability, and undocumented citizenship status. The role of weak social institutions in facilitating vulnerability to sex trafficking victimization is also delineated, including weak education systems, family systems, and the role of social structures that facilitate low economic status. The role of weak social safety nets, including access to health care to treat substance and mental health issues as well as social programs to address child poverty, intimate partner violence, homelessness, and other aspects of economic disenfranchisement are also detailed. Recruitment into sex trafficking and ways traffickers target vulnerabilities resulting from identity-based oppression and exposure to weak social institutions are explored as well. The chapter closes with a description of common barriers to leaving a sex trafficking/commercial sexual exploitation (CSE) situation, which are also intertwined with weak social safety nets and identity-based oppression.

Risk Factors: Identity-Based Oppression

Age

The intersectional perspective, described in chapter 2, holds that we all occupy unique identities, such as race, class, gender, age, sexual orientation, ethnicity, and religious identities. These various identities intersect to produce our own unique set of experiences. Such identities are interrelated with risk factors for sex trafficking, particularly in terms of identity-based oppression and increased vulnerability to exploitation. A variety of studies show that sex trafficking/CSE typically begins in adolescence, with slight variances shown across the research. Accordingly, age is an identity that is associated with sex trafficking risk. Linda Smith and colleagues (2009) found the average age of survivors at the time of their first trafficking experience to be between 13 and 14. Similarly, Ric Curtis and colleagues (2008), in examining homeless youth in New York, found the average age of entry to be 15, for both boys and girls, but noted that nearly 20% of boys and 15% of girls entered the commercial sex industry prior to age 13. Yet, in an analysis of 123 survivors who contacted the organization for services, the Polaris

Project (2014a) found an average age of entry of 19, and 56% were over the age of 17. The Polaris Project (2014a) indicates that existing statistics indicating an average age of entry between 12 and 14 may be skewed because they are based on research studies that exclusively examine minors. Accordingly, research examining both adults and minors is needed for accurate representation to determine average age of entry. For example, Amy Farrell and colleagues (2012) noted that in prosecuted cases including both adults and minors, 24% of survivors were under the age of 16, 33% were between 16 and 17 years old, and 22% were between the ages of 18 and 20. An Urban Institute study (Dank et al. 2015) reported that age of entry into commercial sex markets ranges from 7 to 22, with an average age of 17, with cisgender (or nontransgender) girls starting slightly earlier than boys and transgender girls. Synthesizing these various research sources, individuals between 14 and 25 are at heightened risk of sex trafficking victimization (Dank et al. 2015; Polaris Project 2014a). Individuals will typically "age out" of sex trafficking by their mid-twenties, as they are less desired by buyers and less profitable for traffickers. Some remain in the commercial sex industry much longer and may not be seen as sex trafficking victims once they have left their trafficker and are engaged in commercial sex in order to survive (Oselin 2014; Smith, Vardaman, and Snow 2009). In addition to age, one's sex is also a risk factor.

Sex

In intersectional perspective, sex is one identity that impacts typical experiences of sex trafficking and CSE. Women and girls are thought to compose the vast majority of sex trafficking survivors, as evidenced by prosecuted cases, cases brought to the attention of law enforcement, and those identified in various social service organizations. Women and girls are overrepresented in prosecuted cases, composing 94% of survivors (Banks and Kyckelhahn 2011). The Polaris Project (2014b) indicates that, of the 141 individuals who contacted them for services, 96.5% were female, and hotline calls showed 94.5% involved female survivors. Girls also compose the majority of juvenile prostitution arrests. In 2012, 601 girls were arrested and 189 boys were arrested for juvenile prostitution (i.e., sex trafficking). Studies that exclusively focus on homeless or transient youth paint a different picture, finding that half or more of homeless youth engaged in the sex industry are young men, boys, or transgender girls (Curtis et al. 2008; Dank et al. 2015). The boys are disproportionately gay, bisexual, or identify as a sexual minority group.

Each of these statistical sources provides understandings of various facets of sex trafficking victimization. The different sampling methods and areas of focus used in these studies result in examining different populations. Boys and young men who are victimized in sex trafficking are most likely to be found among the homeless or transient youth population (Curtis et al. 2008; Dank et al. 2015). Several studies find young men and boys engaged in "survival sex" due to homelessness and lack of options. As noted in chapter 1, survival sex can be viewed as a form of sex trafficking when minors are involved and can be viewed as CSE when adults are involved. In contrast, those who interact with social services and law enforcement are more likely to be women or girls.

A sex identity–related issue that may correspond to the overrepresentation of women and girls in sex trafficking statistics could be that they experience greater exploitation and, as a consequence, are more likely to be seen in social and legal services. Both researchers and practitioners report that boys and transgender people are much less likely to have a pimp (Curtis et al. 2008; Heil and Nichols 2015). Curtis and colleagues (2008) found that only one boy and no transgender individuals in their study had a pimp. In another study, practitioners who worked with commercially sexually exploited youth similarly reported that they rarely came across LGBTQ* individuals who were working for a pimp (Heil and Nichols 2015). The Urban Institute (Dank et al. 2015) indicated that, of men and boys in the commercial sex industry, only 4% had "exploiters" (e.g., pimps). In contrast, in the same study, 81% of those with a trafficker/exploiter were female. This study and others (Curtis et al. 2008; Dank et al. 2015) indicate that men and boys and transgender females are more likely to experience trafficking and exploitation in the form of survival sex; as such, the exploitation is much less likely to be identified and labeled as sex trafficking by law enforcement compared to pimp-controlled exploitation characterized by higher levels of coercion, fraud, and force. Further, social services for sexually exploited men, boys, and transgender people are limited. Thus, trafficking in the form of survival sex is much less likely to be reflected in sex trafficking statistics derived from the justice system and social services. However, the exploitation is apparent in these studies examining young men and boys in the commercial sex industry, and minors in these cases are legally deemed sex trafficked. Overall, different sampling frames contribute different pieces of the puzzle, reflecting various facets of sex trafficking/CSE.

LGBTQ Youth*

Intersectional perspectives acknowledge unique experiences based upon intersecting identities. At times such identities reflect societal marginalization and consequent increased risk of violence and abuse, including sex trafficking. Research indicates that LGBTQ* youth may be particularly vulnerable to sex trafficking largely due to an increased likelihood of homelessness. There are an estimated 500,000 homeless youth in the United States. The National Network for Youth and other researchers report that, while composing roughly 10% of the youth population, and 5% of the general population, 20–40% of homeless youth identify as LGBTQ* (Ferguson-Colvin and Maccio 2012; Frederick 2014; Ray 2006). Thus, the number of sexual minority homeless youth is disproportionately high (Frederick 2014; Ray 2006). Because homelessness is a primary risk factor for sex trafficking, between 75,000 and 200,000 homeless LGBTQ* youth are at risk of sex trafficking or CSE.

Children who are rejected by their parents or who have heightened difficulty in foster homes because of their foster parents' reactions to their LGBTQ* identities are disproportionately runaways or throwaways who have nowhere to go. "Indeed, the youth's lesbian, gay, or bisexual identity has been identified as a risk factor for youth homelessness" (Ferguson-Colvin and Maccio 2012, 10). Lynn Rew and colleagues (2005) found that of homeless gay or lesbian youth, nearly three-quarters ran away from or were forced out of their homes because their parents did not accept their sexual orientation. Similarly, the same study found that one-quarter of bisexual homeless youth left home because their parents disapproved of their sexual identities.

This homelessness is directly correlated with increased risk of sex trafficking in the form of survival sex. Erin C. Heil and Andrea J. Nichols (2015) found that LGBTQ* individuals, particularly gay male teens and teen transgender girls are involved in the commercial sex industry due to parental rejection, running away, or being kicked out of their homes, resulting homelessness and a need for survival. A study in New York City found a disproportionate number of LGBTQ* youth involved in the commercial sex industry; survival is their primary motivation (Curtis et al. 2008). Yet another study also found disproportionate numbers of LGBTQ* youth engaged in commercial sex; lack of stable housing, employment, and need for survival facilitated entry and sustains their involvement (Dank et al. 2015).

Additional traumas that LGBTQ* youth may experience and that may facilitate running away, homelessness, and consequent vulnerability to pimps and buyers include negative school experiences, such as homophobic bullying (Frederick 2014; Dank et al. 2015). The National School Climate Survey indicates that more than 55% of LGBTQ* youth report feeling unsafe at school because of others' reactions to their sexual orientation, and nearly 40% feel unsafe due to others' reactions to their gender expression. Nearly one-third report missing school because of feeling unsafe or uncomfortable at school. A sizable majority report verbal harassment, 36% report physical harassment, and just over 16% report physical assault targeting their sexual orientation.[1]

Longing for acceptance and for relief from family conflicts, bullying, or abuse, LGBTQ* youth disproportionately find themselves living on the streets with limited means of survival. Once on the street, they experience challenges that are both similar to and distinct from non-LGBTQ* homeless youth. Issues with gaining legitimate employment, finding adequate shelter, and finding food are similar to non–sexual minority children who are homeless. Yet research shows that gaining access to employment may be even more difficult for transgender youth, who may be discriminated against if their gender identity is apparent. Similarly, shelters for sex trafficked girls may not accept transgender girls whose biological identity is male but whose gender identity is female. Transgender girls may not feel comfortable going to a shelter for boys, where the risk of victimization may be higher and male identity is not consistent with their feminine identities. Thus, transgender girls experience barriers to going to shelters. Because of heightened risk of homelessness compounded with other aspects of employment discrimination and reduced access to shelter, LGBTQ* youth are at increased risk of sex trafficking (Dank et al. 2015).

The relative agency and victimization of LGBTQ* youth is complex. The discussion of survival sex and CSE applies, but with heightened vulnerability based on the marginalization and unique experiences highlighted in this section. Some researchers hold that such survival-generating activities are

an expression of agency and a form of sex work. Prostitution, stripping, pornography, or escort services are viewed by neoliberals as a legitimate form
of work. Pimp control is less common among LGBTQ* youth; thus, such
individuals are more likely to choose their clients and keep their own profits
or simply to form sexual relationships in order to access food and shelter.
For example, Jan Browne and Victor Minichiello (1996) found that gay and
bisexual youth purposefully develop relationships with older men, including
emotional attachments, as a survival strategy. Similarly, Michael D. Smith
and Christian Grov (2011) describe male escorts as empowered sex workers
who made a conscious choice to sell sex, albeit largely for economic need.
Moreover, research examining male and transgender sex workers finds that
they often engage in such work to satisfy desire, to sexually experiment, to
gain social status, to gain sexual experience, to express agency, or to have
an adventure (Frederick 2014). Without a pimp or a trafficker engaging in
force, fraud, or coercion, trafficking is more difficult to ascertain. Yet exploitation of vulnerability, whether by a buyer or a trafficker, is clearly a form of
CSE. With minors, the lines between sex trafficking and sex work are clear.
In situations involving minors who have few alternatives for employment
and who do not want to access social services or resources to avoid returning to an abusive home, the expressed agency is simply about survival. This
reveals exploitation and—legally, due to their age—sex trafficking. Yet an
adult who has better access to legitimate employment, who is not under
pimp control, and who is aware of the resources and social supports available may view sex work as a legitimate and informed choice (Frederick
2014). In sociological perspective, marginalized identities are intertwined
with various forms of inequality; such power imbalances result in higher
levels of exploitation by those with more power, status, and money. While
sexual orientation and gender identity are identities that hold unique and
distinct experiences, race and ethnicity are other socially marginalized identities that show increased risk of sex trafficking victimization.

Race and Ethnicity

The bulk of the research literature examining sex trafficking in the United
States is color-blind; race is not included or examined. Such literature
claims, either directly or indirectly through omission, an "everyone is at
risk" model. To some extent this is true; sex trafficking and CSE are seen

across all demographic groups. Researchers note that sex trafficking survivors stem from a wide variety of socioeconomic backgrounds, geographic areas, racial backgrounds, sexual orientations, and sex, gender, and ethnic identities (Busch-Armendariz, Nsonwu, and Cook Heffron 2009; Curtis et al. 2008; Martin et al. 2014; Smith, Vardaman, and Snow 2009; Dank et al. 2015). While it is true that anyone could potentially become a victim of sex trafficking, there are factors that may increase one's vulnerability to sex trafficking, and some groups are more vulnerable to victimization than others.

If individuals were truly at equal risk across racial and ethnic identities, the number of survivors would "match" the proportion of population by race and ethnicity in the United States, but this is not the case. Overall, black, Latino/a, and Native American individuals are disproportionately represented among survivors in the United States (Dank et al. 2015; Farrell et al. 2012; Martin et al. 2014; Banks and Kyckelhahn 2011). This is likely because those who are racially marginalized in society are disproportionately exposed to the risk factors for victimization in the form of weak social institutions. Economic marginalization, exposure to unequal opportunity in education, and increased involvement in child protection or foster care systems are among the weak social institution implicated.

Richard J. Estes and Neil Alan Weiner (2001) are the most commonly cited when the "everyone is at risk" model is used. To determine trends in commercial sexual exploitation of children (CSEC), Estes and Weiner measured the percentage of youth who were using selected outreach services for any reason in only one to two outreach programs in selected cities and found little racial disproportion in this sample. The sampling is questionable as the limited number of programs used is not a representation of national trends. Moreover, their study is not a valid measure of CSEC; rather, it is a measure of the use of youth services to assess risk. Using a limited number of programs (one to two) in a limited number of cities (three provided data for) to examine the use of youth services by race to determine demographic patterns of CSEC in the United States is problematic at best.

In data that does directly measure sex trafficking, Farrell and colleagues (2012) found, in an analysis of 119 confirmed sex trafficking cases in six study sites across the United States, the racial composition of the group to be 47% white, 32% black, 16% Hispanic, and 13% Asian. Given the population projections provided by the U.S. Census Bureau, even though white individuals made up the majority of those who are sex trafficked in this study, black individuals are disproportionately at risk, showing more than twice the proportionate rate, 13.2% of the population, and white individuals show decreased risk compared to what would be proportionate to population, 62.6% of the total population (not including Hispanics or Latinos). Moreover, Asian individuals are also disproportionately victimized, composing 13% of those trafficked but only 5.3% percent of the population. Hispanics are slightly underrepresented in this study, as the U.S. Census Bureau shows population demographics for this group at 17.1% of the total population.[2]

Other "hard" data directly measuring sex trafficking is illustrated through "juvenile prostitution" arrest statistics. What is criminalized as "juvenile prostitution" is in fact sex trafficking because it meets the criteria of the U.S. Trafficking Victims Protection Act, in that anyone under the age of eighteen involved in a commercial sex act is considered sex trafficked. In the year Estes and Weiner conducted their research, 2001, black children composed the majority of juvenile prostitution arrests nationwide. According to these statistics, 68% of those arrested for juvenile prostitution were black, 30% were white, 2% were American Indian/Alaska Native, and zero were Asian/Pacific Islander.[3] Also, it should be noted that these racial groups are the only choices in FBI arrest statistics. Hispanic or Latino are viewed as ethnicities, not races; thus, white Hispanics (Mexican, Cuban, Puerto Rican) are tabulated as white, and black Hispanics (Dominican, Haitian, Jamaican) are generally tabulated as black. In 2012, 40% of those arrested for juvenile prostitution were white, including white Hispanic, and 58% were black/African American. None were American Indian/Alaska Native, and .01% were Asian or Pacific Islander.[4] Juvenile prostitution statistics clearly show heightened victimization of black/African American youth, both in their criminalization and as sex trafficking victims.

In addition, another U.S. Department of Justice report specifically examining sex trafficking reports that while African Americans make up roughly 13% of the population, they compose more than 40% of confirmed sex trafficking victims (Banks and Kyckelhahn 2011). The same report found that 25.6% are white, 23.9% are Hispanic, 4.3% are Asian, and 5.8% are "other." In addition to black Americans, Hispanic-identified people are also overrepresented in the Department of Justice statistics while white individuals are underrepresented. Multiple research studies conducted in Chicago, Minneapolis, Los Angeles, New York, St. Louis, Miami, and Hartford also show disproportionate victimization of people of color (Hughes 2005; Martin et al. 2014; Oselin 2014; Raphael, Reichert, and Powers 2010; Raphael and Myers-Powell 2010; Reid 2015). An Urban Institute study

(Dank et al. 2015) found that, among those engaged in survival sex, all but 5% are racial minorities, composing the majority of sexually exploited youth in New York; 37% are black/African American, and 30% are Latina/o. In Minneapolis, among cases involving sex trafficked girls, more than half of sex trafficked girls are black/African American (Martin et al. 2014). According to the U.S. Census Bureau, the population demographics in Minneapolis is 18.6% black/African American. Latinas and American Indians are also overrepresented, and whites are underrepresented (Martin et al. 2014).

Local contextual dynamics are important to acknowledge when examining the relationship between race and sex trafficking; different sites have different demographics of sex trafficking, which could be important for prevention and outreach. For example, one study indicates that, in New York City, sexually exploited youth tend to be "female and black, having sex with strangers in hotel rooms or outside" (Smith, Vardaman, and Snow 2009, 9). In contrast, "upstate, the youth [are] younger, more likely to be white, and [are] often exploited at home by adult friends or acquaintances" (Smith, Vardaman, and Snow 2009, 9). Estes and Weiner (2001) point out that acknowledging population demographics on a local level is important in analyzing disproportionate rates of victimization on a local level, meaning that analyses of sex trafficking specifically in El Paso, or San Francisco, or New York, which have widely different population demographics, should also involve the population demographics of those specific cities. At the same time, applying research findings from specific organizations in specific cities nationally is problematized by the same rationale—population dynamics of specific cities may vary widely from the national demographics. Hard statistics of sex trafficking indicate disproportionate risk across race and ethnic groups, negating the "everyone is at equal risk" model. Black/African American individuals are the group at most heightened risk; ignoring this dynamic is a manifestation of color-blind racism.

Immigrant Status

Those from other countries who are sex trafficked in the United States experience vulnerability to exploitation, particularly those of undocumented status. "People fall victim to trafficking for many reasons. Some may simply be seeking a better life, a promising job, or even an adventure"

(U.S. Department of State 2012, 1). Yet, upon their arrival, immigrants are at risk of exploitation, including sex trafficking. Debt bondage is common among sex trafficking survivors originating from other countries. One study showed how South Korean women were smuggled into the United States via Canada and incurred a debt to their trafficker for the transportation fee—the women in this study were then trafficked into brothels in California (Farrell et al. 2012).

Moreover, survivors with roots in other countries may face vulnerabilities specifically related to their immigrant status and increased likelihood of poverty. The U.S. Department of State's *Trafficking in Persons Report* found in 2013 that boys who migrate from Mexico and Central America seeking work are particularly vulnerable to sex trafficking on their way into the United States and may be vulnerable upon arrival as well due to their exploitable poverty or, in some cases, undocumented status. For example, in 2014, Victor Manuel Rax, originally from Guatemala, was arrested for human trafficking (Reavy 2014). More specifically, Rax was accused of trafficking teenage boys in Salt Lake City, Utah. The ages of the boys ranged from 15 to 19 years old, and the trafficking is reported to have spanned at least two years. Rax reportedly sexually abused the teen boys and regularly stated when he did so that he "owned them." The boys were vulnerable as undocumented immigrants. Rax used fear tactics to get the teens to sell sex and drugs, using their undocumented status against them as well as against their parents. Rax is reported to have used threats toward the boys' family members as a form of coercive control, indicating he would go to federal authorities to report undocumented status if the boys did not do what he wanted them to do.

Immigrants are also more vulnerable to labor trafficking, and labor trafficking at times co-occurs with sex trafficking. Labor trafficking itself is a risk factor for sex trafficking because individuals working to disentangle themselves from a situation of debt bondage may sell sex in order to escape a labor trafficking situation. Further, domestic servitude, a form of labor trafficking, may also involve sex trafficking. For example, Heil (2012) illustrated a case in Florida in which a young woman was labor trafficked and simultaneously subjected to sexual servitude along with her domestic servitude. The case of Alex "Cowboy" Campbell depicted in chapter 1 is also a labor trafficking case—the women were forced to work in his massage parlor in addition to being forced to sell sex for his benefit.[5] In yet another case, Aleksandr Maksimenko brought young women from Eastern

Europe, who thought they would be working in a restaurant, to instead work in his strip clubs in Detroit. They experienced forced labor as exotic dancers, which also overlaps with sex trafficking because it is a form of sexual labor. The young women experienced debt bondage, physical violence, threats, and confinement. Maksimenko was eventually sentenced to 14.5 years in prison on charges of involuntary servitude, money laundering, and immigration conspiracies.[6] Yet the circumstance reflects both labor and sex trafficking victimization. Immigrants from low-income nations are particularly vulnerable to these bait-and-switch tactics due to their poverty and may also be vulnerable due to undocumented status.

Intellectual Disability

In intersectional perspective, an intellectual disability is an identity that occupies a unique space that heightens vulnerability to various abuses. Specifically, having a disability in the form of a low intelligence quotient (IQ) increases susceptibility to sex trafficking (Hammond and McGlone 2014). Researchers find an overall higher rate of victimization of youth with intellectual disabilities, including sex trafficking (Harrell and Rand 2010; Clawson et al. 2009; U.S. Department of State 2012). Inge B. Wissink and colleagues (2015) report that the risk of sexual abuse is significantly higher among minors with intellectual disabilities. Those with an intellectual disability are more likely to have limited understandings of their right to decline sex or sexual exploitation and are consequently particularly susceptible to sex trafficking victimization (Wissink et al. 2015). Heil and Nichols (2014) indicate that those with an intellectual disability are vulnerable to exploitation because traffickers purposefully target vulnerable populations. As noted by Joan A. Reid and Alex R. Piquero (2013) traffickers do not want to get caught and may choose minors with an intellectual disability purposefully because they are less likely to be believed if they do seek out assistance from others, including police (see also Wissink et al. 2015).

One case illustrates the vulnerability of youth with intellectual disabilities. In 2010 Mario Alberto Laguna-Guerrero, age 25, was arrested for sex trafficking his 16-year-old girlfriend throughout migrant labor camps in southern Florida over a two-year period. He was facing difficulties paying a smuggling debt and used his underage girlfriend with an intellectual disability, with an IQ of 58, to get the money. He was convicted in 2012 and is currently in prison. The girl told detectives that she did not want to sell sex. Laguna-Guerrero would cut himself and would manipulate her into thinking it was her fault. He also told her he lost his job because of her and that smugglers would cut off his fingers if he did not pay the debt, consequently pressuring the girl into selling sex.[7] An individual with an IQ of 58 faces difficulty in making decisions and is more easily manipulated compared to a person with an average IQ (about 100). This example illustrates how an intellectual disability can heighten risk of manipulation and vulnerability to traffickers. In sociological perspective, vulnerable identities and weak social institutions combine to form an interlocking system of oppression.

Risk Factors: Weak Social Institutions

In the field of sociology, a social institution is commonly referred to as any system involving a set of interrelated social norms centered upon basic and essential human needs. Economic systems, political/governing systems, the criminal justice system, health care systems, education systems, and family systems are among those commonly included in the sociological discourse examining social institutions. Any weaknesses within these social institutions can cause or be related to social problems more generally, including sex trafficking/CSE. In sociological perspective, examining weak social institutions and their impact on sex trafficking susceptibility is important because such environments, combined with a lack of social safety nets, create a climate in which sex trafficking/CSE can flourish. The weak institutions identified in the research literature that increase the risk of sex trafficking/CSE include family systems, the justice and child welfare systems, education systems, and economic systems. Combined with a lack of social safety nets to address such problems, risk to already vulnerable populations is heightened. Lack of social safety nets related to sex trafficking identified in the extant literature include the lack of a minimum wage as a living wage; inadequate access to substance abuse and mental illness-related health care; lack of services to address intimate partner violence, homelessness, child abuse, and child sexual abuse; and weaknesses within social services for trafficked/CSE people.

Family Systems

Problematic home lives are directly related to runaway or throwaway status as well as to susceptibility to a "boyfriend" pimp or survival sex. Runaway, throwaway, or otherwise homeless youth are particularly vulnerable to sex trafficking. Runaway youth are those who choose to leave home for any period of time, whether it is occasionally staying out all night without parental permission or choosing to leave home permanently (Ferguson-Colvin and Maccio 2012). Children run away from home for a variety of reasons including, but not limited to, physical, verbal, sexual, or psychological abuse in the home; parent or child substance abuse issues; or parental neglect or rejection. Throwaways are those whose parents have abandoned or "kicked them out" of the family home. Children may be "thrown away" by parents with serious addiction issues, or by parents who are reacting to the child's substance abuse or who reject their child's identity as LGBTQ*. In the United States, statistics indicate more than a million and a half children under 18 were reported as homeless, largely as a result of running away or being rejected from their households (Ferguson-Colvin and Maccio 2012).

Smith and colleagues noted in their multicity study that "a common factor is the history of child physical and sexual abuse in the home or the extended family. In Las Vegas, Nevada, statistics indicate that from January 2004 through December 2006, nearly 41% of juveniles suspected of being involved in prostitution-related offenses had been victims of sexual assault. Additionally, 21% were victims of familial molestation" (Smith, Vardaman, and Snow 2009, 9). Child sexual abuse invites the risk of sexual exploitation and trafficking for a number of reasons. Among them, youth who experience sexual abuse may have incorrect ideals of a healthy relationship, are more likely to draw their worth from their sexuality, and have control issues. Controlling one's own sexuality, whether in the commercial sex industry or otherwise, is initially seen as a form of empowerment by some because they, not the abuser, are controlling their sexuality (Oselin 2014). Additionally, "youth who were previously sexually abused by exploitive adults become confused about what constitutes kindness, intimacy, and safety, which may result in greater vulnerability to subsequent exploitation by adults (e.g., pimps) who initially seem kind, protective, and safe" (Cole et al. 2014, 14). Survivor Holly Austin Smith, who was sexually abused as a child and recruited by a pimp at a local mall at the age of 14, stated, "I didn't think I needed help, I thought Greg and Nicki [her traffickers] has already rescued me" (Smith 2014, 99). As a child, Smith confused kindnesses for belonging and acceptance, likely related to the prior sexual abuse she experienced: "I felt like these women accepted me without judgement. I felt lucky. I felt like I was finally good at something. . . . I felt like one of them. I was born to be a prostitute" (Smith 2014, 98). Notably, child sexual abuse that is not addressed results in risk of exploitation and sex trafficking. Adding an additional layer of difficulty, unaddressed victimization simultaneously results in distrust of adults and social rules, impeding assistance from adults as well as increasing the likelihood for delinquency, creating further risk of sex trafficking (Cole et al. 2014).

Growing up in homes in which children view their mothers being beaten by husbands and boyfriends is also a factor in sex trafficking victimization as it may be a catalyst to running away or a reason to view violence as a normal part of an intimate relationship (Raphael and Myers-Powell 2010). Thus, intimate partner violence in the home reflects a weak family system and increases risk particularly in getting involved with a "boyfriend pimp," whose violence and abuses are normalized. Alternatively, this is another influence on the decision of youth to run away from home, increasing risk of getting involved in survival sex.

When children or teens run away from abusive or conflict-ridden families, they typically do not want to be found. This makes seeking legitimate employment or education difficult. If runaways attend school, they fear being sent back to their abusive households. If they seek a job, they may have no address or consistent phone number to list, which may interfere with a call-back from the potential employer. Further, runaways or throwaways may not be of the legal age for employment, which is typically 16 years old in most states or 15 with permission from a guardian and a note from the teen's school. It is unlikely that a runaway or throwaway would be able to or would desire to access such permissions from their parent, guardian, or school. When faced with difficulties accessing legitimate employment, some youth will either seek out illegitimate employment or will be a target for those wishing to take advantage of economic and other difficulties. When teens have nothing else, they have their bodies to sell.

Homeless youth are particularly likely to engage in survival sex, as runaways or throwaways typically do not want to be found. "According to researchers and child advocates, the CSEC issue mostly affects: runaway and homeless youth who trade sex as a means of survival; children who have been sexually, physically and emotionally abused; juveniles with minimum education who are unable to find legitimate employment; and children who are vulnerable and easily controlled and manipulated by an adult looking to make a profit" (Curtis et al. 2008, 1). Problematic home lives, including a background of child abuse, neglect, and sexual abuse as well as domestic violence in the home and parental substance abuse, are among the common reasons why children run away from home (Hammond and McGlone 2014; Reid 2010; Kotrla 2010; Wilson and Dalton 2008). Abuse and neglect in the home leads to risk of runaway status and homelessness and to involvement in survival sex, but it also increases vulnerability to a pimp, who may initially pose as a boyfriend offering romance, affection, love, and general caretaking—things that are lacking in the home life (the boyfriend pimp and types of trafficking that survivors experience are detailed in the following chapter).

While problematic home lives are associated with sex trafficking vulnerability, it should be noted that children from homes with loving families, where substance abuse, child abuse, intimate partner violence, or sexual abuse are absent, can also be trafficked (Cole et al. 2014; Heil and Nichols 2015). At times parents are desperately searching for their children (Heil and Nichols 2015; Schisgall and Alvarez 2008). Recognizing disproportionate risk does not negate the trafficking of those who do not hold disproportionate risk.

Weak Child Welfare Systems: Juvenile Justice and Foster Care Involvement

Juvenile justice system involvement is relatively common among trafficked youth because of involvement in the commercial sex industry or because of problematic home lives, runaway status, or truancy (Cole et al. 2014; Reid 2010). When a runaway youth is recovered, or a youth who is found selling sex is discovered, the typical response often is to channel the youth into the juvenile justice system. From there the youth will be placed in a juvenile detention facility or at times may even be unknowingly returned to the problematic home life that was the source of the situation. In cases involving supportive families, the child will be returned to the home and possibly referred to outpatient therapeutic services. Few cities offer other alternatives (see chapter 9). Accordingly, it is not only unsurprising but expected that research indicates disproportionate involvement of children in the juvenile justice system in sex trafficking. A potential challenge arises when there are weaknesses within the juvenile justice systems.

Juvenile detention facilities are known recruitment sites for traffickers, either through other girls in the facilities or found within or outside such facilities by recruiters (Smith, Vardaman, and Snow 2009; Polaris Project 2015b). Reid (2015) noted that girls with links to a trafficker recruited other girls within juvenile detention facilities. In uncommon cases, girls may be recruited by traffickers with legitimate ties to the juvenile justice system. In one case four men, one a former juvenile probation officer and another a former University of Texas football player, were convicted of sex trafficking–related crimes. Timothy McCullouch Jr., Richard "Crenshaw" Gray, Deion "Memphis" Lockhart, and Emmanuel "E Jay" Lockhart were found guilty of sex trafficking a 16-year-old and three other women over a seven-month period spanning 2012–2013 (Martinez 2015). McCollouch had worked with two of the survivors as an El Paso County juvenile probation officer when they were underage girls. This indicates a weakness within the juvenile justice system, in that such individuals have access to vulnerable girls to exploit.

In addition to juvenile justice system involvement, research indicates a substantial proportion of sex trafficked youth have prior backgrounds in other child welfare–oriented systems as well (Cole et al. 2014; Kotrla 2010; Raphael, Reichert, and Powers 2010; Oselin 2014). There is some overlap as placement in juvenile detention facilities is one option within the juvenile justice system; placement in foster care or group homes are other alternatives. Involvement in the child welfare and foster care systems among sex trafficked youth is relatively common and can be considered a risk factor for vulnerability to sex trafficking; such involvement is likely a reflection of problematic home lives, and implicates involvement due to status offenses such as running away, truancy, and curfew violations. One study found 64% of survivors of sex trafficking had experiences in foster care and group homes as children (Nixon et al. 2002). An abundance of research shows disproportionate victimization among children in foster care, who also show a heightened runway risk (Hammond and McGlone 2014). Further, despite screening procedures, and the fact that there are many wonderful foster parents, there is a record of increased exploitation of youth in foster care. Reid (2015) found traffickers actually recruited outside known group homes.

In one illustration, Robert Gonzales, 39, trafficked a 14-year-old foster child. He met her through a foster placement with his sister-in-law (Garrison 2015). He first romanced the girl, started having sex with her, convincing her that he was in love with her. He also gave her methamphetamines and alcohol, then began forcing her to sell sex for money or drugs, and also made child pornography, another form of sex trafficking, with her. Physical abuses, such as punching, kicking, burning her with cigarettes, were also uncovered in the court case. The victim's sister found the relationship troubling, took pictures of them, and contacted police. Gonzales was sentenced to 112 years in prison. This is just one example among many to indicate weaknesses in social services that are intended to help and support children. More often, foster care systems are related with sex trafficking as an artifact of already existing family problems and related childhood trauma.

Weak Education Systems

High student mobility rates, teacher mobility rates, drop-out rates, and truancy rates as well as low graduation rates, low academic performance, and schools that have lost their accreditation are reflections of weak education systems. They are also indicators of vulnerability to sex trafficking. The mobility rate relates to student population turnover, or moving in and out of school districts, which overlaps with poverty or low socioeconomic status. Essentially, when families cannot afford the rent for their apartments, they move or are evicted. They are then in search of the next low rental property, which often means moving to another school district. This impacts a child's learning and attachment to schools, teachers, and peers. When youth have fewer attachments to their schools, they are more likely to be truant or drop out. When they are not at school and unsupervised during school hours, then they have increased exposure to pimps and buyers who are actively seeking them out (Heil and Nichols 2015). In addition, in weak education systems, academic performance and graduation rates are lower, which impacts job opportunities and salaries in adulthood and increases sex trafficking through resulting low socioeconomic status.

Fulton County School District, just outside of Atlanta, Georgia, and St. Louis Public Schools illustrate weak education systems and the ways mobility rates are intertwined with academic success and graduation rates. There are sixteen high schools in the Fulton County School District; six have mobility rates greater than 50%. Of those six, only one met Adequate Yearly Progress (AYP), stipulated by the No Child Left Behind Act in the 2010–11 school year, and graduation rates for five of the schools were below 70%.[8] In contrast, of the three high schools with mobility rates lower than 15%, all three of them met AYP, and graduation rates all exceeded 96%. Unsurprisingly, there is a correlation between mobility rates and student success rates, including placement tests and graduation rates. This is no doubt conflated with social class. The St. Louis Metropolitan area is known for having some of the worst schools in the nation, and many have even lost their accreditation. Thirty-six schools had mobility rates higher than 50% in the St. Louis Public School system between 2011 and 2012.[9] In addition to high student turnover rates, there is high teacher turnover as well, with a quarter of the teachers not returning after the first year. The graduation rates in the St. Louis Public School District overall showed an average of only 45.9% in the 2013 school year, and a drop-out rate of nearly 15%.[10]

High student mobility, drop-out, and truancy rates are characteristic of schools in low-income areas; weak education systems are intertwined with low socioeconomic status. Most schools get the majority of their funding through local property tax revenues. Since less affluent areas collect lower property tax revenues, they have lower levels of funding. This translates into larger class sizes, less qualified teachers, out-of-date textbooks, insufficient numbers of textbooks so they cannot be taken home for study, poorer quality of facilities, and less access to technology in the classroom, all of which are associated with lower academic success. This lowered academic success impacts graduation, standardized test scores, and the ability to get into a college or university, impacting life chances and subsequent generations' exposure to weak education systems.

Research consistently shows that sex trafficked adults tend to have lower levels of education, and trafficked youth have higher rates of drop-out status and truancy. These are all risk factors for sex trafficking. When kids are not in school because they have no connection to the school, teachers, or other kids as a result of constantly changing school districts, or when the education is poor, kids are more likely to be truant or drop out. In that case, they are exposed to pimps and traffickers, who are actively seeking them out in neighborhoods, public parks, outside of schools, and on social media. Adults with lower levels of education have fewer opportunities in higher education or in job opportunities, increasing vulnerability to sex trafficking/CSE. Interestingly, Reid (2015) noted that the major difference between those who were sex trafficked in their youth, who sustained commercial sex-industry involvement in adulthood, and those who did not was educational attainment. Simply put, poverty drives unequal opportunity in education and unstable living conditions, producing weak education systems, leading to sex trafficking vulnerability through resulting truancy, drop-out status, and lack of opportunity. Traffickers are waiting to take advantage of this vulnerability, from less educated adults with few job opportunities to truant and drop-out youth who see little point in attending schools they have no connection with.

Weak Economic Systems

The research makes clear that poverty or low economic status is not only associated with weak education systems but it is also related to sex trafficking/CSE in the form of survival sex or sex-work-turned-sex-trafficking. When minors engage in survival sex, this is sex trafficking, as discussed previously. Homeless youth engaging in survival sex are absolutely in poverty, which is the reason for their exploitation/sex trafficking. When adults engage in survival sex, this is CSE, but at times survival sex can turn into a sex trafficking situation when pimps do not allow survivors to stop commercial sex-industry involvement. Multiple prosecuted cases exemplify this dynamic. One such case involved Michael Johnson and Samantha Ginocchio, who were charged with sex trafficking in 2013 (Fazal 2013). They had recruited two young women trying to support their children as single mothers on low salaries, initially soliciting one of the women from a restaurant where she was earning a low wage. Both women, aged 18 and 19, initially agreed to sell sex to supplement their income, with Johnson and Ginocchio as their pimps. The business arrangement quickly went sour when both women decided that they wanted to quit, and Johnson and Ginocchio would not allow it (Fazal 2013). Deception and coercion were implicated in this case, qualifying it as a sex trafficking situation. Research indicates those who come from backgrounds of poverty are vulnerable to sex trafficking. In some cases, poverty is intertwined with parental substance abuse and with parental involvement in selling sex (Heil and Nichols 2015; Oselin 2014). Lauren Martin and colleagues (2014) examined sex trafficking in Minneapolis, writing, "The cases present a picture of the girls as living in poverty. Generalized residential addresses in Minneapolis police department cases show girls living in neighborhoods with very high poverty rates."

Poverty is also a driving factor for those trafficked in the United States who are originally from other countries. Global stratification as well as social stratification within a nation are "push" factors, causing individuals to seek out better opportunities in other countries. At times, these opportunities are false fronts for a trafficking situation. Push and pull factors influence particularly vulnerable people, including those from poverty stricken nations with little opportunity for upward mobility. Push factors may also include a low cultural value on women, which is associated with lowered opportunity for economic mobility for women. Other push factors include a country suffering from economic instability and issues such as massive unemployment, political instability, and social stratification (Kara 2010). Pull factors essentially center around the promise of money and opportunity for upward mobility in the new country, which also increases susceptibility to a trafficking situation.

Weak Social Safety Nets

Lack of access to health care related to mental illness and substance abuse is an example of a weak social safety net, which increases sex trafficking vulnerability (Heil and Nichols 2015). Without access to health care, it is difficult for individuals to hold legal employment because of untreated mental illness, unaffordable medications for physical and mental illness, or untreated substance abuse issues, and entrée into the commercial sex industry may then manifest in the form of survival sex or exploitation by a pimp (Oselin 2014).

Survivors struggling with addiction also report being approached during transitional periods, such when they are discharged from rehabilitation facilities or are evicted from their residence due to substance use. Survivors also state that health-related issues including medical and mental health conditions, cognitive impairments, and physical disabilities contributed to their exploitation. These conditions prevented some survivors from maintaining steady employment and financial security. Survivors with health issues reference challenges accessing health services and prescription medication (Polaris Project 2015b).

When individuals lack access to substance abuse rehabilitation, or access to treatment for mental illness or health issues, this prevents recovery options and reinforces sex trafficking vulnerability. In the case of substance abuse, individuals are caught in the cycle of use—the need for money to support their habit, survival sex, and sustained abuse (Oselin 2014). Moreover, many shelters will not accept an individual who presents with addiction, indicating another gap in services that adds a layer of difficulty in exiting the sex trade. Lack of health care may particularly impact transgender individuals as well, who do not have access to health care related to their needs, such as hormone therapies and expensive cosmetic surgeries, and may engage in survival sex to pay for it.

Accordingly, weak social institutions increase risk of sex trafficking/CSE. Weak education systems increase risk factors of truancy and drop-out status for minors, and the lack of higher education and employment opportunities for adults. Weak economic systems produce a low minimum wage and lack of survival options. Challenges within juvenile justice and the child welfare system also increase risk. Problematic family systems can lead to sex trafficking, at times facilitated by parents-as-traffickers (chapter 6); in other circumstances various abuses lead to running away and becoming homeless with limited survival options, producing an environment at high risk for sex trafficking. Combined with insufficient social safety nets, including inadequate services to address child abuse and neglect and intimate partner violence, failure to provide a minimum wage as a living wage, and limited access to mental health or substance abuse rehabilitation, the environment is primed for traffickers to recruit and exploit those who are most affected.

Recruitment

There are multiple ways individuals can become involved in a trafficking situation, such as through friends, family members, buyers propositioning and initiating them into the commercial sex industry, or pimps or "boyfriends" (Curtis et al. 2008; Dank et al. 2015; Martin et al. 2014; Nichols and Heil 2014; Reid 2010; Williamson and Prior 2009). Pimps are routinely looking for individuals to recruit in juvenile detention centers and outside of courthouses, homeless shelters, and group homes as well as in schools, public parks, bus shelters, chat rooms, social media, and neighborhood streets. Often pimps form a romantic relationship with young women or girls first, and then facilitate their involvement in the commercial sex industry. Girls report pimps hanging out around shelters and group homes, ostensibly because it is known that vulnerable girls are staying there, and shelters are not ideal living situations (Curtis et al. 2008; Reid 2015; Smith, Vardaman, and Snow 2009). Curtis and colleagues (2008) reported that pimps offered girls better living alternatives than their family homes, shelter, foster care, or group homes that they came from. In such circumstances, girls often do not initially know their new boyfriend is a pimp and end up falling in love, only to be subjected to prostitution and violence in the end.

Getting propositioned by strangers—buyers in the street—is another form of entrée into a sex trafficking situation or survival sex. One study in New York (Curtis et al. 2008) found that nearly one-quarter of teens in the sample were recruited into prostitution through buyer propositions, particularly homeless boys and transgender youth. The teens reported clients coming up to them in the street, hanging around bus stops and shelters. Getting out of the cold was a reason for taking up clients' offers, in addition to getting food and a place to sleep. Another study found over one-quarter of youth were approached by a buyer, marking their entrance into the commercial sex industry (Dank et al. 2015). "A survey of runaway and homeless youth in Salt Lake City in February 2008 found that of the 32% of youth who had been victimized through 'survival sex,' 50% indicated that they had been sought out and solicited by the adult perpetrator" (Smith, Vardaman, and Snow 2009, 18). Similarly, in St. Louis, Heil and Nichols (2015) found that buyers routinely sought out homeless youth in areas where LGBTQ[*] youth were known to go for "safe" spaces, including a popular coffeehouse and a homeless shelter.

Recruitment by friends is associated with sex trafficking/CSE as well. Teen girls hanging out with delinquent peers, truancy, and a desire for an exciting lifestyle are associated with peer recruitment (Curtis et al. 2008). Other men and girls report that an older female mentor taught them the business—how to be safe and how to make as much money as possible (Curtis et al. 2008; Raphael, Reichert, and Powers 2010). Research also shows girls running into other girls on the street who got them involved in prostitution to help them survive. Recruitment of transgender youth is mostly through peer groups, when the teen needs money or to get out of a group home or bad living situation. In an Urban Institute study (Dank et al. 2015) largely composed of homeless or transient youth, nearly half the sample was recruited by peers or friends.

Recruitment of individuals from other countries is both similar to and distinct from recruitment of those who are domestically trafficked. Similarly, recruitment in the international arena works to exploit vulnerabilities, particularly poverty. In international trafficking, however, typically a trafficker is the recruiter, rather than peers, buyers, or friends. A common recruitment theme among trafficked people from other countries is the bait-and-switch technique. Traffickers use fake employment agencies and false-front businesses to entice women and girls, who think they will get legitimate work in nail salons, massage parlors, or bars, or in domestic work as cooks, nannies, or housekeepers. After this recruitment, they are then sex trafficked. Debt bondage combined with bait-and-switch recruitment techniques is commonly implicated in cases involving those who are trafficked internationally. An individual may have to pay a fee to cover transportation and the connection service as well as a fee for food and housing, and commercial sex-industry involvement then becomes seemingly inevitable in the face of mounting debt and lack of other options (McCabe and Manian 2010; Heil 2012).

Mail-order bride schemes may also hold potential for sex trafficking, although the relationship is unclear (McCabe and Manian 2010). There are more than two hundred international mail-order bride or international matchmaking services operating in the United States, with between four thousand and six thousand women coming to the United States as mail-order brides each year (McCabe and Manian 2010). Donna M. Hughes and colleagues (2007) note marriage fraud schemes in South Korea facilitated by U.S. servicemen as facilitating entrée into sex markets in the United States. Erin Heil (2012) found that labor trafficking overlapped with sex trafficking. In Heil's Florida case study, women were at times recruited/trafficked by their husbands or boyfriends to pay off a smuggling debt or to get money for basic needs as a result of labor trafficking victimization. This environment is also intertwined with barriers to exiting a trafficking/CSE situation.

Barriers to Leaving

There are multiple factors that prevent survivors from leaving trafficking situations, including emotional barriers, stigmatization, abuses, debt bondage, cultural beliefs, and gaps in services. Emotional barriers, such as feelings of low self-worth, perhaps the result of emotional abuses in an intimate partner relationship with the trafficker/pimp, can serve as barriers to exiting the commercial sex industry. Love for the trafficker and trauma bonds also serve as barriers to leaving. For victims of domestic trafficking in the United States, one of the primary barriers to leaving a trafficking situation is love for the trafficker. Domestic minors, in particular, who are in a relationship with their boyfriend pimps may be too attached to their trafficker to leave them.

Emotional barriers may also be intertwined with the stigmatization felt from peers, family, and society (Curtis et al. 2008; Oselin 2014). Shame may be an issue, with individuals afraid to go home or to go back to school because of the stigma, the resulting shame, and nonacceptance. In international context, survivors may be ashamed to go back to their home country, where they may be not only ostracized but also subjected to violence and abuses for violating sexual and gender norms, and blamed for their abuse and victimization.

Fear of physical violence or other retaliation from the trafficker/pimp as well as threats of violence to family and friends may prevent a sex trafficking survivor from leaving the trafficking situation. In relatively uncommon cases, individuals may experience confinement or physical constraints. Further, as discussed earlier, debt bondage may be present; for those trafficked into the United States, this may include coverage of a "transportation fee" that is difficult to pay off, or fees for room and board or clothing, which serve as a barrier to leaving. For domestically trafficked people, debt bondage related to drugs, clothing, or housing may represent challenges to leaving a trafficking situation. Addiction and lack of access to substance abuse rehabilitation may also present a barrier.

For victims who are trafficked into the United States from other countries, cultural beliefs may also present a barrier. A case in Florida found that a sex trafficking victim believed she was tied to her trafficker through an amulet containing her hair. She believed he possessed her soul, and misfortune would befall her family if she displeased him (Heil 2012). Another issue specific to international victims occurs when the trafficker has taken documents or identification needed for travel and employment, such as a passport or worker visa. Moreover, if survivors are in the United States and undocumented, they may fear of deportation as well as ramifications of the legal system in destination country (see chapter 9). Regardless of legal status, immigrants are also exposed to threats to family members in the home country; this psychological coercion presents a barrier to leaving the trafficking situation (Hopper 2004; Farrell et al. 2012). Smuggling debts, confiscated identification, and limited English-speaking abilities may create dependencies on the trafficker and serve as barriers to leaving the trafficking situation (Nichols and Heil 2014; Hopper 2004).

In addition, sex trafficking survivors may have nowhere to go. Trafficked people might be dependent on the trafficker for basic needs, such as food, housing, and clothing. This prevents them from seeking help, as individuals may not have resources outside of the trafficking situation (Farrell et al. 2012; Nichols and Heil 2014). Unavailability of services is a notable barrier to leaving a trafficking situation, including a lack of safe shelter and other resources (Heil and Nichols 2015). Finding steady employment that pays a higher wage than sex work, education, substance abuse rehabilitation, stable housing, and access to trauma informed care are among the services in demand (Curtis et al. 2008). Importantly, in an analysis of commercially sexually exploited homeless youth in New York, "when the youth were asked if they would like to leave 'the life,' an overwhelming majority, 87% (n = 211), stated that they would like to exit if given the opportunity" (Curtis et al. 2008). Another study showed that 93% of 283 youth involved in survival sex had recently stopped or wanted to stop commercial sex industry involvement (Dank et al. 2015). Addressing the barriers that prevent exit from the commercial sex industry is necessary to assist individuals who want to leave it.

Chapter Summary

This chapter began by examining risk factors for sex trafficking, including identity-based oppression and heightened exposure to weak social institutions. Individual identities that serve as risk factors are age, sex, sexual orientation, gender identity, race, ethnicity, immigrant status, and intellectual disability. Weak social institutions are reflected in weak economic systems in the form of a failure to provide a living wage as a minimum wage, and resulting exposure to poverty or low-wage work. Weak education systems produce higher mobility rates, higher drop-out rates, and higher truancy rates, which increase exposure to exploitation through a pimp/trafficker. Lower educational attainment breeds further poverty through a lack of economic mobility and increases vulnerability. Weak family systems increase exposure to intimate partner violence in the home, child abuse or neglect, child sexual abuse, or parental rejection, leading to runaway or throwaway homeless youth, also increasing risk of exploitation by a trafficker or buyer. Lack of access to health care, particularly substance abuse and mental health care as well as health care specific to transgender people's needs, is a risk factor. Last, weaknesses within the juvenile justice system and foster care produce environments for recruitment. Barriers to leaving include fear of deportation, traffickers' reprisals, stigma and shame, lack of stable employment and housing, lack of money to meet basic needs, and lack of availability of social services.

Discussion Questions

1. Define and provide an example of a weak social institution. How are weak social institutions implicated as risk factors for sex trafficking?

2. How does identity-based oppression related to risk of sex trafficking vulnerability? Provide at least three examples.

3. What are some potential solutions or ways of addressing weak social institutions? Be sure to discuss social safety nets.

[6]

Traffickers

Keosha Renee Jones once had dreams of being a pediatrician. She was a middle school cheerleader hopeful for the future. When her mother's long-time boyfriend, her father figure, left the family, Keosha described suffering emotionally at the loss. By chance, Derrick Hayes happened along at this vulnerable point in her life. Keosha explained that charismatic Derrick filled the hole in her life that her father figure's absence created. Derrick told her he loved her, and she quickly fell in love with him. As it turned out, Derrick was a pimp, working with the St. Petersburg, Florida, gang 8Hype, and the relationship soon became abusive. Keosha described how he coercively took her virginity by beating her until she "complied" (Silvestrini 2015, 1). Shortly after, Derrick sent her into a bar patronized by white men looking for sex-for-sale. She was coerced into having sex with one of the men in a public park and handed the money over to Derrick. This incident marked the first time Keosha was trafficked, at the age of 15. The next six years for Keosha would be full of beatings, manipulation through drug addiction, and coerced prostitution at the hands of Derrick. Derrick abused her to the point of hospitalization several times, beat her and threatened her family when she tried to run away, and pulled a gun on her brother when he tried to intervene. Yet Keosha's psychological bonds to Derrick were strong, and she continued to love him. Derrick brought other girls into his trafficking ring but told Keosha that she was special—the other girls were just for sex and business. After a brief stint in prison on a weapons charge, Derrick introduced her to two runaways. They told her they were 17 and had no place to go, and Derrick wanted to "put them in the game." Keosha became a sex trafficker herself, as partner to Derrick. The girls were actually 14. Keosha was the one who arranged their first "date," bought them clothes, collected the money, and put ads of the girls online. Keosha was later arrested by the FBI six months after reporting the crimes herself, when she found out the girls were 14 and not 17, after seeing the girls' pictures on a missing persons flier posted in the neighborhood. Keosha was charged with conspiring to engage in sex trafficking of children. One of the girls recounted callous treatment from Keosha in a letter to the judge who heard the case when it came to trial, "I let her know that I was hurt, but she didn't care." One of the girls also wrote, "She continued to make me do awful things with awful people." Another written statement indicated, "I never saw a dollar," "The most we would get is a bar of soap to make sure we were clean for the next job." One girl even indicated Keosha's responsibility for the physical violence she received, stating that she "hired a man that hurt me real bad. I could not walk or anything." Keosha was sentenced to six months in jail, five years of supervised release, and is currently a registered sex offender. She was also required to get her high school equivalence diploma, maintain full-time employment, take random drug tests, and complete one hundred hours of community service. Derrick Hayes was sentenced to 30 years in prison.

The reader at this point may be wondering how Keosha could become a trafficker, after going through the horrific experience herself. Stories like Keosha's are not unusual among traffickers; they are actually typical of women traffickers (see text box 6.1). One Chicago-based study found that, of women who pimp, 100% had sold sex or were trafficked themselves (Raphael and Myers-Powell 2010). This dynamic of "trafficked-to-trafficker" seems to be at least one pipeline for creating future traffickers. Traffickers can be formerly trafficked people like Keosha or a boyfriend-as-pimp like Derrick, but they can also be parents, buyers, or pimps who are not intimately involved with their victims. There are very few research studies that specifically examine sex traffickers. Of these, the majority largely focus upon trafficking operations (detailed in chapter 7). Consequently, this chapter synthesizes the limited body of work specifically

BOX 6.1
Typology of Female Traffickers in the United States

Sex Trafficking Victims as Traffickers

University of Minnesota Law School professor Mark Kappelhoff stated that he has seen both men and women prey upon vulnerable victims; he believes "sex trafficking is an equal-opportunity crime." For most women who traffic, the story begins with personal victimization. Researcher Lauren Martin states that "past victimization is critical to how and why women are involved" (Rosenblum 2013, 1). The common story is that female traffickers were prostituted in their teens and later moved into work as traffickers themselves. In fact, many female suspects arrested for their role in the trafficking of another person for sex are current or former victims of sex trafficking. They become offenders when they recruit other young women and children into trafficking situations for their pimps, traffickers, or boyfriends, or when they start their own "business." The role of female pimps, including women who have transitioned from victim to victimizer throughout involvement in the sex industry, requires further study (Roe-Sepowitz et al. 2014). Based on what is known, the following overlapping typologies emerge.

Pimp-Coerced Female Trafficking

A pimp will sometimes use an older woman in "the life" to gain a girl's trust and convince her to come along with them. A National Institute of Justice (2012) report found that these women were typically in their mid-forties, the age of most teenagers' mothers. Media reports show cases like this with women in their twenties as well (Rosenblum 2013; Silvestrini 2015). Teenage victims with troubled upbringings may be more responsive or trusting with an older seemingly "mother figure." Those who simultaneously traffic and are trafficked recruit other women and girls for their pimp, with promises of their own release upon replacement. Still other former victims begin to identify with their traffickers after an extended period of abuse and become recruiters, in some cases because of affinity or because they have been desensitized as a result of their own trafficking (Surtees 2008).

Partners and Couples as Traffickers

Jody Raphael and Brenda Myers-Powell (2010) showed 50% of female pimps were coerced into pimping, and 57% of these women entered pimping at the request of their boyfriends. Bionca Elizabethelen Mixon was charged with playing a key role in the seven-day kidnapping of a 17-year-old Iowa girl forced to have sex with about thirty men in a St. Paul hotel room. It was said that "Mixon did most of the coercing going from being tangentially involved to substantially involved." A point of interest in this case is that Mixon was deemed a victim by an area program that advocates for girls and women involved in sex trafficking. This signifies the complex nature of these crimes and the role of victimization in traffickers' lives.

Familial Traffickers

The National Report on Domestic Minor Sex Trafficking (Smith, Vardaman, and Snow 2009) describes familial trafficking in which a mother prostitutes her daughter in exchange for drugs. Children are unfortunately used in cases where parents' addictions trump the responsibilities of being a parent. In 2009 human trafficking was a growing mom-and-pop business, with couples being arrested, including a minister and his wife (Buchbinder 2013).

Lone Female Traffickers

While some formerly trafficked women go on to advocate for their rights and the rights of other survivors, others become independent traffickers. These women are typically former victims of sex trafficking who decide to go into their own business. Raphael and Myers-Powell's (2010) study of ex-pimps found that 100% of females sold sex prior to pimping. They had firsthand knowledge of what "the life" meant, as they had personally been threatened, abused, demeaned, isolated, confined, demoralized, medically neglected, drugged, dominated, and controlled, but they subsequently survived to become the next generation of traffickers (Buchbinder 2013).

—Deanna McPherson, LMSW, MSW, MPH

examining sex traffickers. Specifically, this chapter investigates the characteristics and backgrounds, including a typology, of sex traffickers as well as an examination of the social conditions that increase the risk of becoming a pimp or trafficker. The chapter concludes with a discussion of the glorification of pimp culture in the United States and its relationship to sex trafficking.

Types of Traffickers

Pimps as Traffickers

Where is the line between pimping and trafficking? Recall that the Trafficking Victims Protection Act (TVPA) defines trafficking as the inducement of a commercial sex act by force, fraud, or coercion, or involving anyone under 18. Accordingly, pimping that contains any of these elements legally equals trafficking. As indicated in the previous chapter, pimps are more common in cases involving cisgender women and girls compared to transgender women and girls, and men and boys (Curtis et al. 2008). Several research studies reveal that the majority of pimp-controlled prostitution in the United States involves some level of force, fraud, or coercion; minors; or commercial sexual exploitation. The terms "pimp" and "trafficker" will be used interchangeably throughout this section; use of the term "pimp" henceforth refers specifically to forms of pimping involving the components of the TVPA. Not all pimping meets the legal definition of sex trafficking (Marcus et al. 2014). Such cases may involve exploitation or may be based on a consensual non-exploitive business arrangement. Various types of pimp-controlled prostitution that do overlap with sex trafficking are detailed below, including strong-arm pimps, boyfriend pimps, non-intimate partner pimps, and international traffickers. Familial traffickers and buyers as traffickers are also delineated. Note that some of these "types" may overlap and manifest simultaneously.

The Strong-Arm Pimp

Some pimps essentially operate through forced or coerced prostitution. This includes abduction, threats, and physical violence to gain economically from conditions of forced or coerced prostitution. Although less common, abduction can be part of this form of pimping. In such cases, youths and adults are taken from the streets and forced to sell sex for the profit of the pimp. For example, in the documentary *Very Young Girls* (Schisgall and Alvarez 2008), 14-year-old Nicole described how a car pulled up next to the bus stop where she was waiting for her bus. She was grabbed and forced into a car, taken to a private home, and forced to have sex with multiple men over a three-day period by the pimp who abducted her.

Celia Williamson and Michael Prior (2009) conducted a study in Toledo, Ohio, and interviewed survivors of sex trafficking. One survivor who participated in their study described being forced to sell sex through both physical and psychological coercion. Sherry, vulnerable as a chronic runaway, said:

> I was walking down the street having fun, just recently got out of here [detention] in January. And all of the sudden this black Yukon rides up. He tried to talk to me, at first, but I told him how old I was and then he rolled up around the corner and jumped out the car and just started hitting on me for no reason. . . . [He] started beating me and just for no reason and he told me I was going to be his ho. And just started basically abusing on me and threatening me. . . . He took me to the car and told me that I was going to make his money or he was going to kill my little brother and sisters and my mom. He said I've been watching you.
>
> (Williamson and Prior 2009, 51)

In a notorious case of sex trafficking involving abduction, Christian Dior "Gucci Prada" Womack, a Philadelphia-based pimp, trafficked two women and one minor in Atlantic City, Virginia Beach, and Philadelphia. He used methods of abduction and force, characteristics of a strong-arm pimp. Womack had a girlfriend as his partner, Rashidah "Camille" Brice, 24. Womack and Brice found a 16-year-old at an Atlantic City casino who had been left there by her friends. They took her to the Trump Plaza Hotel, and Brice coerced her through physical violence into selling sex to an adult male. The pair videotaped the encounter and then extorted money from the buyer (Logue 2014). The trafficking duo then posted an ad of the girl on Backpage.com and took her to Virginia Beach, where Womack forced the minor to have sex with fifteen men in a single incident, threatening her with a handgun to gain her compliance (Logue 2014). The next stop was the Red Roof Inn in Tinicum, a small town about an hour's drive from Philadelphia, where they forced her to sell sex for five days to numerous men, repeatedly threatening her life with a gun if she tried to escape. Womack and Brice continued to sell her for another nine months, largely arranging dates over the Internet. Eventually, the girl was able to get $50 from a customer; she then took a cab home and contacted her mother. Her mother then called the Philadelphia police. Another woman was similarly coerced into Womack and Brice's prostitution ring, also meeting them in Atlantic City. She needed a ride to Pennsylvania, and Brice and Womack offered her one. Once in the car, the duo first drugged her, then asked her if she wanted to sell sex. When she refused, Brice and Womack took her belongings, including her driver's license and phone, and also threatened to kill her. They posted ads of her on Backpage.com as well, but she was able to escape after two days without being forced to engage in prostitution. Yet another woman fell victim to Womack and Brice, telling investigators that Womack drugged her and attempted to rape her. She managed to escape while the trafficking pair was asleep, and she reported them to local authorities in Marcus Hook, Pennsylvania. After this incident the two were finally located and arrested by police. Womack was sentenced to life in prison, and Brice was sentenced to nearly fifteen and a half years in prison.

Pimping through abduction or force is not nearly as common relative to survival sex or boyfriends pimping out their girlfriends. A study of trafficking in St. Louis, Missouri (Heil and Nichols 2015), notes that strong-arm trafficking is often represented nationally in awareness campaigns but is described by police, prosecutors, and social service providers as infrequently occurring. Similarly, Anthony Marcus and colleagues (2014), who examined sex trafficking in Atlantic City, also describe this type of trafficker as relatively uncommon. Ric Curtis and colleagues (2008) likewise maintain that pimping through abduction, force, and extreme coercion is not prevalent in New York City. The Polaris Project (2015b) found about 7% of cases involved kidnapping, force, or abduction. While these cases do occur, this type of pimp represents a relatively small proportion of sex traffickers. These cases do tend to draw the most media attention because of the atrocious nature of the crime and the serious and overt physical and psychological harm done to the survivors.

The Boyfriend Pimp

Like strong-arm pimps, boyfriend pimps, one of the most common types of traffickers, often engage in acts of coercive control, including violence and threats of harm, but in ways that revolve around psychological manipulation and emotional abuses. The boyfriend pimp is literally what the term implies—a pimp who is simultaneously the boyfriend of the trafficked person. Often this involves an older man with a teen girl (Reid 2010;

Lloyd 2012; Heil and Nichols 2015). In such cases, the pimp first becomes involved in an intimate relationship with the girl or young woman and establishes a "love" relationship. "Through a series of calculated and methodical stages, the trafficker establishes trust, and psychologically and physically bonds with the victim through a web of deceit and lies, securing her allegiance—even after the relationship changes drastically into one of violence, torture, and abuse" (Smith, Vardaman, and Snow 2009, 8). The boyfriend pimp recruits minors into prostitution by initially posing as a boyfriend and romancing young women and girls. He may buy her clothes, take her out to restaurants, provide love and affection, and seem to take care of her. The boyfriend pimp's goal is to fill any missing holes in the girl's life. Sometimes this hole includes basic needs like food, shelter, and clothing, and other times this includes fulfilling an emotional need due to lack of parental support or presence, or other family troubles— like Derrick in the opening to this chapter. Yet in some cases girls may come from homes with supportive relationships with their parents; the boyfriend pimp simply makes her feel loved and otherwise romances her (Heil and Nichols 2015). Once the love relationship has been established, then the pimp reveals what his line of work is and otherwise convinces the girl to sell sex. Commonly, the boyfriend pimp will indicate that he really loves her and does all of these things for her, and he tells her that if she sold sex, she would be doing it for them or returning the favor she owes. They could go to nicer dinners, have more shopping trips, and otherwise improve their lives (Heil and Nichols 2015; Lloyd 2012; Raphael, Reichert, and Powers 2010; Raphael and Myers-Powell 2010; Smith, Vardaman, and Snow 2009).

This could be seen as a form or extension of intimate partner violence in that the boyfriend pimp is typically abusive within the intimate relationship, and engaging his partner in commercial sex is another manifestation of the coercive control typical in cases of intimate partner violence. For example, Raphael and colleagues (2010) found that a majority of women selling sex in Chicago entered sex markets through a boyfriend pimp, and violence and abuse were present and escalated in a majority of cases as well. Linda Smith and colleagues (2009) indicated that the Clark County Public Defender's Office reported that of the 103 minors arrested under prostitution-related charges, 30 indicated that they had boyfriends as their pimps. There are multiple prosecuted cases, research studies, and accounts from social service providers indicating that boyfriend pimps compose a large proportion of traffickers in domestic sex trafficking cases (Heil and Nichols 2015; Reid 2014; Smith 2014; Smith, Vardaman, and Snow 2009; Williamson and Prior 2009). While the boyfriend pimp often involves an older man with a younger woman or girl, cases in which similar-age boyfriends are pimping out their girlfriends have been found as well, among minors as well as adults (Heil and Nichols 2015; Busch-Armendariz, Nsonwu, and Cook Heffron 2009).

Additional cases have found that young gay men and boys also enter into intimate partner relationships with adult men who convince them to sell sex or who exploit them by taking the money earned from engaging in the commercial sex industry (Heil and Nichols 2015). This is another manifestation of the boyfriend pimp. For example, in a recent Urban Institute Study examining commercial sexual exploitation in New York City, one respondent, a 21-year-old gay-identified male, after being asked how much he typically earned, stated, "Oh my goodness like $1,000, $1,500. . . . But people were taking it from me. Like my friend, he used to . . . I was dating him so, while I was working them [the customers], he was working me" (Dank et al. 2015, 49). His boyfriend made his appointments, arranging his dates for him. The same respondent indicated that when he started dating someone new, this new boyfriend played a nearly identical role to his old boyfriend, pimping him while simultaneously taking his money and living off him. The boyfriend pimp represents a loved one trafficking/exploiting the survivor, yet pimps who traffic may be non-intimate partners as well.

Non-Intimate Partner Pimps

In many cases, a pimp trafficker is not romantically involved with those who are being trafficked or exploited. Keosha's example at the beginning of this chapter illustrates both the boyfriend pimp, in Derek, as well as an example of a non-intimate partner pimp, in Keosha's own involvement in trafficking. Women who are partners with their boyfriend pimp, or who are otherwise coerced into recruiting and trafficking other women and girls, are found in about a third of federally prosecuted sex trafficking cases (Farrell et al. 2012). According to a recent study by the Polaris Project (2015b), while more than a third of the cases they came into contact with involved a boyfriend pimp, a romantic situation, or a marriage proposal, about 10% involved someone posing as a benefactor, about 10% were those offering a job, and about 7% involved the strong-arm pimp using tactics of kidnapping and abduction. According to this study, many cases involve some type of pimp or third-party exploitation. The strong-arm pimp or pimps engaged in debt bondage, bait and switch, or sex-work-turned-sex-trafficking are types of non-intimate partner pimps. Familial traffickers can also serve as non-intimate partner pimps.

Familial Traffickers

Research suggests that parents sometimes traffic their own children. This may involve the intergenerational transmission of prostitution, in which prostitution and pimping are normalized, or it may involve selling their children to settle a drug debt or to obtain drugs (Oselin 2014). For example, Erin Heil and Andrea Nichols (2015) found that parents with substance abuse issues, such as addiction to heroin, methamphetamines, or prescription pills, were essentially trafficking their children to pay for the drugs. The researchers also found that social service providers working with trafficked people indicated that parents in both rural and urban areas sold their children to pay bills. Further, Smith and colleagues (2009) report that Hillsborough Kids, Inc., a private foster care service in Florida, had several cases involving caregivers producing pornography of their child, mothers being paid for the sexual abuse of their child, and one case of a mother selling her child to another trafficker. Moreover, the same researchers report that a shelter for high-risk youth in Las Vegas, WestCare Nevada, found nearly 30% of minors receiving services were commercially sexually exploited by family members, often for drugs or something else of value, or money. Raphael and Myers-Powell (2010) similarly indicate that of the twenty-five ex-pimps that they interviewed, many had first been exploited by their parents. Jennifer Cole and colleagues (2014, 17) maintain that familial sex trafficking is reported in "nearly all communities where needs assessments of sex trafficking of minors have been conducted and may be more common than expected." The Polaris Project (2015b) reports that nearly 10% of their clients had experienced some form of familial trafficking.

Heil and Nichols (2015) found reports of children being sold in their homes, neighborhoods, and even church basements in exchange for drugs. Parents who sell their children for drugs are sex traffickers because there is a commercial sexual exchange involving a minor. Parents are trading the sex of their minor children for something of value—usually drugs. Survivor and antitrafficking advocate Asia Graves described her experiences with being sex trafficked for drugs beginning at the age of 6 (Muhammad 2014). She explained that her mother's drug dealer sexually abused her until she was 10 years old, when her mother was finally able to conquer her addiction. Asia noted that, on the occasions of her mother's relapses, "that same drug dealer kept coming back and my mom knew that this man was touching me. She allowed him to touch me so that she could get her drugs, and that made me feel as if I was only worth sex" (Muhammad 2014). In another case, husband and wife Kentuckians Anthony and Kathy Hart solicited clients for their teenage daughters in movie theaters, restaurants, and grocery stores in exchange for money or other valuables (Kocher 2014). In 2009 a Missouri man was arrested in Niagara Falls, New York, by the FBI for sexually exploiting a girl for more than five years beginning at the age of 12 (Smith, Vardaman, and Snow 2009). Among a variety of sexually exploitive acts, he appeared to be training the girl to become a dominatrix. In Missouri, he was charged with seven felony counts of commercial sex trafficking of a minor. In this case the mother was involved in the sexual exploitation of her own daughter; she was given money for allowing her daughter to be sold. These are just a few examples of cases in which family members have been implicated in sex trafficking/commercial sexual exploitation.

In addition to parents profiting from the exploitation of their children, researchers also find intergenerational transmission of involvement in the commercial sex industry. At times entry is facilitated by parents who are involved in the industry themselves, either as pimps or selling sex (Oselin 2014; Raphael and Myers-Powell 2010). Consequently, those whose parents are in the industry are at a higher risk of entering themselves. In such cases selling sex is viewed as normal, as it is a "family business," or individuals who are abused and exploited in their homes may runaway and become retrafficked in the form of survival sex (Oselin 2014).

Parents may serve as the "third party," facilitating commercial sexual exploitation of their own children. Yet a third party is not necessary to label a situation as sex trafficking, and the third party is not always the trafficker. In some areas, buyers themselves are being charged with sex trafficking when no third party is present and they are purchasing sex from children, typically teens engaging in survival sex.

Buyers as Traffickers

Important court cases in the U.S. Circuit Court of Appeals, *United States v. Jungers* and *United States v. Bonestroo,* involved an appeal from the United States District Court for the District of South Dakota. This appeal has serious implications for U.S. policy as it sets the precedent for buyers to be prosecuted as sex traffickers. Initially, separate jury trials ended in the convictions of the buyers, Daron Lee Jungers and Ronald Bonestroo, for the attempted sex trafficking of minors. Both were caught in sting operations in 2011 in Sioux Falls, South Dakota. Federal law enforcement officers posted an ad online pretending to be a man offering his girlfriend's underage daughters for sex while his girlfriend was out of town. The two men, in separate instances, responded to the ad. Jungers thought he was getting an 11-year-old girl to perform oral sex on him, and Bonestroo thought he was getting two 14-year-old twin girls to have sex with him for an hour. In both cases, the defendants were found guilty by juries, but they were acquitted by the district court judges.[1]

In both Jungers's and Bonestroo's overturned cases, the district court judges justified acquittal by stating that it was not the intention of Congress to prosecute purchasers of sex as traffickers; the intention of the TVPA was to punish pimps or other third parties as traffickers, not to punish buyers. Yet the federal government appealed both decisions, arguing that no customer exception is indicated in the law, which indicates "a commercial sex act induced by force, fraud, or coercion, or in which the person induced to perform such act has not attained 18 years of age" (TVPA, sec. 8a). Brendan V. Johnson was the U.S. attorney representing the government in the appeals case in which the judges reversed the acquittals of both men, reinstating the initial jury verdict and consequent sentencing. In part because of this ruling, buyers can continue to be prosecuted as sex traffickers. Shortly after winning this appeal, nine buyers attending the Sturgis Motorcycle Rally in South Dakota were prosecuted as sex traffickers, each facing a ten-year sentence and $250,000 fine for knowingly agreeing to pay for sex with minors (Bartenstein 2015). Buyers have been prosecuted on federal and state levels throughout the United States.

However, it should be noted that, just as with the TVPA more generally, law and implementation of the law vary considerably from jurisdiction to jurisdiction (Farrell et al. 2012; Nichols and Heil 2014). A different decision by a different circuit court could potentially change this dynamic.

The End Sex Trafficking Act of 2013 attempted to specifically broaden the definition of traffickers in federal law to address any definitional issues and to clearly include those who patronize and solicit sex acts with minors. The bill was introduced but not voted upon or enacted by Congress. Consequently, the future of buyers of minors as sex traffickers remains unclear as this book goes to press. At the same time, the Jungers and Bonestroo case outcomes do provide precedent on a federal level to prosecute buyers as traffickers.

International Traffickers

Sex traffickers operating in the United States who are working between nations are described here as international traffickers, which includes those who are involved in trafficking rings internationally and with the United States as the destination, source, or transit country. This type of trafficker may overlap with other types of trafficking described in this chapter. As one example of an infamous international pimp, Joaquin Mendez-Hernandez, who also goes by the name "El Flaco," is a U.S. citizen, formerly of Mexico, who was sentenced to life in prison for his involvement in an international sex trafficking operation. This case was part of a larger investigation that uncovered twenty-three perpetrators and worked to assist twelve sex trafficked people. The international sex trafficking ring spread from Mexico to Georgia, first defrauding women from Mexico and Nicaragua, promising them legitimate employment and an opportunity for a better life. After entering the United States, the women were physically and psychologically forced into prostitution throughout the southeast United States, particularly in Savannah, Georgia. The women reported to have been forced to sell sex to up to fifty men a day. Members of the sex trafficking ring used psychological coercion, threatening their children, who were held hostage in Mexico. The women were also traded among other members of this crime ring, in Florida, Georgia, North Carolina, and South Carolina. All twenty-three defendants pled guilty. Their sentences ranged from twenty-two months to life, depending on the severity or level of their involvement. Two additional defendants, Eugenio Prieto-Hernandez and Daniel Ribon-Gonzalez, remain at large.[2] International traffickers are more likely to be a part of organized crime rings rather than individual operations. Such dynamics are discussed in more depth in chapter 7.

Who Are They, and Why Do They Do It?

Survivors of sex trafficking often experience various forms of abuses, including emotional, economic, sexual, and physical abuses, both as a precursor to and during their commercial sexual exploitation. Yet traffickers themselves frequently come from backgrounds of victimization. Studies examining pimps find a history of problematic home lives as children, including domestic violence, sexual abuse, pimping and prostitution, and substance abuse issues within the home. This discussion may be difficult for some readers, as it may be easier to think in dyadic terms of "good" and "evil." However, traffickers are not created in a vacuum, and various social conditions more or less "create" traffickers, or certainly create social environments in which traffickers are more likely to be produced. This conversation is important because in order to prevent sex trafficking, the social conditions that create traffickers themselves must be addressed (Raphael and Myers-Powell 2010). The more popular response is simply to address sex trafficking after the fact and emphasize arrest, prosecution, and conviction of buyers and traffickers with the hope of marginal or specific deterrence. But deterrence research suggests this is shortsighted, and it is prevention that may be key to addressing sex trafficking.

There is some research that supports the concept of intergenerational transmission of sex trafficking/prostitution (Oselin 2014; Raphael and Myers-Powell 2010). Such research suggests that domestic traffickers who are pimps are more likely to come from homes in which prostitution is normalized. Drawing from interviews with twenty-five ex-pimps, Raphael and Myers-Powell found that a majority of them, while growing up, had family members who were involved in prostitution. Prostitution was essentially a family business, with the mother or father pimping or selling sex. More than half indicated their mothers sold sex, were pimped, or both during their childhoods. The majority of ex-pimps in this study stated that their mothers, uncles, sisters, and cousins had pimped them out at young ages; many were trafficked themselves by their parents. This study also suggested emulation of fathers who were pimps, or of mothers who got them involved in pimping.

Notably, research indicates a majority of pimps experienced physical abuse while growing up and were also victims of childhood sexual assault at an average age of 9.5 years old (Raphael and Myers-Powell 2010). High rates of childhood substance abuse also indicates a neglectful or problematic home life, with a majority of the ex-pimps reporting to have regularly used alcohol as a child, beginning at about 12.5 years old. Significantly, a majority of ex-pimps in one study reported witnessing domestic violence in the home: "The overwhelming majority of ex-pimps suffered physical abuse and sexual assault while growing up and watched their mother being physically assaulted by their fathers, stepfathers or boyfriends" (Raphael and Myers-Powell 2010, 2). Likely related to this abuse and neglect within the home, running away from home or foster care was described as common. These factors are ironically parallel to the risk factors highlighted for sex trafficking victimization.

Importantly, one study found that, of ex-pimps, 100% of female ex-pimps and 56% of male ex-pimps sold sex themselves prior to pimping. The average age these pimps gave for the first time they sold sex was about 14.5 for women and about 15.5 for men (Raphael and Myers-Powell 2010). Similarly, another study found in an analysis of 379 sex trafficking suspects, about one-third were female and a majority had been or were being trafficked themselves, thus becoming traffickers when recruiting for a pimp (Farrell et al. 2012). A background of commercial sexual exploitation was a catalyst to women becoming pimps, like Keosha's story depicted at the beginning of this chapter, and for a small majority of men as well. Importantly, research indicates that pimping also gave the pimps a sense of power, control, and respect that had been missing from their tumultuous lives of victimization at the hands of others, particularly their mothers and their mothers' boyfriends. They also did it for survival and to make a living. In addition to coming from households with a family background of prostitution and pimping, or abusive or neglectful homes, which result in running away and selling sex to survive and eventually becoming pimps themselves, community factors may also play a role in leading people to become pimps.

In the Raphael and Myers-Powell study (2010), a majority of those they interviewed had people in their neighborhood involved in prostitution. Likewise, Sharon S. Oselin (2014) indicates that community normalization is related to engagement in selling sex. Social environments with relatively high rates of prostitution seem to be implicated in one's likelihood of becoming a pimp/trafficker. In neighborhoods where prostitution is normalized, it may be viewed as a viable opportunity for survival or wealth—a job opportunity, so to speak (Smith 2014). Community factors such as poverty appear to be intertwined with prostitution being visible in neighborhoods.

In turn, men in the neighborhood with nice cars, clothes, and who seemed to have a lot of money and girlfriends may serve as role models. Exposure to poor quality education or a lack of education is another potential community-level factor. One study found that a majority of men and women who were ex-pimps had no high school degree (Raphael and Myers-Powell 2010). This may also be intertwined with community-level factors involving poverty because the schools with the highest drop-out rates and lowest graduation rates are disproportionately located in impoverished communities.

The majority of women involved in pimping describe being coerced into pimping, most often by boyfriends, who threatened them with physical violence if they did not comply. In some cases this was because male pimps did not want evidence traced to them (Farrell et al. 2012). Simply put, women often became traffickers by default or as their best option, when their own traffickers coerced them to engage in pimping to avoid getting caught. While some women were coerced by their male pimps, who were often their boyfriends as well, others began pimping to exit exploitation and violence. As one woman stated, "You call it pimping, I call it surviving and being smart. You either get in this world or you get got. No one will get me again like my mother did" (Raphael and Myers-Powell 2010, 4). In contrast, men who were coerced into pimping cited gang coercion. "I was raised in the game. It was a way of life in my household and neighborhood. It was almost hereditary" (Raphael and Myers-Powell 2010, 3).

These factors all involve intersecting vulnerabilities, with each factor increasing the likelihood of involvement in pimping, and they overlap considerably—poverty, lack of educational opportunities, community and intergenerational normalization of pimping, childhood neglect and abuse, domestic violence—these are not distinct categories. Perhaps most striking is the fact that the risk factors for pimping are almost identical to that of victimization. Consequently, in order to address sex trafficking, risk factors for both victimization and pimping should be ameliorated through prevention efforts targeting these sources of victimization. This would call for increased resources for domestic violence services. Researchers have pointed out for decades that the safety of children is inextricably linked to the safety of their mothers (Banks, Dutch, and Wang 2008; Nichols 2014a). Witnessing domestic violence in the home normalizes violence and may relate to the way one sees the value of women as subordinate (Nichols 2014a). Working to prevent and address childhood sexual and other physical abuse in the home is imperative as these factors lead to running away, becoming trafficked, and then becoming a trafficker oneself. Education systems must also be improved, providing resources to parents and children. Increased access to substance abuse prevention and rehabilitation is also called for. Lastly, poverty must be addressed. The United States has the highest rate of childhood poverty of all the high-income nations. These conditions "are precursors of pimping and trafficking, contributing to a process by which victims become victimizers" (Raphael and Myers-Powell 2010, 9).

The Glorification of Pimping in Pop Culture

Yet another cultural manifestation creating a social environment conducive to sex trafficking is the glorification of pimping in pop culture. Several researchers have written about the glorification of pimp culture in mainstream society, although this work is limited and not generally the focal point of analysis (Kotrla 2010; Smith, Vardaman, and Snow 2009; Zimmerman 2012). The glorification of pimping in pop culture is impacted and represented by multiple social factors. There is a high level of value attached to the multiple meanings that the word "pimp" currently holds. Historic, iconic, and celebrity figures of pimps perpetuate the glorification of pimping in popular music, books, movies, T-shirts, and even Halloween costumes. These factors serve to normalize and celebrate the figure of the pimp. Yet there are some important critiques of this glorification, including the perpetuation of androcentric and often racist depictions that consequently negatively impact sex trafficked or commercially sexually exploited people and perhaps even the traffickers themselves. Sex trafficked people, who are exploited to provide the means for pimps to live up to this venerated image, bear the brunt of this glamorization of the pimp. The pimp subculture, in part facilitated by white power structures and disproportionately negatively impacting people of color, is detailed in the following section.

Language

Language evolves over time, and words may acquire new meanings. The word "pimp" has morphed over time to take on at least two meanings, and both reflect a high level of value and status. In some representations of pop culture, "pimp" simply means "really cool," achieving success, or upgrading to the top of the line with no association to commercial sex (Zimmerman 2012). Manifestations of this use of language include phrases such as "pimped out" to describe upgrades to the highest status; "that's so pimp" to describe something really cool; or "you are such a pimp," meaning one is really awesome. Take, for example, the MTV hit show *Pimp My Ride*. The show clearly uses the word to represent the upgrade to the best (Kotrla 2010). Yet another meaning of the word additionally signifies images of power, wealth, and respect through managing women and girls who sell sex for profit. The term dates back to the 1600s and means an individual who coordinates the sale of sex for his own profit, has many sexual conquests, commands respect, and has savvy street smarts with the end result of wealth and high social status (Zimmerman 2012).

While neither of these definitions may immediately hold negative associations for some, both distort or ignore the reality of what pimping entails for many women, girls, men, and boys. By blurring the lines between the two definitions, culturally, we not only condone but normalize exploitation. While some pimping arrangements involve a mutual contractual agreement and may not involve violence, coercion, fraud, or minors (i.e., sex trafficking), the research indicates that such dynamics as well as physical, verbal, economic, and sexual abuses are represented in the majority of pimp-involved, prostitution-related research studies and scholarly work (Raphael and Myers-Powell 2010; Dempsey 2011; Lloyd 2012; Martin et al. 2014), with some exceptions (e.g., Marcus et al. 2014). Yet this dynamic is absent from the "pimp discourse" in pop culture. Simply put, both usages of the word deny or ignore the practice from the perspective of those who are pimped by only representing the facet of pimping from the pimp's perspective or centered solely upon the pimp, or by reshaping language to use the term to describe anything "cool" or of high value and status.

Iconic Figures

Iconic pimps also contribute to the glorification of pimping. There is a long history of pimps who are figures of respect, status, and power and who are still regarded as popular idols and role models within pimp culture today. Perhaps most notable is the iconic Stagger Lee, who was a St. Louis-based musician and pimp in the late 1800s (McCulloch 2006). Lee belonged to an infamous group of pimps known in St. Louis as the "Macks," who were famed for their ostentatious and expensive clothing, participation in the St. Louis underworld, and partying lifestyle. Lee ran a highly successful prostitution business catering to prominent men in St. Louis in what is now known as Laclede's Landing, located on the riverfront in St. Louis, Missouri (McCulloch 2006). Lee was known for embodying a representation of masculinity that included money, respect, power, disdain for authority, and independence, which remain modern-day desirable qualities of pimps. Lee would eventually be imprisoned for shooting and killing a man who won his hat in a night of gambling. The incident has since been the topic of folklore, hit songs, and books written about Lee (McCulloch 2006; Price 2002), situating his story as a famous pimp in historic memory.

Notably, Iceberg Slim, another key figure in pimp culture, was a fan of and influenced by Stagger Lee. Iceberg Slim was known for pimping from about 1940–60 in the Milwaukee and Chicago areas. Iceberg Slim's autobiography has become a part of pimp culture, and his writings are revered by many modern-day pimps. This infamous quote from his book indicates the power and control that may be involved in pimping: "Fast, I got to find out the secrets of pimping. I really want to control the whole whore. I want to be the boss of her life, even her thoughts. I got to con them that Lincoln never freed the slaves" (Iceberg Slim [1969] 2011). This technique of control and manipulation, which Iceberg Slim describes in some detail in his book, is used by some pimps today, some of whom credit Iceberg Slim for influencing their philosophies. For example, one of the most publicly known and revered pimps, Don "Magic" Juan, stated: "I'd see a pimp, so I'd pattern myself after that. I'd read Iceberg Slim. I'd watch *Superfly*, with the flashy cars and clothes. I went for all of that. When I came to the game I was 16" (Hoekstra 2000, 1).

Don "Magic" Juan, like Stagger Lee and Iceberg Slim, is also seen as a "founding father" of pimp culture. Don "Magic" Juan ran a large-scale national prostitution ring in the 1970s and early 1980s and is known for his savvy entrepreneurial skills in developing this nationwide enterprise. He is also known as Bishop "Magic" Juan as he became a minister in 1985 after he found God. As Don "Magic" Juan, he is known for developing the Players Ball, which is an award ceremony for pimps, characterized by their wealth, flashy clothing, and cars. Some of the awards administered at the ceremony include "Pimp of the Year," "No. 1 International Pimp of the Year," and "No. 1 Super Player" (Bales and Soodalter 2009). Don "Magic"

Juan himself was the winner of the Pimp of the Year award for thirteen consecutive years. The criterion for winning these titles is reportedly directly correlated to the annual income earned for that year. The Players Ball is derived from the 1973 film *The Mack* (presumably taken from Stagger Lee and the St. Louis Macks). In this film, the main character, Goldie, attends a Players Ball, an award ceremony recognizing and honoring the most successful pimps in the nation. Since the film's premiere, the ball has taken place every year on the birthday of Don "Magic" Juan, and celebrities and others nationwide come to celebrate the founder's birthday and attend the extravagant awards ceremony.

Many famous artists have attended and even received awards at the Players Ball, including Snoop Dogg (also known as Snoop Lion) and P. Diddy (formerly known as Puff Daddy). This event is also endorsed by radio stations, corporate sponsors, and even local mayors, indicating that "pimping" is a culturally normalized and celebrated practice, given the background of Don "Magic" Juan. The Players Ball is represented in mainstream culture as well, depicted in the documentary *Pimps Up, Hoes Down*, shown on HBO, as well as the documentary *American Pimp*. The DVD *Master Players Ball* was also released and distributed in 2006, with live footage from the Players Ball.

While pimping does not always necessarily equal sex trafficking, and the ceremony is thought to use the word "pimp" to characterize wealth and status, not pimping per se, this awards ceremony glorifies the pimp as an elite figure of admiration (Bales and Soodalter 2009). But this glorification relates to sex trafficking because some cases of sex trafficking–related convictions implicate involvement with the Players Ball. For example, Matthew Thompkins was indicted for sex trafficking in 2006. He was a Players Ball award winner, receiving two Pimp of the Year awards. In addition to Players Ball award winners receiving sex trafficking sentences, sex trafficking is known to have occurred at the ball itself. In 2003 in Atlanta, several pimps were arrested for having minors working as prostitutes; one case involved a 10-year-old girl. The Players Ball was also a site of protest by sex trafficking survivors in 2005, in the Chicago area. One protester, a sex trafficking survivor who was recruited into prostitution by a pimp at the age of 14, told the media that the ball was a "ball for child molesters" (Briggs 2005). Celebrity involvement also increases the status of the ball. In addition to Players Ball–related activities, celebrity figures who discuss their lives as pimps more generally may also be related to a culture that romanticizes and normalizes pimping.

Celebrity Pimps

Celebrities have also glamorized pimping. For example, chart-topping rapper, *Girls Gone Wild* host, and Players Ball awardee Snoop Dogg described pimping at the height of his career and explained why he did it. In an interview with *Rolling Stone*, Snoop Dogg stated, "I put an organization together . . . I did a *Playboy* tour, and I had a bus follow me with ten bitches on it. I could fire a bitch, f—k a bitch, get a new ho: It was my program. City to city, titty to titty, hotel room to hotel room, athlete to athlete, entertainer to entertainer" (qtd. in Weiner 2013). He further indicated that he did not do it for the money, rather, for the glamor. "I'd act like I'd take the money from the bitch, but I'd let her have it" (qtd. in Weiner 2013). He said that pimping allowed him to realize a dream he had since he was a kid of having material items and women. "As a kid I dreamed of being a pimp, I dreamed of having cars and clothes and bitches to match. I said, 'F—k it—I'm finna do it" (qtd. in Weiner 2013). He told of making arrangements for high-profile athletes and entertainers, who would "come hang out, pick and choose, and whichever [woman] you like comes with a number. . . . A lot of athletes bought p—-y from me" (qtd. in Weiner 2013). While there is no evidence that sex trafficking was involved in Snoop Dogg's prostitution operation, it does reflect and reproduce the glamorization of pimping, in both Snoop Dogg's own reflections of childhood visions of himself as a pimp and his view of the lifestyle as glamorous as well as in his representation of this facet of his life to mainstream society. He internalized glamorous images of pimping as a child and as an adult worked to manifest this image in his own life. In his public declaration describing his pimping activities, he depicts pimping as a normal behavior of a celebrity figure. Because some pimping involves sex trafficking, and much pimp-controlled prostitution involves aspects of abuse, this celebrity endorsement of pimping is problematic. At the very least, it contributes to a social environment glorifying pimping, which is implicated in a sizable proportion of sex trafficking.

Snoop Dogg is not the only celebrity to describe his experiences as a pimp. James Lipton, host of *Inside the Actor's Studio*, told of being a pimp in Paris as a young man, stating that it was a "great year" of his life. In an interview, he described working in Paris in the 1950s as a pimp in order to make a living. "It was only a few years after the war. Paris was different then, still poor," he explained in the interview (Rader 2013). "Men couldn't get jobs and, in the male chauvinist Paris of that time, the women couldn't get any work at all. It was perfectly respectable for them to go into *le milieu* [i.e., prostitution]" (qtd. in Rader 2013). Lipton said he made enough money to live by managing a bordello, having been recruited for this work by a woman he knew who sold sex, and taking a cut of the women's earnings. While Lipton stated in his interview that the women were not exploited, he also stated that there were no other jobs for women to do. The reality for these women likely falls into the "shades of gray" area of exploitation, as they became involved in the sex trade through a lack of choices, and their story is told only through Lipton's words. Like Snoop, Lipton contributes to the celebrity pop culture that romanticizes pimping. The celebrity endorsement of pimp culture extends to music artists and is reflected in lyrics.

Music Lyrics

Intertwined with celebrity pop culture and pimping are popular music artists, particularly artists in rap and hip-hop, who also glorify pimping. However, just like the double meanings of the word "pimp" in language described earlier, the use of the word "pimp" is represented differently by various artists. Some use the term with the meaning of "really cool" while others use the word for someone who manages and controls women in prostitution to make money. Just like the language discussion earlier, this blurs the lines between coolness and exploitation in a way that normalizes it and never offers perspective from the women who are exploited.

Nelly is an example of an artist who uses the word "pimp" in ways other than as a representation of commercial sexual exploitation. In the song "Pimp Juice," Nelly explains pimp juice as something that the opposite sex finds appealing, "money, fame, or straight intellect" (Lorber and Haynes 2002). Thus, this definition plays into the meaning of being able to attract the opposite sex, being really cool, or having qualities or characteristics that represent power, seemingly absent from the commercial sexual exploitation of women (Zimmerman 2012). Nelly notes that the applied label of "pimp juice" does not discriminate based upon sex—women can have it, too.

Ludacris's 2005 single "Pimpin' All Over the World" appears to use a definition of pimping distinct from commercial sex as a way of complimenting and romancing a woman and showing her a good time (Bridges,

Scantz, and Jones 2005). In contrast, Ice-T's "Pimp or Die" uses a meaning of "pimping'" involving commercial sex, and the song is wrought with extreme violence, abuse, psychological manipulation, and exploitation directed toward pimped women. He also overtly refers to various aspects of pimp culture, including Iceberg Slim, Bishop "Magic" Juan, the Macks, the book *The Pimp Game*, and the film *Pimps Up, Hoes Down*, in which he played himself (Ice-T 2006). Ice-T's role in the glorification of pimping is multifaceted; in addition to being a popular rapper, he had his own reality television show, and is widely known as an actor playing an NYPD detective on the prime time NBC show *Law & Order: Special Victims Unit*. He is also the winner of two NAACP image awards, in 1996 and 2002, for his role on the *Law & Order* series. Likewise, Lil Jon's "Can't Stop Pimpin'" clearly describes commercial sexual exploitation for his profit, involving schoolgirls, psychological manipulation, physical violence, control, and more (Norris et al. 2001). Lil Jon was on *Celebrity Apprentice*, a reality show with Donald Trump, in 2011 and 2013. Although "Can't Stop Pimpin'" came out in 2001, he continues to be a commercial success. His "pimp cup"— a 44 oz. black glass goblet embossed in gold with "pimp" written across it—is also popular and even notorious; one can buy a pimp cup on Amazon.com. Similarly, 50 Cent's "P.I.M.P." was also a hit commercial success, earning the number three spot on Billboard's Hot 100 in 2003. 50 Cent provides a meaning of pimping that absolutely entails getting women involved in commercial sex for his profit, describing a scene in which he meets a woman stripping at a club, and soon has her earning money for him in a hotel and on the track. He describes living large off the pimped women's profits while the women get a much smaller cut, and he describes use of psychological manipulation by being a father figure, friend, and confidant, until the woman/girl is "confused" (Porter, Jackson, and Parrot 2003). This is a well-known pimping tactic that is commonly reported in sex trafficking research (Heil and Nichols 2015; Martin et al. 2014; Raphael and Myers-Powell 2010; Williamson and Prior 2009; Romo 2013).

"It's Hard Out Here for a Pimp" by Three 6 Mafia was represented in the 2005 film *Hustle & Flow* and also won Best Original Song at the 78th Academy Awards. The song lyrics and film situate pimping within the context of racialized and class-based marginalization as well as the social pressure for men to have material items and money (Coleman, Beauregard, and Houston 2005). While not ostensibly a representation of sex trafficking, it is androcentric in its representation in that the verse and the film highlight the hardships for pimps, but the struggles of the women themselves are not acknowledged (Romo 2013). As many black feminists have noted throughout the history of feminism and of various movements advocating for racial equality and rights, black women often take a back-seat to black men, from the Black Nationalist movements of the 1960s, to the Battered Women's Movement, to voting rights (Beal 2013; Crenshaw 1991; hooks 2014). Pimping is depicted as a strategy in surviving poverty in disenfranchised black communities, but without perspective from or acknowledgment of the black women who are pimped in these circumstances (Beal 2013; hooks 2012; Romo 2013).

Pimp Manuals?

In addition to learning aspects of pimping from celebrities, music, and iconic figures, would-be-pimps can also buy well-known guidebooks. Transmission of pimping tips from successful pimps can be passed along in this way. *The Pimp Game: An Instructional Guide* is a centerpiece of pimp culture. This book was implicated in the case of Alex "Cowboy" Campbell, who received a life sentence for sex trafficking, as discussed in chapter 1. The pimp guide describes techniques that pimps can use to manipulate young women and girls to sell sex for them (Smith, Vardaman, and Snow 2009).

> You'll start to dress her, think for her, own her. If you and your victim are sexually active, slow it down. After sex, take her shopping for one item. Hair and/or nails is fine. She'll develop a feeling of accomplishment. The shopping after a month will be replaced with cash. The love making turns into raw sex. She'll start to crave the intimacy and be willing to get back into your good graces. After you have broken her spirit, she has no sense of self value. Now pimp, put a price tag on the item you have manufactured.
>
> (qtd. in Smith, Vardaman, and Snow 2009, 23)

This is just one of many books popularized in pimp culture. Multiple books serve to glorify pimping and educate the would-be pimp entrepreneur. Iceberg Slim's autobiography remains popular, and perhaps the next best-known books on pimping include *Pimp Tales, Book One: The Gospel of* the Game by James Robinson, *The Pimp's Bible: The Sweet Science of Sin* by Alfred Bilbo Gholson, and *Pimpology: The 48 Laws of the Game* by Pimpin' Ken. These books are easily accessible, available on sites like Amazon.com. The reviews are interesting to read as well, and reveal the unquestioned normalcy and desirability of pimping in U.S. pimp subcultures. This glorification of the pimping lifestyle, and even the guidebooks that can be bought online, not only reinforce the glamorization of the pimp but also provide instructions for trafficking operations, the topic of chapter 7.

Normalization

Various aspects of pop culture outside of iconic figures, celebrities, music, and books also contribute to the normalization of pimping. Pimps may also be viewed as an object of amusement, if not an iconic figure, as represented in Halloween costumes. Halloween costumes of pimps for men, women, boys, and even dogs include accessories like sunglasses, gold chains, hats, canes, and ostentatious fur coats. This costume also depicts a racist image. In an online search through the top-selling Halloween costumes, there were only two costumes in which the model was a black male; one of them was of a pimp. Viewing pimps as funny or cool may be problematic as much pimp-controlled prostitution involves sex trafficking or commercial sexual exploitation. Beyond Halloween costumes, there is a wide array of apparel also depicting "pimp." Onesies for infants with the word "pimp" on them, in various fonts and colors, are available as well as onesies with "pimp my trike" and "pimp my bike." Amazon.com offers ten different choices. Zazzle.com also offers multiple options for all ages and sexes. "Pimp" T-shirts for both men and women are also available in a variety of different styles. "Pimp Slap That Bitch," "Irish Pimp," "Pimpin' Ain't Easy," "Got Hos?" (a mockery of the "Got Milk?" ads), "Pimps Up, Hoes Down," "Slap That Ho Like a Domino," "Pimp Daddy Mack," and "McPimpin, #1 Big Mac Daddy Supersized" (a play on McDonalds) are some of the varieties the shirts can be purchased. References to slapping and derogatory words combined with "pimp" further problematize these products. This may be harmless fun for some, and arguments finding no fault with this line of products would likely suggest that the intended meaning of the language here is "really cool." For others, it privileges the pimp, and its meaning makes a mockery of the commercial sexual exploitation and violence experienced within the sex industry.

Resistance in the Black Community

Glorification of the pimp subculture has been critiqued by multiple facets of the black community. There are many related sites of activism and resistance generated by black scholars, hip-hop artists, documentarians, student groups, and more. This critique primarily targets the music industry and is generated from perceptions of the negative impact on the black community more generally, and on black women and girls in particular. Such groups are critical of the power dynamics implicated in contemporary rap and hip-hop music, including white power and black male power, which manifest in the disempowered status, sexual objectification, and violence directed toward black women.

Black feminist theorists Terri M. Adams and Douglas B. Fuller (2006) critique rap lyrics for marginalizing the experiences of black women. They describe rap lyrics as cultural forms that work to reflect experiences of oppression and resulting marginalization but from androcentric views that render black women virtually invisible (Adams and Fuller 2006, 943; Romo 2013). Thus, while depictions of black male struggle are present in rap music, the simultaneous depiction of the struggles of black women is largely absent. Erasure of struggle works in tandem with the oppression of black women by black men in rap music lyrics, which is facilitated by white-owned record labels. The result is multiple manifestations of oppression—from race-based oppression by white power structures to sex-based oppression by black men. This critique works to address arguments that the music is merely a reflection of the marginalization and struggle of poverty-stricken black communities by pointing out that black women are largely absent from this discourse.

Similarly, while the disproportionate number of pimps and traffickers who are African American cannot be taken out of the context of marginalization within multiple institutional structures, black feminists point out that the victimization of black women and girls cannot be ignored under the guise of identity politics (Crenshaw 1991; Adams and Fuller 2006). This race-, sex-, and class-based marginalization is reflected in sex trafficking statistics; in federally prosecuted cases, a disproportionate number of convicted sex traffickers are African American, and mostly men (Banks and Kyckelhahn 2011). Amy Farrell and colleagues (2012) found that "of 379 suspects in 119 sex trafficking cases, 39% were white, 39% were black, 18% were Asian, and 31% were Hispanic." Notably, the buyers are disproportionately white men, reflecting another layer of oppression (see chapter 8). Yet those who are trafficked are disproportionately black women and girls (see chapter 5). *The Root, The Grio, Essence, Ebony*, and other media outlets catering to a largely black audience are critically analyzing the disproportionate rate of victimization of black women and girls in sex trafficking and prostitution and working to bring this dynamic to public and political attention.

This oppression is also facilitated by white consumers and white power structures in the perpetuation of pimp culture via commerce. Documentarian Byron Hurt describes the origins of hip-hop, from which rap is derived, as an artistic response to racial marginalization. Hurt notes that hip-hop music at one time held important political and intellectual messages and analysis, and was a site for artistic manifestations of resistance from oppression. Yet, over time, as record labels were purchased by large corporate conglomerates largely operated by white, upper-class men, these messages were lost in favor of music revolving around killing, disrespecting women, and pimping to cater to the tastes and interests of a largely white audience. Today, 70–80% of sales of hip-hop and rap albums are purchased by a white audience, and it is the consumers that guide the music (Hurt 2006; Hart 2010). The corporatization of hip-hop also includes advertising using the music by groups such as McDonald's, Coca-Cola, Nike, and MTV (Rose 1994). Would-be rap artists describe the struggles of creating music because record labels will not pick up politically astute or other socially conscious music that does not include lyrics involving killing, drugs, or sex (Hurt 2006). Chuck D, of Public Enemy and co-author with Yusuf Jah of *Fight the Power: Rap, Race, and Reality*, is known for socially conscious and politically motivated rap music. He is also critical of the current dynamics of race, power, and oppression depicted in the music industry today, advocating strongly for peer-to-peer music sharing networks to essentially take back hip-hop and rap music from white power structures.

In addition, student groups at historically black colleges and universities have also attempted to address sexual commodification of black women in hip-hop and rap. For example, students at Spelman attempted to engage Nelly in a dialogue about the commodification of black women depicted in one of his music videos, "TipDrill," in which Nelly swipes a credit card through a woman's ass-crack. Disappointingly, Nelly cancelled his appearance and did not participate in the conversation (Hurt 2006). More recently, Jefferson High School students in Portland, Oregon, organized a series of events through the Black Students Union to address marginalization and inequality more generally, and sexual objectification of black women more specifically, showing activism and resistance among students (Shaw 2015).

Importantly, it should be noted that the various aspects of pimping described here, such as using language and purchasing "pimpified" hip-hop and rap music, T-shirts, and Halloween costumes, are engaged in and facilitated by the white community and white power structures. Additionally, the purchasers and creators of the products and music glamorizing pimping are largely white, and the customers of sex trafficked people are disproportionately white as well. Thus, resistance to glorification of pimping must come from people of diverse backgrounds to have a larger impact. Glorification of pimping is just one facet of this conversation.

Further, multiple racial groups engage in pimping and sex trafficking, regardless of the disproportionate portrayal of pimping in music, books, and idolization of historic figures as race-based. Richard Estes and Neil Weiner (2001) note that trafficked people are typically of the same racial and ethnic background as their trafficker. While anyone is at risk (see chapter 5), ignoring the disproportionate victimization of black women and girls is a form of color-blind racism and oppression through omission. There is a higher percentage of black traffickers as well as black victims while buyers are disproportionately white (Banks and Kyckelhahn 2011). Thus, a larger conversation about sex trafficking, recognizing heightened vulnerabilities through an intersectional lens, is called for.

Counterarguments to critiques of the cultural glorification of pimping might suggest that homogenizing all pimping is problematic. Not all pimping entails violence or oppression. Such arguments rely on the assumption that pimping is inherently negative and needs to be changed. Further, the agency of sex workers who willingly work with pimps is also not recognized in antiglorification arguments. Thus, for some, the glorification of pimping is not a problem. Yet the already-existing glorification of pimping also homogenizes pimping, albeit in a positive way. This model also fails to recognize the many nuances involved in pimping and the harmful forms it can take as well as the experiences of those victimized or exploited in systems of pimping. The critiques of each perspective are rendered identical in that each view loses nuanced understanding and voice from those who have the most at stake. The reality is that the caricature of the glorified pimp in pop culture and pimp culture does not necessarily reflect the life of the pimp, it excludes women who are pimps, and it marginalizes the experiences of those who are trafficked or otherwise exploited or abused by pimps. Taking these arguments together, resisting homogenization and providing nuanced understandings of pimps, traffickers, and survivors/victims/sex workers finds some common ground.

Chapter Summary

This chapter delineated types of traffickers, backgrounds of traffickers, and the glorification of pimp culture. Types of traffickers include familial traffickers, strong-arm pimps, boyfriend pimps, international traffickers, and buyers as traffickers. Traffickers come from backgrounds of victimization, including domestic violence, abuse, and neglect in the home; prostitution and pimping in the home and in the community; and substance abuse as well as poverty and lack of educational opportunity. A small majority of male traffickers were trafficked or exploited themselves, and, overwhelmingly, women who are traffickers were previously trafficked themselves. The glorification of pimp culture can be found in modern manifestations of language usage, celebrity pimps, iconic historical figures, music lyrics, and even T-shirts, Halloween costumes, and infant clothing. Glorification combined with marginalization and victimization creates a social environment primed for sex trafficking.

Discussion Questions

1. Discuss the use of the term "pimp" in contemporary language and music lyrics. Is this problematic? In what ways?

2. Do an Internet search for "pimp T-shirt." Click on images, and describe what you see. Do the same for "pimp Halloween costume." What might such images represent to people who have been trafficked or exploited?

3. Explain the role of white consumers in perpetuating music lyrics that disproportionately marginalize and victimize black women.

4. Do an Internet search and analyze the lyrics of any of the songs depicted in this chapter.

7

Sex Trafficking Operations

In 2014 twenty-four gang members were indicted in San Diego for a sex trafficking operation spanning forty-six cities and twenty-three states. Women and girls were initially recruited from the streets in San Diego as well as through various social media, including Facebook, Twitter, Instagram, and YouTube. The recruiters used "bait and switch" methods to attract the women and girls through rap videos with promises of a glamorous lifestyle. Yet, after recruitment, the women and girls were not provided this glamorous life; instead they were alleged to have experienced violence, threats, and intimidation resulting in forced or coerced involvement in the commercial sex industry. The women and girls were tattooed with the gang's name, pimps' names, and barcodes to illustrate their ties to the gang. Arrests were made in San Diego, Arizona, and New Jersey. Over sixty survivors were recovered, including eleven minors. They were all offered social services to assist with their recovery (Ponting 2014).

This chapter specifically examines sex trafficking operations like this one and investigates various venues where trafficking or solicitation take place, such as hotels, truck stops, private parties, the Internet, street-level work (the "stroll"), escort, massage parlors, and strip clubs. The use of interstate circuits in various parts of the United States is also investigated, including the Midwest, Northeast, and Pacific Northwest and at the Canadian border and Mexican border. The role of technology and trafficking is specifically examined. Other trafficking techniques to avoid detection, such as exploitation of the "bottom girl," are described. The role of organized crime rings, small-scale operations, and individual "entrepreneurs" is also detailed as are the various roles of those involved in trafficking operations.

Venues for Trafficking and Commercial Sexual Exploitation

There are multiple venues in which sex trafficking and commercial sexual exploitation (CSE) take place, including hotels, truck stops, private parties, street-level work, massage parlors, private residences, and strip clubs, and may be facilitated through the Internet, escort services, or false-front businesses. Various venues impede identification in different ways. Sex trafficking/CSE conducted through the "stroll," or street-level sex work, is much more visible, but individuals working in this area are often misidentified as criminals, and their victimization is rendered invisible due to their stigmatized status. One study found in an analysis of sex trafficking cases that 13% involved street-level sex work (Farrell et al. 2012). Other venues offer near anonymity, operating in hidden venues largely closed from public view or occurring in relatively insular communities. Hidden venues provide an added layer of challenge in identification of and outreach directed toward survivors.

In Florida research found that traffickers used hidden brothels temporarily set up in makeshift bars (Heil 2012). In Texas researchers found that false-front spas and clubs were used for sex trafficking/exploitation (Busch-Armendariz, Nsonwu, and Cook Heffron 2009). Massage parlors, while widely reported as sex trafficking venues, were a component in only 3% of cases in Amy Farrell and colleagues' (2012) analysis. Similarly, the Polaris Project (2015b) reports that commercial front brothels were used as venues in just 3% of cases. Adding another layer of difficulty to identification in false-front businesses, police face difficulty when investigating in insular ethnic neighborhoods, where outsiders are easily recognized (Farrell et al. 2012; Nichols and Heil 2014).

Several studies implicate truck stops and travel plazas as venues for trafficking. The Polaris Project (2015b) reported that, in 2014, of 21,431 calls to the National Human Trafficking Resource Center hotline, 230 involved truckers. The trucking industry is a relatively insular community, which potentially impedes identification of traffickers. Several studies find that girls are moved from city to city to avoid getting caught, and one of the ways they are being trafficked is through the use of semitrucks (Nichols and Heil 2014; Roe-Sepowitz et al. 2014; Williamson and Prior 2009). Truckers make up both a consumer base for trafficked women as well as a means for interstate trafficking. Commercial sex involvement at truck stops is a long-standing practice and well known in the trucking community. In an industry that is dominated by men, the large numbers of single men present at truck stops and travel plazas offers an opportunity for traffickers to make money. At one point in time, citizens' band radios were used to solicit, but this may have been displaced to the Internet and cell phones used today. When a truck driver known to the author of this book was asked about selling sex at truck stops, she replied,

Not anymore. It's like they all disappeared. But years ago like up until 2007 it was all over the place. They were called "lot lizards" then. They would get on Channel 19 on the CB radio and advertise "Would anyone like some female company? Go up to say Channel 27." Well, out of curiosity I followed one up there once just to hear what was going on. Then she would tell her price. The driver would say what truck he was in and that was that. Even transgender [people] got into that game in the 90s. But this past year I haven't really heard much. With GPS in everyone's truck and cell phones, drivers don't even have CBs in their trucks hardly. But it was nationwide spread back when I first started driving in 1988 up until 2007.
(Personal communication with anonymous trucker, 2015)

This example, while only anecdotal, represents the possibility of movement of solicitation to less noticeable modes of communication, and not as openly conducted, or could represent a decline in commercial sex in the trucking industry due to the activism of Truckers Against Trafficking (see chapter 11).

In addition to truck stops, traffickers use hotels as sites for sex as another form of "keeping it indoors." Many prosecuted cases and sting operations reported on in the media involve hotels, with the "dates" set up on the Internet, typically through popular sites like Craigslist.com or Backpage.com. More systematic research, in an analysis of 119 sex trafficking cases across six study sites, found that a substantial number of cases involved use of the Internet for solicitation, and 10% took place in a hotel (Farrell et al. 2012). The Polaris Project (2015b) reported hotels as the most common venue, followed by the street or "stroll," residential brothels, and escort services. Another study found nearly 60% of youth most commonly went to buyers' residences or hotels for a commercial sexual exchange (Dank et al. 2015).

Farrell and colleagues reported that nearly half of their analyzed sex trafficking cases occurred in private residences. Private parties are a relatively hidden venue for sex trafficking. In examining social service providers' experiences with trafficked youth, one social services provider explained:

> Where, there's a whole other side of this, and this was [Sherri's] world, where it was, for the lack of better word, had higher clientele. . . . She would be taken to parties, you know. She wasn't made to walk the streets. And someone said, "while you were there, why didn't you tell someone or run?" Besides the whole fear and manipulation and that sort of thing, she said "who do you tell?" she said, "when the clients that are there are attorneys and judges."
>
> (qtd. in Nichols and Heil 2014, 12–13).

A key challenge is that when sex trafficking occurs indoors or in relatively private or hidden venues, it is more difficult to uncover. Street-level sex work is increasingly moving indoors with the advent of the Internet. Internet solicitation makes conducting transactions easier, and it produces less risk of getting caught by police. Such dynamics delineate the nearly hidden nature of the crime, with the exception of relatively infrequent "sting" operations targeting Internet solicitation, and the difficulty of identifying and investigating sex trafficking cases and offering services to survivors.

Technology as a Trafficking Tool

Technology is known as both a recruitment tool and a solicitation tool for traffickers and pimps. Joan A. Reid (2010) indicated that in the southern United States, trafficking solicitations occurred primarily through use of the Internet, and transactions were conducted primarily indoors. Similarly, Linda Smith and colleagues (2009) examined ten cities in the United States and found that all of them evidenced trafficking on the Internet. In Ohio, Celia Williamson and Michael Prior (2009) found that minors were commonly advertised online. Nichols and Heil (2014) note that in the St. Louis area, pimps would look for vulnerable homeless youth, offer them shelter, and soon post them on the Internet for sex. The Internet offers pimps the opportunity to reach more customers more quickly, as opposed to meeting a more limited pool of customers in a particular locale and waiting for them. In addition to sales online, recruitment also occurs online on Facebook, in chatrooms, and on other social media sites. Traffickers look for women and girls who have a financial need or personal vulnerability, or young girls looking for love, romance, or attention.

Technology is perhaps one of the most publicly and politically contentious areas of debate in antitrafficking work. The debate is centered upon censoring websites that offer sex for sale. Those in favor of censoring or eliminating sections of websites that offer escort services, adult services, and similar things indicate that, of identified sex trafficking cases, a substantial portion of survivors were trafficked or exploited on sites like Craigslist and Backpage.com. This is viewed as a legitimate reason to eliminate these sections of websites. Those that are not in favor of censorship suggest that it interferes with individual freedoms of the website providers as well as those who buy and sell sexual services that do not involve minors or adults engaged by force, fraud, or coercion.

The reality is that closing down one site at a time has little to no effect on overall Internet-based trafficking due to criminal displacement. Site shut-down simply moves it to another site, or even a different section of the same site (Heil and Nichols 2014). For example, after years of antitrafficking activism, Craigslist shut down its adult services section, which was implicated in a substantial portion of trafficking cases. Immediately following, there was a rise in sex-for-sale ads on Backpage.com as well as multiple other local and national sites offering similar services. Shortly after there was in increase in solicitation ads on Craigslist itself—simply under a different section, notably, the personals section. This "squeezing the balloon" effect is reminiscent of the displacement theory, which maintains that closing down one site at a time does not deter solicitation; it simply moves it and makes it even more difficult to detect. Prior to the shut-down, Craigslist required a phone number and credit card for such ads, which could then be traced if a suspicious ad was flagged. This offered an opportunity to identify traffickers. Tracing traffickers became more difficult when the solicitations moved to other sites that did not offer such monitoring. Accordingly, in order for the shutdowns to be successful, they would have to simultaneously implicate all sites offering sex for sale. This is unpopular with anticensorship activists. Encrypted sites or sites located in other countries could also thwart such attempts. While this is a difficult issue to rectify, research indicates without a doubt that technology plays a significant role in trafficking operations, and increasingly so, as street-level sex work continues to move online (Curtis et al. 2008; Farrell et al. 2012; Kotrla 2010; Kunze 2010; Heil and Nichols 2014; Dank et al. 2015). The technique of soliciting online is often accompanied by interstate movement, another common trafficking technique used in the United States by traffickers and pimps.

Interstate Circuits

There is much evidence to suggest that interstate circuits are often part of trafficking operations in which traffickers move survivors from city to city, usually through personal vehicles traveling on interstate highways. Trafficking circuits have been uncovered in multiple research studies, prosecuted cases, and reports by social service providers, survivors, and law enforcement. Interstate circuits appear to be mostly regional but sometimes cover a larger national spread. Traffickers essentially move girls from city to city to avoid detection, to draw from a new consumer base, and to isolate the women and girls they work with from their communities and personal contacts to prevent them from seeking help. As indicated in a previous chapter, males are significantly less likely to work with a pimp, and research has not uncovered as much interstate movement involving men and boys in the commercial sex trade. Multiple research studies find that use of travel in trafficking operations is purposeful: to prevent getting caught (Smith, Vardaman, and Snow 2009; Williamson and Prior 2009; Nichols and Heil 2014). Young women's and girls' pictures would appear on Backpage.com in one city for a short period of time, then would return a month or two later (Nichols and Heil 2014). Smith and colleagues also report that, "in an effort to evade law enforcement, traffickers/pimps will often stay in cities for a short period of time" (Smith, Vardaman, and Snow 2009).

Interstate circuits of domestic victims tend to be regional; there is a Pacific Northwest circuit, a Midwestern circuit, a Northeast circuit, and a Southern California circuit, among others. Smith and colleagues (2009) describe a particular circuit, the Western circuit, including movement between Seattle, Portland, San Francisco, Los Angeles, San Diego, Hawaii, Phoenix, Denver, and Salt Lake City and even crossing international borders into Vancouver, Canada. In reality, interstate or trafficking circuits are unpredictable. They are known to sometimes involve a chain of cities within a state or smaller geographic territory but can also involve a chain of states or can function nationally, such as the case described at the beginning of this chapter. At times trafficking circuits may even extend beyond national borders. Even on regional circuits, the ordering of the city-to-city travel is not consistent or necessarily planned. This makes identification more difficult.

One case, among many, exemplifies a multistate East Coast trafficking circuit. Atlanta native Joshua Dumas, nicknamed "Hitman," was 21 when he pled guilty to sex trafficking minors in Maryland, Virginia, North Carolina, South Carolina, Georgia, and Florida. He partnered with leader Edwin Barcus Jr., who also pled guilty to "founding and leading a child exploitation enterprise."[1] Dumas admitted to a "managerial role" recruiting minors for Barcus's business. Dumas's technique was to serve as the "boyfriend pimp," romancing the girls and then glamorizing commercial sex. Authorities alleged that members of this trafficking operation used a semiautomatic pistol for intimidation purposes and offered the girls drugs to keep them compliant. A juvenile boy was also involved as a "lookout" for police and to run errands. The girls were advertised on Backpage.com, and buyers called throwaway cell phones to schedule dates. Using throwaway phones is a technique to avoid traced calls. Buyers would then meet with girls at a hotel, paying $80–$200 for sex with the minors depending on how much time they bought. The girls made between $500 and $3,000 per day and gave all the profits to Barcus, Dumas, or another partner in their scheme.

Smith and colleagues (2009, 22) state that "the transient nature of the trafficking markets keeps traffickers/pimps below the radar of most law enforcement as they move with their victims from city to city evading detection and preventing the girls from becoming identified minors to law enforcement or service providers." Knowledge of use of interstate circuits is important as it could have implications for interstate and highway patrols in terms of training related to identification. Multiple cases have been uncovered by happenstance on interstates in regular policing of minor traffic violations, which suggests an opportunity for identification with better awareness and training. Importantly, while trafficking circuits are known to be prevalent in trafficking operations and they tend to be regional, they are otherwise unpredictable. At times a trafficking circuit can include crossing national boundaries, making it an international circuit. Yet sometimes transnational or international movement does not follow a repeated circuit; rather, it involves travel to get to a destination point. Essentially this entails a trafficking flow, or transnational trafficking movement, typically from low-income countries to high-income countries.

International Trafficking Movement

As described in chapter 1, survivors who are trafficked internationally may be sex trafficked through the Canadian or Mexican borders and may even have been trafficked through multiple countries before arriving at the destination of the United States. For example, Kimberly A. McCabe and Sabita Manian (2010) describe the trafficking of survivors from various European countries to London and then to the United States. Researchers also report transport from Scotland to Canada and then into the United States via air travel. The states that are thought to have the highest rates of internationally sex trafficked women include California, New York, Nevada, and Texas (McCabe and Manian 2010). Source countries of those who were internationally trafficked in 2013 most frequently came from Mexico, the Philippines, Thailand, Honduras, Guatemala, India, and El Salvador, often via the Mexican border (U.S. Department of State 2014). Recently prosecuted cases in the United States and trafficking cases on the FBI's most wanted list involve sex trafficking survivors from Mexico, Guatemala, and Honduras. Importantly, these are nations that are experiencing a surge in violent crime and are ranked as low- or medium-income countries. Honduras and Guatemala are labeled as low-income nations, and while Mexico ranks as a middle-income nation, social stratification facilitates the perseverance of a large underclass. These countries also score in the bottom half of the gender equality index, meaning that it is more difficult for women and girls to find economic opportunities.[2]

To illustrate transnational movement in supply–demand chains in international context, there is the case of Severiano Martinez-Rojas, who, in 2006, along with others, began trafficking to Atlanta, Georgia, young girls from Mexico and Guatemala who were seeking a better life. The girls were smuggled into the country and were then forced into the commercial sex industry. It was not until 2013 that Martinez-Rojas was indicted on sex trafficking–related charges.[3] In another example, Roger Galindo-Sepeda and Maria Isabel Cruz are currently on the FBI's most wanted list for trafficking more than thirty young women and girls into the United States from Honduras and forcing them first to work in bars owned by the duo and then forcing them into engaging in commercial sex acts with the bar's customers.[4] The young women and girls thought they would be working as waitresses or maids, but upon arrival in Texas they were told they owed seven to ten thousand dollars to pay off their transportation fees and had to work off their debt before they could be released. They first worked in the bar to pay off these transportation fees, a form of debt bondage as repayment for being smuggled into the country, and were shortly channeled into selling sex. Isolated in houses and businesses kept by the traffickers, the women and girls reported being forced to wear excess makeup and to go to the clubs and bars managed by the traffickers scantily clad, and then forced to sell sex to the customers to pay off their debt. Traffickers threatened reporting them to U.S. authorities for illegal entry into the country, where they were told they would be locked up in U.S. prisons. Their family members in rural areas of Honduras were also threatened. Galindo-Sepeda, who is facing sex trafficking–related charges in the United States, is currently thought to be residing somewhere in Honduras.

The U.S. Attorney's Office in the Southern District of Texas placed Alfonso Angel Diaz-Juarez on the FBI's most wanted list for sex trafficking–related charges for his alleged role in an international sex trafficking operation running between the United States and Mexico. He was indicted along with thirteen others for his role in this operation. Undocumented Mexican women and minors were sex trafficked between 1999 and 2013, one of the longest-running known international trafficking operations. Diaz-Juarez is accused of recruiting women and girls for sex trafficking operations in brothels, bars, and cantinas owned by his thirteen co-conspirators. Force, fraud, or coercion were implicated in this case, including locking the women and girls in rooms so they could not leave and using violence to threaten and control their activities.[5] Even U.S. servicepersons have been implicated in international sex trafficking operations in relatively complex international networks. Donna M. Hughes, Katherine Y. Chon, and Derek P. Ellerman (2007) found that military personnel based in South Korea gained entry of South Korean women into the United States through false marriages. The women were then channeled into the commercial sex industry in the United States.

Meeting the Demand

Internet solicitation, interstate circuits, international flows, and hidden venues work to meet the demand of buyers. To buyers, trafficking survivors are indistinguishable from willing sex workers, although occasionally a trafficked person will ask a client for assistance, with varying results (see chapter 8). The demand for sex-for-sale drives such markets. In some instances, this demand is heightened. Locations with large numbers of single men are known venues for sex trafficking and commercial sex, including oil fields, sporting events or other large events, conventions, military bases, hotels near airports used by commuters, truck stops, and agricultural fields with large numbers of temporary field workers. Large concentrations of men appear to increase the demand for sex for sale, or at least concentrate it in a particular locale. While such events and circumstances may not increase the number of sex trafficked people, it increases the number of buyers and transactions in a given night. Smith and colleagues (2009) found that girls were trafficked up to forty-five times in a single night in the "peak demand times" such as the Sundance Film Festival in Salt Lake City, the Ultimate Fighting Championships in Las Vegas, and the Super Bowl. Smith and colleagues report traffickers moved women and girls to these locations expecting higher demand for sex, which resulted in the higher number of prostitution-related arrests. Other researchers have found sex trafficking occurring in the field tents of migrant workers or in nearby makeshift brothels to sell sex to migrant workers (Ugarte, Zarate, and Farley 2003; Heil 2012).

Amy Dalrymple and Katherine Lymn (2015) report heightened sex trafficking in the Bakken region of North Dakota largely due to the relatively new and booming oil industry and the demand of male workers for purchased sex. When a missing persons report on a girl is filed in Minneapolis, police officers report that they check Backpage.com in North Dakota to attempt to find her. Sex workers report high profits and plentiful buyers but also indicate that sex trafficking occurs alongside willing sex work. Sex trafficking–related arrests have increased related to the North Dakota oil industry's surrounding sex trade. In one sting operation, officers posted ads posing as underage sex workers and found eleven men who were interested in purchasing sex from girls between the ages of 10 and 16 (Lymn 2015). Several federal court cases are pending as well. Trina Nguyen and Loc Tran first faced state-level charges related to operating an illegal brothel in Minot, North Dakota, and they currently, after moving their brothel and attempting to cover it up as a false-front massage parlor in nearby Dickinson, North Dakota, face federal human trafficking charges. In another recent case revolving around North Dakota and the Bakken region, Keith Graves faces five counts of sex trafficking involving five adult women. Yet another case involves Prince Jones and Eyeesha Hinton, who are charged with sex trafficking a 13-year-old girl whom they advertised on Backpage.com. These examples suggest that pimps and traffickers work to supply the demand, which may be heightened or concentrated in circumstances involving a large number of single men looking to purchase sex.

Structure of Trafficking Operations

Types of Operations

In the United States, sex trafficking operations can take the form of intricate organized crime rings, small-scale operations, or individual business. Traffickers in the United States tend to be associated with small criminal groups, gangs, or individuals. The bulk of the research suggests that trafficking most often involves a male pimp (sometimes a female pimp who is a "partner" to a male pimp and who is often a trafficking victim as well) and one or more women or girls (sometimes boys) as trafficking victims. While domestic traffickers can have links to transnational or international organized crime, this is less common than individual enterprise. The majority of trafficking operations in the United States are small-scale operations involving one to five people (McCabe and Manian 2010). For example, Otis Washington, his brother, and two uncles ran a sex trafficking operation that was essentially a family business. The brothers are reported to have victimized nearly fifty young women and girls over a decade, reportedly seeking out those with mental health issues or those from conflict ridden homes. They were charged when a 15-year-old told her grandmother about her victimization at the hands of the Washingtons, and the grandmother reported it (Xiong 2014). The Washingtons ran their operation in various parts of Minnesota, soliciting largely online. Otis Washington received a 40-year sentence for multiple convictions. Trafficking operations range in size, from smaller family-run operations like the Washingtons' to large-scale operations. In Chicago, one study found pimping operations that had two to thirty women working at any given time (Raphael and Myers-Powell 2010). Some worked for large escort services or strip clubs; others had their own small- or medium-sized escort services, and one owned a brothel.

Some operations are larger and include networks of key players, sometimes involving bribes to law enforcement. In one Chicago-based study, 60% of pimps said that they bribed law enforcement, including vice and beat cops, and a captain as well as detectives and even an alderman. One female pimp described giving sex to a cop to keep out of trouble with the law (Raphael and Myers-Powell 2010). Cab drivers, bellhops, hotel clerks, bartenders, and convention information centers also were on the payroll for referring customers (Raphael and Myers-Powell 2010). Gang members are also known to be hired for security purposes, particularly by female pimps (Raphael and Myers-Powell 2010).

While criminal gangs have traditionally been associated with drugs or arms trafficking, they are increasingly being associated with sex trafficking. Smith and colleagues (2009) report gang-led sex trafficking rings in Boston and Oakland. The prevalence or relative proportion of gang-involved trafficking remains unknown, but such cases are known among prosecuted cases and cases that are brought to the attention of social service providers. They may also appear in news reports. For example, one 14-year-old girl from the Bronx, New York, ran away from home and shortly thereafter was allegedly picked up by two members of the Crips and forced into prostitution in Queens. Police found her in an abandoned house five months later, after she got ahold of a cellphone and called 911 and her grandmother while the traffickers were sleeping.[6] The case uncovered in San Diego that opens this chapter involved gangs affiliated with the Crips (Ponting 2014). An East Side Piru gang member in Washington State, Marteze Ravoine Clair, was charged with sex trafficking multiple women and girls, posting hundreds of ads on Backpage.com, giving them drugs, keeping their money, and threatening them with violence.[7] Gang involvement, both small and large scale, is implicated as a facet of sex trafficking operations in the United States.

International sex trafficking operations have been known to be larger and may involve organized crime rings, as in the cases of Alex "Cowboy" Campbell, El Flaco, and Severiano Martinez-Rojas, discussed previously in this book. In some cases, this may include networks of more than fifty people

(McCabe and Manian 2010). Like larger domestic trafficking rings, such networks may include pimps, cab drivers, bellhops, and hotel staff, but may also include those providing false documents and even law enforcement, immigration officials, and border guards (McCabe and Manian 2010). Individuals who play smaller roles in trafficking rings are referred to as facilitators.

Facilitators

Facilitators in trafficking operations can be described as those who are "helpers" or supporters in trafficking enterprises. They include connectors, who connect buyers to those who are selling sex or who are sold for sex. Connectors can be cab drivers, hotel staff, or even those who "advertise" in the street or in businesses. Recruiters are those who initially get survivors into the sex trafficking operation. Recruiters can be the pimps and traffickers themselves, or they can be a survivor who has been with the pimp for a long time (often called a "bottom" or "bottom girl," who is legally viewed as a trafficker). Groomers prepare a survivor for their exploitation by getting them clothes, telling them how to solicit, telling them what to do sexually, how much to charge, and more (Smith 2014). Groomers can be a "bottom," another survivor, or the pimp or trafficker. Watchers may also be paid essentially as a "lookout" for police, other pimps, or to make sure the survivor is doing what they are supposed to. Watchers can be hotel staff, taxi drivers, other survivors, the traffickers or pimps themselves, or an individual whose sole job is to "watch." All of these roles can take a variety of different forms and can involve a combination of overlapping roles (Williamson and Prior 2009).

Facilitators are often not the focal point of a trafficking investigation, but they profit from, make possible, and contribute to the trafficking and exploitation of adults and children. One study found that a "connector" cab driver earned $100 for each "connection," or a third of the overall profit (Smith, Vardaman, and M. Snow 2009). Facilitators may be charged with conspiracy to commit sex trafficking if they are caught. One recent case in which a facilitator was implicated in Philadelphia involved Adrian Palmer, who was sentenced to 80 months in prison for his role as a watcher. Palmer was on hotel staff at the Days Inn in Philadelphia as a security guard and was also on the payroll of sex trafficker Craig Johnson, who provided Palmer with a daily fee, typically $60–100, for helping Johnson avoid police.

Quota Systems

Traffickers may also use quota systems, indicating a particular dollar amount that each individual is supposed to bring in a night. At times, in larger crime rings, recruiters may have quotas as well, leading to a chain of quotas that ultimately profits those at the top of a tiered system. Sometimes survivors will not be allowed to come home until they meet their quota, thus denying them shelter, food, and sleep. They may also be subjected to violence if they do not make enough money. Research suggests that the quotas vary widely, ranging from $50 to $3,000 a night (Polaris Project 2015b, Raphael and Myers-Powell 2010). These studies also show a range in the earnings that trafficked or exploited people are able to keep; anywhere from 30% to 100% of earnings will typically be taken by the pimp, most typically 50% to 100%. The pimp will keep some or all of the profits but may offer food, shelter, clothing, and other material items. This "exchange" gives the appearance of caretaking and mutual reciprocity of caretaking or contribution, although the reality is that the trafficker or pimp is buying/offering these comforts with money that the trafficking victims earned. The victims would be able to buy all of these things and more if they kept their own earnings. This is why the pimp/trafficker needs other mechanisms of control. The pimp wants to maximize profits. Money is the ultimate goal, and controlling "operations" and actors in "operations" is what makes money. In reality, trafficking does not entail a regular or predicted salary. The salary depends on how many individuals are part of the trafficking enterprise, what their quota is, even what the region of the United States the operation is located in. For example, pimps operating out of truck stops tend to make less than those offering escort services on the Internet. Girls advertised online typically make more than girls on the street. There are many variables at play related to a pimp's annual salary.

Importantly, what we know about traffickers and trafficking operations comes from interviews or case studies with traffickers, reports from survivors, and cases uncovered by law enforcement. Studies examining traffickers tend to have small sample sizes and may not be representative of traffickers and trafficking operations overall. Survivor reports are based on clinical samples; those who have sought out or were otherwise referred to services may have different experiences from those who do not. Cases uncovered by law enforcement are limited by the officers' ability to identify trafficking situations and do not include unidentified cases that could be distinctly different. Simply put, all existing studies or sources of information on traffickers are limited in their capacity to provide generalizable results, and there may be much that we do not know about trafficking operations.

Chapter Summary

Trafficking operations range in complexity and take a variety of forms. Trafficking enterprises can involve intricate organized crime schemes or smaller-scale operations managed by an individual pimp or pimp with a partner. The use of interstate circuits tends to be regional but unpredictable and is a technique to avoid detection. Moving survivors from place to place makes identification more difficult and impedes help-seeking by isolating them from friends, family, and communities. International movement typically channels impoverished women and girls into sex trafficking operations through fraud and debt bondage. Technology is used to gain a larger consumer base and to advertise and recruit for trafficking operations. Hidden venues, such as false-front businesses, hotels, private parties, and residences, or venues in relatively insular communities, such as truck stops or ethnic residential neighborhoods, also impede detection. Trafficking operations may also extend to include a variety of key players, including connectors, recruiters, watchers, "bottom girls," and others. Importantly, it is the unregulated demand for prostitution, which buyers do not distinguish from sex trafficking, that drives sex trafficking and exploitation. Trafficking techniques, such as force, fraud, and coercion create a system of coercive control that makes it difficult for survivors to exit the commercial sex industry.

Discussion Questions

1. Describe the different types of trafficking operations evident in this chapter.

2. What are some limitations to identification that specific trafficking techniques pose?

3. What are some creative ways of addressing such limitations in terms of outreach to survivors?

8

Buyers

Decades of research in the United States shows disproportionate punishment of those who sell sex compared to those who buy it (Carmen and Moody 1985; Fairstein 1993; Lutnick and Cohan 2009; Maher 1997; Miller 1997, 2009; Sanchez 2001). While selling sex remains illegal in the United States, with few jurisdictional exceptions, traditionally and presently those who sell sex receive the brunt of criminalization. This is evidenced by disproportionate arrest rates, fines, and incarceration for prostitution. Research also uncovers rape, coerced sex, and violence by law enforcement directed toward those who sell sex, while buyers often pay a small fine or are not a focus of investigation at all (Maher 1997; Miller 1997, 2009; Sanchez 2001). In a turn of events, buyers have received increased attention from the antitrafficking movement, particularly by abolitionists and radical feminists, whose argument centers on demand. If there were no demand for bought sex, then sex trafficking would not exist. The U.S. criminal justice system is beginning to shift, and an increased number of sting operations now target buyers as well as sellers of sex in an attempt to identify sex trafficking victimization and to deter demand for prostitution through penalty. In particular, those who would willingly buy sex with anyone under 18 are under particular scrutiny. Increased investigation, enforcement of already existing laws, John schools, and John shaming practices are among the efforts to curtail demand on a structural-cultural level.

John schools and John shaming are programs intertwined with the justice system and are intended to reduce the demand for bought sex. In addition, laws are being implemented in some jurisdictions to charge buyers as sex traffickers when the case involves a minor. Despite the academic and public debate, and despite shifts in law enforcement, relatively little is known about those who buy sex. The available research shows variability in buyers' backgrounds and their interactions with those engaged in the commercial sex industry as well as their motivations to purchase sex (Jordan 1997; Monto 1999, 2004; Monto and Milrod 2014; Weitzer 2007, 2010). This chapter examines characteristics of buyers, prevalence of bought sex in the United States, buyers' interactions with those they buy sex from, their motivations to buy sex, survivor views of buyers, criminal justice responses addressing demand, and buyers' efforts to avoid detection.

Research on Buyers

Research examining those who buy sex is limited, particularly in the United States. This is perhaps unsurprising due to the illegality of prostitution and the related social stigma (Monto 2004). The extant research is derived from interviews, content analysis of online forums, and national surveys. Online forums that provide ratings or reviews of those in the commercial sex industry have been evaluated by researchers either through content analysis of their comments, or as a source for selected research participants (Holt, Blevins, and Kuhns 2014). Qualitative work relying on in-depth interviews examines the motivations, backgrounds, and experiences of those who purchase sex (Bernstein 2001; Jordan 1997; Monto 2004). Interview-based data as well as analyses of online forums have been critiqued for their lack of representativeness—one could argue that those who are willing to be interviewed as well as those who use Internet forums to discuss or rate sellers of sex may not be reflective of the general population of buyers. In addition, researchers can use data that those in the commercial sex industry give them, also typically through in-depth interviews, which are subject to similar limitations in their applicability (Curtis et al. 2008; Martin et al. 2014; Dank et al. 2015). Survey data derived from convenience samples from those who had been arrested also work to uncover the experiences, backgrounds, and motivations of those who purchase sex but are similarly methodologically challenged by lack of representativeness

(Monto 1999; Monto and Hotaling 2001; Monto 2004, Monto and Milrod 2014). In contrast, the probability-sample national surveys have the benefit of being statistically representative, yet such surveys are limited in their depth, largely examining prevalence of buying and basic demographic characteristics (Monto 2004; Monto and Milrod 2014). In sum, the research is limited by both the lack of studies available and the methodological challenges associated with them. The following sections examine the major research findings derived from the existing literature.

Buyers of Sex in Prostitution and Sex Trafficking Are Indistinct

A buyer of sex has no way of knowing whether the person they are buying sex from is trafficked, exploited, or a willing sex worker, which makes a buyer of prostitution indistinct from a buyer of sex trafficking. "Some may engage in sex with minors unknowingly. The perpetrators may assume that a prostituted individual is an adult. Alternatively, they may or may not inquire about the age of that individual and may still decide to engage in a sex act even if she or he is a minor" (Finklea, Fernandes-Alcantara, and Siskin 2015). Janice G. Raymond (2004, 1165) contends that "most male consumers do not stop to ask whether women and girls elect or are forced into prostitution." The same could be said for purchasing sex from men and boys. Further, even if buyers did inquire about consent and age, it is unlikely that a trafficked or exploited person would answer honestly because of the need for money or because of adherence to a pimp/trafficker. As buyers always consent to purchasing sex, and those who sell it do not always consent (such as those who are trafficked) or cannot consent (such as minors), then "demand" arguments maintain that it is the buyer who is accountable on some level for the trafficking or exploitation.

Demographics of Buyers

Research indicates that buyers come from all demographic groups, including those of various ages, races, ethnicities, social classes, and sexes. Yet research also indicates that a majority of buyers are white men. This includes those who buy sex from men, women, adults, children, lesbian, gay, bisexual, or transgender people (Curtis et al. 2008; Frederick 2014; Dank et al. 2015).

For example, when asked about characteristics of buyers, 65% of youth in the commercial sex industry in New York City indicated that they typically sold sex to white males. In the same study, youth indicated that about a third of their buyers were known to be married; many also had children, and most buyers were thought to be between 25 and 55 (Curtis et al. 2008). In Minneapolis, buyers of minor girls were between the ages of 23 and 65, with an average age of 42 (Martin et al. 2014). Lauren Martin and colleagues (2014, 35) also noted, "In more than half of our interviews, participants described wealthy white male sex buyers seeking commercial sex with juveniles in Minneapolis but residing in the suburbs." In an analysis of prosecuted sex trafficking cases in the St. Louis bi-state area, it is apparent that buyers are mostly white and from rural or suburban areas. Such demographics reflect a power imbalance between the purchaser of sex and those who sell it, in that buyers are typically older, white, male, and wealthier. In contrast, those who sell sex are disproportionately African American or Latina, in poverty, younger, women or girls who are pimp-involved, or those identifying as LGBTQ[*] who are engaging in survival sex (Dank et al. 2015; Martin et al. 2014).

Average Joe or Depraved Predator?

Researchers have been interested in examining characteristics of buyers for a variety of different reasons. Some researchers have been interested in examining whether buyers are disproportionately criminal or are otherwise misogynistic or whether they support rape myth mentalities (Raymond, Hughes, and Gomez 2001; Raymond 2004; Weitzer 2007; Monto and Milrod 2014). If buyers were depraved in any of these ways, this would tell us that exceptional men who are violent, criminal, or otherwise mentally flawed purchase sex. Yet researchers generally find that this is not the case—men who buy sex are not typically distinct in terms of criminal records, rape myth support, or overt misogyny. What this reveals instead is that some combination of culture, socialization, or circumstance is likely implicated in the normalized views of bought sex among buyers. Both neoliberals and abolitionists alike laud this finding, albeit for different reasons. Neoliberals suggest that this means there is nothing wrong with buyers or their motivations for buying sex. This normalization condones the purchase of sex. Abolitionist and radical feminist arguments suggest that the fact that "normal" men buy sex reflects greater cultural inequalities and the devaluation of women by the "common man" as part of culture, thereby reflecting and perpetuating gender inequality.

Researchers report, based on probability samples, that buyers and non-buyers of sex are largely indistinct—the only differences found were that buyers were more likely to have a military background and were more likely to be white, single, and employed (Monto and Milrod 2014). The finding of the military background may indicate that initiation into purchased sex was fueled by military culture. It is widely known that prostitution and sex trafficking occur at higher levels around military bases (Raymond Hughes, and Gomez 2001; Hughes, Chon, and Ellerman 2007). Another study also found that in the United States, men who had served in the military were overrepresented as buyers (Sullivan and Simon 1998; Raymond, Hughes, and Gomez 2001). In a recent national survey, buyers did not have criminal records nor did they support rape myths any more than the general population (Monto and Milrod 2014).

Those who inhabit online forums are a bit more distinct, suggesting that the sample is unique in its characteristics and is not generalizable to the larger population. Such men are more likely to be married, white, better educated, and upper class (Monto and Milrod 2014). They are also more likely to say they would marry a sex worker, and they believe that those in the commercial sex industry enjoy prostitution. Such findings are contrasted by other research using smaller samples and confined to specific geographic regions. For example, one study comparing buyers to nonbuyers in San Francisco, who were otherwise demographically similar, found that buyers were more likely to have a criminal record, to say they would rape if they could get away with it, and to have coerced sex from women in the past (Farley et al. 2011). More recent work by Melissa Farley and colleagues (2015) using a larger sample of more than a hundred men in Boston shows similar findings—that buyers are more likely to be misogynistic and have a history of sexual aggression and rape.

Social factors, like the intergenerational transmission of buying, might facilitate normalization of purchasing sex, just as sex workers indicate fathers sometimes initiate their sons into purchasing sex (Raymond, Hughes, and Gomez 2001). "These reports indicate that the main users of women in prostitution are regular men who are in regular marriages, study in regular educational programs, and have regular jobs, some of whom are entrusted with upholding the very laws that they violate" (Raymond 2004). The only highly significant finding is that buyers are overwhelmingly men.

Importantly, just because there is no profile and buyers do not appear to be deviant criminals does not mean purchasing sex is a normal or common aspect of male behavior, nor is it rapidly increasing. In fact, a minority of adult men in the United States purchase sex (Monto and Milrod 2014).

Prevalence of Men Who Buy Sex

One of the earliest studies examining the prevalence of buying sex was conducted in 1948 by Kinsey, Pomeroy, and Martin. This study is often cited by supporters of sexual commerce because it depicts purchasing sex as a normal and inevitable part of men's lives, reporting that 69% of men bought sex (Monto 2004). Similarly, in the early 1960s Harry Benjamin and R. E. L. Masters (1964) reported that 80% of men bought sex. Both samples were nonrepresentative and have been critiqued for nongeneralizability and selective sampling, and that Kinsey and colleagues were not social scientists and did not use scientific methods (Monto 2004). In contrast, research in the 1990s based on national probability samples, which are statistically representative, countered such claims, finding that only about 16–20% of men in the United States had ever purchased sex, with less than 1% having done so in the past year (Monto 2004; Laumann et al. 1994; Smith, Marsden, and Hout 2011). One study (Sullivan and Simon 1998) drawn from a nationally representative sample found that 17% of men had purchased sex in their lifetime, with less than 1% having done so in the past year. The 2000 General Social Survey (GSS) reported that 17% of men had purchased sex in their lifetime; 3% had done so in the past year (Weitzer 2007). Ten years later the 2010 GSS reported that 14% of men had purchased sex in their lifetime, and only 1% in the last year (Monto and Milrod 2014; Smith, Marsden, and Hout 2011). Similarly, the most recent study measuring prevalence of purchasing sex in the United States, conducted by Martin A. Monto and Christine Milrod (2014), found in a meta-analysis of data from the GSS, public domain data on arrestees, and data from the Internet forum *Erotic Review* that 14% of men in the United States had bought sex at some point in their lives, with 1% having done so in the last year. Thus, there is much consistency in research conducted over the last two decades. So what accounts for the wide gap in prevalence-reporting in the 1940s and 1960s compared to the 1990s and 2000s? One explanation, taking these statistics at face value, is that men are simply less likely to purchase sex in the contemporary world.

This is supported by data in one national survey finding that younger men were less likely to describe their first sexual experience as with a sex worker compared to older men. Speculatively, perhaps the feminist movement in the United States has had some impact on the cultural value of women and men's decreased likelihood of purchasing sex. More likely, the methodological challenges with the earliest studies resulted in misreporting. Thus, there is no evidence that prostitution use is a rapidly growing crime, at least in the United States (Kara 2010). The market of buyers appears to be relatively stable or even declining.

Continuum of Buyer Motivations

Informal Relationships and Companionship

Buyers of sex can be viewed as representing various spaces on a continuum, from those who want companionship, to those whose motivation is purely the commercial sexual exchange, to violent predators. Based on interview data with both buyers and those engaged in the commercial sex industry, motivations of some buyers indicated a desire for companionship and informal relationships, reflecting a facet of those who purchase sex. Several studies show that friendships and informal relationships occur between those in the commercial sex industry and regular buyers (Curtis et al. 2008; Dank et al. 2015; Oselin 2014). Positive interactions with buyers seem to be exclusively with regulars and make up a minority of experiences. Many individuals in the commercial sex industry report having regular buyers who they rely on for steady income (Curtis et al. 2008; Oselin 2014; Dank et al. 2015). One study found 15% of youth in the commercial sex industry described their buyers as friends or providers of emotional support (Dank et al. 2015). Research indicates that at times buyers care about and form relationships with those they buy sex from. For example, Sharon Oselin (2014, 3) stated, "One woman exiting prostitution indicated that one of her regular buyers encouraged her to leave prostitution, because 'she was worth more than that.'" This statement is interesting as the buyer himself seemed to find the act of selling sex detrimental, yet he continued to purchase it. Some individuals described their regular buyers as a point of contact in case of emergencies—someone to call when in need of shelter, food, or money. Youth in one study described "sugar daddies" who could be counted on to support their economic needs, including offering food, money, and shelter (Curtis et al. 2008). Others indicated that their regular buyers at times simply wanted conversation and companionship. A 17-year-old female in Ric Curtis and colleagues' (2008) study indicated that some men wanted someone to party with, including using drugs together or simply offering companionship: "So we was goin' for the rich, white guys. It's not just fuckin' and suckin', some of them just want you to sit there and smoke with them. Or if you do the type of drug that they do, that's what they like. Or they wanna talk to you—they can't talk to their wives—they need somebody to talk to" (Curtis et al. 2008, 78). Similarly, in an Urban Institute study, a gay-identified male said,

> Sometimes they don't even want sex, sometimes they just crave the attention, and sometimes they just want that person to be next to them. I guess they just like, feed off of the attraction or whatever but, it's cool, like they, they're very nice, take me out to eat, chill, watch a movie, sometimes of course there have been sexual encounters, but like it doesn't really—it's not so strong. Not like how regular dates would be if you wanted to just have sex, you just want sex and then money and that's it.
>
> (Dank et al. 2015, 28)

Another gay-identified male in the same study indicated similar feelings: "Yeah like I feel I can talk to him about anything, you know, have somebody else's outlook on important things, and he's like older. So it's like he's a friend he's like older he's been through things in his life since I find to talk to him about stuff like school or anything else like that" (Dank et al. 2015, 29). About 15% of the sample in the Urban Institute study saw some of their buyers—and only their regular buyers—in a positive light; 85% did not (Dank et al. 2015).

Research examining buyer narratives reports similar results to those indicated in the narratives of those who sell sex. The desire for companionship is represented as a motivation among some buyers of sex. Julia O'Connell Davidson (2002) found that buyers described their relationships with those they purchased sex from as friendly or as love relationships, saying they believed the relationships were mutually satisfying. "Some clearly feel that their prostitute partners are special people and that they themselves are seen as special in the eyes of prostitutes" (Jordan 1997). Some researchers describe buyers wanting "the girlfriend experience," which includes characteristics valued in a girlfriend, such as conversation, generosity with time, cuddling, and foreplay, along with some element of romance (Weitzer 2007). Research also indicates that many buyers choose to be blind to the issue of consent and power because they choose to believe that those whom they buy sex from freely consent and enjoy sex with buyers (Davidson 2006; Monto 2004). At the same time, such relationships cannot be romanticized because there are power dynamics at play in terms of social background—age, race, class, sex, and the absence of better choices. Moreover, one person is buying sex from another—the person with the power to buy it has more power than the person who needs to sell it for the money.

Commercial Sexual Exploitation

Commercial sexual exploitation represents another aspect of the continuum of buyer behaviors, regardless of buyer motivations, which is reflected in the way that a majority of those in the commercial sex industry describe their interactions with buyers. Survivors of sex trafficking and commercial sexual exploitation consistently describe in the research motivations for selling sex that are economic in nature. The vast majority, 87–93%, would prefer to do something else if better alternatives were available (Curtis et al. 2008; Dank et al. 2015). In one study, youth engaged in sex markets indicated that they did not like providing sex to strangers and found buyers disgusting, and they did it for survival (Dank et al. 2015). The following two narratives from Curtis and colleagues' (2008) study also illustrate this:

> The fact that I have to have sex with somebody I don't know. Like . . . it's uncomfortable 'cause you don't wanna look at the person . . . you don't wanna look at yourself—you don't wanna look! The whole time you're doin' it, you gotta think, the money, the money, the money—'cause otherwise, I couldn't do it.
>
> (104)

> I just gotta do what I gotta do and so I can eat every day. I don't like the fact that I have to be with another man, just to survive. That's what I hate the most.
>
> (105)

Similarly, in an Urban Institute study (Dank et al. 2015), 91% of youth indicated that they disliked trading sex, including how it made them feel dirty or degraded, and they disliked the buyers. Buyers with bad hygiene and those who were unattractive or verbally disrespectful were described as a part of the negative aspects of selling sex.

Violence and Abuse by Buyers

On the other end of the continuum, violence against those who sell sex is rampant. Masses of research spanning decades show the disproportionate victimization of those in the commercial sex industry. More recently, in an Urban Institute study (Dank et al. 2015), youth who sold sex indicated various forms of abuses perpetrated by buyers, including refusal to wear a condom, physical abuse, and nonpayment for services rendered. "The degree of these altercations covered the full spectrum of violence and ranged from verbal arguments to threats at gunpoint and rape" (Dank et al. 2015, 40). Youth also "saw others face situations that were frequently violent and exploitative at the hands of clients as well as exploiters" (Dank et al. 2015, 56). Similarly, Curtis and colleagues (2008) note that fear of being raped, killed, or being otherwise harmed made youth want to do something else to earn money. "Just last week, that was the first time that happened to me in a long time, but it happened a lotta times before—guys force themselves on me—and stuff like that. That's what I dislike the most" (Curtis et al. 2008, 105).

The most severe forms of buyer violence found in the extant research include "physical violence, sadistic sex, and use of weapons to threaten or harm women" (Raymond 2004, 1174–75). Those in the commercial sex industry, particularly street-level sex workers, are also disproportionately targets of serial killers; multiple cases within the last decade show this to be the case in various locations across the country, such as Kansas City, St. Louis, Long Island, and other places, among street-level sex workers as well as those soliciting online. Overall, violence is a part of sex-for-sale, particularly street-level work and sales arranged online. Violence against sex workers in the United States is reduced in the few legalized and regulated brothels compared to street-level or online sexual commerce. The opportunity to enact abuse or violence may be a motivation among some who buy sex.

Other Buyer Motivations

Motivations for purchasing sex, as opposed to finding sex partners though other means, vary widely. As indicated earlier, these motivations range from finding companionship to finding an individual to perpetrate violence against. Researchers also report that buyer motivations include things like getting sex acts that their partners are not willing to do, such as oral sex, anal sex, domination and submission, or fetishized sex; lacking a sex partner; wanting convenient sex while on a business trip; or desiring sex without a need for commitment, relationship, or other effort (Monto 2004; Farley et al. 2015). Youth in one study by Curtis and colleagues (2008) indicated that buyers came to them for fetishized sex or acts that might otherwise be seen as atypical. Two examples from different respondents in this study illustrate: "There are crazy people. I had this [white] guy come up to me and he wanted me to rub his knee for $200 while he jacked off" (78). "I have had Caucasian guys come up to me, ask about the most outrageous things, like shittin' on 'em, pissin' on 'em" (78).

Moreover, some buyers may specifically be seeking out a youthful body: "65% of the johns that go on the Internet are more responsive if the ads have age descriptors like 'young' or 'barely legal' attached to them—65% are more responsive to that" (quoted in Smith, Vardaman, and Snow 2009, 19). This indicates that, like fetishized or atypical acts, gaining access to a youthful body may be a factor specifically sought out by buyers, which would be difficult to access without purchasing sex.

Addressing Demand: Structural Responses Targeting Buyers

It is well documented that women involved in prostitution in the United States were typically those punished by law through arrest, fines, and jail time while their male buyers were largely ignored (Monto 2004; Smith, Vardaman, and Snow 2009). This dynamic is in the process of changing in the United States. Evidence of this newer focus on male buyers is suggested by the emergence of demand-reduction efforts in various parts of the United States and federal funding earmarked for such efforts. Part of the Trafficking Victims Protection Reauthorization Act (TVPRA) of 2005 included funding to address demand reduction under the premise that targeting buyers was necessary to slow markets for sexual commerce, thereby reducing sex trafficking. The TVPRA of 2005 provided $25 million to police departments across the United States for demand-reduction efforts.

There are different forms of demand-reduction initiatives. Reverse stings, which have been implemented in 826 cities and counties across the United States, involve undercover officers posing as sex workers and have been conducted in street-level sex work, Internet-based sex work, and brothel-based sex work. In the Cook County/Chicago area, police take part in regular sting operations, ticketing those who attempt to buy sex from undercover police officers. With brothels, police initially make arrests of brothel operators, then plant decoys in their place, continuing to monitor calls and make arrests of walk-in buyers. A limitation is that the vast majority of decoys are women officers; accordingly, buyers of men and boys are not a focal point of such investigations. Another limitation is that such efforts are limited in number by resources and funding. Further, if trafficking is not identified or involved, those in the sex industry are criminalized.

In addition, John shaming programs have been implemented in some cities as well. Those buying sex who are caught by police may be publicly shamed through placing the buyers' photos and/or names in news reports, on billboards, on police websites, and in local newspapers. In St. Louis, Missouri, a rather large billboard at a major bridge exchange at the intersection of multiple major interstates publicizes this information, complete with picture, name, and offense. Shaming can also include "dear John" letters or postcards sent to the buyers' homes, indicating that they were caught purchasing sex, and some also provide information about health risks and the harm done to survivors. Some areas may place a modified form of a restraining order on a buyer, restricting the buyer from areas in which sexual commerce is known to occur. Community awareness and education may also be viewed as a form of demand reduction, primarily targeting men and boys, indicating the harm to survivors of sex trafficking/ CSE with the goal of changing cultural attitudes about bought sex. In other cases, demand reduction is limited to community service typically ranging from four to forty hours, in some cases with buyers cleaning streets where sex work is known to occur, intending to deter future purchasing. Surveillance cameras also provide some form of demand reduction, at least insofar as they provide evidence used to arrest or fine buyers.

Perhaps the most widely known of demand-reduction programs are the John schools, which work to provide education and awareness to those who have been arrested for buying sex. A John school can be a diversion program to avoid formal charges or can be combined with other charges. They vary widely in their implementation, in some cases limited to a one-day class, in other cases involving classes over an extended period of time. In still other formats, some John schools involve simply watching a video or receiving a handout with a short presentation by an officer. Typically a fine is also paid, on average $400. In some cases the fines are channeled into social services for survivors. John schools often involve the provision of education about health risks and the harm done to survivors. Accordingly, the form and content and the implementation vary widely. As a result, the relative success of John schools also varies widely, with some claims of success and other claims of uselessness.

Another form of demand reduction is charging adults who purchase sex with minors as sex traffickers (see chapter 6). This is becoming increasingly popular, although it is still limited in its implementation. For example, one buyer of a minor selling sex was sentenced to ten years. Twenty-nine-year-old Louis Edward Cooke was a Clayton resident, an elite upper-class area just outside St. Louis, Missouri. In an undercover sting operation, Cooke answered an ad on Backpage.com that depicted two "young and irresistible" sisters. Through e-mail correspondence, Cooke was informed that the girls were 13 and 15 years old. "Cooke chose the older girl, adding that he would choose the younger if there was a special discount being offered, court documents show" (Patrick 2011). He went to a residence in Kirkwood, Missouri, a largely middle-class suburb also just outside of St. Louis, for sex with the 15-year-old girl. The FBI and Kirkwood police were waiting for him and arrested him at the residence. He was later convicted of two counts of attempted sex trafficking of a minor. Charging buyers as sex traffickers is discussed in more depth in chapter 9.

In a National Institute of Justice report, Michael Shively and colleagues (2012) indicate in their overall analysis of demand-reduction programs that "little research or descriptive information is available about the vast majority of interventions." They also note that a majority of communities working to address demand typically did not use evidence-based practices, resulting in "initiatives [that] had struggled or failed when faced with problems that had been solved elsewhere" (Shively et al. 2012, i). Research findings indicating failure or struggle among those not using known best practices calls for evidence-based practice in order to prevent the known challenges affiliated with demand-reduction initiatives. Despite this limitation, there are several studies that examine demand-reduction efforts, which were reviewed by Shively and colleagues (2012). For example, Weisburd and colleagues (2006) report a 75% reduction in prostitution in Jersey City, New Jersey, following a series of reverse stings. Displacement was factored into their analysis, and increased prostitution was not seen in other areas of the city. At the same time, the researchers were not able to measure whether sexual commerce was moved indoors and facilitated online instead. A program in St. Petersburg, Florida, involved both arrest and shaming and reported a 25% decline in calls to police from community members to address sexual commerce. Shaming in this case included sending a "dear John" letter to the home address and providing information on sexually transmitted diseases (Shively et al. 2012). At the same time, the evaluation of the relative success of this demand-reduction initiative measured calls to police, which is not a direct measurement of sexual commerce. The buyers could have simply altered their tactics to become better at avoiding detection (Holt, Blevins, and Kuhns 2014). Similarly, a program in Raleigh, North Carolina, also combines arrest with shaming and notes a 38% reduction in calls to the police for assistance addressing the sex trade in their community. This study has the same limitations as the St. Petersburg study and is also complicated by the fact that the calls to police increased after a community awareness effort and dropped following. This temporary community interest due to the awareness effort could also be implicated in the success rate. One of the best-known demand-reduction programs is based in San Francisco and includes a John school. The evaluations show a nearly 40% drop in re-arrest, with the drop held for more than a decade.

Shively and colleagues report that "the impact is unlikely to be attributable to johns moving their activities online. While it is true that commercial sex solicitation has been shifting from the streets to online venues, the shift to online solicitation has been gradual rather than abruptly occurring in one year, and has been widespread rather than occurring only in San Francisco" (2012, vi). Yet the program is not able to examine whether buyers are simply being more careful or whether they have stopped purchasing sex altogether. Research indicates that buyers are becoming savvy at avoiding detection.

Buyers Avoiding Detection

Criminological research indicates that, instead of deterring particular behaviors, illegality and enforcement of the law often simply moves it or perpetrators alter their tactics to avoid detection (Heil and Nichols 2014). According to criminal displacement theory supported by recent research, demand-reduction efforts result in altered tactics of buyers as well as displacement of commercial sex activities. Instead of deterring behaviors, research indicates that some buyers work to preserve their anonymity and avoid criminal justice system involvement (Farrell et al. 2012; Holt, Blevins, and Kuhns 2014). Amy Farrell and colleagues (2012) note that buyers used websites that review individuals in the commercial sex industry to make sure their confidentiality was preserved by avoiding decoys and stings and only buying sex from those who were labeled as legitimate on such websites. Buyers also communicate via Internet, phone, and even citizens' band radios, telling each other where police are present (Farrell et al. 2012). Thomas J. Holt and colleagues (2014) indicate increased movement to indoor settings that are less identifiable. One critique of demand reduction is that it often is measured based on reoffending. Accordingly, the assessment is limited in that it cannot determine whether lack of re-arrest is attributed to the demand-reduction technique—such as arrest, fine, John school, community service, or public shaming—or to being more careful not to get caught. Holt and colleagues (2014) indicate that buyers are using Web forums to trade information and tips on ways to avoid getting caught by police. This includes information about sting operations in the area, suspected decoys, suggestions for observing an area, and "tests" to see if an individual is an officer or someone in the commercial sex industry. The "cop test" typically involves getting a potential seller to show her breasts or take part in initial fondling before a discussion of the transaction. "For example, one of the users from the Baltimore forum stated that when a prostitute would enter his car, 'I am usually ready to "check their ID" which for me means for them to show me their rack'" (Holt, Blevins, and Kuhns 2014, 270).

When law enforcement is known to have increased patrols, buyers also change their tactics, which may mean coming out at different times of night or going to a different location. One study showed that knowledge of increased patrols was relayed on John sites, offering information to avoid detection (Holt, Blevins, and Kuhns 2014). This simply displaced the behavior as opposed to deterring it. Prostitution might be moving from busy streets into neighborhoods and private residences, facilitated online to avoid detection. As increased patrols appear to have moved sexual commerce indoors and online, buyers have also developed techniques for not getting caught online. Such techniques to avoid decoys and sting operations include looking up phone numbers online and telling each other on online forums about sex workers they had encounters with who were considered "safe" (Farrell et al. 2012; Holt, Blevins, and Kuhns 2014).

Chapter Summary

Buyers are not a monolithic group; they come from all demographic backgrounds. Yet middle-aged white men are disproportionately represented as buyers in multiple research studies. The motivations to buy sex vary, ranging from those seeking friendship and companionship, to those seeking a commercial sexual exchange, to those looking for fetishized or atypical sex acts, to those seeking a target for violence. What they share in common is that they purchase sex. Various demand-reduction efforts include public shaming, John schools, arrest, fines, community service, and reverse sting operations. Programming varies widely across jurisdictions, as does evaluation and assessment of outcomes. Outcomes are limited to evaluation of re-arrest rates or calls to police and are limited in their ability to account for criminal displacement. Moreover, research indicates that buyers are developing and accessing methods to avoid sting operations, including online and street-level stings. Abolitionists and radical feminists maintain that demand for purchased sex must be addressed in order to combat sex trafficking, such as through the various demand-reduction programs and law enforcement efforts focusing on buyers. Neoliberals maintain that buyers are targets of abolitionist demand-reduction efforts, indicating that the U.S. government is moving toward this form of policy.

Discussion Questions

1. Describe the motivations of buyers to purchase sex.
2. What power dynamics are implicated in the relationship between buyers and sellers of sex?
3. Describe various demand-reduction programs, and discuss their relative benefits and challenges.

Part III

Responses to Sex Trafficking

[9]

Criminal Justice System Responses

In 2014 a national sting operation resulted in an investigation of 201 suspected pimps and uncovered 168 children, many of them teenagers under the care of the U.S. child welfare system, who had not been reported missing. This was the eighth in a series of annual sting operations set up by the U.S. government known as Operation Cross Country, which involved more than 400 state and local law enforcement offices. Since its inception, the initiative has uncovered more than 3,600 children who meet the legal criteria for sex trafficking. Most recently, in February of 2015, a national two-week-long sting operation across 17 states and 70 jurisdictions uncovered 570 buyers of sex-for-sale, 23 traffickers/pimps, and 54 women and 14 girls identified by law enforcement as sex trafficking survivors. All were taken into police custody. The buyers were charged with buying sex and traffickers/pimps were charged with sex trafficking, pimping, or promoting prostitution. The women and girls identified as survivors were referred to social services and were not charged with crimes (Bellware 2015).

Large-scale sting operations like these tend to make national headlines, but the efforts of those in the criminal justice system go beyond such initiatives. Such efforts include identifying sex traffickers and survivors as well as investigating, reporting, and prosecuting sex trafficking–related crimes. There are both benefits and challenges associated with criminal justice system responses to sex trafficking. Benefits include legal recourse for victimization, justice seeking, and potentially preventing traffickers from causing further harm to survivors/victims. At the same time there are challenges to identification, prosecution, and implementation of the law. Various components of justice system involvement can have the latent consequence of revictimization, which results from misreporting and criminalizing survivors, putting conditions on services, or exposing the victim to the trafficker/pimp in court. Accordingly, while efforts are being made and progress is seen, there remain some important areas of contention.

This chapter describes the background and development of federal anti–sex trafficking legislation, including a detailed account of the 2000 U.S. Trafficking Victims Protection Act (TVPA) and the key components of its reauthorizations. The chapter also provides a general description of the functions and challenges of state-level antitrafficking laws and their relationship to the U.S. TVPA. The ways sex trafficking cases are prosecuted are explained, including federal and state prosecution and the difficulties associated with each. Current challenges to implementing federal and state laws are examined as well, including key issues with identification, investigation, and reporting and the latent consequence of revictimization of sex trafficked/exploited people.

U.S. Federal Law: The Trafficking Victims Protection Act

In 2000 the United States adopted the Trafficking Victims Protection Act (TVPA), indicating that already existing criminal law was ineffective and insufficient at protecting survivors and prosecuting traffickers (Albonetti 2014). As mentioned in chapter 1, the TVPA defines a severe form of trafficking as:

a) A commercial sex act induced by force, fraud, or coercion, or in which the person induced to perform such act has not attained 18 years of age; or

b) the recruitment, harboring, transportation, provision, or obtaining of a person for labor or services, through the use of force, fraud, or coercion for the purpose of subjection to involuntary servitude, peonage, debt bondage, or slavery.[1]

The adoption of the U.S. TVPA coincided with the development of international antitrafficking legislation, commonly known as the Palermo Protocol (see chapter 1). The TVPA, and its reauthorizations in 2003, 2005, 2008, and 2013, takes a four-pronged approach including prevention, protection, and prosecution (known as the 3Ps) and monitoring other nations' anti-trafficking efforts (Clawson, Dutch, and Cummings 2006; Clawson et al. 2008; U.S. Department of State 2014; Farrell et al. 2012; Stolz 2005). The following subsections describe each of these four prongs as well as the benefits and challenges associated with them.

Prevention

The U.S. Department of State describes prevention efforts as including education and awareness, targeted outreach to vulnerable populations, and legislation to address known problem areas. Prevention could be viewed in two ways: preventing sex trafficking from initially occurring and preventing further trafficking of an already-trafficked person. Legislative endeavors for prevention include TVPA-related funding for interagency task forces across the country. Presently, forty-two task forces exist across the nation. One responsibility of the task forces is to provide community education and awareness with the aims of preventing sex trafficking from initially occurring and increasing identification of already existing trafficking through citizen tips. The TVPA also works to provide a federal-level interagency task force whose responsibilities include monitoring and combating human trafficking. Presidential appointees, agency directors, and others are to support the evaluation of trafficking prevention efforts as well as the protection of survivors and prosecution of traffickers (Clawson, Dutch, and Cummings 2006). Over the years, Rescue and Restore Coalitions have been established in various sites, focusing on both community awareness education and training for social service providers, law enforcement, and others likely to come into contact with sex trafficked people (Heil and Nichols 2015). The Department of Transportation and the Department of Human Services also offers training in conjunction with five commercial airlines on how to identify and respond to a suspected trafficking situation.

The National Human Trafficking Resource Center established a national hotline as a means to prevent further trafficking by providing a forum for help-seeking on the part of survivors or for identification tips from concerned citizens. The hotline also takes calls to answer questions about human trafficking and to provide resources for prevention, outreach, and services (U.S. Department of State 2014). The Polaris Project (2015b), which operates the hotline, reported 1,611 potential cases received on the hotline and 292 direct contacts from survivors to their BeFree Textline in 2014.

Strengthening penalties against buyers and traffickers is also a part of prevention efforts, overlapping somewhat with the prosecution prong of the TVPA. Enforcing extraterritorial jurisdiction of child sex trafficking offenses by U.S. citizens is viewed by the United States as a form of prevention, ideologically curtailing demand through deterrence and enforcement of the law. U.S. laws provide extraterritorial jurisdiction over child sex tourism offenses perpetrated overseas by U.S. citizens. Although the deterrent effect remains unevaluated, the Department of Homeland Security made three criminal arrests resulting in eight convictions in child sex tourism cases in 2011, and made fifty-seven arrests in 2013, indicating an increase in the implementation and enforcement of this legislation (U.S. Department of State 2012, 2014).

Efforts to address sex trafficking of at-risk groups is also part of the prevention aspect of the TVPA. Prevention initiatives involving at-risk groups in 2014 targeted American Indian and Alaskan Native populations, who disproportionately experience sex trafficking victimization, as well as areas surrounding newer oil industries, which saw an increase in sex trafficking. This resulted in efforts toward investigation and identification of sex trafficking in Indian Country, and in the oil fields of North Dakota and Montana (U.S. Department of State 2014). The Department of Justice worked with a training institute in Indian Country to create training in human trafficking for state criminal justice workers as well as a curriculum for tribal youth. Despite the work to address sex trafficking in these areas, such efforts were problematized by "lack of collaboration between local law enforcement and tribal agencies, inadequate training for tribal law enforcement, the impact of criminal gangs on indigenous communities, and victims' fear of reporting trafficking to law enforcement" (U.S. Department of State 2014, 402). Accordingly, work in this area needs further improvement.

Prevention efforts and outreach targeting high-risk groups are limited because known high-risk populations are not consistently the focus—or even a focus at all—of outreach and prevention education. Black women and girls show the highest risk of sex trafficking and yet are largely erased from government efforts to ameliorate sex trafficking victimization (Heil and Nichols 2015). Color-blindness results in tacit acceptance of the disproportionate victimization of black women and girls. Latinas also show disproportionate sex trafficking victimization, but prevention and outreach efforts to this population is limited as well. Further, areas with high rates of runaway or truant youth, high rates of school student turnover, and high drop-out rates—identified risk factors for sex trafficking—should be an obvious focal point of outreach and prevention education (Heil and Nichols 2015). Yet they are also not typically a focal point of outreach efforts funded by the federal government. Moreover, LGBTQ* youth are known to be at heightened risk, yet prevention and outreach are extremely limited and services for these groups are difficult to access (Koyama 2011; Heil and Nichols 2015; Dank et al. 2015). Homeless youth also show heightened risk of sex trafficking victimization, but outreach remains limited (Curtis et al. 2008; Heil and Nichols 2015; Dank et al. 2015). While women and girls are disproportionately victimized, boys and young men experience sex trafficking as well (Curtis et al. 2008; Dank et al. 2015). Yet much of the discussion about men and boys is extremely limited in the antitrafficking discourse generally and prevention efforts particularly. Prevention is one aspect of services, largely in the form of outreach, education, training, or hotline use, but once survivors have become involved in a trafficking/exploitation situation, they are in need of additional services. This is where the protection aspect of the TVPA comes into play.

Protection

The TVPA aims to provide protection and assistance to survivors of trafficking. There are benefits and challenges associated with such measures. Major criticisms of the protection aspect of the TVPA are that services to survivors are limited and the focus centers more upon identifying and prosecuting traffickers than assisting survivors. Importantly, the U.S. Department of State acknowledges a lack of funding to support survivors and notes that both child and adult trafficking survivors have been denied appeals for social services funding assistance (U.S. Department of State 2012, 2014). Heather J. Clawson and colleagues (2008) uncovered similar challenges associated with the TVPA, including lack of funding earmarked for shelter for minors and a lack of funding more generally to meet the needs of domestic survivors. This is a consistent finding across various research studies in multiple locations. Sex trafficking–specific services are limited to less than a hundred for girls and adults nationwide, and few specifically invite men, boys, or LGBTQ* individuals (Heil and Nichols 2015). Erin Heil and Andrea Nichols (2015) found in their case study of St. Louis that service providers had difficulty finding safe shelter for trafficked and exploited youth, and that efforts toward identification were limited by the lack of social service options available once a trafficking case was identified as such. Meredith Dank and colleagues (2015) similarly reported that youth were engaged in the commercial sex industry in part due to lack of accessible shelter and services. Services protect survivors from subsequent harm from traffickers/pimps and provide a survival option. Without these services, survivors are vulnerable to traffickers' reprisals, continued involvement in the commercial sex industry in the form of survival sex, and retrafficking resulting from a lack of survival options.

The TVPA does include funding for aftercare services and temporary immigration status to protect survivors who hold undocumented status (Clawson, Dutch, and Cummings 2006; Stolz 2005). The primary goal is to prevent deportation, so survivors can be available as witnesses for prosecution. Temporary immigration status is determined in this instance by the T visa. "The T nonimmigrant status visa (T visa) is set aside for those who are or have been victims of human trafficking, protects victims of human trafficking and allows victims to remain in the United States to assist in an investigation or prosecution of human trafficking."[2] The T visa "allows for valid immigration status for up to four years for victims who are physically present in the United States and who comply with any reasonable law enforcement requests for assistance with an investigation or prosecution of a human trafficking case" (U.S. Department of State 2012, 362). Eligibility is determined by whether the trafficking survivor is physically in the United States or a U.S. territory as a result of sex trafficking; if the person is a victim of a severe form of trafficking as indicated in the TVPA; if the victim has cooperated in investigation and prosecution of traffickers; or if the person would experience substantial harm upon leaving the United States. (Clawson, Dutch, and Cummings 2006). The TVPA and the Immigration and Nationality Act work in tandem to certify trafficking survivors through the Office of Refugee Resettlement. Once a survivor is certified, benefits may be offered, such as employment authorization, housing, mental and medical care, and supplemental security income. In some cases benefits may also extend to family members. "The Immigration and Nationality Act allows the Attorney General to give T-visas to the victim's spouse and children and to the victim's parents if the victim is younger than 21 years of age" (Clawson, Dutch, and Cummings 2006, 7). After three years survivors can apply for permanent residency and citizenship.

In some cases, a U nonimmigrant status visa (U visa) might be preferred because they are thought to be easier to access for those whose cases do not entirely meet the criteria for a T visa. The U visa "allows for legal immigration status for up to four years for victims of certain crimes, including trafficking, who have suffered substantial physical or mental abuse as a result of such crimes and who cooperate or are willing to cooperate with reasonable law enforcement requests in the investigation or prosecution of the qualifying criminal activity" (U.S. Department of State 2012, 362). Permanent residence is an option for some trafficking survivors and their immediate family members who do not have citizenship, but this is discretionary and determined by the U.S. attorney general (Heinrich and Sreeharsha 2013). Despite these benefits, there are limitations to the protections for immigrants offered under the TVPA.

One challenge is that the T visa is capped at five thousand, and the U visa is capped at ten thousand per year. The U visa applications have reached the cap and applicants have been denied. Further, those over 18 are required to cooperate with prosecution in order to access the protection benefits; thus, the benefits are conditional. Some researchers argue that there is a coercive element to prosecution and social service provision because of this requirement (Hopper 2004). If adult survivors are unwilling to testify, they may not receive assistance or protection. Benefits are largely provided only during the prosecution process as well. Those under 18 do not have conditional benefits; children are not required to participate in a prosecution to access services. Adults may get an exception if they can show extensive physical or psychological trauma (U.S. Department of State 2012).

In addition, "the eligibility requirements have been questioned, as well as the omission of awarding punitive damages, attorney fees, and litigation expenses" (Clawson, Dutch, and Cummings 2006). Protections are limited for those who are trafficked but still do not qualify for benefits. "The severe form of trafficking definition is the operational definition; that is, meeting this definition triggers the benefits and services provided under specified federal and state programs" (Stolz 2005). Thus, those whose cases are difficult to prosecute or whose cases fall more closely on the lines of exploitation rather than trafficking will not get the TVPA-provided protections.

Prosecution

The third "prong" of the TVPA is prosecution. Sex trafficking cases are typically prosecuted on a federal level, although cases can also be prosecuted on a state level as well. If there is a strong case with sufficient evidence of force, fraud, or coercion, or if the case involves a minor, and if there is a cooperating victim(s), the federal prosecutor's office will generally take the case. In states with weak antitrafficking laws, less prosecutorial experience, or reduced capacity for investigating such cases, the preference is to refer to the federal level (Clawson et al. 2008; Farrell et al. 2012). Cases that are prosecuted on a federal level are prosecuted by the U.S. Department of Justice's Offices of the United States Attorneys. The United States is divided into ninety-four federal districts, each with their own federal district courts and federal prosecutors. Federal prosecutions for sex trafficking remain relatively static, in the hundreds annually. In 2013, for instance, 222 defendants were charged with sex trafficking in federal courts, a slight increase over the preceding year (see also chapter 1) (U.S. Department of State 2014).

If there is insufficient evidence or if a victim is unable or unwilling to testify, then the case is typically prosecuted on the state level, where the case may be charged as a lesser crime. In some cases, the evidentiary burden may actually be less for a sex trafficking charge depending on the state law, so prosecution on a state level might be preferred in such circumstances (Heil and Nichols 2015). In 2011 state-level prosecutions were in the dozens (Heinrich and Sreeharsha 2013). Two major studies, by Heather Clawson and colleagues (2008) and by Amy Farrell and colleagues (2012), found that sex trafficking was prosecuted at a state level relatively rarely because many state prosecutors were unaware of state trafficking laws, were otherwise reluctant to prosecute under a relatively new law or charge, or continued to prosecute as other related crimes under charges they were used to. Clawson and colleagues (2008) also found lack of resources for state prosecutors; as such, cases tend to be extremely lengthy and time consuming. Because of these challenges and those mentioned above, sex trafficking cases are typically referred to and prosecuted on the federal level. Farrell and colleagues (2012) found that about half of cases are prosecuted in federal court and half in state courts. Yet, of those cases prosecuted on a state level, only 17% involved an official charge of sex trafficking, and the remaining cases were prosecuted as other crimes. Accordingly, while state prosecutions appear low, if related charges were counted as sex trafficking prosecutions—such as pimping, pandering, juvenile prostitution, enticement of a minor into prostitution, promoting prostitution, and child pornography—this number would be much higher. The number of state prosecutions appeared to increase somewhat, from dozens in 2012 to over one hundred state prosecutions of human trafficking in 2013; the majority of these human trafficking cases were sex trafficking cases (U.S. Department of State 2012, 2014). This indicates that state prosecutors may be becoming more aware of the laws and more comfortable with prosecuting under state antitrafficking laws as time progresses. This may also reflect improvement in state-level statutes. However, about 30% of cases are dismissed by prosecutors on a federal level and about 20% on a state level (Farrell et al. 2012), which demonstrates the challenge of prosecuting these crimes. While prosecution efforts are improving, challenges remain, including but not limited to: victim/survivor cooperation, adequate survival resources for victims, and proper trauma training and social services.

CHALLENGES TO PROSECUTION

There are multiple challenges associated with prosecuting sex trafficking cases. First and foremost, if cases are not identified, they will not be prosecuted. As indicated in more depth later in this chapter, there are many barriers associated with identifying sex trafficking situations, including law enforcement's lack of knowledge about sex trafficking, lack of resources, time constraints, misreporting as another crime, deportation of victims and traffickers, and other criminalization of survivors. Such barriers impede the investigation and the gathering of the evidence prosecutors depend on for a successful case. Further, sex trafficking cases appear to take much longer to prosecute than other serious crimes prosecuted on the federal level, taking two to three times as long (Clawson et al. 2008). This can prove taxing for survivors who wish to move on with their lives and may consequently drop out of participating in prosecution due to the lengthy commitment of time (Nichols and Heil 2014).

Survivors may not want to prosecute for reasons other than time constraints. Some survivors may not wish to prosecute so they will not have to see their trafficker in court. Revictimization in court is an issue—the accused has the right to face their accuser in court. Facing the trafficker can be extremely traumatic for survivors, who may not want to prosecute to avoid such revictimization and trauma. Lack of services to survivors is also related to prosecution; if survivors do not have their basic needs met and do not have access to trauma treatment (see chapter 10), then they are not in a stable position to cooperate with prosecution. They may even return to the trafficking situation in order to support survival needs or due to trauma bonds (Clawson et al. 2008; Hopper 2004). Moreover, the trafficker might be a husband or boyfriend, or there may be children involved and further dependency for survival needs (Smith 2014). Fear of retaliation in the form of physical violence, homicide, or harm to family and friends is another reason survivors may be reluctant to cooperate in a prosecution. Even with a survivor who wants to prosecute, challenges remain that must be addressed through needs-based advocacy and social service provision.

Notably, trauma effects can also pose challenges for survivors and prosecution efforts. Trauma can lead to fragmented memories or confused chronologies of events, so survivors may provide inconsistent statements—the perfect fodder for the trafficker's defense attorney (Nichols and Heil 2014). Thus, calling in expert witnesses to relay to the court the effects of trauma and the reason for possibly inconsistent stories is warranted. Further, victims may not be truthful in initially recounting their stories, for a variety of important reasons, including fear of their trafficker's reprisals to themselves and family members, lack of options to meet basic needs or dependency on the trafficker, fear of criminalization, and love for the trafficker.

Victim-centered techniques that work to ameliorate revictimizing experiences in the justice system include the use of closed circuit television for testimony. Exposure to the trafficker in court can be traumatic, and in order to avoid this trauma, recorded testimony places less stress on the survivor. Unfortunately, such techniques are little used (Smith, Vardaman, and Snow 2009). First, prosecutors argue that jurors are more likely to identify with the survivor if the survivor is present in court. Second, in *Crawford v. Washington*, the federal court decided that testimony was not admissible unless the defense had the opportunity to cross-examine. As a result, in order to avoid invoking *Crawford v. Washington*, survivor presence is preferred, regardless of the trauma and revictimization associated with facing the trafficker/pimp in court. Linda A. Smith, Samantha Healy Vardaman, and Melissa A. Snow (2009) note that prosecutors may prefer a plea bargain in order to prevent this revictimization in cases where children are involved. Alternatively, the court process can be empowering, if conducted with appropriate therapeutic treatment.

A language barrier may pose a challenge to survivors and prosecution, inhibiting communication and understanding between them both. This can also pose a barrier to survivors' ability to tell their stories and to tell them consistently. Cultural factors related to communication may offer challenges as well. For example, Hopper (2004) notes that among some groups, repeated questioning is considered culturally impolite, yet this is the standard procedure of the U.S. criminal justice system. "The legal process in the United States involves not only repeated questioning by law enforcement, prosecutors, and judges, but also cross-examination by an adversarial defense attorney" (Hopper 2004). Because of cultural dynamics, trafficked individuals might not provide a consistent story, shifting their responses as a consequence of repeated questioning. Another challenge to prosecution is that both survivors and traffickers alike are known to have been deported, making prosecution and justice seeking for survivors impossible (Heinrich and Sreeharsha 2013; Hepburn and Simon 2010; Nichols and Heil 2014). Deportation of trafficking perpetrators and victims is likely due to issues with overlapping jurisdictions and lack of coordination among Immigration and Customs Enforcement (ICE) and the various U.S. Attorney's Offices handling the cases (Hepburn and Simon 2010; Nichols and Heil 2014). ICE is responsible for deporting undocumented immigrants, while the U.S. Attorney's Offices are responsible for prosecuting trafficking cases. Lack of communication and collaboration between these entities results in the deportation of undocumented victims and perpetrators, both before and during the prosecution process. Importantly, when survivors of sex trafficking are deported, or when their traffickers themselves are deported before a prosecution can take place, this revictimizes survivors and provides an added layer of trauma to their already traumatic experiences. Addressing criminalization of trafficked immigrants who are undocumented and instead supporting access to a T visa or U visa is called for.

The age of the survivor may also call for victim-centered approaches. Children who are questioned repeatedly often think they are being re-asked questions because they gave an incorrect response. "Children may not understand adults' questioning, may not disclose the entire story, and may respond incorrectly even when they are certain of the right answer. Young children may change their story if asked the same questions repeatedly, because they interpret their answers as being wrong" (Hopper 2004, 132). In addition, adolescents involved with a boyfriend pimp are less likely to cooperate with prosecution. Social service provision for this group is vital in addressing the trauma bonds such individuals hold with their trafficker. Without support from the survivor, prosecution will not be as successful and a lesser charge or dropped charge may be inevitable. Smith, Vardaman, and Snow (2009) note that for children who have trauma effects from involvement in the commercial sex industry, advanced interview techniques by someone educated in trauma care and victim-centered interviewing (or child interviewing) is important. They note that most law enforcement agencies currently lack this capacity.

Perhaps most important is the question of what the goal is. Prosecution is generally assumed to be the goal of the U.S. justice system, punishing traffickers to prevent them from engaging in further harm and getting justice for survivors. Yet survivors themselves may not want to prosecute, and supporting survivors' needs and goals is important. Perhaps these are not mutually exclusive categories. Supporting survivor needs serves both survivors and prosecution efforts. Supporting victims and using a survivor-centered approach leads to cooperation with prosecution and testimony in court (Clawson et al. 2008; Farrell et al. 2012; Nichols and Heil 2014). Kelly Heinrich and Kavetha Sreeharsha (2013) write that "both making available victim assistance and working in conjunction with service providers are critical to rebuild trust with victims and ensure their cooperation in the criminal justice system." Clawson and colleagues, in examining successful prosecution endeavors, report that 90% of their sample of prosecutors indicated prosecution was rarely to never successful without victim testimony. It is in the best interests of prosecutors to gain trust and to provide resources to support survivors' needs. Addressing reasons why survivors may not wish to cooperate would be helpful to both survivors and prosecution endeavors. When survivors' needs are supported and respected, then they are more likely to be in a position to cooperate (Nichols 2014a). In contrast, when survivors' needs are not supported, cooperation with prosecution is less likely. They may recant their statements and may even return to the traffickers (Clawson et al. 2008). "Law enforcement is learning that victim assistance is necessary to stabilize traumatized victims so that they are physically and mentally able to assist investigators and prosecutors"

(Heinrich and Sreeharsha 2013). Needs might include trauma-informed care, safe housing, safety planning, or substance abuse treatment (Macy and Graham 2012).

SENTENCING

Following a successful prosecution, sentencing is also influenced by the TVPA. The TVPA resulted in increasing the mandatory minimum sentence for sex trafficking offenses to 10 years, 15 years in cases involving those under 14 years of age, and changing the maximum sentence to life in prison without parole (Albonetti 2014; Heinrich and Sreeharsha 2013; Stolz 2005; U.S. Department of State 2012). Life sentences have been issued in multiple cases involving both adults and children as victims. An analysis of post-TVPA sentencing found a "substantial increase in the mean length of imprisonment in FY [Fiscal Year] 2005, followed by further increases in subsequent years" (Albonetti 2014). The TVPA also established a 5-year sentence related to the destruction, holding, or keeping of another's identification documentation (Clawson, Dutch, and Cummings 2006). Sentencing may include restitution as well, in which a trafficker is required to pay survivors damages and losses, assessed at the court's discretion. The legislation itself appears to be sufficient and sound, as the sentences are similar to those of other serious crimes in the United States (U.S. Department of State 2012). Yet there remain challenges to this legislation, particularly in terms of identification and prosecution. The increase in penalties corresponds with the theoretical premise of deterrence theory—the idea of making the punishments for a crime severe enough to deter the crime. However, research indicates that the sentence must be swift and certain, and the risks must outweigh the rewards. Given the elusive nature of sex trafficking and challenges to identification and prosecution, these criteria are limited, rendering the deterrent effect limited as well. In terms of the deterrent effect, researchers indicate that, despite relatively harsh punishment for sex trafficking, the crime is still viewed as having relatively little risk (Busch-Armendariz et al. 2009; Heil and Nichols 2014; Smith, Vardaman, and Snow 2009). Often lesser charges are used, such as pimping, pandering, or enticement of a minor into prostitution. When cases are misidentified as juvenile prostitution, state-level pimping and pandering laws are typically used, which usually offer much lower sentences, such as probation or six months in jail (Smith, Vardaman, and Snow 2009).

Sentencing in child pornography is important to include in an analysis of sex trafficking because it fits the legal definition of sex trafficking as a form of commercial sexual exploitation of minors (see chapter 3). Yet cases involving child pornography are seldom prosecuted as sex trafficking cases. Instead, they are prosecuted as they have been traditionally, as child pornography cases. This is likely because the charge of possessing, producing, or distributing child pornography is much more direct, and prosecutors are more likely to win. Prosecutors have traditionally used these charges to prosecute possession of child pornography and simply continue to use them because they have been successful in the past. Sentences are roughly similar to or longer than a typical sex trafficking–related charge, depending on the dynamics involved. The federal sentence for transporting child pornography is between 15 and 30 years in prison. The federal sentence for each count of possessing child pornography is 10 years in prison and/or a fine of up to a quarter of a million dollars. Federal sentences for producing pornography are generally 10 to 30 years. Child pornography–related charges are prosecuted at the state levels as well, also with lengthy sentences attached to them.

Monitoring Other Nations' Activities

The last prong of the TVPA provides a stipulation involving the monitoring of other nations' activities. The United States sets minimum standards for the elimination of trafficking, with which countries that receive any type of economic or security assistance from the United States are expected to comply. The minimum standards broadly include establishing antitrafficking legislation and providing assistance to survivors. More specifically, "Tier placement in the annual Trafficking in Persons Report is dependent upon set criteria, including how vigorously a state investigates and prosecutes traffickers, protects identified victims, shares trafficking data, punishes public officials accused of trafficking, educates the public about prevention, monitors itself, and improves upon these efforts from the previous year" (Smith 2011, 17). Countries that get assistance from the United States are expected to provide an annual report to the United States describing and assessing outcomes of efforts to address various types of human trafficking, including sex trafficking (Clawson, Dutch, and Cummings 2006). Countries that do not get assistance may also submit reports in order to participate in a global analysis of nations' progress in meeting the minimum standards. Evaluation of country reports is based upon the criteria described earlier, and each country is then evaluated and placed into "tiers" by the U.S. Department of State (U.S. Department of State 2014). This prong of the TVPA also offers limited provisions for assistance to other countries to meet the minimum standards but threatens sanctions against those who fail to meet the standards (Clawson, Dutch, and Cummings 2006).

Tier 1 countries are largely determined by evidence of sustained anti-trafficking legislation and provision of assistance to survivors (Smith 2011). Tier 2 countries are those that do not fully meet the minimum standards set by the TVPA. They are identified as destination, transit, or origin countries for trafficked people, but they do not have adequate laws or victim assistance in place (Smith 2011). There is also a tier 2 watch list, for countries in which there has been a notable increase in the number of trafficked people or countries that fail to show evidence of antitrafficking efforts. Alternatively, if a country has agreed to make a sustained effort, there is a respite period of a year in order to comply with the minimum standards, with placement on the tier 2 watch list (Smith 2011). Nations that fall into tier 3 are those who do not comply with the minimum standards, do not report to the United States, or do not otherwise agree to make an effort to improve. The majority of countries fall in the tier 2 category, making an effort but not able to or failing to comply with the minimum standards of the TVPA.

While the tier system provides some basis for data collection on human trafficking on a global level and facilitates development of legislation and services, there are critiques of the system. First, global stratification is clearly implicated in the tier system. The high-income nations are generally on the tier 1 list, and lower-income countries are more likely to be on the tier 2 or tier 3 lists. A majority of those countries categorized on the tier 3 list or tier 2 watch list are among the poorest nations. This suggests that such nations may lack the resources necessary to address human trafficking on a legislative or social services level.

Another related critique of the tier system is that the United States imposes sanctions on tier 3 nations. When the U.S. imposes sanctions against nations who do not have sufficient resources to address the problem, those nations will face further economic difficulties, making it even more difficult to create and sustain antitrafficking endeavors, and it puts survivors at further risk due to increased vulnerability. This works in a way similar to the No Child Left Behind Policy created to address education gaps in the United States. Poor-performing schools—typically concentrated in the lowest income areas, which need the resources most to improve test scores—are denied resources because they did not make the grade, making it even more difficult to meet the standards.

In addition, the policy has been critiqued on aspects of global power dynamics other than global stratification. Critics suggest that countries should not be expected to adhere to U.S. legislation. The United States is often accused of "arrogance," and requiring other countries to submit an antitrafficking report to and be monitored by the United States is viewed as hierarchal or as violating the sovereignty of nations. Unsurprisingly, some nations in conflict with the United States do not submit reports, and the U.S. Department of State automatically labels them as tier 3 nations, regardless of any other contrary evidence. Thus, the criticism is that sanctions are imposed in a subjective, politicized manner (Smith 2011).

The policy has also been criticized for creating a situation that encourages underreporting of human trafficking. Heather Smith (2011, 16) writes, "Governments that receive aid from the U.S. have a particularly acute need to demonstrate that they are tough on trafficking. In short, governments have incentives to underreport incidences of sex trafficking, potentially limited resources to collect data, and strong motivations to exaggerate their efforts to curb it." Other challenges include a lack of resources to collect data and a lack of focus on addressing the poverty that fuels sex trafficking as well as the preponderance of corrupt criminal justice systems that accept bribes from traffickers in order to preserve trafficking operations while simultaneously covering up the problem (Kara 2010). Moreover, just because antitrafficking laws exist does not mean they are being enforced or that the reports that countries submit are a holistic, objective analysis of the accomplishments and remaining challenges. For example, Smith (2011) indicates that nearly 40% of nations with antitrafficking laws had not used them, indicating an enforcement gap (see also UNODC 2009). Accordingly, while there are benefits to monitoring other nations' antitrafficking efforts, such as facilitating the development of antitrafficking legislation and services and engaging countries in a global analysis of these efforts, there are some remaining challenges that are difficult to address. These challenges both in the United States and internationally are partly addressed through various reauthorizations of the TVPA.

Reauthorizations

The various reauthorizations of the TVPA brought further structural changes that advocates and their political partners have worked to accomplish. First, the Trafficking Victims Protection Reauthorization Act (TVPRA) of 2003 gives survivors the right to sue their traffickers, adds human trafficking to the list of crimes that can be charged under the Racketeering Influenced Corrupt Organizations (RICO) statute, and provides additional protections to survivors and their families from deportation (Polaris Project 2014a; Smith, Vardaman, and Snow 2009). "The 2003 Trafficking Victims Protection Reauthorization Act (TVPRA) also encouraged the use of International Law Enforcement Academies to train foreign law enforcement authorities, prosecutors, and members of the judiciary about human trafficking" (Smith, Vardaman, and Snow 2009). The 2003 reauthorization has been criticized because it places a restriction on awarding federal grants to programs, organizations, and researchers who support legalization of prostitution (Stolz 2005; Weitzer 2007, 2011). This "gatekeeping" is problematic because organizations directly serving sexually exploited and trafficked people are denied from applying for certain grants if they have advocated for decriminalization or legalization (Alvarez and Alessi 2012). The Sex Workers Project in New York, for example, is one of the largest and longest-standing organizations that provide services to sex trafficked and exploited people, and their perspective is that decriminalization would best support the needs of their clients. Yet funding is restricted from this group and others.

In the face of criticisms that implementation of the TVPA had an almost exclusive focus on immigrant survivors, despite the much higher numbers of domestically trafficked people, the TVPRA of 2005 emphasized protections and increased service provision to domestic minor sex trafficking (DMST) survivors. The 2005 TVPRA funded grant programs for state and local law enforcement to increase their antitrafficking efforts in the area of DMST (Polaris Project 2014a; U.S. Department of State 2006). For example, additional funds for investigating and prosecuting cases involving

U.S. citizens were allocated. In addition the 2005 reauthorization "funded anti-human trafficking task forces, intended to increase community partnerships and coordinated community responses between social service providers and law enforcement, thereby increasing identification and assistance to trafficking survivors" (Clawson, Dutch, and Cummings 2006).

The TVPRA of 2008 requires law enforcement to collect and report human trafficking data to the Federal Bureau of Investigation (FBI) (Heinrich and Sreeharsha 2013). Specifically, the Uniform Crime Report is a national data collection set of crime statistics representing cases that are uncovered by law enforcement and reported to the FBI by police departments across the United States. Prior to this reauthorization, the U.S. Department of Justice only collected human trafficking data that was voluntarily provided. Thus, the available statistics were extremely limited (Heinrich and Sreeharsha 2013). Increased protections with the T visa, increased penalties for trafficking, and expanded definitions of various types of trafficking with the aim of benefiting prosecution efforts are also a part of the 2008 TVPRA (Polaris Project 2014a; U.S. Department of State 2008).

Last, the primary benefit of the 2013 TVPRA to trafficking victims within the United States is increased provisions for collaboration with federal, state, and local law enforcement to address challenges associated with charging and prosecuting traffickers (Polaris Project 2014a; U.S. Department of State 2013; see also Farrell et al. 2012; Clawson et al. 2008; Nichols and Heil 2014). Criticisms of the TVPA and its reauthorizations still remain, primarily in that the emphasis is on law enforcement and prosecution and much less so on direct assistance to survivors of human trafficking. Research bears out that increased access to a myriad of social services is much needed (Dank et al. 2015; Heil and Nichols 2015, Macy and Graham 2012; Macy and Johns 2011; Smith 2014). The TVPA has resulted in benefits, but challenges remain to be addressed on the federal level. Meanwhile, states can and do create their own antitrafficking laws, with benefits and challenges as well.

State Law

Every state has now criminalized sex trafficking; Wyoming was the last state to pass legislation in 2013. State laws vary widely in both their definitions of sex trafficking and in their implementation. Farrell and colleagues

(2012) found that "state anti-trafficking laws differ widely in both the definition of what actions constitute a human trafficking crime and the focus of the state response to the problem." In some states the law only addresses DMST, and others conflate smuggling and sex trafficking, stipulating that some type of movement across state or international boundaries or status as an undocumented immigrant are required (Heinrich and Sreeharsha 2013). Importantly, the majority of state-level antitrafficking laws do not include adequate assistance to survivors, the right to sue their trafficker for damages in civil cases, or protection from criminalization (Heinrich and Sreeharsha 2013).

There are also differences between states in terms of how sex trafficking is handled. Some states have antitrafficking task forces; implement statewide coordination efforts, evaluation, and assessment of needs; or offer or mandate training to law enforcement, and other states do not do any of these things (Heinrich and Sreeharsha 2013). The Polaris Project (2015c) issues state rankings each year based upon ten criteria:

Does the state have a statute criminalizing sex trafficking?
Does the state have a statute criminalizing labor trafficking?
Does the state mandate asset forfeiture and inclusion of trafficking in the RICO statues?
Does the state offer training on human trafficking for law enforcement or the development of a task force?
Does the state lower the burden of proof for minors?
Does the state post the national human trafficking hotline?
Has the state passed a Safe Harbor law decriminalizing child victims?
Does the state offer victim assistance?
Does the state provide victims with access to civil damages?
Does the state vacate convictions for sex trafficking survivors?

The report indicates significant progress by most states in each year. Another group, Shared Hope International, also produces annual state evaluation reports, in the form of a state report card.[3] The report cards are based on six criteria:

Does the state criminalize DMST?
Do criminal provisions address demand?
Are there criminal provisions for traffickers?

Are there criminal provisions for facilitators?

Are there protections for child victims?

What are the criminal justice tools for prosecution and investigation?

This report also shows progress across states over the years. There are groups that are working to address remaining challenges with state-level laws. For example, the Uniform Law Commission works to create more uniformity in antitrafficking law between and among the states, including to address definitional issues, provide consistency between states, and more accurately reflect the dynamics of sex trafficking throughout the United States (Heinrich and Sreeharsha 2013). Ultimately, laws are only as good as the actors on the ground implementing them. The best-designed system can fail or succeed depending on those who are responsible for enacting it. Notably, while state legislation varies, the implementation of the law itself varies even within a state, from jurisdiction to jurisdiction, which has a significant impact on identification and misreporting (Nichols and Heil 2014).

Identification

Investigation of sex trafficking on the federal level is typically conducted by the FBI, although in cases where the survivor or trafficker is from another country, the U.S. Immigration and Customs Enforcement, the U.S. Department of Homeland Security, and the U.S. Department of State's Human Trafficking Unit may become involved (Heinrich and Sreeharsha 2013). At times federal investigators will collaborate with local law enforcement as well. While cases are typically investigated and prosecuted at the federal level, most are initially identified at a local level (Farrell et al. 2012). There are nearly eighteen thousand full-time law enforcement agencies in the United States, creating a situation rife with a lack of uniformity in education, training, and protocols and resulting in discordant practices throughout the United States (Wilson, Walsh, and Klueber 2006; Farrell et al. 2012; Nichols and Heil 2014).

How Law Enforcement Identifies Cases

Multiple studies show that law enforcement, from a local to federal level, is primarily reactive rather than proactive in investigating sex trafficking

(Farrell et al. 2012; Heinrich and Sreeharsha 2013; Hopper 2004). Proactive identification involves law enforcement seeking out sex trafficking cases, whereas reactive identification involves reacting to already-identified cases, such as through victim self-reporting, tips from community members or organizations, or cases discovered in the course of other crime investigations. Research indicates that police identification is largely reactive due to lack of resources and time constraints (Clawson, Dutch, and Cummings 2006; Farrell et al. 2012).

Many sex trafficking cases are identified by law enforcement accidentally or as a matter of circumstance. For example, there was a case just outside of Harrisburg, Pennsylvania, in which state troopers searched a car following a stop for a traffic violation. They found thousands of baggies of heroin but also found four teenage girls who were allegedly engaged in commercial sex acts under the direction of Robert Middlebrook (Sheppard 2015). Middlebrook was charged with sex trafficking of minors and drug-related offenses. Had it not been for the traffic violation stop, this case would not likely have been identified. Research studies find that cases are often identified by happenstance on seemingly innocuous traffic stops. Heather Clawson, Nicole Dutch, and Megan Cummings (2006) examined the ways in which sex trafficking cases came to the attention of law enforcement and found that about a third were uncovered during investigations of other crimes. More recently, Farrell and colleagues (2012, 78) found that 18% of cases came from ongoing investigations of other crimes; police commonly "stumbled upon cases of human trafficking during the course of their routine patrols." Similarly, Nichols and Heil (2014) note that police identified sex trafficking through routine traffic stops by running the identifications of minor girls and consequently finding that they were the subjects of missing person reports. Accordingly, identification of sex trafficking in the course of regular policing activities accounts for a proportion of identified cases.

As another form of reactive investigation, parents have identified their own sex trafficked children, searching for them on escort/adult services ads on popular websites and then going to law enforcement for assistance (Nichols and Heil 2014). Keith Eldridge (2015) reports that a mother in Olympia, Washington, found her 14-year-old daughter on the website Backpage.com, soliciting sex under the name "Diamond." The mom responded to the Backpage.com ad by asking what $200 could get her; the response was "good sex." At this point, the mom essentially set up her own "sting" operation, setting up a "date" at a Tacoma motel. Once she saw the trafficker's car, she contacted police from the motel office, who then arrived and arrested the traffickers. In this case Curtis Escalante and accomplices Michael Williams II and Mikael Williams were all charged with human trafficking–related crimes. One study (Farrell et al. 2012) notes that while tips from family members occur, they are relatively uncommon, finding in a review of 119 sex trafficking cases that only 3% are reported to law enforcement by a survivor's family member. This might be a consequence of the fact that many engaged in the commercial sex industry are runaway or "throwaway" youth; thus, many parents of trafficked youth are not seeking them out. Alternatively, parents who are concerned about their missing children may seek out other forms of assistance, such as filing a missing person report, rather than seeking out their children in the commercial sex industry themselves and then going to police.

In addition to parent-provided information, tips from ordinary citizens and referrals from community organizations also serve as a catalyst to identification. Clawson, Dutch, and Cummings (2006) found about a third of identified cases in law enforcement originated from citizen tips. Interestingly, referrals from task forces, social service providers, or other community based organizations were uncommon sources of referrals in this study. At the same time, six years following the Clawson, Dutch, and Cummings study, Farrell and colleagues (2012) reported that nearly 40% of 119 cases of sex trafficking were identified based on tips from community and social services organizations. Education and awareness in the community, supported in part through federal funding, was heightened during this time period. Although a direct relationship is unclear, this suggests the possibility that education and training of social service providers and the general community produces identified cases.

Aside from these reactive methods of identification, police may also engage in proactive policing techniques. A typical proactive approach of law enforcement practices involves searching sex-for-sale advertisements on the Internet, looking for young faces, and setting up "sting" operations to arrest traffickers and offer survivors services (Farrell et al. 2012). The challenge to this technique is that investigators are not likely to identify individuals who are trafficked who do not look particularly young. Men and boys are also typically not included or identified in these searches. Researchers reported in twelve study sites that about 12% of sex trafficking cases were identified through such sting operations (Farrell et al. 2012). The number of identified cases produced through sting operations varies from year to year and is influenced by available resources and the consequent number of sting operations conducted. National sting operations typically produce varying numbers of survivors, traffickers, and buyers with each initiative, often in the hundreds (Heil and Nichols 2014). Sting operations are somewhat controversial because, while they do uncover trafficked minors, they also simultaneously lead to the arrests of adults engaged in the commercial sex industry who cannot or are not willing to reveal force, fraud, or coercion, or otherwise implicate their pimps. There are limitations to the legal definition of sex trafficking, which does not protect exploited people who do not fit its label, nor does it protect willing sex workers. Moreover, minors are also typically arrested in sting operations and later channeled into services, which often includes juvenile detention or foster care, because other resources are limited or inaccessible. Some argue that sting operations revictimize the survivors, particularly when adequate services and trauma-informed care are not offered.

Farrell and colleagues reported that survivors of sex trafficking self-reported their victimization to law enforcement in only 10% of cases. This is important because the onus is generally on the survivor to come forward for assistance (Clawson, Dutch, and Cummings 2006; Farrell et al. 2012; Hopper 2004). According to the extant research, a limited number of sex trafficked people seek assistance from law enforcement. There are various barriers that prevent both self-reporting and other modes of identification of sex trafficking in the justice system.

Barriers to Identification in the Criminal Justice System

Multiple barriers exist that pose challenges to identifying sex trafficking in the justice system. Such barriers include those that inhibit survivors' help-seeking as well as barriers present within the criminal justice system. In addition, trafficking techniques themselves make identification much more difficult for law enforcement because much effort is put into ensuring nondetection and reducing risks of getting caught (see chapter 7). Barriers that inhibit survivors' self-reporting include distrust of law enforcement, fear of criminalization for prostitution or for undocumented immigration, love for the trafficker/boyfriend/pimp, and fear of the trafficker/pimp (see chapter 5). Barriers posed within various aspects of law enforcement include definitional issues, misreporting as another crime, and officers' attitudes, all of which are associated with a lack of education and training about the issue.

DEFINITIONAL ISSUES

There are definitional issues that may pose challenges to the identification of sex trafficking by law enforcement in terms of the way sex trafficking is operationalized and translated into practice. These issues include a lack of officers' knowledge about what the TVPA and state-level antitrafficking laws are as well as a lack of knowledge even about what sex trafficking is and what it encompasses (Farrell et al. 2012). Jeremy M. Wilson and Erin Dalton (2008) found wide variations in the definitions of sex trafficking that officers held from city to city, even within the same state. As mentioned earlier, with interpretations of state laws, officers may have an incorrect definition of sex trafficking, assuming that some type of movement across international borders or state lines is required. Despite the TVPA and even state law that holds the same or a similar definition, sex trafficking may be confused with smuggling, migration, or otherwise crossing borders. One study found that 20% of officers viewed trafficking and smuggling as synonymous (Clawson, Dutch, and Cummings 2006). As discussed in chapter 1, this is not the case; in jurisdictions in which officers hold such definitions, domestic survivors are completely ignored and "missed" in identification efforts. This is problematic because the majority of sex trafficking in the United States is domestic. Similarly, Deborah Wilson, William Walsh, and Sherilyn Klueber's (2006) study indicated that police had incorrect ideas about the dynamics of sex trafficking, showing lack of education, awareness, and training in this area. For example, nearly three-quarters thought trafficking was a part of international organized crime, showing the incorrect belief that a typical trafficking survivor was an immigrant (Wilson, Walsh, and Klueber 2006). More recent research also shows lack of understanding of legal definitions resulting in officers' misidentification and reporting (Farrell et al. 2012; Nichols and Heil 2014; Heil and Nichols 2015). The cases that are identified as sex trafficking also tend to have higher rates of violence, including physical, sexual, and emotional abuse, as well as threats of harm and exploitation. Cases that are exploitive or involve psychological manipulation and include lower rates of violence may not be labeled as sex trafficking by officers but as other crimes (Farrell et al. 2012). This is especially important because several studies indicate that psychological manipulation or dependency for basic needs are primary components of sex trafficking rather than severe physical violence. Thus, the legal definition of sex trafficking, regardless of the presence of severe violence, may not be used in police investigations and reporting practices. As a consequence of definitional issues, law enforcement may fail to identify sex trafficking. In addition, the misidentification and misreporting of sex trafficking that result from definitional issues at times results in the criminalization of victims themselves (Heil 2012; Hopper 2004; Rand 2010).

MISREPORTING

Lack of thorough investigation in other commonly co-occurring crimes also serves as a barrier to identifying sex trafficking in the criminal justice system and results in misreporting. Paradoxically, while research finds that a proportion of sex trafficking cases are uncovered in the course of routine investigations or patrols, research simultaneously finds that officers are not thoroughly investigating crimes that often co-occur with sex trafficking, which could lead to even more identified cases. Intimate partner violence, rape, and sexual assault and undocumented immigration are among the crimes that may occur alongside sex trafficking. In addition, sex trafficking is often misreported as prostitution or juvenile prostitution.

Some researchers find that sex trafficking survivors are criminalized as undocumented immigrants, resulting in deportation of survivors without uncovering or further investigating the trafficking situation (Hepburn and Simon 2010). As indicated in chapter 1, sometimes a smuggling situation can develop into a sex trafficking situation. Research indicates that such cases are handled only as undocumented immigration, further exacerbating distrust of law enforcement while simultaneously contributing to misidentification and misreporting. Those without identification or whose identification has been taken by the trafficker may be viewed as criminals and not screened for trafficking. Researchers have found that officers refer such individuals to Immigration and Customs Enforcement, who may then deport them before the identification of the sex trafficking situation can take place (Hopper 2004; Heil and Nichols 2014;

Hepburn and Simon 2010). Limited English-speaking abilities also pose a challenge for survivors in interactions with law enforcement. Immigrants who hold limited English-speaking abilities depend on others to tell their stories, which sometimes results in misreporting as offenders of crimes. At times officers unknowingly use the survivor's trafficker as an interpreter (Hopper 2004).

In addition to not identifying sex trafficking because of focusing on undocumented immigration, prostitution is another area where officers often miss the opportunity to identify a trafficking situation. Clawson, Dutch, and Cummings (2006) found that officers admitted it is easier to assume an individual is willingly engaged in the sex industry rather than trafficked, an attitude that impedes investigation and identification and ultimately results in the criminalization of sex trafficking survivors. Consequently, a lack of thorough investigation inclusive of sex trafficking screening leads to both lack of identification and misreporting. Similarly, Jody Raphael, Jessica Ashley Reichert, and Mark Powers (2010) found that domestic trafficking of women in Chicago was misidentified and misreported as prostitution. Heil (2012) notes that once an individual in Florida reaches the age of 18, they are no longer considered by police as potentially sex trafficked. Police there view women over 18 as willingly engaging in the sex industry, precluding any involvement with a trafficker; these cases are "missed" by police. Farrell and colleagues (2012) found in an analysis of fifty incident reports of prostitution, about 10% had elements of sex trafficking. This is consistent with a 2008 study by Newton and colleagues, who also found that nearly 10% of prostitution cases across four jurisdictions had elements of sex trafficking. The number could be higher, as these are elements that law enforcement officers noted and included in reports while simultaneously misidentifying the case as prostitution. Such elements may depend on subjective determinations of officers and the officers' willingness to identify them and include them in reports. Moreover, the fact that there are hundreds of juvenile prostitution cases reported annually by law enforcement offices across the nation to the FBI suggests that the federal law—and state law as well—is not being implemented locally by some officers.

Intimate partner violence is among the crimes that are in need of further investigation to uncover potential sex trafficking (Nichols and Heil 2014). In terms of co-occurring domestic violence, researchers indicate that sex trafficking is in some cases an extension of intimate partner violence

(IPV). In an abusive relationship, abusers engage in multiple forms of coercive control, which can manifest in the form of sex trafficking. This is characteristic or inherent to the cases involving the "boyfriend pimp" for minors. Other researchers and practitioners note that this overlap between IPV and sex trafficking is pervasive among trafficked adults and minors.[4] One Chicago-based study found that 20% of 222 prostituted women were pimped by boyfriends (Raphael, Reichert, and Powers 2010). Another study found that 16% of 54 trafficking victims were pimped out by boyfriends with whom they had an emotional bond (Kennedy and Pucci 2007). Reid (2010) also notes that trauma bonds between minors and their boyfriend pimps are prevalent. The Polaris Project (2015b) indicated intimate relationships are implicated in over a third of sex trafficking cases. Lauren Martin and colleagues (2014) highlight IPV commonly co-occurring with sex trafficking of minors in Minneapolis as well. Multiple case studies and prosecuted cases indicate this relationship. As such, when finding prostitution overlapping with IPV, law enforcement should handle it as both a case of IPV as well as a potential sex trafficking case. Lack of further investigation in these areas results in misreporting crimes as a single charge of domestic violence or prostitution, whereas sex trafficking may also be present.

Reporting as another crime, such as prostitution, IPV, or undocumented status as opposed to trafficking poses significant challenges to identification. This also facilitates greater distrust in legal systems, creating even further barriers to identifying and assisting sex trafficked people. Correcting the misreporting involves a shift in definitions, attitudes, and practices. Police need a working definition of sex trafficking consistent with the TVPA. Uniformity across state laws is needed as are protocols to recognize indicators and investigate commonly co-occurring crimes further, screening for a trafficking situation. This would result in better police identification of sex trafficking more generally as well as identification in the course of investigations of other crimes.

OFFICER ATTITUDES AND THE NEED FOR TRAINING

Coinciding with these definitional issues and issues of identification and misreporting is a lack of education and training as well as some officers' attitudes about sex trafficking and even about survivors themselves.

Farrell and colleagues (2012) found that the majority of those most likely to come into contact with victims within the criminal justice system were front-line or patrol officers as opposed to detectives, FBI investigators, or specialized vice officers. They were also the least likely to receive training in sex trafficking. Farrell and colleagues (2012) found little to no training among front-line officers. Typically the trainings were an hour long, so even those who did receive training received incredibly limited training. A lack of protocols to refer cases to specialized investigators was also limited, as was the very presence or availability of such investigators. Accordingly, an investigation might end with a report of a patrol officer, and a charge for another crime. Similarly, Wilson, Walsh, and Klueber (2006) also found that 92% of front-line officers had received no training, and the trainings for those who did attend were limited to about two and a half hours. In the same study, 98% had no policy directly associated with trafficking. Another study found that while a majority of federal investigators were educated about the issue of trafficking, only a third of front-line officers reported being knowledgeable about trafficking (Clawson, Dutch, and Cummings 2006). In terms of familiarity with the TVPA, more than a third were unfamiliar with the TVPA, and less than half described themselves as being very familiar with the TVPA. Moreover, more than a third did not know if they had a state trafficking law (Clawson, Dutch, and Cummings 2006).

Wilson, Walsh, and Klueber (2006) found that a majority of local law enforcement believed sex trafficking was a problem in other areas, but they did not think it was a problem in their own area. Heil and Nichols (2015) found similar officer attitudes in their case study, with some officers reporting sex trafficking as unimportant, low priority, or just the hype item of the moment. "Whether human trafficking is viewed as a serious problem or considered a priority crime can affect law enforcement's capacity to respond" (Clawson, Dutch, and Cummings 2006). Wilson, Walsh, and Klueber (2006) found that, among 163 police departments, only 12% thought trafficking was an important issue in their jurisdictions. More recently, Amy Farrell, Jack McDevitt, and Stephanie Fahy (2008) found in their study that almost three-quarters of local, state, and federal law enforcement reported that they thought trafficking did not exist or was rare in their jurisdictions. Wilson, Walsh, and Klueber (2006) also indicated that local police felt sex trafficking was a federal issue and should be handled at a federal level.

Officer attitudes may also lead to revictimization. Farrell, McDevitt, and Fahy (2008) found that in more than three-quarters of 166 interviews, police believed survivors were partly responsible for their victimization. Farrell and colleagues (2012, 124) quote an officer, who said, "prosecutors, law enforcement, period, that they just don't really believe a lot of these people are victims. I mean, they're just never going to believe it, they saw these girls and all they saw were stripper whores." In the same study, in describing the "ignorance" of some of the officers' attitudes, another officer stated:

> People seem to think that even when dealing with minors, it's the classic pimp and ho type of investigation. Why should I care about some pimp beating a ho or why should I care about some pimp putting a girl on the streets. She could have made another choice. Whatever. Or it is the ignorance of they are all illegal, they shouldn't be here. To the hell with them. I mean they get what they get.
>
> (Farrell et al. 2012, 125–26)

This perception was heightened for those who returned to the commercial sex industry. A consequence of this blame-the-victim attitude is the criminalization of adult and minor sex trafficking survivors with charges of prostitution and their revictimization. The prevalence of this attitude among law enforcement also means that help-seeking or officer investigations may not result in assistance. In contrast, in places where officers are well trained, survivors are more likely to be identified and more likely to cooperate with law enforcement (Clawson, Dutch, and Cummings 2006; Reid 2010).

Criminalizing Trafficking Survivors

Perhaps the most important challenge to protecting survivors and prosecuting traffickers is that survivors may be criminalized themselves, most typically for prostitution or undocumented immigration. According to the TVPA, survivors should not be penalized, including fines, arrest, incarceration, or other penalties. Yet research indicates that the justice system penalizes survivors in multiple ways. In a review of 119 sex trafficking cases, Farrell and colleagues (2012) found that 35% of survivors had initially been arrested.

In order for cases to be properly identified as human trafficking, investigators must recognize the reasons victims are engaged in illegal activity and believe in the credibility of the victim. When misclassifications occur, they affirm the victims' worst fears and fulfill the prediction victims heard from their trafficker, that the police would not be there to help them (Farrell et al. 2012, 90).

The U.S. Department of State (2012) reported that in 2010, 112 males and 542 females under the age of 18 were arrested for prostitution. In 2012 there were a total of 56,575 prostitution and commercialized vice arrests; 790 were under age 18. The FBI reported that nearly 42,000 people were arrested for prostitution in 2013. All of the cases involving minors should have been handled as sex trafficking cases. Some of the cases with adults may have involved trafficked survivors as well, or those experiencing commercial sexual exploitation (Farrell et al. 2012).

Moreover, of the arrests for prostitution and commercialized vice, 41% were African American, indicating structural disadvantage and marginalization increasing the likelihood of commercial sex involvement, since African Americans only compose 13% of the population. Alternatively, or perhaps additionally, this could indicate higher rates of criminalization of African Americans. Fifty-four percent of those arrested for prostitution were categorized as white; however, Latinos may be included in this category as the FBI deems Latino/a or Hispanic to be an ethnicity, not a race; thus, Latino/as who are Mexican American—the vast majority of Latino/as in the United States—are typically tabulated as white; those of Latin American descent who are Dominican or Haitian are typically tabulated as black. Thus, the "white" statistic represented in FBI and local law enforcement arrest reports conflates Latino/as with "white."

In 2012, of the 790 arrests of juveniles, 319 (40%) were white, including white Hispanic; 461 (58%) were black/African American; none were American Indian or Alaska Native; and 10 were Asian/Pacific Islander. This shows that African American minors who are sex trafficked are disproportionately targeted as criminals rather than as sex trafficking victims, and also shows they are at higher risk (see also chapter 5).[5] In 2010 the FBI reported a total of 62,670 arrests for prostitution and commercialized vice; of them, 19,480 were men, 43,190 were women; 1,040 were juveniles, 61,630 were adults; 33,990 were white, 26,590 were black, 430 were American Indian or Alaska Native, and 1,650 were Asian/Pacific Islander. Thus, the rate of arrest of juveniles for prostitution dropped considerably from 2010 to 2012. Yet the arrest rate for prostitution declined considerably overall, by more than half from 1990–2010, and there was a crime drop among nearly every other crime category.[6] The reasons for the decline in juvenile prostitution arrests are likely multifaceted, including a drop in arrest rates for prostitution overall; a crime drop overall; movement to indoor prostitution advertised on the Internet, making it more difficult to uncover; and perhaps shifts in state law and better awareness and education of officers in sex trafficking.

Juvenile Justice System Responses

While so-called juvenile prostitution is clearly a form of sex trafficking under the TVPA and under state laws, at times youth are charged with prostitution. The result is that DMST survivors are in juvenile justice or detention facilities and rehabilitation programs across the nation (Smith, Vardaman, and Snow 2009). There is a high rate of chronic runaway status among DMST survivors, including running from juvenile facilities. Often individuals want to go back to their trafficker because they think there is a love relationship there. Because girls so frequently run from services, those who work in juvenile justice often charge a survivor with a status offense to keep the individual in lock-down care to prevent her from running back to her trafficker/boyfriend pimp or to preserve safety in light of the "fight or flight" responses typical of trafficking survivors (see chapter 10) (Heil and Nichols 2015; Smith, Vardaman, and Snow 2009). Lock-down-care is a contentious area of debate in the antitrafficking community (Smith 2014). Proponents suggest that it is necessary to keep children safe and to prevent running away and further victimization in the commercial sex industry, and that it provides time to engage the minor in trauma-informed care (see chapter 10). Opponents indicate that it is revictimizing, treats survivors as criminals, increases distrust of law enforcement and social service providers, and reduces the likelihood of accessing services in the future. Heinrich and Sreeharsha (2013) also note that because sex trafficking survivors are often misidentified as criminals, they are not typically screened for referrals to services that could identify and respond to such victimization. Further, they note that even if law enforcement does properly identify survivors as sex trafficking survivors, law enforcement may believe arrest and criminalization is a way of supporting them in order to mandate services.

The long-term impact of this is that "the frequent arrest of sex-trafficking victims only reinforces what traffickers tell their victims—law enforcement will not help you" (Heinrich and Sreeharsha 2013, 4). Yet others suggest that lock-down care should be determined on a case-by-case basis (Smith 2014). An alternative would be a pipeline from the point of identification not into the justice system but into sex trafficking–specific residential services, avoiding arrest through crisis response teams in which an advocate or social worker is paired with plainclothes law enforcement (Heil and Nichols 2015; Nichols and Heil 2014). However, social service options for sex trafficked and exploited people, particularly those with shelter or other housing, are extremely limited across the nation, and availability is scarce relative to the need. In the absence of alternatives, placing trafficked youth in juvenile detention centers or foster care remains the norm (Smith, Vardaman, and Snow 2009). A major problem with this is that the survivor often does not receive any therapeutic services in juvenile facilities and, in particular, the interventions known to work best with this population, such as trauma-informed care, motivational interviewing, use of the stages of change model, mentorship models, and transformational relationships (see chapter 10) (Heil and Nichols 2015; Lloyd 2012).[7]

Safe Harbor

Forty-two states and the District of Columbia hold laws that are consistent with the definition of sex trafficking provided in the TVPA, with no force, fraud, or coercion required for minors in the commercial sex trade. Yet, as indicated earlier, these laws are often improperly enforced and result in the criminalization of sex trafficked minors. As a response to criminalization of sex trafficked youth, many states have enacted Safe Harbor laws, which aim to eliminate the criminalization of minors involved in the commercial sex industry, often supplementing state laws (U.S. Department of State 2013). Safe Harbor laws work to maintain consistency between implementation of state law and the TVPA in that any minor involved in commercial sex is a sex trafficking victim/survivor. Under Safe Harbor, the alternative to criminalization is typically diversion into social services rather than the juvenile court system. Safe Harbor laws vary from state to state and may include increased penalties for traffickers and buyers, the right of survivors to sue their traffickers in a civil suit for damages, legal protections for survivors, provision of services, and a focus on prevention. Some states maintain consistency with the TVPA, implementing dropped or no charges for those under 18, while others use age 14 or 15 as a cut-off point (Polaris Project 2015c). Some states only allow noncriminalization for a first time offense. Charges may still be filed and only dropped once the survivor/victim has completed necessary requirements, such as attending a diversionary program. Safe Harbor laws may work to address the issue that, while state laws criminalize adults who have sex with minors under statutory rape laws, in cases where adults buy sex from minors, the laws are not used (Polaris Project 2015c). Criminalization of the buyers of minors as sex traffickers may be included in Safe Harbor laws in some states. Lack of victim assistance is also addressed through Safe Harbor laws, as "only 32 states and the District of Columbia provided designated victim assistance as part of their anti-trafficking framework" (U.S. Department of State 2014). Newer Safe Harbor acts may be modeled after the Uniform Law Commission's recommendations. This provides uniformity of laws from state to state, which is important because many sex trafficking cases involve multiple states. The majority of states have not yet implemented Safe Harbor laws and, despite the TVPA and even their own state antitrafficking laws, continue to criminalize and revictimize child trafficking victims.

Shifting Legislation to Support Adult Survivors

There is no Safe Harbor for adults, but some cities offer diversion programming, prostitution courts, or a pipeline into services as opposed to incarceration. Some states also include eliminating felony prostitution charges from survivors' criminal records. A serious issue with the criminalization of adults is that a criminal record of prostitution—often multiple charges—makes it much more difficult for the victim to gain legal employment with a criminal record. Paying the associated fines without access to legitimate employment is also problematic. Accordingly, the system is designed in such a way that the consequence is a revolving door back into the commercial sex industry, making it extremely difficult to exit. A law passed in New York State in 2010 allows women who can prove they were coerced into prostitution to have their convictions wiped from their records, which removes barriers to accessing housing and employment. In the Cook County/Chicago area, women who attend Prostitution

Anonymous are not charged with prostitution. States are moving toward eradicating the felony prostitution charge to improve the lives of those who sell sex and to remove the barrier to accessing legitimate employment that a felony record often creates (Heil and Nichols 2015). The New York Human Trafficking Intervention Initiative is an example of an alternative that involves a statewide system of specialized courts that exclusively adjudicate prostitution cases of both minors and adults. The human trafficking courts, with specially trained prosecutors, judges, and defense attorneys, work to break the cycle of arrest and retrafficking/exploitation by diverting away from punitive approaches to offering services and opportunities to address any underlying issues, such as shelter, job skills training, education, substance abuse, or mental health treatment.

Chapter Summary

The criminal justice system plays an important role in addressing sex trafficking victimization. On a legislative level, the TVPA addresses protection, prevention, prosecution, and the monitoring of other nations' activities. Protection largely involves aftercare services and immigration benefits to survivors. Protection efforts are primarily challenged by lack of available services and criminalization of sex trafficked people. Prevention includes efforts to address areas and populations known to be at risk, providing community education and awareness, developing legislation to address identified challenges, and maintaining the national hotline. Prevention efforts are significantly challenged by their limited scope in lack of addressing known high-risk populations. Prosecution efforts aim to remove traffickers from general society to prevent them from trafficking, but these efforts are limited by the evidentiary burden, lack of survivor cooperation, initial misidentification and misreporting by local law enforcement, and a lack of education, awareness, and training of state prosecutors and local law enforcement. State-level laws are expanding but may be challenged by definitional issues and available service provision for survivors. Moreover, many state-level laws and the implementation of such laws present challenges to survivors by criminalizing both juveniles and adults in the commercial sex industry, increasing distrust of law enforcement, and making the break from the trafficker more difficult. Law enforcement lacks the resources to engage in a large number of proactive identification initiatives and is limited to occasional sting operations as funding permits. Implications suggest outreach and prevention efforts to known high-risk populations, increased funding for service provision to survivors, victim/survivor-centered prosecution and investigation techniques, increased education and awareness training for local law enforcement, and the decriminalization of minors and adults who sell sex.

Discussion Questions

1. How does your state rank?

   a. Go to http://www.polarisproject.org/what-we-do/policy-advocacy/national-policy/state-ratings-on-human-trafficking-laws and summarize what your state is doing well on and what your state needs to improve.
   b. Go to http://sharedhope.org/what-we-do/bring-justice/reportcards/2014-reportcards/ and summarize what your state is doing well on and what needs improvement.
   c. Describe any discrepancies between these evaluation systems. What criteria are they using? How would you design a state evaluation system based on the information provided in this chapter? (e.g., what criteria would you use?)

2. According to the TVPA, how is sex trafficking defined? What are some limitations to this definition?

3. List the four prongs of the TVPA and the benefits and challenges associated with each.

[10]

Social Services and Health Care Responses

Sex trafficked and exploited people can and do go on to lead fulfilling lives. Access to social services and resources can be pivotal for persons transitioning out of the commercial sex industry or a trafficking situation by addressing the myriad trauma effects that sex trafficked and exploited people are likely to experience. This chapter explores the practices of those who work with or may come into contact with sex trafficking/commercial sex exploitation (CSE) survivors in the social services and health care sectors. The areas examined include the health care industry, rape and sexual assault services, domestic violence services, child protective services, foster care, and those working with at-risk or homeless youth. Organizations that explicitly work with sex trafficking survivors, commercially sexually exploited youth, or those otherwise exiting the sex industry are also explored. Specifically, this chapter examines avenues for identification within health care and social services, barriers to accessing services, and promising practices in working with sex trafficked/CSE people.

Identification

The benefit and primary purpose of identification is that it is a step toward assistance. The assumption presented across the public discourse, particularly as perpetuated by the media, is the need for "rescue," and identification facilitates "rescue" of the victims who are confined, physically restrained, or those who experience severe force or coercion. This may very well be the case in sex trafficking situations involving abduction and these forms of abuses. However, sex trafficking most commonly allows for a high level of mobility, despite the economic exploitation involved or psychological manipulations. Viewing trafficked/exploited people as unable or unwilling to engage in help seeking is inaccurate in the majority of sex trafficking cases. Research shows that trafficked/exploited people are active in help seeking in a variety of different areas and are able to survive under challenging circumstances (Curtis et al. 2008; Dank et al. 2015). In some cases, such as the less frequently occurring cases in which someone is abducted and forced into the sex industry, identification is the moment survivors have been waiting for. In more typical cases of sex trafficking, such as with boyfriend pimps or survival sex, survivors may actually wish to avoid identification for a number of reasons, such as fear of criminalization or retaliation from the trafficker, but would benefit from access to information and resources.

While some sex trafficked/exploited people may wish to avoid identification, research indicates that a majority of commercially sexually exploited people would exit the commercial sex industry if they had better opportunities. Knowledge of available resources and services facilitates this exit (Curtis et al. 2008; Oselin 2014). Importantly, "bridge" people, such as social service providers, are able to provide expanded choices and resources to assist trafficked/exploited people in help seeking and making life changes, either at the initial point of contact or in the future (Oselin 2014). One multisite study examining four organizations found that "bridge" people are key in facilitating decision making and accessing resources to help people leave the commercial sex industry. Importantly, service providers cannot help sex trafficking/CSE survivors with these expanded choices and increased access to resources if survivors are not identified or do not come forward for assistance (Hopper 2004; Nichols and Heil 2014; Macy and Graham 2012).

Even if an individual is already accessing some form of social services, social service providers cannot provide appropriate needs-based services such as trauma-informed care (TIC) without knowledge of the sex trafficking/CSE (Macy and Graham 2012). Consequently, outreach among at-risk populations and increased identification within health care and social service provision is called for. Survivors are not commonly identified by service providers, but research suggests survivors frequently access social services and health care (Macy and Graham 2012; Curtis et al. 2008). Many times health care and social service providers are interacting with trafficked/CSE people without knowing it (Curtis et al. 2008; Kotrla 2010; Macy and Graham 2012; Nichols and Heil 2014).

Rebecca J. Macy and Laurie M. Graham (2012) conducted a content analysis of research articles, organizational documents, and antitrafficking websites and found commonly reported indicators to identify sex trafficking/CSE in social services or health care settings. These indicators included signs that a person is being controlled, signs that a person does not have freedom of movement, and signs of physical abuse, fearfulness, and/or depression (Macy and Graham 2012). Such indicators are widely reported on antitrafficking websites and organizational materials. Some of these indicators are problematic because it is not always readily apparent when someone is being controlled, and survivors often do not want to disclose their abuse. It is also well documented that the vast majority of sex trafficking survivors do have freedom of movement; restrictions on movement resulting from coercive control are not typically visible. While some trafficked/exploited people experience physical abuse, others do not, or the signs may not be in visible places. Fearfulness may not be displayed either, particularly by those engaging in survival sex. Using only the commonly reported indicators, those in health care and social services will identify only a small fraction of sex trafficking/exploitation.

Psychological indicators, such as signs of depression, anxiety, dissociation, and trauma, prove to be more promising indicators as research indicates an increased presence of these conditions among individuals in the commercial sex industry regardless of the type of trafficking experienced. The commonly reported indicators also coincide with other areas of abuse as well as sex trafficking/CSE, such as child sexual abuse and intimate partner violence, problematizing identification specifically of sex trafficking/CSE (Cole et al. 2014). Even so, these areas are just as important to identify, and, if present, the additional trauma within the overlapping areas related to the trafficking/CSE may come out in treatment. In many cases, it is impossible and problematic to separate the trafficking/CSE from other forms of exploitation and abuse that are experienced simultaneously. Backgrounds with multiple sources of trauma are not uncommon among sex trafficking survivors, such as child abuse or neglect, child sexual abuse, intimate partner violence, bullying, parental rejection, refugee status, and more. Individual cases and needs will vary according to the type of trafficking/exploitation the individual has undergone. The experiences of those who are abducted are distinct from the experiences of those with trauma bonds to a boyfriend pimp or those engaging in survival sex. Moreover, sex trafficking victimization of international trafficking survivors, while in many ways similar to those of domestically trafficked people, can be quite distinct, such as for refugees or in cases where the trafficker has organized crime connections to the survivors' family and home community in the country of origin. Accordingly, identification through routine screening and assessment is complex and difficult to address.

Aside from the general indicators, child/youth-specific indicators uncovered in Macy and Graham's research (2012) may also hold more promise. Child/youth-specific indicators for identification include chronic runaway status, chronic truancy or absences from school, untruthfulness when asked about age, possessing hotel room keys, holding a fake ID, involvement with a "boyfriend" who is much older (not school-age), dressing inappropriately for the season, talking about sexual activities that exceed age-group norms, extensive knowledge of the commercial sex industry, signs of physical abuse or substance abuse, and appearing fearful, anxious, or depressed. Many of these indicators are corroborated by multiple original research studies (Reid 2010; Curtis et al. 2008; Heil and Nichols 2015; Lloyd 2012). At the same time, these indicators may not be uniformly present and may not be present in all types of sex trafficking/CSE.

In terms of primary identification, available research suggests that building trust and rapport is key when asking someone about their victimization (Macy and Graham 2012). However, often interactions involving initial identification are limited. Building trust and rapport in a short time is admittedly challenging. Importantly, asking survivors questions must only occur when that person is alone, as survivors are not likely to disclose abuse when their trafficker or a partner of their trafficker is present. Words associated with sex trafficking, such as "force," "coercion," "trafficking," and "slavery," as well as other words used in the antitrafficking arena like "handler," "controller," or "trafficker" should be avoided because the vast majority of sex trafficked/exploited people are not likely to identify with those terms (Macy and Graham 2012; Smith 2014).[1] In cases involving survivors who are from other countries and who have limited English-speaking abilities, using a translator who is educated in trauma care is extremely important in order to communicate as effectively as possible. Most important, the survivor's safety is vital. Preferably, a social worker with expertise in TIC and safety planning should be on site in any location in health or social services to both ask assessment and intake questions and to create safety plans if necessary. Such individuals have the expertise to do so. For example, in many hospitals, there are social workers or advocates on site who are educated in dynamics of intimate partner abuse. When a doctor, nurse, or staff member suspects a patient is experiencing some form of intimate partner abuse, the social worker is asked to speak to the individual and offer assistance and resources. This model shows promise in similarly identifying and responding to sex trafficking/CSE. Survivor-defined advocacy should accompany this practice. The survivors' goals and needs are most important, not a report to law enforcement or a potential prosecution. While justice system involvement might fit the needs of some survivors, for others it might not. Accordingly, calling the National Human Trafficking Resource Center's hotline or calling local law enforcement or anyone else should be a matter of individual choice (Macy and Graham 2012; Nichols and Heil 2014). When minors are involved, this becomes more complex. Service providers should be clear about confidentiality and mandatory reporting throughout service provision. Arguably, children do not have the same capacity as adults to make informed choices, and practice should be guided accordingly.

Identification is the first step in offering appropriate services to the survivor. The point of identification is to provide an opportunity to provide treatment and resources to assist sex trafficked/CSE people, not to force someone into legal or social services. Working to identify CSE/trafficking could be pivotal in a person's life, to help them leave their exploitive situation and get treatment and resources to live a life free from such exploitation and trauma if they choose. The primary aim of identification from a social services standpoint is to offer services to people who want them, or to at least make it known that such services are available for immediate or future use. Even if the individual does not initially want to make a change, identification and outreach is still important, as research shows that knowledge of available resources for future use also provides benefit (Oselin 2014). The following sections highlight identification in specific settings, namely, health care and social services.

Health Care Settings

Research indicates that sex trafficked and exploited people often access multiple public services before coming forward or otherwise being identified. Such spaces hold promise in the potential to identify victims and to offer assistance (Curtis et al. 2008; Farrell et al. 2012; Smith, Vardaman, and Snow 2009; Smith 2014). One facet of public services that sex trafficked/exploited people are likely to access is health care. Multiple prosecuted cases have been uncovered because a trafficked/exploited person visited the hospital. Health care settings offer much potential in identifying and offering services to sexually trafficked or exploited people.

Emergency rooms in particular offer important sites for identification. Sex trafficked people are less likely to have health insurance, indicated by the presence of increased associated risk factors such as poverty, homelessness, and temporary or illegal migrant status. Emergency rooms are one of the most common places for the uninsured to go for health care because they are required to treat those who come seeking health care. As a result, trafficked/CSE people may go to emergency rooms to treat even seemingly innocuous illnesses, like respiratory infections, sore throats, or sinus infections. Trafficked/exploited people may also go to emergency rooms to get treatment for serious physical injuries as a result of physical abuses from their pimps/traffickers, such as sprains, breaks, contusions, and cuts. In addition to injuries received from pimps, there is a large body of research that finds increased victimization associated with selling sex, including physical violence such as aggravated assault, rape, and sexual assault at the hands of clients or other violent people seeking an easy target. In addition to physical injuries and minor illnesses, emergency rooms may see cases of drug overdose among trafficked/CSE individuals.

Health care facilities that work with substance abuse issues are important contact points for survivors. Multiple studies show that sex trafficked/exploited people are disproportionately likely to have substance abuse problems that may have led to their exploitation or may be the result of their exploitation and consequent self-medication (Cole et al. 2014; Heil and Nichols 2015; Oselin 2014). Accidental or purposeful overdose—a form of attempted suicide—may be reasons why a trafficked/exploited person goes to the emergency room. Multiple studies show a relatively high attempted suicide rate among those in the sex industry, ranging from 46% to 75% (Parriot 1994; Joiner et al. 2009; Kidd and Kral 2002). Emergency room nurses and doctors are among the first to provide care to those who have attempted suicide. In addition to areas of the hospital that care for patients with suicide attempts, areas of the hospital specializing in behavioral and mental health issues are positioned to identify sex trafficking/exploitation (as well as other sources of trauma) as trafficked/CSE individuals are disproportionately likely have symptoms of trauma, depression, anxiety, and dissociation (Cole et al. 2014).

In addition to mental health care, individuals may seek care for reproductive health, including sexually transmitted infections (STI), access to contraception, unplanned pregnancy, and check-ups. A trafficked/exploited person may come to the emergency room, a free health clinic, a medical van, or Planned Parenthood to get treatment for an STI. Research indicates that selling sex is associated with a higher rate of STIs. For example, Ric Curtis and colleagues (2008) found that about one-fifth of their sample had contracted an STI, and many youth test for STIs every six months. Trafficked/exploited people may also seek treatment in some of these health care settings for an unplanned pregnancy or check-ups. One study found CSE girls reported regular obstetrician/gynecologist (OBGYN) visits, with half visiting an OBGYN within six months prior to the study (Curtis et al. 2008). Curtis and colleagues (2008) also found that the majority of youth in the commercial sex industry use contraception. Three-quarters reported that they always used contraception, and nearly a quarter said they almost always used condoms or other prophylactics.

Expanded training in identifying signs of trafficking/CSE is recommended in health care settings, for doctors and nurses as well as organization staff. This is particularly the case in emergency rooms and areas of the hospital that treat substance abuse and mental health issues. Referral to an on-site social worker is recommended when possible. Places that offer harm reduction, such as direct outreach and drop-in services, where individuals can get access to free condoms or clean needles, are other areas that may provide avenues for identification. In addition to training to recognize potential signs, related intake or medical assessment should include questions that would allow for a survivor to disclose abuse. Importantly, such questions must be asked in a culturally competent, trauma-informed way by a social worker educated in such areas. The goal of identification in such circumstances is to offer choices and services (Smith 2014). There are some areas related to health care that overlap with other services in the community. For example, while sometimes sex trafficked and exploited people who experience rape and sexual assault access hospitals for assistance, others will go to rape crisis centers for care.

Social Service Settings

Rape and Sexual Assault Services

Because those who sell sex are disproportionately raped and sexually assaulted, rape and sexual assault services is another point of contact for identification. Some research indicates that sex trafficking/CSE is sometimes misidentified by police as rape or sexual assault because trafficking/CSE also co-occurs with these crimes (Nichols and Heil 2014). Data regarding rates of rape specifically among sex trafficked people is unavailable. However, research indicates that among commercial sex workers on the street level, between 68% and 80% of women report being raped. Individuals working in sexual assault and rape crisis centers as well as those in health care settings (e.g., advocates in hospitals, sexual assault nurse examiners) should receive training in identifying sex trafficking that co-occurs with rape or sexual assault in situations where the survivor is involved in the sex industry because they may be at higher risk of being involved in a trafficking situation (Heil and Nichols 2014; also see Macy and Graham 2012). When sex trafficking is identified, it can guide appropriate services, such as TIC, or referral to sex trafficking–specific services. Rape and sexual assault among those in the sex industry is perpetrated by clients, police officers, or community members. Yet at times rape and sexual assault is perpetrated by an intimate partner who is also sex trafficking the survivor. Consequently, intimate partner violence (IPV) services are another area of identification and provision of services; survivors may use such services in order to access resources to assist in responding to multiple forms of abuse.

Intimate Partner Violence Victim Advocacy Services

Because a relatively large proportion of sex trafficked/CSE people in the United States are pimped by a boyfriend, IPV victim services are an obvious point of contact for sex trafficked/CSE people. Multiple studies show that sex trafficking is often an extension of abuse in intimate partner relationships in what is typically referred to as "the boyfriend pimp" form of sex trafficking (Heil and Nichols 2015; Lloyd 2012; Nichols and Heil 2014; Raphael, Reichert, and Powers 2010; Reid 2011; Smith, Vardaman, and Snow 2009; Smith 2014; Martin et al. 2014). Rebecca Macy and Laurie Graham (2012) found that survivors of sex trafficking/CSE accessed IPV services as a form of help seeking. As such, Macy and Graham (2012) suggest that domestic violence service providers should receive training in order to better identify and respond to sex trafficking/CSE survivors seeking assistance. As a result of the battered women's movement beginning in the late 1960s and carrying over into the present day, services for women have greatly expanded. Domestic violence victim advocates and social workers are now found in hospitals, police departments, courthouses, drop-in centers, outreach agencies, transitional housing, nonresidential services, and shelters (Nichols 2014a).

Understanding the legal definitions of sex trafficking and the labeling of the domestic violence–prostitution link as sex trafficking is important for those working with IPV survivors because it may expand available choices, such as legal or social service benefits. Advocates and social workers could potentially recommend a trafficking charge, or an application for a T or U visa, as a tool to assist the survivors they work with if individual survivors determined it served their best interests. Training of social workers and advocates in this area of identification also holds implications for service provision, in that awareness of the increased likelihood of posttraumatic stress disorder (PTSD) or complex trauma associated with CSE could help to identify the best treatment for a particular survivor, in collaboration with that survivor. If the survivor is under 18, social workers and domestic violence advocates are typically bound by mandatory reporting laws and must work with the survivor to see what the survivor's best options are. Child protective services will typically become involved at that point.

Child Protective Services, Juvenile Justice, and Foster Care

Research indicates that many sex trafficked people have multiple interactions with child protective services, the juvenile justice system, and foster care. In many cases the interactions with these institutions are interrelated. A disproportionate number of sex trafficked youth come from problematic home lives and experience child physical or sexual abuse as well as neglect or substance abuse, or they may witness fathers or mother's boyfriends abusing their mothers within the home (Heil and Nichols 2015; Raphael and Myers-Powell 2010; Smith, Vardaman, and Snow 2009). This often leads to runaway or truancy behaviors, which then increases the likelihood of the child going into the juvenile justice system or foster care (Heil and Nichols 2015; Smith, Vardaman, and Snow 2009). If the family home is seen as unfit for the child, the child will be placed in foster care or a juvenile detention facility, which increases vulnerability to sex trafficking/CSE. Research indicates that these places are frequently sites of recruitment into pimp-controlled prostitution. Alternatively, a child may run away from a problematic home life and may be picked up by police for engaging in the commercial sex industry, either induced by a pimp or as survival sex; the child would then go into the juvenile justice system and then may get placed through child protective services into foster care and become retrafficked or may even recruit other girls for a pimp (Heil and Nichols 2015; Reid 2015). These three institutions, child protective services, juvenile justice, and foster care, are intertwined in the lives of many sex trafficking survivors.

Jennifer Cole and colleagues (2014) suggest screening for CSE in juvenile justice facilities. Repeated runaway status is a risk factor for trafficking, and youth in these circumstances often end up in the juvenile justice system for a status offense, such as running away, curfew violations, or truancy. Unfortunately, research indicates that the criminalization of youth involved in selling sex is the typical response, despite the U.S. Trafficking Victims Protection Act's proclamation of inherent sex trafficking victimization among all youth engaged in commercial sex (Cole et al. 2014; Smith, Vardaman, and Snow 2009; Smith 2014). Survivors and service providers indicate that criminalization can be revictimizing, it increases the likelihood of trauma symptoms, and it makes it more likely that such youth will not receive appropriate treatment (Cole et al. 2014; Heil and Nichols 2015; Smith 2014). Importantly, criminalization can also lead to distrust of social services and law enforcement, serving as a barrier to identification, future help seeking, and consequent treatment (Smith 2014).

Some researchers suggest screening for trauma using a trauma inventory, such as the Traumatic Events Screening Inventory or the Child Welfare Trauma Screening Tool (Cole et al. 2014). Such inventories would identify commercial sexual exploitation with the aim of getting the child proper trauma-informed, sex trafficking–specific treatment (Cole et al.

2014; Heil and Nichols 2015). At the same time, this screening is not infallible. Youths may be reluctant to disclose sexual abuse and CSE that has not already been uncovered or disclosed to the juvenile justice system. As survivor Holly Austin Smith (2014) explains, this is intensely personal and not something a young person feels comfortable talking about with just anyone, particularly a person that the child does not trust. Further, Cole and colleagues point out that youth may not see their own experiences as sexually exploitive, which might cause the assessment to be inaccurate. These researchers also state, "Screening for commercial sex may be most effective when conducted by a clinician who has developed rapport with a child" (Cole et al. 2014). As described earlier in this chapter, screening is best performed by someone with the expertise to do it correctly, such as a social worker trained in TIC. As discussed later in this chapter, social work practice with youth is distinct, and particular methods may be more useful with this population (see also box 10.1). If the sex trafficking/CSE that youth experience is not identified and treated within child protective services, foster care, or the juvenile justice system, many remain homeless and sell sex to survive or continue working for a pimp.

Youth-Serving Organizations

Other important areas for identification are agencies that work with homeless youth, such as youth-serving drop-in centers, youth shelters, and those who conduct street outreach to homeless youth or specifically to sex workers who sell sex on the street. Youth-service organizations vary in their form and the services they offer across the country. Services that may be offered include basic needs like food, clothing, shelter, and showers as well as counseling, job search assistance, job training, legal assistance, medical care, and life skills training (Curtis et al. 2008). Multiple research studies find that a large proportion of trafficked people who engage in survival sex experience homelessness or lead an otherwise transient life (Curtis et al. 2008; Heil and Nichols 2015; Martin et al. 2014; Urban Institute 2014). As a result, those who work with such populations are in a position to engage in outreach to identify and consequently assist those who want or are in need of help, including treatment, resources, and legal options.

While youth are trafficked and exploited, it is important to recognize that they simultaneously express agency. Agency is expressed through figuring out day-to-day survival, of which commercial sex may be seen as the best available option as well as the source of their trafficking/CSE. Part of this survival is also help seeking. Running away might be a manifestation of help seeking and survival as well as the trafficking/exploitation itself. Accessing youth-serving organizations is another method of help seeking among homeless youth. One study in New York found nearly two-thirds of CSE youth had accessed a youth-services program at some point (Curtis et al. 2008). Among the youth population of New York City who were selling sex, nearly a third indicated that they had used emergency, month-long, and three-month-long youth shelters and had visited youth-service agencies for food and counseling (Curtis et al. 2008). Yet many returned to the streets because there were few shelters and limited bed space. Some youth also indicated that they went to agencies to hang out with friends in a safe space. Moreover, youth indicated that they had built relationships with staff and counselors at youth-serving agencies in NYC (Curtis et al. 2008). Erin Heil and Andrea Nichols (2015) found similar dynamics in St. Louis, suggesting that youth-serving agencies offer an opportunity for transformational relationships (see box 10.1). Accordingly, it is important that youth-serving organizations provide information about resources to assist youth in getting out of sex trafficking/CSE situations. Despite efforts toward identification, significant barriers to services have been identified in research across the United States.

Barriers to Accessing Services

Barriers to accessing services include a lack of sex trafficking–specific services, shelter, or residential treatment as well as a lack of services providing for other basic needs. In addition, substance abuse, trauma bonds, stigma and criminalization of commercial sex, service providers' lack of cultural competency, and a lack of identification documents serve as barriers to service utilization as well. These barriers can be confounded by identity-based discrimination and other factors, such as discrimination targeting race, class, sexual orientation, immigrant status, or gender identity and expression. In many areas the demand for services exceeds the availability of services (Heil and Nichols 2015). Lack of available services is a significant barrier to help seeking. As indicated in the previous chapter, while

BOX 10.1
Relationships in Therapy

In order to make change with a client, the one variable I rely on the most is the therapeutic alliance I have with an individual. The relationship I have as a therapist with my clients is of upmost importance for making a difference and is especially vital when working with someone who is healing from a complex trauma.

Since complex traumas, especially those like sex trafficking and commercial sexual exploitation, take place inside a relationship, the healing and interventions used also need to be seated within a relationship. The research on the efficacy of clinical interventions since the 1970s has all pointed to the same thing, that 70% of change is based on the relationship a client has with a service provider and only 30% is dependent on the actual techniques a therapist uses.

It goes without saying that a relationship with a client is different from the other types of relationships a service provider has in their life. A strong therapeutic alliance is going to need trust and accountability on both ends, just like other relationships; however, it must also be trauma informed and client centered.

Working from a trauma-informed framework for building relationships with clients will help service providers to first understand the impact trauma can have on an individual's development as well as explain behaviors that might otherwise not make sense. In addition, it reduces the risk of the service provider retraumatizing a client. Building a relationship on a foundation that is trauma informed is the first step in being able to eventually engage the client in interventions that will help to reduce trauma symptoms and increase their ability to self-regulate.

Furthermore, keeping the relationship client centered is vital for building trust in the therapeutic alliance. Being client centered ensures that the therapist is taking into account the client's preferences, beliefs, and needs verses trying to fit the client into the services or framework that the therapist prefers. A client-centered approach puts the therapist in the role of "learner" to the client, which not only builds trust and safety for the client but also empowers them and allows them to experience a sense of healthy control that was nonexistent in the exploitive situation. The client-centered approach also helps the therapist to focus on the "real" versus the "ideal." When dealing with complex trauma, it is not uncommon to see high recidivism rates, which can lead to burnout in a therapist who is focused on goals that she wants the client to meet. When the therapist focuses on the client, the client's goals, and what is realistic, a therapist will more easily be able to walk alongside a client and continue building rapport.

The relationship will also make the interventions more effective. Take, for example, my experience working with "C" a 19-year-old survivor of commercial sexual exploitation who was being prostituted out of a car wash. By using trauma-informed care and a client-centered approach, I was able to begin forming a relationship with the client. This allowed me to use the technique of motivational interviewing in order to increase my alliance with her and increase the client's willingness to use services with a street outreach program. The intervention on its own might have fallen short, but when used with the strong rapport, the intervention had more sticking power with the client.

—Abby Howard, MSW, LCSW, Youth in Need

the TVPA called for the protection of victims, funding for victim services has not been prioritized relative to efforts toward identification and prosecution (Smith, Vardaman, and Snow 2009). This is problematic because once a survivor has been identified and is in need of services, services must be available. Heil and Nichols (2015) found that service providers reported identifying trafficked/exploited youth but did not always have somewhere to send them to access shelter or other housing that was sex trafficking–specific. There are only twenty-nine organizations in the United States that provide services for women exiting the sex industry, and thirty-eight organizations nationwide that serve sex trafficked girls under 18 (Heil and Nichols 2015; Oselin 2014). The majority are not residential services. Moreover, services to men and boys and those who identify as gay males or transgender people are extremely limited. Typically, homeless shelters or drop-in centers are the only available options. There is a lack of services for those of marginalized identities; inability to access services based on immigrant status is another related barrier.

If someone's first language is not English, and if that person has limited English-speaking ability, this can be a barrier to accessing services. Trying to get information about resources with limited or no ability to read the language is challenging. If an organization is accessed, trying to speak with individuals in order to get services is similarly challenging. Individuals without proof of legal identity also experience heightened difficulty accessing services (Kurtz et al. 2005). Various public services often—not always—require proof of identity and citizenship to access services. This poses a barrier, particularly for sex trafficking survivors who are undocumented. For example, Kurtz and colleagues (2005) found in Miami that illegal immigrants selling sex who were not able to provide identification faced difficulty accessing services. The same study also found that those who lived on the streets for a long time did not have a valid address; many did not have a driver's license and did not have a social security card or did not know where it was. Consequently, inability to access identification documents posed a barrier to citizens who were trafficked as well.

In addition, not knowing one's rights as a victim/survivor, either international or domestic, might serve as a barrier (Macy and Johns 2011). This is intertwined with a history of others viewing victims as criminals and bearing the social stigma of involvement in the commercial sex industry or being an illegal immigrant (Hopper 2004; Kurtz et al. 2005; Lutnick 2009). Stigma associated with selling sex and with substance abuse is also identified as a barrier to accessing services, and accessing appropriate services. Kurtz writes that "women often attempt to hide their sex work and drug use to increase the likelihood of receiving services although, in fact, hiding the very aspects of their lives that most harm their health is self-defeating because providers may well remain unaware of their greatest needs for care" (Kurtz et al. 2005, 355). Heil and Nichols (2015) report a lack of access to substance abuse treatment is also a barrier to accessing services and exiting the commercial sex industry. Many shelters have rules about being drug-free in order to access shelters. Fear of arrest, fines, or jail also serve as a barrier to accessing assistance (Lutnick 2009; Kurtz et al. 2005). Linda Smith, Samantha Vardaman, and Melissa Snow (2009) indicate that youth survivors may not be able to access services because of criminalization and resulting detention.

Another barrier to identification and accessing services is misguided antitrafficking awareness and outreach campaigns. Outreach and community awareness initiatives often depict adolescent girls in chains, or with bar codes on their heads, using the language of modern-day slavery or sex trafficking (Heil and Nichols 2015). While perhaps useful for drawing attention and public and political support to the issue, the danger is that community awareness campaigns are funded in part to increase identification through citizen tips. If ordinary citizens think sex trafficking typically involves ropes, chains, inhibited freedom of movement, or branding, then they will not recognize suspicious circumstances to report a tip (Heil and Nichols 2015). Such images project the perception of the "ideal victim," and those who fall outside of that image may not be labeled as victims/survivors in need of assistance. Author and survivor Holly Austin Smith (2014, 36) recalled posters in antitrafficking campaigns "of little girls crying, some in pigtails and some holding teddy bears with slogans touting lost innocence. *This was not me.* By eighth grade I was angry, undisciplined, and sexually active. Did this make me less of a victim?" Other researchers have problematized notions of the ideal victim as well, illustrating that individuals who do not meet the image of the ideal victim, like Holly, are less likely to be identified and viewed as in need of care and may be criminalized instead (Hoyle, Bosworth, and Dempsey 2011). Accordingly, identification using these images as criteria will only capture a small fraction of sex trafficking/CSE.

In addition to mischaracterizing typical cases of sex trafficking and reducing the likelihood of tips from ordinary citizens, there is also a negative impact when such images are used in direct outreach to survivors, and survivors are speaking out about this. For example, Smith stated, "If an anti-trafficking advocate had reached out to me on the street and used the words 'trafficking' or 'slavery,' I would have turned up my nose. If someone offering street outreach showed me pictures of kids in chains, I would have told them they were talking to the wrong person" (Smith 2014, 98–99). Outreach materials have to be relatable to the people they are intended to reach out to. This might include not using legal terminology, like "sex trafficking," or using language intended to draw attention to the issue, such as "modern-day slavery." Language such as "selling sex" or "trading sex," along with "looking for other options?" is more relatable to those involved in both survival sex and pimp-controlled prostitution. For example, the Polaris Project recently developed a new outreach poster with the language "Get help to get out. I did. I was caught in the life and I thought there was no way out. Then I found help." This wording was accompanied by a nonsensationalistic image. Following an intersectional perspective, images must also be diverse and reflect the populations they are intended to reach. For example, most images are of white girls. Yet young men and boys make up a substantial portion of those trafficked in street-level commercial sex (Curtis et al. 2008; Heil and Nichols 2015).

African American, Latina/o, Native American, and transgender women and girls are disproportionately victimized in sex trafficking. Accordingly, their images should appear on outreach materials, particularly in areas known to exploit these individuals. Additional barriers to accessing services can be found in chapter 5.

Aftercare

Research indicates that basic needs are among the myriad of needs a sex trafficking/CSE survivor may have, and meeting these needs are essential to exiting the commercial sex industry (Dank et al. 2015; Kurtz et al. 2005; Macy and Johns 2011). Steven Kurtz and colleagues (2005), following interviews with 586 sex workers in Miami, Florida, identified basic needs as shelter, access to drinking water, transportation, crisis intervention, and drug detox. Noël Busch-Armendariz, Maura Busch Nsonwu, and Laurie Cook Heffron (2014) add safety, crisis intervention, and trauma-informed mental health services to the list of basic needs. In a content analysis of available research studies and organizational documents, Macy and Johns (2011) list crisis safety services, shelter services, language services, emergency medical care, and crisis legal advocacy among the immediate needs of sex trafficked people.

Means for survival, like food, shelter, medical treatment, and clothing, must be discussed with survivors to assist in finding resources to meet these basic needs (Hardy, Compton, and McPhatter 2013). A lack of options in meeting basic needs is a primary barrier to leaving a sex trafficking/ CSE situation (Hardy, Compton, and McPhatter 2013; Lloyd 2012). Many survivors of sex trafficking/CSE have substance abuse issues and may need detox as a part of initial care as well. Curtis and colleagues (2008) reported that more than 80% of commercially sexually exploited youth in their study said they would do something else if they had better options. Accordingly, the inability to otherwise meet immediate or basic needs is a catalyst to both entering and perpetuating sex trafficking. Veronica L. Hardy, Kevin D. Compton, and Veronica S. McPhatter (2013) suggest the development of goals within service provision to address both immediate needs and aftercare needs. Importantly, the emotional, physical, and psychological consequences of sex trafficking are directly related to the aftercare needs of survivors.

Promising Practices

Promising practices for social service provision include TIC, survivor-informed care, survivor-defined/client-centered practice, cultural competency or intersectional practice, strengths-based practice, the stages of change model, community-based responses (CBR), the single point-of-contact model, motivational interviewing, sex trafficking–specific services, transformational relationships, safety planning, eye movement desensitization and reprocessing (EMDR), and cognitive behavioral therapy. Note that many of these practices overlap or are interrelated, and this is not an exhaustive list. Some of these practices are thought to work best with sex trafficked/CSE youth who are sex trafficked by a boyfriend pimp or who sell sex to survive. In turn, some of these approaches will not likely be appropriate for someone who is abducted or forced into commercial sex trafficking.

Trauma Effects

Psychological trauma manifesting as complex PTSD, suicidal ideation, anxiety, depression, dissociation, substance abuse, or trauma bonds is implicated in sex trafficking victimization, which impacts well-being, development, trust, impulse control, and future relationships (Cole et al. 2014; Hardy, Compton, and McPhatter 2013; Heil and Nichols 2015; Williamson, Dutch, and Clawson 2008; Clawson, Dutch, and Williamson 2008). Complex trauma can also result in "disorganized memories, inability to self-soothe, attachment problems, and difficulties with appropriate interpersonal boundaries" (Cole et al. 2014). Trauma responses typical of sex trafficking/CSE also include fight-or-flight reactions to triggering events or stimuli (Heil and Nichols 2015).

The trauma that sex trafficked people experience is distinct in that it involves repeated exposure to traumatic events that are difficult or impossible to avoid. Heil and Nichols (2015) note that sex trafficking trauma is unique because it is perpetrated by a larger number of people, such as traffickers/pimps and multiple buyers, and over an extended period of time. Furthermore, the trauma is repeated daily and often is facilitated by a loved one—a boyfriend, parent, or other caregiver. Cole and colleagues (2014) note that sex trafficking–related trauma is not only unique in its form but distinct in its heightened symptoms. The researchers compared the trauma of commercial sexual exploitation of children (CSEC) to the trauma of sexually assaulted youth with otherwise similar backgrounds and found that exploitation in commercial sex elicited heightened trauma symptoms compared to other types of sexual abuse. Cole and colleagues (2014, 14) also found "that involvement in commercial sex, over and above the effects of sexual abuse and assault, is associated with emotional, developmental, psychological, and behavioral dysregulation in those involved." The primary difference between the two comparison groups in this study is that youth involved in commercial sex "had significantly higher overall scores on the UCLA PTSD-RI [i.e., PTSD symptoms], and on the subscales measuring avoidance and hyperarousal compared with the matched group, [which] suggests that exploitation in commercial sex may have unique effects on youth's trauma symptoms, which may require modifications to treatment" (Cole et al. 2014, 16). In addition to increased avoidance, hyperarousal, and PTSD, dissociation is also an effect of sex trafficking/CSE. Dissociation is a survival response to traumatic stress in which an individual distances oneself during and following traumatic events by compartmentalizing or burying memories of traumatic events. Such individuals may even detach from consciousness while experiencing the trauma or may describe out-of-body experiences (Cole et al. 2014; Roe-Sepowitz 2012). Dissociation is a coping or survival mechanism, but it is an unhealthy coping mechanism, as individuals are distanced from their trauma in a way that allows it to continue unaddressed and results in negative psychological effects. In addition to heightened trauma, certain types of sex trafficking may include distinct or additional trauma.

In cases involving sex trafficking as an extension of IPV such as with the boyfriend pimp, trauma bonds, also called Stockholm syndrome, must also be addressed through trauma-informed therapy. This adds another layer of complexity to treatment. At times survivors might defend or protect their pimps/traffickers/boyfriends. Generally speaking, trauma bonds most likely occur in cases where there is a perception of threat to one's survival, isolation from others, or a perceived inability to leave the situation. Regardless of other victimization, and even if the victimization is caused by the trafficker/pimp, a trauma bond may form if the trafficker provides some affection, kindness, or material items related to survival. In addition, threats of harm, threats of harm to loved ones, physical violence, and economic abuse are additional traumas that sex trafficked/CSE individuals may experience at the hands of the boyfriend pimp (Heil and Nichols 2015; Hopper 2004; Heffernan and Blythe 2014). These are all "textbook" elements of the boyfriend pimp. Importantly, CSE often involves feelings of guilt, shame, stigma, and nonacceptance from others in society, but the pimp will always accept the survivor. As one survivor stated in the documentary *Very Young Girls*, "I'll always have him" (Schisgall and Alvarez 2008).

Sex trafficked/CSE youth can be challenging survivors to work with (Cole et al. 2014; Hardy, Compton, and McPhatter 2013; Heil and Nichols 2015; Smith, Vardaman, and Snow 2009; Smith 2014). The disruption of development caused by complex trauma makes this so, and this can even create a barrier and aversion to effective therapy. As a result, it is important to make complex trauma therapy a centerpiece of therapy for youth in order to respond as effectively as possible to sex trafficking/CSE (Cole et al. 2014; Heil and Nichols 2015; Smith, Vardaman, and Snow 2009). Cole and colleagues (2014, 20) found that "treatment goals must target these issues of trust, intimacy, and safety, and service environments must offer refuge from exploitive, unsafe conditions if recovery is to occur." Heil and Nichols (2015) also found that issues of trust, intimacy, and safety as well as shame and guilt were key points to address in treatment—for youth as well as adults. The ability to gain trust in any relationship is undermined by repeated trauma from multiple people over a period of time.

While research studies find multiple forms of trauma and PTSD present among trafficked/exploited people, less is known about trauma-informed therapy among this population. Kristin Heffernan and Betty Blythe (2014) conducted a study with sex trafficking survivors in which service providers adapted a survivor-centered model to include TIC. The study found that, of seven survivors in one organization who received this care, feedback from all survivors indicated that "they feel safe, respected, and confident to live independently in an environment of their choosing" (Heffernan and Blythe 2014, 1). Heil and Nichols (2015) examined social work practice with trafficked/CSE people, and social service providers indicated that TIC was an effective approach. However, this work is extremely limited and lacks adequate evaluation of both short-term and long-term outcomes specifically among sex trafficked/CSE populations. At the same time, this is absolutely an evidence-based practice with other areas of trauma exposure (Jordan 2010; Edmond, Sloan, and McCarty 2004; Schubert and Lee 2009; Mendelsohn et al. 2011; Fritch and Lynch 2008). Additional components of TIC, such as EMDR and cognitive behavioral therapy also offer promising avenues for practice (See boxes 10.2 and 10.3).

BOX 10.2
Using EMDR with Survivors of Sex Trafficking

One of the most highly researched and effective trauma treatments available is eye movement desensitization and reprocessing (EMDR). It has been found to be effective in treating PTSD, depression, and anxiety in survivors of child sexual abuse, sexual assault, and intimate partner abuse. In addition, specialized treatment protocols have been developed to use EMDR with complex trauma survivors struggling with borderline personality disorder, dissociative disorder, attachment disorders, and substance abuse disorders. Because these are common diagnoses for sex trafficking survivors, and because sex trafficking survivors often experience child sexual abuse, sexual assault, and intimate partner abuse, a strong case can be made for using this evidence-based trauma treatment with survivors of sex trafficking.

The basic treatment structure involves eight phases that incorporate a three-pronged approach that targets past traumatic events, current trauma triggers, and future possible challenges. It incorporates elements of psychodynamic, cognitive-behavioral, and body-centered psychotherapies, making it easy to integrate into a wide range of clinical approaches.

After obtaining a thorough client history and providing psychoeducation on trauma and the process of EMDR therapy, an assessment is conducted on the target event that is generating distress. This involves identifying the core elements of the traumatic experience that need to be processed to facilitate resolution. The client is asked to identify an image that best represents the distressing memory, to describe the primary negative self-belief connected to that image, and a desired alternative positive self-belief. With the image in mind, the client is asked to describe the primary emotion they feel and to scan their body for any physical sensations that might also be present. Once the image, thoughts, feelings, and physical sensations related to the trauma have been activated, desensitization is initiated by the therapist facilitating bilateral stimulation though eye movements, hand taps, or alternating auditory sounds delivered through head phones. The client is instructed to "just notice whatever happens" during bilateral stimulation, which only lasts for about twenty to thirty seconds at a time. The therapist then will ask the client to report whatever came up for them, which might be a thought, a body sensation, an image or a feeling. That then becomes the focal point for the next set of bilateral stimulation. This form of processing continues with periodic checks to assess the level of distress the target memory is generating, which will usually decrease during the session. The number of sessions needed to eliminate distress and reach a place of adaptive resolution varies with each client, but clinically significant change has been shown to occur in as few as one to twelve sessions.

One of the advantages of EMDR is that, while it facilitates trauma processing, it does not require the client to recite a detailed trauma narrative; consequently the approach to processing can be less distressing for both the client and the therapist. In addition, there is minimal homework required outside of the therapy session, thereby reducing potential barriers to treatment engagement.

Service providers need trauma treatments for children, adolescent, and adult survivors that are effective across diverse groups. EMDR has been used with male and female trauma survivors from fifty-four countries located on six continents. It has been found to be effective for trauma survivors as young as 6 to as old as 79, across different levels of education and social economic status. Within the United States, EMDR has been found to be effective with survivors who identify as white, African American, Latino, American Indian/Alaskan Native, and Asian Pacific Islanders. Although there are other evidence-based trauma treatments available, none have demonstrated superiority over EMDR. Furthermore, it has also been found to produce clinically significant results quite rapidly, making EMDR both effective and efficient.

—Dr. Tonya Edmond, Ph.D., MSW, associate professor, Brown School of Social Work, Washington University in St. Louis

BOX 10.3

Cognitive Processing Therapy in Trauma Care: Potential Treatment for Sex Trafficked and Exploited Individuals

Cognitive processing therapy (CPT) has gained empirical support as one of the most effective treatments for PTSD, particularly related to rape and sexual assault. CPT was developed by Patricia A. Resick and Monica K. Schnicke (1992, 1993) and adapted from social cognitive therapies for PTSD targeting information processing, emotional reactions, and the impact of trauma on a person's beliefs and expectations within a social context (Rothbaum et al. 2000). Multiple studies show evidence of elevated PTSD in survivors of sexual exploitation and trafficking, with rates ranging from 27% to 69% (Farley and Barkan 2008; Twill, Green, and Traylor 2010; Wells and Mitchell 2007).

CPT targets one's "stuck points," manifestations of PTSD that one is unable to accommodate or process, and helps integrate the trauma experience into the individual's life (Vickerman and Margolin 2009). The goal is to decrease avoidance and intrusions of aspects of the trauma (e.g., flashbacks, nightmares) through this integration process. It can be provided to individuals in both group and individual formats and has been adapted successfully to reflect the interests and needs of the individual (Galovski et al. 2012).

Of existing cognitive-behavioral techniques and other trauma treatments, CPT was found to have established the most support for effectiveness with women sexually assaulted during adolescence or adulthood (Vickerman and Margolin 2009). Findings indicate that 42–80% of clients will show significant improvement in PTSD symptomology, with approximately 50–70% no longer meeting diagnostic criteria for PTSD at the end of treatment (Bradley et al. 2005; Foa et al. 1999; Resnick et al. 2002).

CPT has also been tested and produced successful outcomes with multiple foreign-born populations, such as Bosnian refugees in a Midwestern city (Schulz, Huber, and Resnick 2006; Schulz et al. 2006) and female Congolese survivors of sexual violence (Bass et al. 2013).

Given the state of the evidence, CPT is considered an evidence-based treatment for survivors of rape and sexual assault and should be considered as a potential treatment for trafficked and exploited people who are known to experience symptoms of complex PTSD.

Particular attention should be paid to the characteristics of the target group, as one study suggests that CPT may be more effective with individuals with higher depression and guilt at the time of pretreatment and less effective with younger age, lower intelligence, and less education (Rizvi, Vogt, and Resnick 2009). This may be of considerable importance given that education status and age are risk factors for trafficking.

Nonetheless, CPT is an important intervention to consider when designing future treatments for sexually trafficked and exploited individuals and holds great promise for effective treatment.

—Lara Gerassi, MSW, LCSW, National Institute on Drug Abuse, TranSTAR Pre-Doctoral Fellow, Brown School of Social Work, Washington University in St Louis

Trauma-Informed Care

Trauma-informed care is generally understood to reflect an outlook or perspective of social service provision that includes an understanding and awareness of trauma; such understandings should guide practice, programmatic design, and organizations themselves (Heffernan and Blythe 2014). There are several components of TIC, including an understanding and awareness of trauma, safety, cultural competency, empowerment and rebuilding control, and using survivor-centered and strengths-based approaches (Elliott et al. 2005; Hardy, Compton, and McPhatter 2013; Heffernan and Blythe 2014). A strengths-based approach is exactly what the term implies—the strengths of the individual are acknowledged and used to guide practice in building safety, empowerment or control, and trust. Strengths can include resiliency, specific talents, goals, values, and one's outlook on the future, among other things. Strengths can also include one's unique cultural or social identities. Various components of TIC are described in the following sections.

Physical Environment

The physical environment and the latent as well as overt messages that are sent through décor and setup are important to a healing environment. Positive images of survivors and images of future success as well as images of people who demographically look like those the organization serves are part of a trauma-informed environment.[2] Security measures to provide a sense of safety are also important as some survivors may have traffickers who are stalking them or may otherwise provide a threat. An environment that one feels safe in is key to a trauma-informed environment. Even the awareness of the potential for music to be a trigger is important as well. Girls Educational & Mentoring Service (GEMS) executive director Rachel Lloyd, in her Victim, Survivor, Leader training webinar, stated, "When a young person walks in, even though we're a youth friendly program, we're not going to be playing something that is going to potentially be triggering or be exploitative or bring up issues for a young person, and so being really conscious about that kind of stuff [is important]." Some practitioners providing services for women and girls call for a gender-specific space in environments that serve women and girls in the initial healing process because the interactions many sex trafficking survivors have had with men as clients and as pimps have been traumatic. In addition to the physical environment, trauma-informed staff contribute to a trauma-informed environment as well.

Trauma-Informed Staff

Trauma-informed staff across the organization is important to creating a trauma-informed environment. While those who engage in direct practice may be educated in trauma-informed therapy, others in the organization also must be educated in trauma triggers, the potential for therapeutic moments, and related dynamics. This includes all players in the organization who have any contact with survivors. While various staff members are not engaging directly in trauma therapy, using a trauma-informed lens to "recognize the value in everything having a therapeutic and healing and empowering lens" is important to TIC.[3]

It is important to establish a trauma-informed organization that includes everyone working in the organization, regardless of their roles or duties. For example, Holly Smith (2014) said she had been unwilling to disclose to professional staff about her sexual exploitation, prior childhood sexual abuse, and sexual behaviors more generally—disclosure that was key to her recovery because each of those prior incidents shaped or led to the sex trafficking. Smith recalled an interaction with an orderly who seemed genuinely concerned about her well-being. She described him as an older man who expressed no attraction or desire for her; he asked her why she behaved the way she did toward men and asked her to write a list of every person she had any type of sexual encounter with prior to arriving. He said the list was connected to her current trouble and asked her to think about each person and the circumstances surrounding each encounter. She wrote the list and was in control of it; it was private unless she chose to share it. Smith described this as a therapeutic moment that allowed her to better understand her history and its relationship to her victimization. This example illustrates how therapeutic moments within organizations can occur outside of an actual therapy session. In her webinar, Rachel Lloyd notes that therapeutic moments can happen when staff are driving survivors to appointments, waiting with them at the Department of Motor Vehicles, or accompanying them in simple, everyday activities. Any of these events could include developing trust, a transformational relationship, or even a pivotal moment. As a result, it is important that all staff in an organization are trauma informed. In addition to trauma-informed staff, interactive language used to describe the relationships between service providers and survivors is important.

Research examining various facets of the battered women's movement shows that early grassroots advocates found fault with the term "client" in individual-level advocacy/service provision because it reinforced a hierarchal relationship or power dynamic between the advocate and the women seeking assistance. "Advocates initially maintained that such hierarchal interactions put abused women in a position of reduced power, mimicking the same power dynamics that are conducive to domestic violence" (Nichols 2014a). Similarly, GEMS suggests avoiding client labels as well. Lloyd says in her webinar:

> We don't use the term "client," we talk about "members," the client term often tends to make people feel like we're the smart ones and we're there to provide for you and put our expert opinion on you. Our young people have experienced being clients and patients and those kinds of things in other systems and institutions and so being a member is being part of our program, that we are in a community.

Lloyd even suggests rethinking how organizations use terminology surrounding staff positions because those terms may trigger feelings associated with staff positions in child protective services, foster care, and juvenile detention, with which many survivors are likely to have multiple and negative experiences. Accordingly, being viewed as a member of a collaborative community is key for both survivors and staff.

Aside from avoiding language regarding organizational positions, rescue language should also be avoided. Rescuing survivors is thought to be inaccurate in most instances because survivors are finding ways to survive while simultaneously experiencing victimization and exploitation. In addition, such language could also be viewed as demeaning and as nonadmission of agency, help seeking, survival, and long-term goals. Lloyd stated, "This isn't about your ability to rescue somebody and that's why we push back so much on the rescue language, because it's so unhelpful and because it's really demeaning and unhelpful for the young people and the adult survivors that we serve and it's not a strategic way of addressing someone's long term life goals in any way." Keeping in mind these potential triggers surrounding language, music, safety measures, the physical environment, images in decor, and the feelings such things arouse are part of TIC. Regardless of efforts to create a trauma-informed environment, triggers will arise, and teaching self-care skills are key in responding to trauma triggers.

Self-Care

Self-care, self-soothing, or finding ways to cope is another important piece of TIC, allowing survivors to develop their own stability and peace. Learning self-care can be a critical piece to avoiding fight-or-flight responses to a trauma trigger. Many girls run from services in the fight-or-flight responses characteristic of trauma survivors (Heil and Nichols 2015). Lloyd says in her webinar,

> One of the most critical things that we can do for young people is to be able to give them the tools and this comes along with that stability piece too, when people are ready to engage in counseling and those kinds of things, we want to make sure that people have the ability to be able to self-care, too, and not just rely on us, the service providers, the clinicians, or other people in their support network, that they know how to practice and some grounding techniques when they're feeling really triggered and really traumatized, that they know how to do some deep breathing and they know how to take themselves out of those really tough moments.

Importantly, self-care techniques that are effective for people will vary on an individual basis. What makes one person feel safe or able to self-regulate is distinct from what another person might need. This could be deep breathing, writing, drawing, listening to music, gardening, doing yoga, or something else. Lloyd continues:

> So, thinking about with this young person she liked poetry but that wasn't really this thing that super calmed her, and so we ended up buying her a skateboard and so when she would get triggered and when her mom would call and upset her she would take off on her skateboard and so I learned about all this stuff and I'd be like Oh, dear God please don't hurt yourself like that, but it was her way of being able to feel free and do something therapeutic for herself.

Tailoring service provision to individual cases and needs, whether in self-care or other areas of therapeutic approaches, are generally referred to as survivor-defined approaches.

Survivor-Defined Approaches

Survivor-defined practice is interrelated with cultural competency, strengths, self-care, and TIC in that collaboration between the survivor and the service provider is viewed as key—social workers should seek out how survivors view their individual situations and what their individual needs are, incorporating each survivor's voice throughout the process. Survivor-centered approaches, also referred to as victim-centered, survivor-defined, or woman-defined models, work to combine the expertise of social service providers with the goals, needs, and experiences of survivors. In this collaborative partnership between the social service provider and the survivor, service providers supply information about resources and give feedback based on survivors' individual cases and needs, but the survivors make and guide their own choices (Nichols 2014a). Services are individually tailored to meet the unique needs of each survivor, rejecting a "one size fits all" approach. A central tenet of survivor-centered approaches is that services are determined based on what the survivor wants and needs rather than what other institutional structures and actors may want, such as arrest, prosecution, or leaving an abusive partner (Nichols 2014a).

Much of the research in this area is in the field of study examining IPV (Macy et al. 2010; Kulkarni, Bell, and Rhodes 2012; Zweig and Burt 2007; Nichols 2014a; Goodman and Epstein 2008). The outcomes indicate that when survivor-centered approaches are used, women have a lower rate of re-abuse, lower rate of depression, better sense of well-being, greater satisfaction with services, and greater likelihood of using services in the future. Limited work examines this approach specifically within the context of sex trafficking and commercial sexual exploitation. When asking social service providers about responses that seemed to work well, Heil and Nichols (2015) found that social service providers indicated the survivors they worked with had varied needs and goals, and providers consequently tailored individual services depending on each person's needs and goals. Even those with very similar experiences had different needs. For example, one social service provider indicated that feeling safe was an important part of service delivery in individual and group therapy to commercially sexually exploited people, but the specific things needed for one girl to feel safe was distinct from another's. In the same study, social service providers indicated that sensory therapy could be geared toward each individual's interests; for one girl, that might be painting; for another, horticulture; and yet another, cooking, equine therapy, or running (Heil and Nichols 2015). As Lloyd described in her webinar, self-care and coping mechanisms can also be individually tailored. While this work is limited and while rigorous evaluation of this technique is lacking in the context of sex trafficking, it is evidence-based in other areas of practice.

Importantly, sex trafficked/CSE people are not a monolithic group. The reasons they become involved in selling sex are key to understanding individualized aftercare or treatment. For some, sexual abuse is a precursor to trafficking/exploitation, and for others, there may be a background of rejection from their families for sexual orientation or gender identity. Vulnerability as a refugee or undocumented immigrant may lead others into sex trafficking/CSE, and others were abducted or sex work turned into sex trafficking. Examining catalysts for entering into commercial sex is important for children who are trafficked as well as for adults. Research indicates those who start selling sex as adults often have substance abuse problems that precipitated entry into the commercial sex industry (Oselin 2014). "All of these differences must be considered when weighing options for residential treatment vs. outpatient services, closed vs open facilities, and CSEC-specific programs vs. youth focused programs that include services for victims of CSE" (Smith 2014, 161). Because needs and experiences vary, services must vary as well. Similarly, while many youth who are trafficked come from problematic home lives, some have supportive, loving parents at home, who may be able to assist with recovery in the home setting (Heil and Nichols 2015). For others, a safe residential treatment home may be a better option, particularly if there are problems in the home and the youth does not wish to return (Smith 2014). Some may need substance abuse treatment, and others may not. Refugees may have additional trauma experiences that should impact treatment. In some cases people who are sexually exploited by their partners may want to leave their partners, but others might not be ready or might not want to for a variety of reasons (Lloyd 2012). This requires individually tailored services within the context of different safety planning techniques, options for therapy (such as residential/shelter or drop-in options), and more. Heffernan and Blythe (2014, 2) write that "each victim interprets and creates her or his own reality of human trafficking. . . . The emotions felt by each client, along with the client's cultural responses to her or his experiences, may be different for each victim or survivor of human trafficking." As a result, service providers in Heffernan and Blythe's study aimed to provide case management in a form that allowed for survivor voice in talking about and acknowledging each survivor's perspective and experiences in a nonjudgmental environment (Heffernan and Blythe 2014).

This work extends beyond social service provision as a survivor-centered model can be engaged in by other community partners as well. Research on survivor-centered practices with sex trafficked/CSE people in the justice system (typically called a victim-centered approach in this area of study) find that a victim-centered approach in interviewing by law enforcement and prosecutors facilitates better results, including increased cooperation with prosecution, while simultaneously meeting the needs of survivors (Smith, Vardaman, and Snow 2009; Nichols and Heil 2014). There are multiple approaches that are interrelated with a survivor-centered approach. In order for services to be truly survivor-defined, it is necessary to recognize individual identities and the potential impact on trauma, barriers to services, experiences with trafficking/exploitation, and service provision. This calls for cultural competency within service provision.

Cultural Competency

Cultural competency includes a familiarity with the social identities survivors occupy as well as specific needs based on these social identities and the barriers and experiences with social systems and trauma that may be impacted by such identities. This is also referred to as intersectional practice (Crenshaw 1991; Collins 2008; Nichols 2014a). For example, research indicates that unique forms of trauma may be experienced by sex trafficked/CSE people who are LGBTQ[*], including things such as the heinous practice of "corrective" rape as well as parental rejection, marginalization from social institutions, and school bullying. Cultural competency and understandings of these potential forms of trauma are necessary to address them. Researchers also find that a need for translators is a part of cultural competency, as is a need for cultural understandings of each individual's background. Trafficked people originally from other countries may have distinct needs based upon cultural norms from the country of origin that must be incorporated into practice.

Some researchers suggest that holistic knowledge about human trafficking itself and its effect on survivors is a form of cultural competency (Busch-Armendariz, Nsonwu, and Heffron 2014). The argument could be made that understanding the specific and multiple traumas that may be present in the experiences of sex trafficked people is important to social work practice. Consequently, a holistic understanding of sex trafficking/ CSE, a survivor subculture, or "the life" is important to providing services, whether it is acknowledged as a form of cultural competency or as something else (Lloyd 2012). Cultural competency is viewed as a cornerstone of TIC and is interrelated with strengths-based and survivor-centered approaches. Cultural competency "takes into account the whole human being which means that attributes such as age, culture, ethnicity, and the like . . . are viewed as strengths" (Heffernan and Blythe 2014, 3). Accordingly, cultural competency is central to the strengths perspective, and both are intertwined with TIC.

Survivor-Led Approaches

A growing body of work suggests that survivor-involvement in organizations serving trafficked and CSE people produces better outcomes, largely through transformational relationships (Lloyd 2012; Heil and Nichols 2015; Oselin 2014).[4] This includes survivor-led advocacy, survivor mentorship, an established community of survivors, and survivor-informed programmatic design. For example, drawing from interviews with survivors and social service providers, Heil and Nichols (2015) note that establishing a community of survivors is important in creating a climate of rapport and nonjudgment, which survivors feel is imperative to healing. Similarly, by comparing four "prostitute-serving organizations," Oselin (2014) found that the most successful outcomes come from organizations in which long-term residential care is combined with mentorship from survivors who can provide a positive outlook on the future and serve as role models for change and accomplishing goals to leave the commercial sex industry. Lloyd (2012), executive director of GEMS and a survivor herself, also indicates that the successful program at GEMS is largely attributed to their survivor-leader model. When women and girls are exposed to others who have been through the same or similar experiences, this creates an understanding, bond, and atmosphere of nonjudgment and acceptance. GEMS boasts nearly a 75% success rate, indicated by women and girls who receive services and successfully leave the commercial sex industry. Similarly, the Nashville Model, used by Magdalene House sites in the United States, reports a 72% success rate. The community of survivors, reestablished trust, and a nonjudgmental atmosphere are central to this model. In her survivor account, Holly Smith describes meeting another survivor as life-changing. Her efforts toward help seeking began when she came into contact with Courtney's House, led by survivor Tina Frundt. Holly had previously thought—for nearly twenty years—that she was the only one. "Their unconditional friendship, love, and support was the platform from which my true healing from Atlantic City [where she was trafficked at 14 years old] was launched" (Smith 2014, 185).

Sex Trafficking–Specific Services

One key point of concern in working with juveniles who have been commercially sexually exploited, particularly those with a boyfriend pimp, is that when "rescued" from the streets, many run away from services to return to the streets. Accordingly, it is of central importance to acknowledge this reality, which gets little to no attention in the public, political, and academic discourse, and then to further determine why this is the case and what can be done to address it. Very little work examines this issue (see Heil and Nichols 2015; Reid 2010; Smith 2014). The small body of work that does exist suggests that girls are placed into services inappropriate to their needs, such as juvenile detention, foster care, psych wards of hospitals, rehab, or with people they cannot connect to. Children may be involved in these organizations for a wide variety of reasons, including substance abuse, anger management issues, and more. Essentially, trafficked youth may be getting treated for conditions they do not have in some settings, like anger management or substance abuse issues, while simultaneously they are not getting treatment related to sexual exploitation/trafficking. This work suggests that placement in sex trafficking– or CSE–specific services, with a community of survivors and using TIC is a promising direction for future practice (Heil and Nichols 2015). At the same time, while some organizations have very high success rates when they incorporate such practices, others fail miserably. This suggests that implementation is as important as programmatic design. For example, Kennedy (2013) reports that a short-term safe house in Miami-Dade County was only open for a few months before it closed because juveniles ran away within days of getting into the short-term shelter. The safe house was located in a crime-ridden neighborhood described as a "hotbed" of sex trafficking, and girls could freely come and go (Kennedy 2013). Ensuing debate following the closure centered on whether sex trafficking–specific services for youth should be locked down (see chapter 9) or should be in rural or more isolated settings (Reid 2015). Girls may be more comfortable with what they know, a lifestyle that is consistent with what they are used to, and the understandings of others who also live with them on the street. Girls run because they run from everywhere, according to Kristi's House director Mary Faraldo (Kennedy 2013). Heil and Nichols (2015) indicate that running from services is a result of the trauma typical of sex trafficked/CSE people. Coming to terms with trauma and real life changes is a huge stress, and fight-or-flight reactions are not uncommon; they are expected (Heil and Nichols 2015). Any safe home should have people and programs the girls can relate to. TIC is necessary to "reprogram" fight-or-flight responses, to prevent running away from services, and to address the trauma that trafficked or exploited people experience. Long-term care shows the most positive outcomes, likely because it takes a long time—more than two or three months—to get to a point that a person can even talk about trauma after building a relationship with a therapist and to begin the process of trauma-informed therapy. Above and beyond sex trafficking–specific services, survivor-led care and TIC are important. In order to address the multiple needs survivors may have, community-based responses are important as well.

Community-Based Responses

Community-based responses (CBR) to sex trafficking are forming throughout the country, including a collaboration between various facets of the justice system, social services, and other community partners. They can take the form of interagency coalitions, task forces, or informal or formal community partnerships. Much has been written about community-based responses (also called coordinated community responses) in the field of IPV. Research indicates that such systems show better outcomes for survivors, including lower rates of re-abuse, higher satisfaction with services, lower rates of depression, greater sense of well-being, and increased likelihood of using services again in the future. Survivors have myriad needs, and such systems support those needs (Nichols 2014a). Less work in this area has been done in relationship to sex trafficking.

Ostensibly, such models would improve outcomes for sex trafficking survivors as well, as researchers also find a number of needs that CBR can work to address. Essentially, this model involves wrap-around or holistic service provision. Having a single point of contact in CBR models may benefit survivors as well. For example, in examining a CBR model with trafficked people in Texas, Busch-Armendariz, Nsonwu, and Heffron (2014) found that a survivor-defined approach is useful to meet the individual goals and needs of the survivor, and the CBR model is beneficial to address complex needs. Essentially, a single point-of-contact social worker assists the survivor in accessing multiple community resources, navigating legal systems, and meeting other individualized needs (Busch-Armendariz, Nsonwu, and Heffron 2014). The authors explain that before this CBR model was implemented, communication between CBR members was disjointed, and it was the addition of the single point-of-contact social worker that created a streamlined system, providing benefit to trafficked people to better and more efficiently meet their needs and goals.

In addition to providing individual case management and providing information and resources based on individual needs, the model in this study was distinct in that the social worker was included in aspects of law enforcement and policy decisions, allowing the social worker to develop innovative strategies in collaboration with survivors (Busch-Armendariz, Nsonwu, and Heffron 2014). Respondents in this study reported better responses from those they needed help from when the social worker advocated for them. This model may also work to build trust between the survivor and law enforcement, which may be damaged for a number of reasons.

The single point-of-contact social worker sits in a strategic position to see the nested environments of survivors and/or professionals. It is analogous to a kaleidoscope where the understanding of multiple reflections (perspectives and needs of survivors, professionals, and systems) mirror and intersect (needs of survivors, professionals, and systems) and provide a unique and optimal image. From this vantage point, social workers can understand how a survivor's experiences and needs may impact and be impacted by the criminal justice system, legal, social and medical service providers, the survivor's family, social service eligibility policies, and social and political movements about immigration, to name a few.

(Busch-Armendariz, Nsonwu, and Heffron 2014)

Rebecca Macy and Natalie Johns (2011) found that a comprehensive continuum of care services is necessary to meet the needs of trafficked people. In a meta-analysis, the researchers found that the following were likely to be needed to address the needs of trafficked people: crisis care; immediate and crisis needs; basic necessities such as food, shelter, and clothing; physical and mental health care; legal services; immigration services; job and life skills training; and substance abuse services (Macy and Johns 2011). CBR models can work to provide wrap-around services to address such needs. In sum, a community-based response model integrating multiple forms of services available to survivors through a single point-of-contact social worker to assist in navigating and accessing the services the survivor wants and needs is suggested, as informed by this prior research. Researchers also indicate that immediate, ongoing, and long-term care is necessary. Importantly, survivor-centered approaches are necessary to integrate with CBR models so the social worker is providing assistance navigating various systems, acting in collaboration with the survivor, not on behalf of the survivor.

Motivational Interviewing

Developed by psychologists William Miller and Stephen Rollnick, motivational interviewing (MI) works to establish internal motivation to change behaviors, particularly when the survivor is ambivalent about working with a therapist (Miller and Rollnick 2012). MI has been found to be successful in areas in which the survivor has a dual diagnosis or feels undecided or has negative feelings about being in therapy. The technique is also particularly successful with adolescents who are resistant to therapy or working with a therapist (Miller and Rollnick 2012; Naar-King and Suarez 2010).

For sexually exploited people, particularly children who do not acknowledge themselves as exploited or as victims and who do not wish to work with a therapist, and for those who have a dual diagnosis (such as Stockholm Syndrome and PTSD), MI may be a promising technique for counselors, psychologists, therapists, and social workers. One survivor stated that "because of prior experiences, prostitution honestly made so much sense to me that I was actually confused by everyone's attempts to dissuade me from it" (Smith 2014, 154). Some survivors of sex trafficking/CSE have experienced multiple forms of trauma prior to the trafficking experience. Survivor Holly Smith points out, "It may take months or years to reverse these effects, so try to be patient if the child is uncooperative while in immediate aftercare" (2014, 153). She further pointed out that if staff had been trained in sex trafficking/CSE, they would be more likely to have discovered the sexual abuse history that was the root of the experiences that led to her trafficking experience.

> It is important for anyone working with victims of CSE to realize that this population is usually very reluctant to reveal anything personal or sincere to adults, especially adults in professional positions. As I have said before, many victims have been in circumstances in which adults consistently let them down. But victims of CSE are especially unlikely to share prior sexual activity. Many victims have been conditioned to conceal early childhood abuse and many find it painful to recall any sexual encounters before the CSE. It will likely take several sessions with a victim, especially a "willing victim" before he or she even considers the idea of trusting a professional.
>
> (Smith 2014, 142)

MI is a goal-oriented, survivor-centered technique that attempts to draw out the goals of the survivor in situations where survivors otherwise would not be willing to discuss them themselves. The therapist is directly attempting to get survivors to think about and consider making changes in their behaviors and lives. Importantly, while MI is a directive approach, it is also nonjudgmental and nonconfrontational. The therapist is not telling the survivor what to do or what to say; rather, the therapist asks open ended questions to draw out a response, provides affirmations of the responses, and engages in active listening. Asking the survivor questions about goals for the future, getting them to talk about the importance of change and contrasting the future to the past, and weighing consequences of actions and the potential problems and risks are key to MI. The idea is to draw out and get the survivor to analyze their behaviors when they might otherwise be reluctant to do so. Sylvie Naar-King and Mariann Suarez (2010) note that when attempting to persuade and direct adolescents, adolescents are more likely to resist. They suggest that MI is a more productive technique with youth. Sex trafficked/CSE juveniles who are court ordered to therapy, particularly those with a boyfriend pimp (see chapter 5) and exploited people who see little change or hope for their future, may particularly benefit from this approach. Therapists can assist survivors by helping them to see a better future and creating goals to attain that future, which motivates the survivor to work toward those goals and to see a better future that they may not see through nondirective interviewing. Simply put, the technique attempts to get survivors to think about changing behavior, with a better outlook on the future as they define it, motivating them to set goals and change behavior so they can get to that better future. Developing a relationship with the survivor is central to MI, including nonjudgment, empathy, and acceptance (see box 10.1). In sum, the goal is to directly engage survivors and facilitate talk about change (Freedman and Combs 1996). The consequence is that the motivation for change comes from the survivor. This model is likely to be successful with sex trafficked and exploited youth who are engaged in survival sex, work with a boyfriend pimp, or "willingly" work with a pimp. The practice is less likely to be applicable to youth who were abducted or are refugees or migrants who were defrauded or coerced into the commercial sex industry. This is also the case with the stages of change model.

Stages of Change Model

The stages of change model is known to be a good model to use with sex trafficked or exploited youth. This model is a cornerstone of the programmatic design of one of the better-known and most successful programs in the nation, GEMS. The stages of change model essentially recognizes that making life changes, including leaving CSE, can be a step-by-step process. The model recognizes the internal and external factors that youth experience when leaving the commercial sex industry and acknowledges how these factors may impact their progression in leaving a boyfriend pimp or the commercial sex industry altogether. The stages include precontemplation, contemplation, preparation, action, and maintenance. In the precontemplation stage, the survivor does not want help or feels that they do not need it. Survivors might feel that they are in love with their boyfriend pimp want to make him happy, or feel like they owe him and need to earn money for them to live off of. Survivors may think they have a future with the boyfriend pimp, as Lloyd describes in her webinar. In the contemplation stage, survivors are processing the information in their own minds and considering change. This typically includes acknowledging the harms of selling sex as well as general unhappiness and then considering action. The preparation stage involves making a plan and literally preparing for change. The survivor may move belongings to a place that is accessible, save money, access services, or work with a safety plan for an exit strategy. In the action stage, the individual actually makes the change, exiting the commercial sex industry and/or the relationship with the boyfriend pimp. In maintenance, the survivor maintains the life change. GEMS describes maintenance period as six months or more of the changed behavior.

Some people are able to permanently change their life the first time they go through the stages and reach maintenance. Many more people, particularly in the context of sex trafficking/CSE, find themselves going back, which GEMS refers to as relapsing. In a GEMS webinar, executive director Rachel Lloyd calls for social service providers to recognize that relapse is a part of the stages of change. The stages of change are not necessarily progressive; rather, they are fluid, and someone may backtrack. Relapse may occur because the survivor missed her trafficker/pimp/boyfriend, got lonely, needed money, or was triggered in some other way. The stages of change model is also used in substance abuse rehabilitation and is considered an evidence-based practice in this context.

There are obviously factors that are distinct in sex trafficking/CSE that shape "relapse." There are many external forces involved in addition to internal forces. The boyfriend pimp/trafficker might be calling, saying he loves her. The trafficker/pimp may be coming to the house, or sending texts, emails, or Facebook posts. Former friends in the life might be trying to get her to come back to the "family." Further, external events or even seemingly innocuous things may trigger fight-or-flight responses characteristic of complex trauma. The stages of change model recognizes that there is a continuum of change. There are different stages that survivors reach in their readiness to change, and different feelings about change. Some survivors may progress through the stages quickly, and for others it might take weeks or months or years. Survivors encourage service providers to be patient with that process (Smith 2014). But relapses may happen. Lloyd says, "Then when they might fall backwards, the shame can keep them away, and often will keep them away. It will keep them away from the very services and people that they need in their lives." It is imperative for survivors to know that, if they go back to their pimps, or back into the commercial sex industry, they will be accepted back with nonjudgement at any point by the service providers and the program they are working with. Lloyd suggests maintaining a balance, showing affirmation of success in progressing through the stages but acknowledging that it is normal and okay to relapse, and the provider and organization are always there to help. Lloyd notes that, for social service providers, helping survivors identify the triggers that prompted them to go back can be important, as is reminding survivors to think about positive aspects of changing their lives. It is important to move past the "victim" stage; addressing basic and immediate needs is imperative. "Nobody who's a victim wants to stay feeling stuck as a victim forever," Lloyd says. Long-term care shows better outcomes for trafficked/exploited people in the trajectory of their lives.

Long-Term Care and Residential Care

Education and career counseling, health awareness, literacy education, and financial management training are among the long-term needs of some survivors of sex trafficking/CSE, along with ongoing TIC (Hardy, Compton, and McPhatter 2013). Long-term ongoing needs include safe transitional and long-term housing; legal services; extensive, ongoing trauma therapy; job and life skills training; education; substance abuse services; immigration advocacy; and language services (Macy and Johns 2011). Kurtz and colleagues (2005) found among nearly six hundred sex workers in Miami that long-term needs include mental and physical health care, ongoing drug rehabilitation, and legal aid and job search assistance. Busch-Armendariz, Nsonwu, and Heffron (2014) report long-term needs such as "independent and permanent housing, and ongoing mental health care." Survivors originally from another country may also need English-language speaking education and assistance with family reunification. Access to long-term resources for international victims/survivors can be accessed through prioritized funding provided by the Office for Victims of Crime and the Office of Refugee Resettlement. Notably, survivor needs vary, and "survivors' needs change substantially over time," indicating a need for a "continuum of care" (Macy and Johns 2011, 89).

A small but growing body of work suggests that long-term care improves the outcomes for sex trafficked/CSE people. For example, in comparing organizations that served women exiting the commercial sex industry, Oselin (2014) notes that those who engaged in outpatient short-term services were much less likely to successfully exit the commercial sex industry compared to those who accessed long-term residential care organizations. This format allows the individual who wishes to leave sex work the opportunity to be around others with similar experiences in a supportive setting that provides resources to leaving and limits contact with others who may influence the individual to go back into the life. Limited work examines transitioning from residential care to the outside world in the United States (Smith 2014; Hardy, Compton, and McPhatter 2013; Oselin 2014). Oselin found that those who maintain ties to the program are more likely to be successful, also finding support for extended long-term care.

Addressing all of the needs for CSE/trafficked people cannot be accomplished short term. Transitioning to intermediate or long-term care is recommended (Macy and Graham 2012; Smith 2014). For example, if minors are in a closed facility, transitioning to an open facility before transitioning straight into the community is recommended. After describing going back into the commercial sex industry as a 14-year-old, after short-term interactions with services, Holly Smith stated, "without long term specialized counseling, I wasn't 'fixed.' I wasn't 'rescued.' I still believed I was a sexual object and that money and material things equaled personal value and achievement. Following my suicide attempts, I should have been stabilized in the hospital and then transferred into a residential program" (Smith 2014, 148). Oselin (2014) also notes that women exiting the sex industry show better outcomes when transitioning out of the program by first accessing transitional housing, then maintaining contact with the organization long term.

Chapter Summary

This chapter examined identification of sex trafficking/CSE in health care and social services, barriers to accessing services, and promising practices working with survivors. Identification using documented indicators is problematic as such indicators will only pick up a fraction of cases. Identification is challenged by survivors' unwillingness to disclose, short time frames for identification, and a lack of qualified professionals to make an initial identification. Respecting survivors' individual wants and needs is key. The point of identification is the time to offer expanded choices and resources for those who want them, not to force an assumption or to meet some other institutional goal. Safety planning and provision of appropriate resources is important. Barriers to accessing services include a lack of identification, a lack of resources to meet basic needs, and a potential for a language barrier. Barriers also include a lack of services more generally but specifically for those who have substance abuse issues and for men, boys, and gay and transgender populations. Promising practices include trauma-informed care, survivor-led practice, eye movement desensitization and reprocessing, cognitive behavioral therapy, culturally adapted cognitive behavioral therapy, cognitive processing therapy, sex trafficking–specific services, strengths-based approaches, survivor-centered practice, cultural competency, motivational interviewing, the stages of change model, transformational relationships, long-term care, and community-based responses with a single point-of-contact advocate.

Discussion Questions

1. What is the primary purpose of identifying sex trafficking/CSE in health care and social services?
2. What are some key components of trauma-informed care?
3. If you were to design outreach for the purposes of identification, what would that look like?

11

The Anti–Sex Trafficking Movement
in the United States

Although the topic of sex trafficking has garnered both public and political support in recent years, little academic research focuses on anti–sex trafficking activism or examines this activism specifically within a social movements framework. This chapter describes current antitrafficking activism in the United States and its grassroots origins. While sex trafficking/exploitation has always existed, other language was used to describe it, such as juvenile prostitution, child prostitution, or prostitution more generally. Awareness of sex trafficking emerged as activist networks formed, along with the language and definitions provided by the U.S. Trafficking Victims Protection Act (TVPA). Anti–sex trafficking activism in the United States expanded greatly in the 1990s, in part as an extension of renewed political interest in combating violence against women internationally and in part due to needs-based grassroots advocacy (Boxill and Richardson 2007; Kalergis 2009; Dempsey 2011; Outshoorn 2005). Yet little work specifically documents the antitrafficking movement in the United States (Boxill and Richardson 2007; Kalergis 2009). This chapter examines grassroots activism and the anti–sex trafficking movement in the United States. Specifically, antitrafficking activism is described, beginning with the grassroots efforts of survivors, professionals in the legal and social services, and their political and community partners. Next, the chapter depicts grassroots organizations that developed awareness and training for identification, such as in truck stops, travel plazas, airports, bus stops, train stations, and hotels. Activism in the political arena leading to the development of legislative accomplishments on the federal and state levels aiming to protect and prevent revictimization of trafficking victims is then discussed. Moreover, the chapter then details international antitrafficking organizations that have had an impact on antitrafficking efforts in the United States, with some organizations specifically operating or holding influence in the United States. Last, several media organizations that have lent their support to antitrafficking activism by providing news coverage, documentaries, and exposure of antitrafficking activists' efforts are described.

"The Roots" of Grassroots Antitrafficking Organizations

Practitioner-based literature uncovers a theme of grassroots activism in developing anti–sex trafficking organizations. Grassroots activism to address some issue is characterized by a "ground-up" approach, usually started by an individual or small group. Some grassroots antitrafficking organizations developed from a professionally recognized need. Children of the Night, in Van Nuys, California, is the first organization known to provide services for sexually exploited youth, that is, sex trafficking survivors. Children of the Night was founded in 1979 by Lois Lee through grassroots efforts.[1] Lee was a Ph.D. student working in the courts to examine court challenges and conduct related research when she became involved in a case in which a serial killer was targeting those in the commercial sex industry as his victims. One evening a woman called Lee at work, concerned about a missing girl she knew who was selling sex. This woman had contacted the police, who failed to follow up on the missing person's report that she filed. The missing girl later turned up dead. Lee was incensed by the lack of law enforcement response. After posting her home phone number on a local station trying to gain information about this serial killer, adolescent girls involved in commercial sex began to call her for assistance. This laid the groundwork for Children of the Night, as Lee subsequently invited these homeless girls into her home because they had nowhere else to go. "Over 250 children passed through her apartment over the course of the next 3 years. From these humble beginnings, Children of the Night was born."[2] The organization describes successfully providing services for over ten thousand sexually exploited children in the United States between the ages of 11 and 17. The organization first officially provided shelter beginning in 1992, although Lee had taken children into her own home beginning in 1979.[3] While sex trafficking only relatively recently came into the public eye, activism surrounding it goes back more than thirty years—evidenced in this example of Children of the Night—just using different words, such as "prostituted children" or "commercially sexually exploited children."

Like Children of the Night, Civil Society is another example of an anti-trafficking grassroots organization that developed from a professionally recognized need. Linda Miller founded Civil Society in 1996 when she recognized, based upon her experience as an attorney, a need for an organization in St. Paul, Minnesota, to combat human trafficking. The nonprofit organization offers legal and social services to victims of trafficking, sexual assault, and abuse. Miller's grassroots activism involved providing individual services as well as social change activism through targeted changes in state-level antitrafficking legislation. She received a certificate of appreciation from the U.S. Department of Justice in 2002 after developing best-practice methods for reaching out to immigrant crime victims, including trafficking survivors. Civil Society also provides presentations to the community regarding human trafficking victimization and identification as well as outreach to human trafficking survivors. The organization also offers medical and dental care, shelter, food, clothing, vocational counseling, legal services for sexual assault and human trafficking survivors, court advocacy/accompaniment, assistance with application to the Minnesota Crime Victims Reparation Board, assistance with orders for protection and harassment restraining orders, and interpretation and translation services for victims of crime.[4]

Nancy A. Boxill and Deborah J. Richardson (2007) describe the beginnings of the antitrafficking movement in Atlanta, Georgia, which resulted in the establishment of the Atlanta Women's Coalition and, later, Angela's House. A court case in Atlanta of 10- and 11-year-old sisters who were commercially sexually exploited by a pimp and other cases like it served as catalysts for grassroots activism. Such grassroots activism included community collaboration between various professional women in the Atlanta area in legal and social services, facilitated by well-known women's colleges and one of the largest women's foundations based in Atlanta. Atlanta's history of grassroots activism in combating racism was also conducive to grassroots activism in the anti–sex trafficking arena as well (Boxill and Richardson 2007). Such grassroots activism led to the development of

Angela's House in Atlanta in 2002, a shelter for underage commercially sexually exploited girls—the first of its kind in Georgia.

Similarly, Lisa Goldblatt Grace, a social worker, also displayed grassroots activism in developing the Boston-based program My Life, My Choice, of which she is co-director (Kalergis 2009). Grace recalls that the death of a minor who was killed by her pimp brought together various professionals in the justice system and social services. This group developed a program that emphasizes evidence-based practice in the prevention of sex trafficking by providing education about sexual exploitation to at-risk girls. The program also addresses education of social service providers and law enforcement, as the girl who was killed by her pimp had interactions with multiple practitioners in various social services sectors, but her trafficking situation was not identified prior to her death. The resulting education program highlights warning signs for the purposes of identification and the ways to respond to a sex trafficking situation once it is identified (Kalergis 2009). The grassroots activism of these pioneers of the antitrafficking movement in the United States is based on their experiences in the justice system and social services, recognizing the necessity for activism and organizations to provide much-needed services to survivors. Antitrafficking activism is also rooted in the grassroots activism of survivors as well (Kalergis 2009).

At times activist organizations are developed by survivors of sex trafficking/exploitation who work to assist others who have been through the same thing. For example, Girls Education & Mentoring Services (GEMS), one of the best-known, highly acclaimed, and pioneering antitrafficking organizations in the United States, began with the work of Rachel Lloyd, a well-known antitrafficking advocate, survivor, and the executive director of GEMS. Lloyd began working with women exiting the commercial sex industry in New York City in 1997 (Lloyd 2012). In doing this work, Lloyd recognized the "overwhelming need for services for young women at risk for sexual exploitation who were being ignored by traditional social service agencies. It became clear that specialized services were essential for this disenfranchised population."[5]

Lloyd's grassroots efforts initially involved offering shelter in her home for other survivors of sex trafficking or commercial sexual exploitation (Lloyd 2011). She recalls, "It started from my kitchen table. Young girls would stay at my house, sleep on my couch. It was a grassroots operation with no funding" (Lloyd, qtd. in Kalergis 2009, 316). GEMS provides services to trafficked and exploited women and girls, sometimes as an alternative to incarceration. The organization is also known for policy-level activism and education and training to service providers across the country.

Activism may come from a professionally recognized need as well as from survivors, and other activists have developed organizations based on humanitarian goals outside of personal or professional experience. The Covering House, based in St. Louis, Missouri, was developed with humanitarian goals in mind. The Covering House is one of only a handful of shelters nationwide to provide explicitly for girls under the age of 18 who are survivors of sex trafficking or commercial sexual exploitation. Like Children of the Night, The Covering House also began with grassroots activism, beginning with one individual's determination to provide services and shelter to girls who are survivors of sex trafficking/exploitation and to provide community awareness about the issue. In 2008 founder Dedee Lhamon saw a need for shelter to serve sex trafficking survivors and commercially sexually exploited youth in the St. Louis area. She was "pierced by the reality of trafficking happening in our country and was heartbroken that there were very few resources available for today's young survivors. From there The Covering House was born."[6] She decided to dedicate her life to working to support sex trafficking survivors and accomplished the goal of setting up her organization a year later as a nonprofit organization. The Covering House currently includes a professional staff as well as a network of grassroots activists—volunteers, interns from area universities, and professionals who are willing to sacrificially give their time. A variety of services are offered at The Covering House: shelter, clinically licensed counseling, an attorney to serve as an advocate for the girls, tutoring and educational support, mentoring and life skills development coaches, and programming developed collaboratively with a trafficking survivor who is also a social worker.[7] One individual's determination began this whole program, recruiting volunteers, professionals, survivors, and activists, because she saw a need for both services and residential care for sex trafficked/exploited survivors in St. Louis, clearly reflecting grassroots activism and origins of The Covering House.

The examples depicted in this section reveal a pattern of activism derived from a combination of survivors, community members, and professionals who recognized a need for shelter and services. Other pioneering organizations with grassroots origins include End Slavery Cincinnati, Veronica's Voice, the Nest Foundation, Courtney's House, Eve, MISSSEY, Rahab's Hideaway, Healing Action, and Breaking Free (see chapter 4), among others. In addition to activist organizations that provide direct services and community awareness, other groups work to provide training in specific venues where trafficking is known to occur.

The Hotel Industry

Perhaps the best-known international antitrafficking organization involving the hotel industry is End Child Prostitution Child Pornography and Trafficking of Children for Sexual Purposes (ECPAT), which was developed in 1990 and claims eighty-two organization-members in seventy-five nations, including the United States. One of their initiatives involves conducting education and training toward recognizing the signs of potential sex trafficking situations and sex trafficking victims/survivors in hotels as part of a larger initiative emphasizing education and awareness in the tourism industry.

Hotels have been identified in media reports as well as in the academic and practitioner-based literature as a venue for sex trafficking. Curtis and colleagues (2008) found in New York City that 44% of commercially sexually exploited youth engaged in prostitution used hotels throughout the city for commercial sexual exchanges. Another study in Washington State investigated sixty-seven police reports and found that 63% of minors involved in sex trafficking reported hotels as venues for such commercial sexual exchanges (Mayock 2012). Andrea Nichols and Erin Heil (2014) also found law enforcement and social service providers who indicated that hotels were a common venue for sex trafficking in the St. Louis area. The types of hotels that sex trafficking occurs in range from elite hotels to small locally owned inns or motels and those owned by organized crime groups (American Hotel and Lodging Association 2012).

Hotels are a convenient location for trafficking to occur in because they are temporary and relatively anonymous (Mayock 2012). Commercial sexual exchanges typically last less than an hour, which makes it unlikely that a trafficker or trafficking victim will be identified in such settings. This makes hotel staff potential front-line, first-exposure identification sources. As a result, both activism and corporate interests have combined to provide education and training in hotels across the United States. In order to address trafficking in hotels, hotel staff receive training to look for possible warning signs in order to identify and respond to a potential trafficking situation.

The American Hotel and Lodging Association (AHLA) also works to provide training in hotels across the United States. The AHLA developed a webinar titled "Child Trafficking: Learn How to Identify and Address" (Mayock 2012). End Slavery Cincinnati, an organization that provides assistance to trafficking survivors, provides a list of such warning signs as well. In hotel settings, sex trafficking operations largely take the form of "in-call" services or "out-call" services. In the case of in-call services, the room is reserved by the trafficker, a partner of the trafficker, or the survivor/victim (Farrell et al. 2012). Clients then come to the room to buy sexual services. Warning signs for in-call services may include frequent movement, with different people coming and going from the room in less than an hour's time. Hotel staff may become wary if other guests complain about frequent knocking and doors opening and closing consistently throughout the night. Other signs may include an increased number of calls to the front desk for a particular room extension from different phone numbers, especially in cases where the caller does not know the guest's name. In addition, housekeeping may take notice of heightened requests for towels and room service, and adolescents or children in the room when school is in session. In situations involving out-call services, victims are relatively mobile and meet clients at hotel rooms for short periods of time for prostitution, then quickly move on. In such cases, warning signs may include a victim who will not make eye contact or may appear fearful or disoriented, or an individual who checks in for short periods of time on different dates—i.e., a returning "customer" who appears to have different guests on each visit.[8] Checking out after a short period of time may also be a warning sign as well as checking in without luggage or paying in cash. Someone—a trafficker or a lookout—may also enter the hotel with the victim and remain in the lobby or bar or outside the room. In addition, young people who are dressed or otherwise made-up to look older, and young girls checking in with an older boyfriend with no luggage may potentially be warning signs. "It may not be one thing that you see . . . but rather it's a few of these indicators together that make it worth contacting law enforcement."[9]

While ECPAT and End Slavery Cincinnati frame hotel training as a form of antitrafficking activism with the aim of identifying more survivors/ victims, the AHLA frames their training within the context of a business model. They note that if trafficking at the hotel is discovered, it could pose a public relations nightmare, may offer consequent financial risk due to the bad publicity, could present safety risks for guests and staff, and may pose legal risks because some jurisdictions, such as Washington State, hold the hotelier liable for trafficking occurring in the hotel if the hotelier is aware of it and does nothing about it (Mayock 2012).

The Transportation Industry

Trucking Industry

The trucking industry is another group that has become involved in anti-trafficking activism. The goal of such activism is to educate truck drivers and truck stop workers about how to spot victims of human trafficking and how to provide outreach to survivors at truck stops (Wheeler 2013). Truckers Against Trafficking (TAT) and Travel Centers of America are the best-known and most active in the trucking industry's antitrafficking efforts. TAT arose from grassroots efforts to address a professionally recognized need. Interstates, highways, truck stops, and travel centers are venues for trafficking, according to the FBI. Several studies also found that trafficking occurs at truck stops in the Midwest (Nichols and Heil 2014; Williamson and Prior 2009). Brice (2013) reports that prostitution is regularly found at truck stops across the nation. In an interview, truck driver Chris Striker stated, "You can turn a CB radio on and drive through these metropolitan areas and it's shocking what kind of marketing, advertising is going on."

TAT is a grassroots activist organization dedicated to raising awareness and action among truckers in the area of sex trafficking.[10] The grassroots efforts of TAT aim to increase the identification and reporting of potential domestic sex trafficking victims. TAT was first developed as a part of another grassroots organization, Chapter 61 Ministries, founded in 2007 by six women located in four states to combat human trafficking. TAT became its own organization focusing specifically on the trucking industry in 2009. In 2011 it became an official nonprofit organization currently led by Kendis Paris.

Truckers across the United States note that truck stops are a common site for prostitution, often with teenage girls sometimes known by the derogatory term "lot lizards" within the insular trucking community. Some truckers who called law enforcement to report these cases garnered national attention when it was learned that some of those selling sex in the truck stops were actually sex trafficked (Johnson 2012). TAT works to educate truckers and those in the travel plaza (truck stop) industry.[11] The aim is for truckers to rethink prostitution at truck stops by identifying these young females selling sex as potential victims of sex trafficking as opposed to "lot lizards," and for the truckers to report these cases to the National Human Trafficking Resource Center (NHTRC) hotline. TAT maintains that truckers are in a front-line position to identify these domestic minor sex trafficking victims and to report such cases to law enforcement with the goal of prosecuting traffickers and getting victims the assistance they need (Johnson 2012). TAT created a training DVD for truckers and travel plaza workers. They partner with multiple trucking companies and travel plazas to provide this training across the nation. Lounges in travel centers across the United States now have information about the warning signs of sex trafficking as well as the NHTRC hotline phone number (Wheeler 2013). TAT also distributes wallet cards and other materials with the NHTRC number on it as a regular part of this training for members of the trucking industry. A representative of the NHTRC hotline stated that truckers provide some of the best tips and referrals because they are uniquely positioned to confront trafficking in their travels since truck stops are a hot spot for prostitution and particularly domestic minor sex trafficking (Johnson 2012). TAT suggests that a warning sign of sex trafficking at truck stops or travel centers is when groups of minors are dropped off by a single car with an older man (Brice 2013). However, there are other warning signs truckers should be aware of as well.

In a recent case in Virginia, trucker Kevin Kimmel reported a suspicious situation in which he saw a young girl's face through the window of a recreational vehicle. The face struck him because he said she looked distraught. Shortly after, Kimmel said, "I saw a guy come up and knock on the door then go inside the Pilot—then quickly came back and knocked again, all of the sudden the thing was rocking and rolling" (in Charters 2015).[12] The girl turned out to be a 20-year-old young woman who was forced to sell sex and was brutally tortured. Court documents allege that the couple who was keeping her withheld food and water, burned her with a hot key, and drove nails into her feet. Court documents also allege that the couple had taken pictures of the woman nude and gagged, and with Clorox bleach sprayed into her wounds to increase her pain.[13] The young woman had been abducted in Iowa on Christmas Eve and then forced into this prostitution. When the police arrived, the young woman told them that Aldair Hodza and Laura Sorensen had been physically and sexually abusing her.[14] This account is not intended to sensationalize this survivor's story; rather, this is an example of the outcome of a trucker's ability to identify and report a potential trafficking situation. The result was that this young woman got legal assistance; it is unclear whether she has accessed the social services she may need for recovery. Aside from activist efforts in the trucking industry, other facets of the transportation industry are engaging in efforts to identify and report potential trafficking as well.

Train Stations

In 2012 Amtrak, the largest passenger train system in the United States, partnered with the Department of Homeland Security and the Department of Transportation in an effort to identify and report suspected incidents of human trafficking. This partnership involves training more than eight thousand Amtrak employees in identifying warning signs of human trafficking, including sex trafficking. Like hotel staff and truckers, Amtrak employees are in a front-line position to identify potential cases of sex trafficking. Amtrak also employs its own police officers who receive this training in identifying and responding to a potential trafficking situation when confronted with it. The Department of Homeland Security and the Department of Transportation developed the training and awareness materials and received political support from the Homeland Security secretary, Janet Napolitano; Transportation secretary, Ray LaHood; and Amtrak president and CEO, Joseph Boardman. These leaders acknowledge the role of trains as a potential source of transport. The Amtrak partnership is part of a larger initiative called the Blue Campaign, created in 2010 to create an interdependent system that works to identify trafficking on multiple forms of public transportation through awareness, education, and training of staff (Seper 2012). In addition to trucks and trains, bus stops are also potential identification spots.

Bus Stops

In 2013 public bus companies began to partner with antitrafficking activists. Metro Transit developed a training program for bus drivers to identify potential sex trafficking situations and worked to implement a public awareness program (Nelson 2013). Transit hubs such as bus stops and train stations may be an area for identifying sex trafficking cases. Research indicates that recruitment occurs at bus stops, and bus stops can also be a location for runaway youth to get out of bad weather. The Twin Cities' Metro Transit police chief, John Harrington, said "police have received calls from people saying prostitution appeared to be happening near bus stops" (Nelson 2013). Metro Transit provides training to bus drivers to identify sex trafficking. The campaign also works to assist victims by posting multilingual signs indicating sources of assistance for sex trafficking survivors/victims. This outreach effort is significant because sites labeled as important for identification are absolutely sites for direct outreach. Posting relatable posters and materials where those engaged in survival sex or under pimp-control are found to go, such as bus stops, is an important avenue for offering assistance.

Airlines

Like truckers and bus drivers, flight attendants have also created activist efforts toward identifying and responding to sex trafficking. While most sex trafficking in the United States involves U.S. citizens, some sex trafficking victims are trafficked from other countries and may enter the United States via airplane (Richard 2000; U.S. Department of State 2014). The Innocents at Risk Flight Attendant Initiative was developed in 2008 by senior flight attendant Sandra Fiorini (Gutierrez 2012). Fiorini noted multiple times in which children flying alone from other countries and who did not speak any English concerned her, particularly after a case was uncovered involving sixteen people who were trafficked to the United States from the Czech Republic (Gutierrez 2013). She wondered how many were literally "flying under the radar" (Gutierrez 2013). The initiative involves training airline employees to identify potential signs of trafficking and to call the NHTRC hotline to report them. The group also passes out wrist bands with the NHTRC hotline number on it so flight attendants can make the call while in flight, so suspects and potential victims can be met at the destination airport for questioning. The Innocents at Risk Flight Attendant Initiative has trained nearly a third of American Airlines flight attendants— approximately twenty thousand people—and has expanded the training to other airlines (Gutierrez 2013).

A variety of airlines claim several success stories, including this one from Delta Airlines:

> Patty McPeak sat down in the boarding area next to a man and a little girl—about four years old. Making small talk, she asked how old the little girl was. The man said the girl was about two years old, he had picked her up from her mother so he wasn't sure. He got very nervous and disappeared for a few minutes and when he returned, the child appeared to be drugged. Patty notified the flight attendants and showed them the Hotline number. Pilots called, and authorities met the flight.[15]

In fact, multiple airlines show success stories on the Airline Ambassadors International Web page. The Blue Lightning Initiative, part of the Blue Campaign described earlier, also emphasizes training staff in the airline industry. The political system is involved in many of the antitrafficking responses, indicated in the Blue Campaign and the Department of Transportation as well as in other areas of the political arena.

Political Activism

In addition to the development of shelters, social services, and work toward identification, grassroots activists worked to change structural conditions with the goal of reducing sex trafficking, commercial sexual exploitation, and revictimization, particularly of minors. Prior to the 2000s, public awareness of and political attention to sex trafficking was limited. Consequently, activists brought the problem to public and political attention (Kalergis 2009; Boxill and Richardson 2007; Heil and Nichols 2015). Through grassroots activism, along with other antitrafficking partners (participants in the movement also included anti–child abuse and anti-rape activists, legal, academic, and political partners, and members of community, student, and faith-based groups), sex trafficking became an object of political interest, and the funding for support services to trafficking victims expanded greatly as a result. Such social change ideology and activism gave rise to the development of the first NHTRC hotline in 2007. Moreover, as part of the Trafficking in Victims Protection Act (2000), the Department of Health and Human Services initiated the Rescue and Restore Victims of Human Trafficking Campaign. Antitrafficking organizations greatly expanded their service provision and became better known publicly throughout the 2000s. Activists gained political ground, and the first task force was established in 2004, with forty-two federally funded task forces implemented nationwide by 2013.

Activists, advocates, and other professionals in the field worked to garner political support to develop and pass antitrafficking legislation (see chapter 9). Further structural-level activism centers on shifts in state laws. As described in chapter 9, state-level law and the way it is implemented varies considerably (Nichols and Heil 2014; Farrell et al. 2012; Clawson et al. 2008). One key area of concern for advocates and activists is that trafficking victims are often criminalized as prostitutes. Several groups have engaged in activism to change these and other laws within their states, including Safe Harbor laws (see chapter 9). On a larger scale of activism, perhaps the best-known antitrafficking organization in the United States, the Washington D.C.-based Polaris Project is an activist organization that advocates for improved federal and state laws as well as better implementation of such laws. The group also runs the NHTRC hotline, created in 2007, and provides education and training as well as direct services to trafficking victims/survivors. The organization conducts research and gathers data, particularly in evaluation of state-level trafficking laws to identify areas in need of improvement, such as the issue that state prosecutors are not using state-level antitrafficking laws. In addition to political support, the antitrafficking movement has gained media support.

Media Support

Power-house media outlets such as MSNBC, CNN, HBO, *Huffington Post*, PBS, FOX, NBC, CBS, ABC, and others have provided media coverage and support for antitrafficking efforts. For example, a simple Internet search uncovered multiple sex trafficking–related news articles by NBC, ABC, FOX, CBS, and their local subsidiaries as well as *Huffington Post*. Some news sites are going further to have ongoing coverage of sex trafficking. Beginning in 2008, MSNBC developed their ongoing series *MSNBC Undercover*, which has produced sixteen documentaries covering sex trafficking. The CNN Freedom Project features a centralized location on the CNN website for blogs, news articles, and documentaries conducted by CNN journalists related to various forms of human trafficking, including sex trafficking in the United States and abroad. The website for this project states: "CNN is joining the fight to end modern-day slavery by shining a spotlight on the horrors of modern-day slavery, amplifying the voices of the victims, highlighting success stories and helping unravel the complicated tangle of criminal enterprises trading in human life."[16] Perhaps the best-known media support comes from Nicholas Kristof of the *New York Times*, who has written extensively on sex trafficking both in the United States and around the world. Kristof's book, *Half the Sky*, co-authored with Sheryl WuDunn, focuses in part on sex trafficking of women and girls. *Half the Sky* was later turned into a documentary. WuDunn and Kristof later developed the four-part PBS series *A Path Appears*, based on another book the duo wrote together; one of the parts emphasizes human trafficking. Note that while news coverage and documentaries draw attention to the issue, the quality of coverage varies. Some of these works are inaccurate, misrepresent the issue, and depict revictimization of survivors.

International Organizations Operating in the United States

In addition to U.S. "ground-up" grassroots organizations, international organizations also have a presence in antitrafficking activities in the United States. International organizations that have a presence in the United States are composed of current and former sex workers, sex trafficking survivors, justice system practitioners, social service providers, and faith-based organizations. The international community of antitrafficking activists and organizations is not a homogenous group. The Coalition Against Trafficking in Women (CATW), the Coalition to Abolish Slavery and Trafficking's (CAST) National Survivor Network (NSN), Shared Hope International (SHI), International Justice Mission (IJM), End Child Prostitution, Child Pornography, and Trafficking of Children for Sexual Purposes (ECPAT), and the Global Alliance Against Traffic in Women (GAATW) all have a presence in the United States and are engaging in anti–sex trafficking activism. The groups vary widely in ideologies and responses to sex trafficking. Some are faith-based/abolitionist; others are based on radical feminist or abolitionist principles; still others are based upon liberal feminist/neoliberal perspectives. The ideologies discussed in chapters 2 through 4 absolutely shape the varying actions of these organizations. SHI and IJM are perhaps among some of the best-known faith-based antitrafficking organizations (see box 11.1). CATW is an international organization providing influence in the United States. This initiative is based on the abolitionist-feminist Swedish model, which views all prostitution as violence against women.[17] CATW also has

BOX 11.1
Faith-Based International Antitrafficking Organizations

International Justice Mission

Many antitrafficking organizations are religious in nature and handle the problem of sex trafficking from a faith-based moral perspective. For example, International Justice Mission (IJM), founded in 1997, focuses on its anti–sex trafficking efforts through religious missionary work. Through biblical grounding, leaders of IJM posit, "We're inspired by God's call to love all people and seek justice."[18] This biblical foundation has led to criticism by secular advocates who argue that the group is fostering religious assimilation in the countries in which it is visible. IJM is known for conducting organized brothel raids and bringing girls into shelters, many of which are Christian-run (Gold and Nawyn 2013). Despite these criticisms, IJM maintains that 90% of their faculty are "nationals of the countries in which they work," reflecting the ideology that work done by those within the nation will have a stronger and longer-lasting effect. The group claims to have assisted millions of people around the globe.

IJM is currently headquartered in Washington, D.C., and has "ongoing operations in 18 cities in Cambodia, the Philippines, Thailand, India, Kenya, Rwanda, Uganda, Zambia, Bolivia, the Dominican Republic and Guatemala, and has Casework Alliance Partnerships in Ecuador and Peru."[19] Operating with more than five hundred lawyers, investigators, social workers, and staff, IJM works under a collaborative casework model that seeks four outcomes: victim relief, perpetrator accountability, survivor aftercare, and structural transformation.[20] IJM's casework model has proven successful in combating victimization both at the individual level and structural level in which the power of the law in victim protection is emphasized. IJM also has branches across the United States that work to educate the public on issues of both domestic and international sex trafficking through community-based chapters.

Shared Hope International

In addition to IJM, another prominent international organization with a religious foundation is Shared Hope International (SHI). SHI's value statement says that, "as Christian stewards, we prayerfully seek to use wisdom and Biblical guidance for every dollar we spend. As Christian leaders, we seek to inspire change by informing and empowering activists, providing strategic guidance to local shelter and service partners, and influencing policy makers and first responders."[21]

Although Christian in nature, SHI clearly emphasizes that the organization will restore and respect victims of trafficking regardless of their "faith or system of belief."[22] Founded in 1998, SHI has played a vital role in restoring the lives of victims of sex trafficking in the United States and abroad. Following a collaborative casework model, the vision of SHI is "a world where every survivor is surrounded by trained professionals, an alert community, just law and policy, knowledgeable service providers and appropriate shelter options."[23] This vision is established through hands-on training and guidance to local advocates in the United States, the Fiji Islands, India, Jamaica, and Nepal. Additionally, the organization participates in education campaigns, policy development, research, and collaborative efforts at all levels of the community. SHI is known for their professional research endeavors, particularly their evaluation and resulting grading system of various nations' responses to trafficking as well as state responses to trafficking within the United States.

—Dr. Erin C. Heil, Ph.D., associate professor, Southern Illinois University
Edwardsville

a presence in the United States and is active in education and legislative endeavors. The CAST developed NSN in 2011 to connect survivors of various forms of human trafficking and to provide a platform for survivor leadership in antitrafficking activism (see box 11.2).

As described earlier in this book, there is much debate within the feminist and antitrafficking communities on the relationship between prostitution and sex trafficking. While the religious (IJM, SHI) or abolitionist-feminist organizations (CATW) described earlier generally view all forms of prostitution as harmful, there are other international antitrafficking organizations with a presence in the United States that note a distinction between sex trafficking and sex work. This distinction is made by those who hold the neoliberal perspective or liberal feminist perspective of sex trafficking, among others.

For example, GAATW draws a line between prostitution and trafficking, stating that trafficking is forced and prostitution/sex work is voluntary.

BOX 11.2
The National Survivor Network and CAST

The National Survivor Network (NSN) is a network of survivors of human trafficking that was founded in 2011. NSN operates to provide community to survivors and to advance survivor-knowledge to government, nongovernmental organizations, law enforcement, and the public, and is dedicated to being survivor led. Members may have experienced any type of human trafficking and originate from or live at any point of origin on the globe. This ethos of inclusion as well as the emphasis on public policy work and a trauma-sensitive method of operation is what attracted me, a survivor of child sex trafficking, to NSN.

At present NSN is supported by the Coalition to Abolish Slavery and Trafficking (CAST) in Los Angeles, which founded the network in 2011. Members have been extremely effective in policy review and advocacy on local, state, and federal levels, and CAST and its partner organizations have provided legal team members to assist with policy training and travel support for survivors to advance advocacy efforts.

In early 2015 NSN membership nominated and elected its first cadre of committee chairs, having until that time been primarily organized by the survivor-organizer Ima Matul, who was hired by CAST into that full-time, paid position in 2012. Committee chairs include a policy chair, two policy champions, a membership chair, a speaker's bureau chair, and a public relations chair.

In my experience as a survivor, and in my evaluation as a psychotherapist specializing in post-trauma phenomena, safe community can be critical to healing. Writing about the powerful effects of his veterans' groups (including private, online discussion forums) on the healing of Vietnam veterans under his care, Jonathan Shay (2002, 162) says, "Restoration of *thumos* and of the capacity for social trust happens only in community," asserting that "our physical brains are biologically evolved to make us culture bearers and users," all of which is of course borne out in current neurobiological studies. While, unlike Shay, I would argue that the one-on-one psychotherapy relationship can also be a healing—if tiny—community, I agree with him that a larger community of others who have shared a common experience unfathomable to wider society can greatly alleviate the deep feeling of alienation and stigmatization experienced when returning "home" from a horrific other world. I find that NSN, for the most part, provides such a milieu.

Perhaps because NSN is a moderated community, it feels particularly safe. My experience in some other venues has been retraumatizing, therefore I am careful about which organizations I enter. A code of conduct, close monitoring of the private Facebook page (which only survivors are allowed to access) for trauma-triggering posts and discussions, available mediation for members in conflict, an open and affirming environment, and a nonsectarian position all contribute to the sense of inclusiveness and containment.

NSN Mission Statement: "To bring together a community of survivors of human trafficking by creating a platform for survivor-led advocacy, peer-to-peer mentorship, and empowerment that embraces all survivors, regardless of gender, age, nationality or type of trafficking experience" (Retrieved from http://nationalsurvivornetwork.org).

—Margaret Howard, MFA, LCSW, is a psychotherapist
in private practice in St. Louis, Missouri

The organization works to abolish trafficking but not prostitution. The International Committee for Prostitutes' Rights (ICPR) supports GAATW. The ICPR advocates for the legalization of prostitution using a harm-reduction framework. ICPR suggests that antitrafficking activists should not just focus on abolishing trafficking; rather, they should work to support prostitutes' rights simultaneously to reduce the harms sex workers are exposed to. The GAATW, founded in 1994, developed as a response to anti-trafficking discourse and activism and because of concern that the voices of trafficking survivors themselves were not being recognized or used to inform policy. In particular, GAATW promotes a human rights approach in its antitrafficking discourse, noting that the cause of trafficking is rooted in intersecting inequalities of "globalisation, expansion of the informal economy, increase in female labour migration and existing inequalities of gender, race, class and nationalities."[24] The group was involved in defining trafficking in the Palermo Protocol and was involved in implementing and monitoring the protocol across various nations. GAATW also emphasizes that trafficking victims are being treated like criminals, as sex workers or as violators of immigration laws, and it directed its activism accordingly, working to create a definition of trafficking that is beneficial to trafficked persons. The GAATW also claims feminist grassroots origins: "The story of GAATW is a women's story; it is a story of women building alliances across borders."[25] GAATW is based in Thailand and includes an alliance of more than a hundred nongovernmental organizations across the globe, including nongovernment organizations practicing in the United States. GAATW partners in the United States include the Sex Workers Project (SWP).[26]

SWP was founded in New York City in 2001 and was the first program in the United States to provide legal services and advocacy to sex workers. SWP upholds the harm-reduction model, focusing on protecting "the rights and safety of sex workers who by choice, circumstance, or coercion remain in the industry."[27] The Center for Women Policy Studies also shares similar views to that of GAATW and is based in Washington D.C., in the United States. Created in 1972, the Center for Women and Policy Studies is known for being the first U.S.-based feminist policy analysis and research organization. The group is among the first organizations to analyze human trafficking from a public policy perspective. Their mission is "to shape public policy to improve women's lives and preserve women's human rights."[28] This policy development, feminist policy analysis, and research orientation includes sex trafficking theory, research, and policy recommendations. Lastly, in Jackson Heights, New York, Safe Horizons, which provides advocacy for crime and abuse victims, is another GAATW partner in the United States, first developed in 1978. Safe Horizons is currently the largest victim services organization in the United States.

Chapter Summary

The aim of this chapter was to review antitrafficking activism in the United States. The antitrafficking movement in the United States is multifaceted and complex. The wide range of participants, including survivors, social service providers, various members of the justice system, community members, facets of the hotel and transportation industries, media outlets and journalists, politicians and policymakers, indicates the widespread reach of sex trafficking and those who confront it as well as the activism that works to respond to it. The movement includes grassroots activism, individual-level advocacy, and large-scale structural change garnering political, community, and media support. International organizations also impact antitrafficking organizations in the United States, indicating a larger social movement manifesting within and outside of the United States. Members, resources, media, and political support as well as the work of those who work with survivors of sex trafficking/CSE and survivors themselves are imperative in responding to sex trafficking/CSE. At the same time, rigorous analysis of the outcomes of activism is limited. Much activism centers on identification and contacting law enforcement. There are some serious challenges to this method, indicated in chapter 9, because contacting law enforcement sometimes results in the revictimization of survivors. As indicated in chapter 10, services for survivors are important for meeting basic needs, long-term needs, and dealing with complex trauma.

Discussion Questions

1. What are the main focal points of various forms of antitrafficking activism? What is the goal, and what is the means for accomplishing this goal? What challenges may be associated with this?

2. What are some other organizations that might be important in identifying survivors of sex trafficking that were not included in the chapter? Why do you think so?

3. Why is grassroots activism important in antitrafficking efforts?

4. Were you surprised to learn that the origin of antitrafficking activism was at least thirty years ago? How does redefining sex trafficking relate to this?

12

New Directions

Up to this point, this book has examined key dynamics of sex trafficking in the United States, the theoretical lenses through which they can be viewed, and criminal justice, social services, and activist responses. The aim of the book, as a whole, is to provide the reader with a broad understanding of sex trafficking and to encourage the reader to become involved in antitrafficking responses. This chapter begins by summing up key areas of concern in the previous chapters, providing recommendations for policy and practice in social services and criminal justice system efforts, and making further suggestions for cultural and structural change. The chapter then closes with a description of the Green Dot initiative, with a "what can you do?" approach. This bystander intervention, first developed to respond to sexual assault and violence against women on college campuses, is applied to sex trafficking, providing responses that can be engaged in by the average person.

Criminal Justice System Recommendations

As indicated in chapter 9, education and training are necessary to facilitate appropriate responses of officers in order to avoid criminalizing survivors or misreporting as another crime and to increase identification.

Moreover, a survivor-centered/victim-centered approach in both policing and the prosecution process is also called for. To best meet the needs of survivors and to support the successful prosecution of traffickers, it is imperative to build trust and rapport and provide the services sex trafficked people need. Officers need education and training to recognize sex trafficking when confronted with it in the course of investigations for random traffic stops as well as in commonly co-occurring crimes. The extant literature indicates that intimate partner violence, rape, and sexual assault of those in the commercial sex industry and victimization of undocumented workers are crimes that commonly overlap with sex trafficking. To address the vulnerability of undocumented immigrants and avoid criminalization, adding resources and easing the immigration process are recommended. Support is also necessary for Safe Harbor laws to eliminate criminalization of sex trafficked children and for other laws that work to ameliorate the penalties that impede those in the commercial sex industry from moving into new areas of their lives. Policy shifts are called for to support decriminalizing the sale of sex, consistent with both the goals of abolitionists and neoliberals, liberal and radical feminists alike. The criminological research makes clear that felony records, imprisonment, arrest, and fines of sex workers do little to deter involvement in the commercial sex industry, in fact, quite the opposite. The great irony is that this results in individuals going *back* into the sex industry in order to pay off fines. Because of lack of options due to criminal records, individuals may become retrafficked or may have little other alternative for survival other than working in the commercial sex industry. Both of these realities are antithetical to the goals of eradicating sex trafficking and supporting the needs of sex trafficked or exploited people as well as sex workers. This revolving door has a negative impact in its revictimization and criminalization of trafficked and exploited people.

Education and Awareness

Identification, in the justice system, in social service organizations, and by community members, is also important in order to offer services to sex trafficked/CSE people. Increased funding is necessary to educate community members on the various types of sex trafficking present in the United States and the common indicators of sex trafficking. This includes education and awareness campaigns in colleges, universities, and schools; faith-based organizations or ethical societies; and other community activist organizations. Education and training of those likely to come into contact with sex trafficked people is essential for identifying trafficked and exploited people in hotels, truck stops, travel plazas, other facets of the transportation industry, hospitals, Planned Parenthood, health clinics, youth services, rape and sexual assault services, domestic violence/intimate partner violence services, child protective services, foster care, and juvenile justice facilities. This identification process in health care and social service settings, or following initial identification by ordinary citizens, should involve a professional educated in trauma-informed care. A reevaluation of commonly reported indicators for inaccuracies should be conducted in order to increase accurate identification of the multiple forms that sex trafficking can take.

Recommendations for Social Service Provision

Importantly, for those who are sex trafficked or commercially sexually exploited, social services are imperative for recovery. This includes social services to meet basic needs, such as access to food, clothing, water, medical care, crisis trauma care, safety planning, and shelter. Social service provision must also include resources for long-term needs, such as education or job skills training, long-term or transitional housing, employment assistance, and legal services. The current availability of social services is not extensive enough to meet the demand for such services. Shelter and housing options are extremely limited. Sex trafficking–/CSE-specific services are recommended, including survivor leadership and mentorship in a community of others who are also recovering from or have recovered from similar trauma in order to better build rapport and trust and to better address the needs of sex trafficked/exploited people. Promising practices, aside from survivor leadership, also include trauma-informed care, survivor-centered practices, cultural competency, the stages of change model, eye movement desensitization and reprocessing, cognitive behavioral therapy/cognitive processing therapy, transformational relationships, motivational interviewing, and community-based responses with a single point-of-contact social worker or advocate. More research is needed in this growing area of study.

Outreach and Prevention

Outreach and prevention must use available research to target high-risk groups and must use language that mirrors the language of those who are being trafficked and exploited. This means identifying high-risk groups, which the research suggests are disproportionately African American, Latina, Native American, LGBTQ* youth, and homeless youth (Dank et al. 2015; Martin et al. 2014; Heil and Nichols 2015). These groups are clearly overrepresented in statistics related to sex trafficking victimization. Such groups are also more likely to be exposed to risk factors such as poor-quality education, low socioeconomic status, and problematic home lives caused by weak social institutions. K–12 education systems with high rates of drop-out, truancy, and student population turnover are key targets for outreach and prevention. This is best addressed in middle school and high school, and in low-income areas with high concentrations of racially or ethnically marginalized groups. At the same time, with the advent of the Internet and with understandings of regional contextual dynamics related to sex trafficking, we do know that anyone is at risk. Consequently, prevention education should be widespread while simultaneously ensuring targeted and increased prevention efforts and outreach to the highest-risk groups. Moreover, outreach materials must reflect the populations they are intended to address. Images on posters should reflect a diversity of racial and ethnic groups as well as sex and gender identities or should otherwise match the populations that are being targeted in specific regions. Inclusive language on such materials, such as specifically highlighting that an organization welcomes transgender individuals, or is a safe zone for anyone of LGBTQ* status, is important in reaching this population. Moreover, images should be relatable to trafficked people. Avoiding chains, ropes, barcodes, and other common images used in the antitrafficking world is imperative in outreach to trafficked and exploited people (Smith 2014). Wording should also include language that survivors would be likely to identify with, like "the life" or "selling sex," as opposed to "slavery" or "sex trafficking."

As stated previously, street prostitution is declining as Internet solicitation increases. The online environment produces less chance for identification and the provision of social services because survivors are less visible and less accessible. Street outreach includes driving a vehicle or going on foot to popular streets on which solicitation is known to occur and offering services, providing information on resources, and providing condoms (Curtis et al. 2008; Lloyd 2012). In current form, outreach to trafficked and exploited people selling sex through the Internet would have to involve making individual calls and arranging to meet with survivors to provide informational and harm reduction materials. Outreach services lack the resources to do this on a large scale, in addition to the practical complications. Accordingly, the population is harder to reach, virtually "hidden in plain sight"—visible on Internet advertisements but difficult to reach due to a lack of resources and survivors' and traffickers' avoidance of any attempt at contact through this venue (Reid 2010). Recall that sex trafficking / CSE takes multiple forms, and survivors, particularly survivors engaged in the commercial sex industry as a consequence of survival sex or involvement with a "boyfriend pimp," may not welcome a call from an outreach worker. In the street venues, there is an opportunity to build a trusting relationship so the survivor, when ready, knows where to go and has an important "bridge" person (Oselin 2014). Yet, as sex-for-sale moves increasingly indoors with solicitation taking place on the Internet, outreach efforts need to become more creative. Some researchers indicate outreach occurring in Internet cafes to address the changing dynamics of the trafficked and exploited population (Dank et al. 2015). Others have posted outreach ads on common Internet sites that advertise sex-for-sale, as survivors often post their own ads. These are examples of creative outreach efforts that need to take place.

Societal Issues

The macrostructural forces that create a social environment where sex trafficking and exploitation can flourish must be addressed in order to get at the root of the problem and to eliminate barriers to help seeking. We live in a society characterized among the high-income nations as fiercely independent—to a fault. The United States lacks the social safety nets that other high-income nations have, resulting in a system that facilitates and sustains an underclass. Social safety nets typically include access to health care, including care related to substance abuse and mental health, affordable medications, and access to transgender-specific health care needs. Safety nets also include financial assistance to prevent poverty, including those which lessen child poverty, day care subsidies, provide a minimum wage as a living wage, and foster equal opportunity and access to education. The United States has the highest rates of child poverty of any other high-income nation. The gaps between our wealthy and our poor are also the greatest. We have the largest number of working poor compared to any other similar nation. Within the last fifteen years, cuts to social service provision and increases in tax breaks for the wealthy, combined with an increased cost of living, declining employment (which is now back on the rise) and employment benefits, have continued to widen the income gap between our wealthy and our poor, facilitating a steady shrinking of our middle class. We do not have equal opportunity in education K–12 because school districts are largely funded by local property tax, which is a direct reflection of the economic status of the school districts' residents. The result is a perpetuation of class inequality. We lack the funding for widespread and equal-access social and health services not because the country cannot afford it but because we are so culturally individualistic that many Americans and the politicians who represent them will not approve it. The Patient Protection and Affordable Care Act (2010), also known as Obamacare, is an improvement in expanding access, but it is a model that is not at all the same thing as universal health care, of which every other high-income nation in the world has some form. We do not have social safety nets that prevent poverty, economic desperation, and sex trafficking anywhere near the extent of other high-income countries.

Known risk factors for sex trafficking and sexual exploitation include homelessness, inequality in schools, poverty, racial/ethnic marginalization, sexism, heterosexism, lack of services for substance abuse assistance, lack of assistance with day care expenses, background of child abuse and domestic violence in the home, and a low minimum wage (Dank et al. 2015; Polaris Project 2015b). Addressing these risk factors involves supporting the funding and political pressure that works to ameliorate them. Weak social safety nets combined with weak social institutions creates a situation rife for sex trafficking and exploitation.

In sum, increased funding for and the availability of shelter, housing, resources, prevention, and outreach for trafficked and exploited people to address weak social institutions and provide expanded education and training to individuals in the criminal justice system, health care systems, and various social services are necessary to address the problem. Modifying policy to reduce the revictimization, criminalization, and retrafficking of sex trafficked and exploited people is also imperative. Continued community activism on multiple fronts, facilitating public and political support, is also needed. Individual-level action also plays a role.

What Can *We* Do?

At this point, after reading all about sex trafficking—experiences of survivors, backgrounds of traffickers, the role of buyers, issues with the varying perspectives and the way they influence policy development as well as challenges with social service provision and criminal justice system responses, the reader might be wondering, *to what end? What can I do?* Embedded within the academic and sociocultural responses to violence against women, there is something called the Green Dot project, which can be applied to anti–sex trafficking/CSE activism. As a model for the average person to get involved in reducing sex trafficking, it provides a useful ideological and action structure in its accessibility and feasibility. Green Dot originally started as a response to violence against women on college campuses and expanded from this base. The initiative was created by Dr. Dorothy Edwards, who stated:

Ten years into my career, which focused one way or another on addressing violence, I looked up, tired and exasperated, and asked myself a simple question, "Am I accomplishing what I set out to accomplish?" My goal was that less women, men and children would become victims of violence as a result of my work. A decade in, I had no evidence that I was even one stop closer to that goal. Despite great job evaluations and almost daily praise regarding another program I had done or speech I had given—I wasn't preventing violence. Period. Furthermore, as I looked around me, I saw my colleagues in the same boat. Conference after conference we sat and listened to each other present on yet another clever poster campaign, another creative one-time-only-mandatory program, and another date-rape skit. There seemed an unspoken agreement that we would resist the urge to cry out in the middle of the presentation "Are you frickin' kidding me? Isn't this the exact same thing I heard 10 years ago, just with a different slogan slapped on the front?" And instead we nodded and smiled—all the while letting our hope for real change slip into tired resignation. This culmination of personal and professional restlessness and frustration triggered a professional crisis of sorts. Here I was, benefiting from the heroic work on intervention and response from those who came before—while simultaneously being acutely aware that I was not building on their successes—but simply maintaining them. . . . Equipped with the best research and theory I could find, I took my newly created strategy to the front lines of my work—at colleges, high schools, and coalitions across the country. There, the best my mind could conjure was subjected to the realities of the front lines: peer pressure, parties, disinterested students, bureaucracy, faculty, teachers, and staff overwhelmed with work-loads and family, message overload, competing issues of equal urgency, we all know the list. I watched with humility (but resiliency) as my initial attempts tanked completely. Then, little by little, the real life experiences and reactions of students and professionals from across fields, along with key community partners, began to shape and mold this model into what has become the Green Dot prevention strategy. By necessity, it is a strategy in process. A strategy that must refine and course correct with each evaluation, stream of data and piece of feedback. By definition, it will be strengthened by the application and scrutiny of others. The story of Green Dot etc. is one thread of many burgeoning around the country, fueled by the same impatient insistence—"this violence has got to stop."[1]

The Green Dot project uses the metaphor of an image of a map, asking participants to imagine all the instances of violence marked by red dots on this map. The red dots are characterized by a moment or choice, when one person makes a decision to harm someone else verbally, psychologically, or physically. The map is quickly covered in red dots. Then the participants are asked to imagine what would happen, in a countermovement of sorts, if each community member contributed just one or two moments of conversation, action, or other intervention to counter instances of physical, verbal, or psychological harm, which are marked by green dots on the map. This could include making a choice to intervene at a college party, looking out for a friend, countering a person making a decision to inflict harm, or simply having a conversation about not tolerating violence and abuse. If each person contributed a green dot or two, the red dots would begin to be overwhelmed by green dots. This is essentially an initiative for cultural change put in the hands of ordinary, average people based on individual decision making to fuel action. This would mean overcoming and having the confidence to intervene, countering peer pressure and the awkwardness of uncertainty. The initiative also recognizes that some may be able to give more than others due to time constraints, level of interest, or other factors. The beauty of Green Dot is that no intervention is too small—any person can find a realistic option that suits what they are capable of or willing to do in an intervention. For example, if someone lacks the confidence to intervene, their green dot might be to find someone else who will. In any circumstance of known harm to others, an individual is faced with a choice—do nothing, check on someone, directly intervene, or find someone who will intervene. In cases where there is an immediate concern for someone's safety, calling the police is likely the best option.

While the purpose of Green Dot was to address and prevent domestic violence and sexual assault on college campuses, others have applied it to sex trafficking responses. I was first exposed to this application by Christina Meneses of the YWCA in St. Louis at a coalition meeting. The central idea of Green Dot is that we all have a role we can play, and we need to meet people where they are. Each individual can decide what their role will be. For myself, awareness through education is the role I have chosen. Yet I also do little things. For example, I was walking with my son in the Delmar Loop area of St. Louis, Missouri. A young man, maybe in his late teens or early twenties, looking like a typical Washington University student, was wearing a T-shirt with an image that resembled a Domino's Pizza box, but instead of saying "Dominoes," his T-shirt had "Pimpin' 'Hos'" printed upon it. I asked the young man if I could take a picture of his shirt on my phone so I could show it in a class I teach. He then asked what the class was, and I told him it was a sex trafficking class at Washington University. I then went on to explain that many cases of sex trafficking involve a pimp who forces, coerces, or otherwise exploits others in the sex trade, or who poses as a boyfriend to a teen girl and then convinces her to engage in prostitution. I told him that I was interested in discussing with the class the way our culture glamorizes pimps, does not take the issue seriously, or otherwise demeans women and those in the commercial sex industry (such as referring to anyone as a "Ho"). He then said, "I guess I should take this shirt off then, huh? I just thought it was funny." Then I asked him to consider why he thought it was funny. He let me take the picture, took off his shirt and put it back on inside out, and we had a good parting. This is an example of a small green dot, but a dot nonetheless. Some of you will directly work with survivors as lawyers, law enforcement, social workers, psychologists, educators, or psychiatrists. Others of you may educate or begin a dialogue with your friends. Some of you may wish to organize events on campus, start a student group, or volunteer for organizations in the community. Some of these items take little but can provide a lot. Imagine all the green dots adding up on a map.

What's Your Green Dot?

The first thing you can do as an antitrafficking advocate is to become educated on this issue. You have started that process by reading this book. Note that this is a rapidly expanding field of study, and new information is becoming available all the time. Keeping up with this information is key to understanding shifts in legislation, the current state of activism, best practices for working with survivors, and the most up-to-date research.

You may also wish to join your local antitrafficking coalition. If there is not one, consider starting one in collaboration with invested community partners. If you are a student, creating a student group on your community college, college, or university campus might be an option, or simply add antitrafficking sessions to your already-existing sociology club, human services club, criminal justice club, or women, gender, and sexuality studies clubs or other clubs or student government–sponsored events. If your classes require research papers and sex trafficking/CSE would be an appropriate topic, consider some aspect of sex trafficking to present to your classmates.

Also keep in mind that many of the risk factors for sex trafficking and commercial sexual exploitation are rooted in various forms of social inequality. This includes racial inequality, sex and gender discrimination, marginalization of LGBTQ* people, anti-immigrant mentalities, and class inequality, among others. Consequently, any work that you do in efforts toward eradicating or improving current dynamics of marginalization and social inequality will benefit trafficked and exploited people.

Contact your governor and state representatives as well as your federal representatives and senators about weak social institutions and the need for expanded social safety nets, and about homelessness, child abuse, domestic violence/intimate partner violence, and unwanted or neglected children, which are factors contributing to sex trafficking. Tell them that you care about these issues and want to support the funding to address them. Such efforts are often referred to as social justice efforts. Addressing social inequalities is both a cultural issue and a social issue. Culturally, this means changing hearts and minds. Education, conversation, mentorship, and leading by example are ways of contributing to cultural shifts. All actions, large and small, will contribute to ameliorating the exploitation and harm done to others. What's your Green Dot?

Discussion Questions

1. Draft a letter to your senators and representatives who sit on our U.S. Congress and indicate the actions you would like taken to address sex trafficking. Send it to them by finding their contact forms here: http://www.contactingthecongress.org/.

2. View this Green Dot campus video and describe what your green dot will be: http://www.youtube.com/watch?v=1V4xna0003Q.

Notes

1. Sex Trafficking: An Introduction

1. "Kansas City Man Pleads Guilty to Federal Sex Trafficking Charge," FBI Kansas City Division, March 26, 2012. http://www.fbi.gov/kansascity/press-releases /2012/kansas-city-man-pleads-guilty-to-federal-sex-trafficking-charge.
2. Trafficking Victims Violence Protection Act of 2000 (TVPA), Pub. L. 106-386, Statutes at Large, 114 (2000): 1464, sec. 103, 8a and 8b.
3. "Former Chicago Massage Parlor Operator Sentenced to Life in Prison for Human Trafficking of Four Women." U.S. Department of Justice, November 26, 2012, http://www.justice.gov/opa/pr/former-chicago-massage-parlor-operator -sentenced-life-prison-human-trafficking-four-women.
4. Civil Society, http://civilsocietyhelps.org.
5. Trafficking Victims Protection Reauthorization Act (TVPRA) of 2013, Pub. L. 113-4, Stat. 54, http://www.gpo.gov/fdsys/pkg/PLAW-113publ4/html/PLAW-113publ4 .htm.
6. "Former Chicago Massage Parlor Operator Sentenced."
7. See also ibid.
8. See also "Victim Survivor Leader Webinar," Rachel Lloyd. *Girls Education and Mentoring Services*, http://www.gems-girls.org/get-trained/webinars.
9. See also "Former Chicago Massage Parlor Operator Sentenced."

10. See also "Sex Trafficking in the U.S.," The Covering House, http://www
    .thecoveringhouse.org/the-issue/

11. See also "Victim Survivor Leader Webinar."

12. Ibid.

2. Theoretical Perspectives and the Politics of Sex Trafficking

1. Howard N. Snyder and Joseph Mulako-Wangota. Bureau of Justice Statistics.
   "U.S Arrest Estimates Arrests of Black Juveniles, Prostitution and Commercialized Vice," and "U.S Arrest Estimates Arrests of Juveniles, Prostitution
   and Commercialized Vice." Generated using the Arrest Data Analysis Tool at
   www.bjs.gov (2012).

2. See also the Magdalene House website, http://www.thistlefarms.org/, and
   the Girls Education & Mentoring Services (GEMS) website, http://www.gems
   -girls.org/.

3. Pornography

1. "Fairview Heights Man Pleads Guilty to Production of Child Pornography,"
   U.S. Attorney's Office, Southern District of Illinois, October 3, 2012. https://
   www.fbi.gov/springfield/press-releases/2012/fairview-heights-man-pleads
   -guilty-to-production-of-child-pornography.

2. "Local Priest Sentenced on Federal Child Pornography Charges," U.S. Attorney's Office, Eastern District of Missouri, August 30, 2013. http://www.justice
   .gov/usao-edmo/pr/local-priest-sentenced-federal-child-pornography-charges.

3. "Former Seminary Student Pleads Guilty to Attempting to Receive Child Porn."
   U.S. Attorney's Office, Eastern District of Missouri, May 31, 2012. http://www
   .justice.gov/archive/usao/moe/news/2012/may/pinkston_nickolas.html.

4. "Local Priest Sentenced."

5. Trafficking Victims Violence Protection Act of 2000 (TVPA), Pub. L. 106-386,
   Statutes at Large, 114 (2000): 1464, sec. 103a.

6. "Poplar Bluff Man Sentenced to 50 years on Child Pornography Charges."
   U.S. Attorney's Office, Eastern District of Missouri, February 13, 2014. http://
   www.justice.gov/usao-edmo/pr/poplar-bluff-man-sentenced-50-years-child
   -pornography-charges.

7. "Child Abductor Sentenced to 120 Years on Child Exploitation Charges." U.S.
   Attorney's Office, Eastern District of Missouri, July 15, 2013, http://www.justice
   .gov/usao-edmo/pr/child-abductor-sentenced-120-years-child-exploitation-charges.

8. "Lincoln County Man Sentenced to Federal Child Pornography Charges." U.S. Attorney's Office, Eastern District of Missouri, November 7, 2013. http://www.justice.gov/usao-edmo/pr/lincoln-county-man-sentenced-federal -child-pornography-charges.

4. Prostitution

1. *Six Arrested in Child Prostitution Ring in Jefferson County*, FBI Denver Division, February 13, 2014. http://www.fbi.gov/denver/press-releases/2014/six-arrested -in-child-prostitution-ring-in-jefferson-county.
2. Breaking Free website, http://www.breakingfree.net/.
3. Ibid.
4. Convention for the Suppression of the Traffic in Persons and of the Exploitation of the Prostitution of Others, December 2, 1949. United Nations Office of the High Commissioner, http://www.ohchr.org/EN/ProfessionalInterest /Pages/TrafficInPersons.aspx.
5. Vienna Declaration and Programme of Action, June 25, 1993. World Conference on Human Rights in Vienna, http://www.ohchr.org/EN/ProfessionalInterest /Pages/Vienna.aspx.
6. Protocol to Prevent, Suppress, and Punish Trafficking in Persons Especially Women and Children, supplementing the United Nations Convention against Transnational Organized Crime, November 15, 2000. United Nations Office of the High Commissioner, http://www.ohchr.org/EN/ProfessionalInterest/Pages /ProtocolTraffickingInPersons.aspx.

5. Survivors

1. National School Climate Survey (2013), Gay, Lesbian & Straight Education Network, http://www.glsen.org/nscs.
2. "USA QuickFacts from the United States Census Bureau," U.S. Census Bureau. http://quickfacts.census.gov/qfd/states/00000.html.
3. Howard N. Snyder and Joseph Mulako-Wangota. Bureau of Justice Statistics. "U.S Arrest Estimates Arrests of Juveniles, Prostitution and Commercialized Vice"; "U.S Arrest Estimates Arrests of Black Juveniles, Prostitution and Commercialized Vice"; "U.S Arrest Estimates Arrests of White Juveniles, Prostitution and Commercialized Vice"; "U.S Arrest Estimates Arrests of American Indian/Alaska Native Juveniles, Prostitution and Commercialized Vice"; and

"U.S Arrest Estimates Arrests of Asian/Pacific Islander Juveniles, Prostitution and Commercialized Vice." Generated using the Arrest Data Analysis Tool at www.bjs.gov (2001).

4. Howard N. Snyder and Joseph Mulako-Wangota. Bureau of Justice Statistics. "U.S Arrest Estimates Arrests of Juveniles, Prostitution and Commercialized Vice"; "U.S Arrest Estimates Arrests of Black Juveniles, Prostitution and Commercialized Vice"; "U.S Arrest Estimates Arrests of White Juveniles, Prostitution and Commercialized Vice"; "U.S Arrest Estimates Arrests of American Indian/Alaska Native Juveniles, Prostitution and Commercialized Vice"; "U.S Arrest Estimates Arrests of Asian/Pacific Islander Juveniles, Prostitution and Commercialized Vice." Generated using the Arrest Data Analysis Tool at www.bjs.gov (2012).

5. "Former Chicago Massage Parlor Operator Sentenced to Life in Prison for Human Trafficking of Four Women." U.S. Department of Justice, November 26, 2012, http://www.justice.gov/opa/pr/former-chicago-massage-parlor-operator-sentenced-life-prison-human-trafficking-four-women.

6. "Final Defendant Sentenced for His Role in International Conspiracy Involving the Forced Labor of Eastern European Women in Detroit-area Exotic Dance Clubs." U.S. Department of Justice. May 23, 2012, http://www.justice.gov/opa/pr/final-defendant-sentenced-his-role-international-conspiracy-involving-forced-labor-eastern.

7. "Hillsborough County Man Arrested by ICE for Sex Trafficking of a Minor," U.S. Immigration and Customs Enforcement, April 14. https://www.ice.gov/news/releases/hillsborough-county-man-arrested-ice-sex-trafficking-minor.

8. Georgia Department of Education website, http://www.gadoe.org/Pages/Home.aspx.

9. "School Data," Missouri Department of Elementary and Secondary Education, http://dese.mo.gov/school-data.

10. Data for 2012 and 2014, ibid.

6. Traffickers

1. *United States v. Junger*, No. 12-1006 (8th Cir. 2013).

2. "Leader of International Sex-Trafficking Ring Sentenced to Life in Prison," United States Attorney's Office, Southern District of Georgia, February 19, 2014, http://www.justice.gov/usao-sdga/pr/leader-international-sex-trafficking-ring-sentenced-life-prison.

7. Sex Trafficking Operations

1. "Atlanta Man Admits His Role in Operating an Interstate Juvenile Sex Trafficking Enterprise," FBI Washington Field Office, March 18, 2013. https://www.fbi .gov/washingtondc/press-releases/2013/atlanta-man-admits-his-role-in-operating-an-interstate-juvenille-sex-trafficking-enterprise.
2. See the World Economic Forum website, http://www.weforum.org/.
3. "Most Wanted—Human Trafficking," FBI website, http://www.fbi.gov/ wanted/human-trafficking.
4. Ibid.
5. Ibid.
6. "Bronx Runaway Teen Found Working As Sex Slave in Queens." *News 12 The Bronx*, February 11. http://bronx.news12.com/news/bronx-runaway-teen-found -working-as-sex-slave-in-queens-1.7033539.
7. "Gang Member Sentenced to 20 Years for Human Trafficking." *Bonney Lake Courier Herald*, August 30, http://www.blscourierherald.com/news/323396841 .html#.

9. Criminal Justice System Responses

1. Trafficking Victims Violence Protection Act of 2000 (TVPA), Pub. L. 106-386, Statutes at Large, 114 (2000), Section 103, 8a and 8b.
2. "Victims of Human Trafficking: T Nonimmigrant Status." U.S. Citizenship and Immigration Services, last reviewed/updated October 3, 2011, http:// www.uscis.gov/humanitarian/victims-human-trafficking-other-crimes/ victims-human-trafficking-t-nonimmigrant-status.
3. *2013 State Report Cards—Protected Innocence Challenge*, Shared Hope International, http://sharedhope.org/what-we-do/bring-justice/reportcards/2013-reportcards/.
4. "Victim Survivor Leader Webinar," Rachel Lloyd. *Girls Education and Mentoring Services*, http://www.gems-girls.org/get-trained/webinars.
5. Howard N. Snyder and Joseph Mulako-Wangota. Bureau of Justice Statistics. "U.S. Arrest Estimates Arrests of Juveniles, Prostitution and Commercialized Vice"; "U.S. Arrest Estimates Arrests of Black Juveniles, Prostitution and Commercialized Vice"; "U.S. Arrest Estimates Arrests of White Juveniles, Prostitution and Commercialized Vice"; "U.S. Arrest Estimates Arrests of American Indian/Alaska Native Juveniles, Prostitution and Commercialized Vice"; "U.S. Arrest Estimates Arrests of Asian/Pacific Islander Juveniles, Prostitution and Commercialized Vice." Generated using the Arrest Data Analysis Tool at www.bjs.gov (2012).

6. Howard N. Snyder and Joseph Mulako-Wangota. Bureau of Justice Statistics. "U.S. Arrest Estimates of all Persons, Prostitution and Commercialized Vice," Generated using the Arrest Data Analysis Tool at www.bjs.gov. (1990–2010).

7. See also "Victim Survivor Leader Webinar."

10. Social Services and Health Care Responses

1. See also "Victim Survivor Leader Webinar." Rachel Lloyd, *Girls Education and Mentoring Services*, http://www.gems-girls.org/get-trained/webinars.

2. Ibid.

3. Ibid.

4. See also ibid.

11. The Anti–Sex Trafficking Movement in the United States

1. See the Children of the Night website, http://www.childrenofthenight.org/.

2. Ibid.

3. Ibid.

4. See the Civil Society website, http://civilsocietyhelps.org.

5. See the Girls Education & Mentoring Service website, http://www.gems-girls.org/.

6. See also "Sex Trafficking in the U.S.," The Covering House, http://www.thecoveringhouse.org/our-story/.

7. Ibid.

8. See the End Slavery Cincinnati website, http://www.endslaverycincinnati.org/.

9. Ibid. Contacting law enforcement is a contentious area of debate. See chapter 10 for information on survivor-centered practice.

10. See the Truckers Against Trafficking website, http://truckersagainsttrafficking.org.

11. Ibid.

12. See also "Trucker Who Helped Save Sex Captive in Virginia: 'I've Got Daughters.'" *CBS News*, February 13. http://www.cbsnews.com/news/trucker-who-helped-save-sex-captive-in-virginia-ive-got-daughters/.

13. "Iowa Couple Pleads Guilty to Sex Trafficking by Force, Fraud, or Coercion." U.S. Attorney's Office, Eastern District of Virginia, May 1, 2015. http://www.justice.gov/usao-edva/pr/iowa-couple-pleads-guilty-sex-trafficking-force-fraud-or-coercion.

14. "Trucker Who Helped Save."

15. "Success Stories," *Innocents at Risk*, Airline Ambassadors International. http://www.innocentsatrisk.org/human-trafficking/success-stories.

16. *The CNN Freedom Project: Ending Modern-Day Slavery*, CNN. http://thecnnfreedom-project.blogs.cnn.com/2011/02/17/more-about-the-cnn-freedom-project/.

17. See the CATW website, www.catwinternational.org.

18. See the International Justice Mission website, "About Us," http://www.ijm.org.

19. Ibid., "Where We Work."

20. See ibid., "What We Do."

21. See the Shared Hope International website, http://sharedhope.org/about-us/our-mission-and-values/.

22. Ibid.

23. Ibid.

24. See the Global Alliance Against Traffic in Women website, http://www.gaatw.org/.

25. Ibid.

26. Ibid.

27. See the Sex Workers Project website, "About," http://swp.urbanjustice.org/.

28. See Center for Women Policy Studies website, http://www.centerwomenpolicy.org/

12. New Directions

1. Dorothy Edwards, *Origin of Green Dot etc.* https://www.livethegreendot.com/gd_origins.html.

References

Adams, T. M., and D. B. Fuller. 2006. "The Words Have Changed but the Ideology Remains the Same: Misogynistic Lyrics in Rap Music." *Journal of Black Studies* 36, no. 6: 938–57.

Akee, R., A. Bedi, A. K. Basu, and N. H. Chau. 2010. *Transnational Trafficking, Law Enforcement and Victim Protection: A Middleman's Perspective.* Ithaca, N.Y.: Cornell University Press.

Akers, R. L., and C. S. Sellers. 2009. *Criminological Theories: Introduction, Evaluation, and Applications.* New York: Oxford University Press.

Albonetti, C. A. 2014. "Changes in Federal Sentencing for Forced Labor Trafficking and for Sex Trafficking: A Ten Year Assessment." *Crime, Law and Social Change* 61, no. 2: 179–204. doi:10.1007/s10611-013-9507-1.

Alvarez, M. B., and E. J. Alessi. 2012. Human Trafficking Is More Than Sex Trafficking and Prostitution Implications for Social Work. *Affilia* 27, no. 2: 142–52. doi:10.1177/0886109912443763.

American Hotel and Lodging Association. 2012. "Industry Principles to Combat Human Trafficking." http://www.ahla.com/uploadedFiles/_Common/pdf/Trafficking_Principles_Industry_Update.pdf.

Bakehorn, J. 2010. "Women-Made Pornography." In *Sex for Sale: Prostitution, Pornography, and the Sex Industry,* ed. R. Weitzer, 91–111. New York: Routledge.

Bales, K., and R. Soodalter. 2009. *The Slave Next Door.* Berkeley: University of California Press.

Banks, D., N. Dutch, and K. Wang. 2008. "Collaborative Efforts to Improve System Response to Families Who Are Experiencing Child Maltreatment and Domestic Violence. *Journal of Interpersonal Violence* 23: 876–902.

Banks, D., and T. Kyckelhahn. 2011. "Characteristics of Suspected Human Trafficking Incidents: 2005–2008." *Bureau of Justice Statistics.* http://www.bjs.gov /index.cfm?ty=pbdetail&iid=2372.

Barron, M., and M. Kimmel. 2000. "Sexual Violence in Three Pornographic Media." *Journal of Sex Research* 37: 161–68.

Bartenstein, B. 2015. "At Sturgis, Police Target Sex Traffickers with Everything They Have." *TwinCities.com.* August 2. http://www.twincities.com/crime /ci_28575977/last-year-another-five-men-were-indicted-after.

Bass, J., J. Annan, S. McIvor Murray, D. Kaysen, S. Griffiths, T. Cetinoglu, K. Wachter, L. Murray, and P. Bolton, P. 2013. "Controlled Trial of Psychotherapy for Congolese Survivors of Sexual Violence. *New England Journal of Medicine* 368, no. 23: 2182–91.

Baumgardner, J., and A. Richards. 2010. *Manifesta: Young Women, Feminism, and the Future.* New York: Farrar, Straus and Giroux.

Beal, F. M. 2013. "Double Jeopardy: To Be Black and Female." *Chicago Women's Liberation Union Herstory Archive.* University of Illinois at Chicago. http://www.uic .edu/orgs/cwluherstory/CWLUArchive/blackandfemale.html.

Bellware, K. 2015. "Hundreds of Johns Arrested in Sex Trafficking Sting." *Huffington Post.* February 2, 2015. http://www.huffingtonpost.com/2015/02/02/national -day-of-johns-2015_n_6595358.html.

Benjamin, H., and R. E. L. Masters. 1964. *Prostitution and Morality: A Definitive Report on the Prostitute in Contemporary Society and an Analysis of the Causes and Effects on the Suppression of Prostitution.* New York: Julian Press.

Bernstein, E. 2001. "The Meaning of the Purchase: Desire, Demand and the Commerce of Sex." *Ethnography* 2: 389–420.

Boxill, N. A., and D. J. Richardson. 2007. Ending Sex Trafficking of Children in Atlanta. *Affilia* 22, no. 2: 138–49. doi:10.1177/0886109907299054.

Bradley, R., J. Greene, E., Russ, L., Dutra, and D. Westen. 2005. "A Multidimensional Meta-Analysis of Psychotherapy for PTSD." *American Journal of Psychiatry* 162: 214–227.

Brice, J. 2013. "Colorado Truck Drivers Keeping Eyes Out for Human Trafficking." *CBS Denver*, July 30. http://denver.cbslocal.com/2013/07/30/colorado-truck -drivers-keeping-eyes-out-for-human-trafficking/.

Bridges, A., and R. Jensen. 2011. "Pornography." In *Sourcebook on Violence Against Women*, ed. C. Renzetti and J. Edleson, 133–47. Thousand Oaks, Calif.: Sage.

Bridges, A. J., R. Wosnitzer, E. Scharrer, C. Sun, and R. Liberman. 2010. Aggression and Sexual Behavior in Best-Selling Pornography Videos: A Content Analysis Update. *Violence Against Women* 16, no. 10: 1065–85. doi:10.1177/1077801210382866.

Bridges, C. B., D. Scantz, and J. F. Jones. 2005. "Pimpin' All Over the World." http://www.azlyrics.com/lyrics/ludacris/pimpinallovertheworld.html.

Briggs, J. E. 2005. "Maywood 'Players Ball' Stirs Protest: Opponents Say Party Glamorizes Pimps." *Chicago Tribune.* December 4. http://articles.chicagotribune.com/2005-12-04/news/0512040421_1_maywood-police-department-pimps-protest.

Browne, J., and V. Minichiello. 1996. "The Social and Work Context of Commercial Sex Between Men." *Journal of Sociology* 32: 86–92.

Buchbinder, S. 2013. "America's Female Sex Traffickers." *Daily Beast.* August 7, 2015. http://www.thedailybeast.com/witw/articles/2013/08/07/when-women-are-found-trafficking-other-women.html.

Busch-Armendariz, N., M. Nsonwu, and L. Cook Heffron. 2009. "Understanding Human Trafficking: Development of Typologies of Traffickers PHASE II." *First Annual Interdisciplinary Conference on Human Trafficking.*

——. 2014. "A Kaleidoscope: The Role of the Social Work Practitioner and the Strength of Social Work Theories and Practice in Meeting the Complex Needs of People Trafficked and the Professionals That Work with Them." *International Social Work* 57, no. 1: 7–18. doi:10.1177/0020872813505630.

Busch-Armendariz, N., M. Nsonwu, L. Cook Heffron, J. Garza, and M. Hernandez. 2009. "Understanding Human Trafficking: Development of Typologies of Traffickers." *Institute on Domestic Violence and Sexual Assault.* Center for Social Work Research School of Social Work: University of Texas at Austin.

Canning, A., and J. Pereira. 2011. "Tot Dressed as Prostitute: 'Toddlers and Tiaras' Blasted for Airing Image of 3-Y-O Pageant Contestant in Racy Costume." *ABC News,* September 12. http://abcnews.go.com/US/toddlers-tiaras-mom-defends-dressing-tot-prostitute-pageant/story?id=14497042.

Carmen, A., and H. Moody. 1985. *Working Women: The Subterranean World of Street Prostitution.* New York: Harper and Row.

Charters, J. 2015. "Trucker Catches Girl's Face Peeking out of RV Window. What He Saves Her from Is Beyond Horrific." *Independent Journal Review,* February. http://www.ijreview.com/2015/02/251159-truckers-instinct-freed-girl-repeat-victim-one-horrid-crimes/.

Cho, S., A. Dreher, and E. Neumayer. 2013. "Does Legalized Prostitution Increase Human Trafficking?" *World Development* 41: 67–82. doi:10.1016/j.worlddev.2012.05.023.

Clawson, H., N. Dutch, and M. Cummings. 2006. *Law Enforcement Response to Human Trafficking and the Implications for Victims: Current Practices and Lessons Learned.* U.S. Department of Justice. https://www.ncjrs.gov/pdffiles1/nij/grants/216547.pdf.

Clawson, H. J., N. Dutch, S. Lopez, and S. Tiapula. 2008. *Prosecuting Human Trafficking Cases: Lessons Learned and Promising Practices.* U.S. Department of Justice. https://www.ncjrs.gov/pdffiles1/nij/grants/223972.pdf.

Clawson, H. J., N. Dutch, A. Solomon, L. G. Grace. 2009. "Human Trafficking into and Within the United States: A Review of the Literature." Washington, D.C.: Office of the Assistant Secretary for Planning and Evaluation, U.S. Department of Human and Health Services.

Clawson, H., N. Dutch, and E. Williamson. 2008. *National Symposium on the Health Needs of Human Trafficking Victims: Background Document.* Washington, D.C.: Office of the Assistant Secretary for Planning and Evaluation, U.S. Department of Health and Human Services.

Cole, J., G. Sprang, R. Lee, and J. Cohen. 2014. "The Trauma of Commercial Sexual Exploitation of Youth: A Comparison of CSE Victims to Sexual Abuse Victims in a Clinical Sample." *Journal of Interpersonal Violence*, November 6, 1–25. doi:10.1177/0886260514555133.

Coleman, C., P. Beauregard, and J. Houston. 2005. "Hard Out Here for a Pimp." http://www.metrolyrics.com/hard-out-here-for-a-pimp-lyrics-three-6-mafia .html.

Collins, P. H. 2008. *Black Feminist Thought: Knowledge, Consciousness, and the Politics of Empowerment.* London: Routledge.

Corrigan, M. J., B. Lonsck, and L. Videka. 2007. "Moving the Risk and Protective Faction Framework Toward Individualized Assessment in Adolescent Substance Abuse Prevention." *Journal of Child and Adolescent Substance Abuse* 16: 17–34.

County Administrative Board of Stockholm. 2014. *The Extent and Development of Prostitution in Sweden.* http://www.lansstyrelsen.se/stockholm/SiteCollection-Documents/Sv/publikationer/2015/rapport-2015-18.pdf.

Cowan, G., C. Lee, D. Levy, and D. Snyder. 1988. "Dominance and Inequality in X-Rated Videocassettes." *Psychology of Women Quarterly* 12: 299–311.

Crenshaw, K. 1991. "Mapping the Margins: Intersectionality, Identity Politics, and Violence Against Women of Color." *Stanford Law Review* 43, no. 6: 1241–99.

Crouch, D. 2015. "Swedish Prostitution Law Targets Buyers, but Some Say It Hurts Sellers." *New York Times*, March 14. http://www.nytimes.com/2015/03/15/world /swedish-prostitution-law-targets-buyers-but-some-say-it-hurts-sellers.html.

Curtis, R., K. Terry, M. Dank, K. Drombrowski, and B. Khan. 2008. *The Commercial Sexual Exploitation of Children in New York City*, Volume 1: *The CSEC Population in New York City Size, Characteristics, and Needs.* U.S. Department of Justice, September. https://www.ncjrs.gov/pdffiles1/nij/grants/225083.pdf.

Dalrymple, A., and K. Lymn. 2015. "When a Minnesota Girl Goes missing, Police Check North Dakota." *Billings Gazette*, January 4. http://billingsgazette.com /news/state-and-regional/montana/when-a-minnesota-girl-goes-missing-police -check-north-dakota/article_ea78afe9-8642-54b7-9b01-76a3aebd9676.html.

Dank, M., J. Yahner, K. Madden, I. Bañuelos, L. Yu, A. Ritchie, M. Mora, and B. Conner. 2015. "Surviving the Streets of New York: Experiences of LGBTQ Youth,

YMSM, and YWSW Engaged in Survival Sex." *Urban Institute*, February 25. http://www.urban.org/research/publication/surviving-streets-new-york-experiences-lgbtq-youth-ymsm-and-ywsw-engaged-survival-sex.

Davidson, J. O'Connell. 2002. "The Rights and Wrongs of Prostitution." *Hypatia* 17: 84–98.

——. 2006. "Will the Real Sex Slave Please Stand Up?" *Feminist Review* 83 (Sexual Moralities): 4–22.

Delson, B., S. Carter, J. Hahn, M. Shinoda, R. G. Bourdon, C. C. Bennington, K. Joshua, and T. Mosely. "Big Pimpin'." http://www.azlyrics.com/lyrics/jayz/bigpimpinextended.html.

Dempsey, M. M. 2007. "Toward a Feminist State: What Does 'Effective' Prosecution of Domestic Violence Mean?" *Modern Law Review* 70: 908–35.

——. 2011. "Sex Trafficking and Criminalization: In Defense of Feminist Abolitionism," *University of Pennsylvania Law Review* 158, no. 6 (November 16). Villanova Law/Public Policy Research Paper No. 2010-20. *Social Science Research Network*, http://papers.ssrn.com/abstract=1710264.

Dines, G. 2010. *Pornland: How Porn Has Hijacked Our Sexuality*. Boston: Beacon.

Doezema, J. 1999. "Loose Women or Lost Women? The Re-Emergence of the Myth of White Slavery in Contemporary Discourses of Trafficking in Women." *Gender Issues* 18, no. 1 23–50. doi:10.1007/s12147-999-0021-9.

——. 2001. "Ouch!: Western Feminists' 'Wounded Attachment' to the 'Third World Prostitute.'" *Feminist Review* 67 (April): 16–38. http://www.jstor.org/stable/1395529.

——. 2005. "Now You See Her, Now You Don't: Sex Workers at the UN Trafficking Protocol Negotiation." *Social & Legal Studies* 14, no. 1: 61–89. doi:10.1177/0964663905049526.

Donovan, J. 2012. *Feminist Theory: The Intellectual Traditions*. 4th ed. New York: Bloomsbury Academic.

Duggan, L., and N. D. Hunter. 2006. *Sex Wars: Sexual Dissent and Political Culture*, 10th ann. ed. New York: Routledge.

Dworkin, A. 1981. *Pornography: Men Possessing Women*. London: Women's Press.

Edmond, T., L. Sloan, and D. McCarty. 2004. "Sexual Abuse Survivors' Perceptions of the Effectiveness of EMDR and Eclectic Therapy." *Research on Social Work Practice* 14, no. 4: 249–58.

Eisenstein, Z. 1983. "The Combahee River Collective Statement." In *Home Girls: a Black Feminist Anthology*, ed. B. Smith, 272. New York: Kitchen Table Women of Color Press.

Ekberg, G. 2004. "The Swedish Law That Prohibits the Purchase of Sexual Services: Best Practices for Prevention of Prostitution and Trafficking in Human Beings." *Violence Against Women* 10, no. 10: 1187–1218. doi:10.1177/1077801204268647.

Eldridge, K. 2015. "Mother Helps Bust Human Trafficking Ring." *WWLP.com*, January 18. http://wwlp.com/2015/01/28/mother-helps-bust-human-trafficking-ring/.

Elliott, D. E., P. Bjelajac, R. Fallot, L. Markoff, and B. G. Reed. 2005. "Trauma-Informed or Trauma-Denied: Principles and Implementation of Trauma-Informed Services for Women." *Journal of Community Psychology* 33, no. 4: 461–77.

Estes, R., and N. Weiner. 2001. "The Commercial Sexual Exploitation of Children in the U.S., Canada and Mexico." University of Pennsylvania, School of Social Work, September 10. http://fl1.findlaw.com/news.findlaw.com/hdocs/docs/sextrade/upenncsec90701.pdf.

Fairstein, L. A. 1993. *Sexual Violence: Our War Against Rape*. New York: William Morrow.

Farley, M. 2004. " 'Bad for the Body, Bad for the Heart': Prostitution Harms Women Even if Legalized or Decriminalized." *Violence Against Women*, 10, no. 10: 1087–1125. doi:10.1177/1077801204268607.

Farley, M., and H. Barkan. 2008. "Prostitution, Violence, and Posttraumatic Stress Disorder." *Women and Health* 27, no. 3: 37–41. doi:10.1300/J013v27n03.

Farley, M., J. Golding, E. Matthews, N. Malamuth, and L. Jarrett. 2015. "Comparing Sex Buyers with Men Who Do Not Buy Sex: New Data on Prostitution and Trafficking." *Journal of Interpersonal Violence*, August 31. doi:10.1177/0886260515600874.

Farley, M., E. Schuckman, J. Golding, K. Houser, L. Jarrett, P. Qualliotine, and M. Decker. 2011. "Comparing Sex Buyers with Men Who Don't Buy Sex: 'You Can Have a Good Time with the Servitude' Vs. 'You're Supporting a System of Degradation.' " Paper presented at Psychologists for Social Responsibility Annual Meeting, Boston, July 15. http://www.prostitutionresearch.com/pdfs/Farleyet-al2011ComparingSexBuyers.pdf.

Farrell, A., J. McDevitt, and S. Fahy. 2008. *Understanding and Improving Law Enforcement Responses to Human Trafficking: Final Report*. Washington, D.C.: U.S. Department of Justice.

Farrell, A., J. McDevitt, R. Pfeffer, S. Fahy, C. Owens, M. Dank, and W. Adams. 2012. *Identifying Challenges to Improve the Investigation and Prosecution of State and Local Human Trafficking Cases*. Washington, D.C.: National Institute of Justice.

Fazal, F. 2013. "Michael Johnson, Samantha Ginocchio Charged for Selling Girls for Sex." *KSDK*, May 29. http://archive-origin.ksdk.com/news/article/382748/70/St-Charles-Countys-first-sex-trafficking-case.

Feinberg, A. 2013. "A State by State Map of America's Filthiest Porn Searches." *Gizmodo*, http://gizmodo.com/heres-all-the-dirty-details-on-americas-thriving-porn-1208587525.

Ferguson-Colvin, K., and E. M. Maccio. 2012. *Toolkit for Practitioners/Researchers Working with Lesbian, Gay, Bisexual, Transgender, and Queer/*

Questioning (LGBTQ) Runaway and Homeless Youth (RHY). National Resource Center for Permanency and Family Connections, September. Available at Family and Youth Services Bureau, http://ncfy.acf.hhs.gov/library/2012/toolkit-practitionersresearchers-working-lesbian-gay-bisexual-transgender-and.

Finklea, K., A. L. Fernandes-Alcantara, and S. Siskin. 2015. *Sex Trafficking of Children in the United States: Overview and Issues for Congress. Congressional Research Service*, January 28. http://fas.org/sgp/crs/misc/R41878.pdf.

Foa, E. B., C. V. Dancu, E. A. Hembree, L. Y. Jaycox, E. A. Meadows, and G. P. Street. 1999. "A Comparison of Exposure Therapy, Stress Inoculation Training, and Their Combination for Reducing Posttraumatic Stress Disorder in Female Sexual Assault Victims." *Journal of Consulting and Clinical Psychology* 67, no. 2: 194–200.

Frederick, T. 2014. "Diversity at the Margins: The Interconnections Between Homelessness, Sex Work, Mental Health, and Substance Abuse, in the Lives of Sexual Minority Homeless Young People." In *The Handbook of LGBT Communities, Crime, and Justice*, ed. D. Peterson and V. Panfil, 473–502. New York: Springer.

Freedman, J., and G. Combs. 1996. *Narrative Therapy: The Social Construction of Preferred Realities*. New York: Norton.

Fritch, A. and S. Lynch. 2008. "Group Treatment for Adult Survivors of Interpersonal Trauma." *Journal of Psychological Trauma* 7, no. 3: 145–69.

Galovski, T., L. M. Blain, J. M. Mott, L. Elwood, and T. Houle. 2012. "Manualized Therapy for PTSD: Flexing the Structure of Cognitive Processing Therapy." *Journal of Consulting and Clinical Psychology* 80, no. 6: 968–81.

Garrison, R. 2015. "Man Sentenced for Pimping Foster Child." *9News*, January 7. http://www.9news.com/story/news/crime/2015/01/07/man-sentenced-for-pimping-foster-child/21403399/.

Gold, S. J. and S. Nawyn. 2013. *The Routledge International Handbook of Migration Studies*. London: Routledge Press.

Gomez, C., and S. Going. 2015. "Serving Trafficking Victims in Immigrant Communities." Office for Victims of Crimes, Web forum, January 21, http://ovc.ncjrs.gov/ovcproviderforum/asp/Transcript.asp?Topic_ID=217.

Goodey, J. 2008. "Human Trafficking: Sketchy Data and Policy Responses." *Criminology and Criminal Justice* 8, no. 4: 421–42. doi:10.1177/1748895808096471.

Goodman, L. A., and D. Epstein. 2008. *Listening to Battered Women: A Survivor-Centered Approach to Advocacy, Mental Health, and Justice*. Washington, D.C.: American Psychological Association.

Gutierrez, T. 2012. "Airline Crews Train to Spot Traffickers" [Video file]. *CNN*, March 17. http://www.cnn.com/videos/us/2012/03/17/pkg-gutierrez-air-trafficking-control.cnn.

——. 2013. "Spotting Human Trafficking on Flights" [Video file]. *CNN*, November 23. http://www.cnn.com/videos/international/2013/11/23/pkg-gutierrez-trafficking-on-flights.cnn/video/playlists/cnn-freedom-project-human-trafficking/.

Hall, G. C. N., R. Hirschman, R., and L. L. Oliver. 1994. "Ignoring a Woman's Dislike of Sexual Material: Sexually Impositional Behavior in the Laboratory." *Journal of Sex Research* 31: 3–10.

Hammond, G. C., and M. McGlone. 2014. "Entry, Progression, Exit, and Service Provision for Survivors of Sex Trafficking: Implications for Effective Interventions." *Global Social Welfare*, March 22, 1–12. doi:10.1007/s40609-014-0010-0.

Hardy, V. L., K. D. Compton, and V. S. McPhatter. 2013. Domestic Minor Sex Trafficking Practice Implications for Mental Health Professionals. *Affilia* 28, no. 1: 8–18. doi:10.1177/0886109912475172.

Harrell, E., and M. Rand. 2010. "Crime Against People with Disabilities, 2008." Washington, D.C.: Bureau of Justice Statistics, Office of Justice Programs, U.S. Department of Justice, December. http://bjs.gov/content/pub/pdf/capd08.pdf.

Hart, W. E. 2010. "The Culture Industry, Hip Hop Music, and the White Perspective: How One Dimensional Representation of Hip Hop Music Has Influenced White Racial Attitudes." Master's thesis, University of Texas at Arlington. Available from Texas Digital Library.

Hartley, N. 2005. "Feminists for Porn." *Counterpunch*, February 2, 2005. http://www.counterpunch.org/2005/02/02/feminists-for-porn/.

Hawkins, J. D., R. Kosterman, R. F. Catalano, K. G. Hill, and R. Abbott. 2005. "Promoting Positive Adult Functioning Through Social Development Intervention in Childhood: Long Term Effects from the Seattle Social Developmental Project. *Archives of Pediatric and Adolescent Medicine* 159, no. 1: 25–31. doi:10.1001/archpedi.159.1.25.

Hawkins, J. D., B. H. Smith, K. G. Hill, R. Kosterman, R. F. Catalano, and R. D. Abbott. 2007. "Promoting Social Development and Preventing Health and Behavior Problems During the Elementary Grades: Results from the Seattle Social Development Project." *Victims and Offenders* 2, no. 2: 161–81.

Heffernan, K., and B. Blythe. 2014. "Evidence-Based Practice: Developing a Trauma-Informed Lens to Case Management for Victims of Human Trafficking." *Global Social Welfare*. April. 1–9. doi:10.1007/s40609-014-0007-8.

Heil, E. C. 2012. *Sex Slaves and Serfs: The Dynamics of Human Trafficking in a Small Florida Town*. Boulder, Colo.: First Forum Press.

Heil, E., and A. Nichols. 2014. "A Theoretical Discussion of the Potential Problems Associated with Targeted Policing and the Eradication of Sex Trafficking in the United States." *Contemporary Justice Review* 17, no. 4: 421–33. doi:10.1080/10282580.2014.980966.

——. 2015. *Human Trafficking in the Midwest: A Case Study of St. Louis and the Bi-State Area*. Durham, N.C.: Carolina Academic Press.

Heinrich, K., and K. Sreeharsha. 2013. "The State of State Human Trafficking Laws." *Judges Journal, American Bar Association* 52, no. 1, http://www.americanbar.org

/publications/judges_journal/2013/winter/the_state_of_state_humantrafficking_laws.html.

Hepburn, S., and R. Simon. 2010. "Hidden in Plain Sight: Human Trafficking Around the World." *Gender Issues* 27, no. 1–2: 1–26. doi:10.1007/s12147-010-9087-7.

——. 2013. *Human Trafficking Around the World: Hidden in Plain Sight*. New York: Columbia University Press.

Hodge, D. R. 2008. "Sexual Trafficking in the United States: A Domestic Problem with Transnational Dimensions." *Social Work* 53, no. 2: 143–52.

Hodge, D. R., and C. A. Lietz. 2007. "The International Sexual Trafficking of Women and Children: A Review of the Literature." *Affilia* 22, no. 2: 163–74. doi:10.1177/0886109907299055.

Hoekstra, D. 2000. "The Happy Hustler." *Chicago Reader*, December 14. http://www.chicagoreader.com/chicago/the-happy-hustler/Content?oid=904137.

Holt, T. J., K. R. Blevins, and J. B. Kuhns. 2014. "Examining Diffusion and Arrest Avoidance Practices Among Johns." *Crime & Delinquency* 60, no. 2: 261–83. doi:10.1177/0011128709347087.

hooks, bell. 2012. "Gangsta Culture—Sexism, Misogyny: Who Will Take the Rap?" In *Outlaw Culture: Resisting Representations*, 134–44. London: Routledge.

——. 2014. *Feminist Theory: From Margin to Center*, 3rd ed. London: Routledge.

Hopper, E. 2004. "Underidentification of Human Trafficking Victims in the United States." *Journal of Social Work Research and Evaluation* 5, no. 2: 125–36.

Hoyle, C., M. Bosworth, and M. Dempsey. 2011. "Labeling the Victims of Sex Trafficking: Exploring the Borderland Between Rhetoric and Reality." *Social & Legal Studies* 20, no. 3: 313–29. doi:10.1177/0964663911405394.

Hughes, D. M. 2005. "Race and Prostitution." Unpublished manuscript. University of Rhode Island.

——. 2007. *Enslaved in the USA*. *National Review*, July 30. http://www.nationalreview.com/article/221700/enslaved-usa-donna-m-hughes.

Hughes, D. M., K. Y. Chon, and D. P. Ellerman. 2007. "Modern-Day Comfort Women: The U.S. Military, Transnational Crime, and the Trafficking of Women." *Violence Against Women* 13, no. 9: 901–22. doi:10.1177/1077801207305218.

Hungarian Civil Liberties Union. 2013. "Where Is the Justice? Sex Work in Hungary." *Hungarian Civil Liberties Union*, March 26. http://tasz.hu/en/hclu-film/where-justice-sex-work-hungary.

Hurt, B., dir. and prod. 2006. *Hip-Hop: Beyond Beats and Rhymes* [DVD]. United States: God Bless the Child Productions.

Iceberg Slim. [1969] 2011. *Pimp: The Story of My Life*. Repr. New York: Cash Money Content.

Ice-T. 2006. "Pimp or Die." http://www.azlyrics.com/lyrics/icet/pimpordie.html.

Jaggar, A. 1988. *Feminist Politics and Human Nature.* Lanham, Md.: Rowman & Littlefield.

Jakobsson, N., and A. Kotsadam. 2011. "The Law and Economics of International Sex Slavery: Prostitution Law and Trafficking for Sexual Exploitation." *European Journal of Law and Economics* 35, no. 1: 87–107.

Johnson, C. 2012. "With a Phone Call, Truckers Can Fight Sex Trafficking." *National Public Radio,* October 19. http://www.npr.org/2012/10/19/163010142/with-a -phone-call-truckers-can-fight-sex-trafficking.

Joiner, T. E., K. A. Van Orden, T. K. Witte, E. Selby, J. D. Ribeiro, R. Lewis, and M. D. Rudd. 2009. "Main Predictions of the Interpersonal-Psychological Theory of Suicidal Behavior: Empirical Tests in Two Samples of Young Adults. *Journal of Abnormal Psychology* 118, no. 3: 634–46.

Jordan, J. 1997. "User Pays: Why Men Buy Sex." *Australian and New Zealand Journal of Criminology* 30: 55–71.

———. 2010. *Relational Cultural Therapy.* Washington, D.C.: American Psychological Association.

Kalergis, K. I. 2009. "A Passionate Practice Addressing the Needs of Commercially Sexually Exploited Teenagers." *Affilia* 24, no. 3: 315–24. doi:10.1177 /0886109909337706.

Kara, S. 2010. *Sex Trafficking: Inside the Business of Modern Slavery.* New York: Columbia University Press.

Kempadoo, K., and J. Doezema. 1998. *Global Sex Workers: Rights, Resistance, and Redefinition.* New York: Routledge.

Kennedy, K. 2013. "Advocates Clash Over Sex Trafficking Treatment." *Associated Press,* August 8.

Kennedy, M. A., and N. J. Pucci. 2007. "Domestic Minor Sex Trafficking Assessment Report—Las Vegas, Nevada." *Shared Hope International.* http://sharedhope.org/ wp-content/uploads/2012/09/LasVegas_PrinterFriendly.pdf.

Kidd, S., and M. Kral. 2002. "Suicide and Prostitution Among Street Youth: A Qualitative Analysis." *Adolescence* 37, no. 146 (Summer):411–30.

Kinsey, A. C., W. B. Pomeroy, and E. Martin. 1948. *Sexual Behavior in the Human Male.* Philadelphia: W. B. Saunders.

Klein, N. 2008. *The Shock Doctrine: The Rise of Disaster Capitalism.* New York: Picador.

Kocher, G. 2014. "Berea Couple Accused of Selling Daughters for Sex Plead Guilty to Lesser Charge." *Lexington Herald Leader,* May 21. http://www.kentucky.com /news/local/counties/madison-county/article44490036.html.

Kotrla, K. 2010. "Domestic Minor Sex Trafficking in the United States." *Social Work* 55, no. 2: 181–87.

Koyama, E. 2011. *Understanding the Complexities of Sex Work/Trade*. Portland, Ore.: Confluere Publications.

Kulkarni, S., H. Bell, and D. Rhodes. 2012. "Back to Basics." *Violence Against Women* 18: 85.

Kunze, E. 2010. "Sex Trafficking Via the Internet: How International Agreements Address the Problem and Fail to Go Far Enough." *Journal of High Technology and Law* 10, no. 2: 241–89.

Kurtz, S., H. L. Surratt, M. C. Kiley, and J. A. Inciardi. 2005. "Barriers to Health and Social Services for Street-Based Sex Workers." *Journal of Health Care for the Poor and Underserved* 16, no. 2 (May): 345–61. doi:10.1353/hpu.2005.0038.

Kyckelhahn, T., A. J. Beck, and T. H. Cohen. 2009. "Characteristics of Suspected Human Trafficking Incidents." U.S. Department of Justice, January. http://bjs.ojp .usdoj.gov/content/pub/pdf/cshti08.pdf.

Laumann, E. O., J. H. Gagnon, R. T. Michael, and S. Michaels. 1994. *The Social Organization of Sexuality*. Chicago: University of Chicago Press.

Lester, T. L. 2012. "OMFG: A Toddlers & Tiaras Contestant Attempts Lady Gaga Meat Dress Replica." *Glamour Magazine*, January 13. http://www.glamour.com /fashion/blogs/dressed/2012/01/omfg-a-toddlers-tiaras-contest.

Levy, J., and P. Jakobsson. 2014. "Sweden's Abolitionist Discourse and Law: Effects on the Dynamics of Swedish Sex Work and on the Lives of Sweden's Sex Workers." *Criminology and Criminal Justice* 14: 593–607.

Limoncelli, S. A. 2009. "The Trouble with Trafficking: Conceptualizing Women's Sexual Labor and Economic Human Rights." *Women's Studies International Forum* 32: 261–69.

——. 2010. *The Politics of Trafficking*. Stanford, Calif.: Stanford University Press.

Lipsey, M. W. 2009. "The Primary Factors That Characterize Effective Interventions with Juvenile Offenders." *Victims and Offenders* 4: 127–47.

Liu, M. 2012. "Chinese Migrant Women in the Sex Industry Exploring Their Paths to Prostitution. *Feminist Criminology* 7, no. 4: 327–49. doi:10.1177/1557085112436836.

Lloyd, R. 2012. *Girls Like Us: Fighting for a World Where Girls Are Not for Sale*. New York: Harper Perennial.

Loftus, D. 2002. *Watching Sex: How Men Really Respond to Pornography*. New York: Thunder's Mouth Press.

Logue, T. 2014. "Chester Man Gets Life in Jail for Sex Trafficking." *Delaware County Daily Times*, December 14. http://www.delcotimes.com/general-news/20141219 /chester-man-gets-life-in-jail-for-sex-trafficking.

Lorber, J., and C. Haynes. 2002. "Pimp Juice." http://www.azlyrics.com/lyrics/nelly /pimpjuice.html.

Lundahl, B. W., J. Nimer, and B. Parsons. 2006. "Preventing Child Abuse: A Meta-Analysis of Parent Training Programs." *Research on Social Work Practice* 16, no. 3: 251–62.

Lutnick, A., and D. Cohan. 2009. "Criminalization, Legalization or Decriminalization of Sex Work: What Female Sex Workers Say in San Francisco, USA." *Reproductive Health Matters* 17, no. 34: 38–46. doi:10.1016/S0968-8080(09)34469-9.

Lymn, K. 2015. "Demand for Sex Is High in the Bakken." *Billings Gazette*, January 4. http://billingsgazette.com/news/state-and-regional/montana/demand-for-sex -is-high-in-the-bakken/article_d2e57e91-0bb1-5454-a2ee-ec91ea62983d.html.

MacKinnon, C. 2005. "Pornography as Trafficking." *Michigan Journal of International Law* 26: 1–15.

Macy, R., M. Giattina, S. Parish, and C. Crosby. 2010. "Domestic Violence and Sexual Assault Services: Historical Concerns and Contemporary Challenges." *Journal of Interpersonal Violence*, 25: 3–32.

Macy, R. J., and L. M. Graham. 2012. "Identifying Domestic and International Sex-Trafficking Victims During Human Service Provision." *Trauma, Violence & Abuse* 13, no. 2: 59–76. doi:10.1177/1524838012440340.

Macy, R. J., and N. Johns. 2011. "Aftercare Services for International Sex Trafficking Survivors: Informing U.S. Service and Program Development in an Emerging Practice Area." *Trauma, Violence & Abuse* 12, no. 2: 87–98. doi:10.1177 /1524838010390709.

Maher, L. 1997. *Sexed Work: Gender, Race, and Resistance in a Brooklyn Drug Market.* New York: Oxford University Press.

Marcus, A., A. Horning, R. Curtis, J. Sanson, and E. Thompson. 2014. "Conflict and Agency Among Sex Workers and Pimps: A Closer Look at Domestic Minor Sex Trafficking." *Annals of the American Academy of Political and Social Science* 653, no. 1: 225–46. doi:10.1177/0002716214521993.

Martin, L., A. Pierce, S. Peyton, A. I. Gabilondo, and G. Tulpule. 2014. *Mapping the Market for Sex with Trafficked Minor Girls in Minneapolis: Structures, Functions, and Patterns. Full Report: Preliminary Findings.* http://uroc.umn.edu/documents /mapping-the-market-full.pdf.

Martinez, A. 2015. "Four Men in Gang-Related Sex Trafficking Case Found Guilty by Jury in U.S. District Court." *El Paso Times*, January 16. http://www.elpasotimes.com/.

Mayock, P. 2012. "How to Identify and Address Human Trafficking." *Hotel News Now*, October 18. http://www.hotelnewsnow.com/Article/9178/How-to-identify-and -address-human-trafficking.

McCabe, K., and S. Manian. 2010. *Sex Trafficking: A Global Perspective.* Lanham, Md.: Lexington Books.

McCulloch, D. 2006. *Stagger Lee.* Berkeley, CA: Image Comics.

McKee, A. 2005. "The Objectification of Women in Mainstream Pornographic Videos in Australia." *Journal of Sex Research* 42: 277–90.

———. 2006. "The Aesthetics of Pornography: The Insights of Consumers." *Continuum: Journal of Media and Cultural Studies* 20: 523–39.

Mendelsohn, M., J. Herman, E. Schatzow, M. Coco, D. Kallivayalil, and J. Levitan. 2011. *The Trauma Recovery Group: A Guide for Practitioners*. New York: Guilford Press.

Miller, J. 1997. "Victimization and Resistance Among Street Prostitutes." In *Constructions of Deviance: Social Power, Context, and Interaction*, ed. P. A. Adler and P. Adler, 444–54. Belmont: Wadsworth.

——. 2009. "Prostitution." In *The Oxford Handbook of Crime and Public Policy*, ed. M. Tonry, 547–77. New York: Oxford University Press.

Miller, W. R., and S. Rollnick. 2012. *Motivational Interviewing: Helping People Change*. 3rd ed. New York: Guilford Press.

Ministry of Health and Social Issues. 2010. "Prohibiting the Sale of Sexual Services: An Understanding." 1999–2008. http://www.government.se/articles/2011/03 /evaluation-of-the-prohibition-of-the-purchase-of-sexual-services/.

Mock, J. 2014. *Redefining Realness*. New York: Atria Books.

Monto, M. A. 1999. "Clients of Street Prostitutes, in Portland, Oregon, San Francisco and Santa Clara, California, and Las Vegas, Nevada, 1996–1999." ICPSR02859-v1. Ann Arbor, Mich.: Inter-university Consortium for Political and Social Research [distributor], 2000. http://doi.org/10.3886.

——. 2004. "Female Prostitution, Customers, and Violence." *Violence Against Women* 10, no. 2: 160–88. doi:10.1177/1077801203260948.

Monto, M. A., and N. Hotaling. 2001. "Predictors of Rape Myth Acceptance Among the Male Clients of Female Street Prostitutes." *Violence Against Women* 7: 275–93.

Monto, M., and C. Milrod. 2014. "Ordinary or Peculiar Men? Comparing the Customers of Prostitutes with a Nationally Representative Sample of Men." *International Journal of Offender Therapy and Comparative Criminology* 58, no. 7: 802–20.

Muhammad, C. 2014. "From Victim to Advocate: Lessons From a Sex Trafficking Survivor." *Final Call*, June 25, 2014. http://www.finalcall.com/artman/publish /National_News_2/article_101547.shtml.

Mulac, A., L. L. Jansma, and D. G. Linz. 2002. "Men's Behavior Toward Women After Viewing Sexually-Explicit Films: Degradation Makes a Difference." *Communication Monographs* 69: 311–29.

Naar-King, S., and M. Suarez. 2010. *Motivational Interviewing with Adolescents and Young Adults*. New York: Guilford Press.

National Institute of Justice. 2012. "Reducing the Demand for Human Trafficking," June 13. http://www.nij.gov/topics/crime/human-trafficking/Pages/reducing-demand.aspx.

Nelson, C. 2013. "Bus Drivers to Look for Trafficking." *Minnesota Daily*, July 24. http:// www.mndaily.com/news/metro-state/2013/07/24/bus-drivers-look-trafficking.

Newton, P., T. Mulcahy, and S. Martin. 2008. *Finding Victims of Human Trafficking*. Bethesda, MD: National Opinion Research Center.

Nichols, A. J. 2010. "Dance Ponnaya, Dance! Police Abuses Against Transgender Sex Workers in Sri Lanka." *Feminist Criminology* 5, no. 1: 195–222.

——. 2014a. *Feminist Advocacy: Gendered Organizations in Community-Based Responses to Domestic Violence.* Lanham, Md.: Lexington Books.

——. 2014b. "Pornography." In *The Encyclopedia of Criminal Justice Ethics,* ed. B. A. Arrigo and J. G. Golson, 680–83. Thousand Oaks, Calif.: Sage.

Nichols, A. J., and E. C. Heil. 2014. "Challenges to Identifying and Prosecuting Sex Trafficking Cases in the Midwest United States." *Feminist Criminology* 10, no. 1: 7–35. doi:10.1177/1557085113519490.

Nixon, K., L. Tutty, P. Downe, K. Gorkoff, and J. Ursel. 2002. "The Everyday Occurrence: Violence in the Lives of Girls Exploited through Prostitution." *Violence Against Women* 8: 1016–43.

Norris, S., M. Goodwin, I. Jefferson, J. Smith, C. Love, and T. Sanders. 2001. "Can't Stop Pimpin'." http://www.cloudlyrics.com/lil-jon-lyrics-cant-stop-pimpin.html.

Oselin, S. 2014. *Leaving Prostitution: Getting out and Staying out of Sex Work.* New York: New York University Press.

Outshoorn, J. 2005. "The Political Debates on Prostitution and Trafficking of Women." *Social Politics: International Studies in Gender, State and Society* 12, no. 1: 141–55. http://muse.jhu.edu/journals/social_politics/v012/12.1outshoorn.html.

Parriott, R. 1994. "Health Experience of Twin Cities Women in Prostitution: Survey Findings and Recommendations." *CURA Reporter* 24, no. 3: 10–15.

Patrick, R. 2011. "Clayton Man Caught in FBI Sting Gets 10 Years." *St. Louis Post-Dispatch,* March 24. http://www.stltoday.com/news/local/crime-and-courts /clayton-man-caught-in-fbi-sex-sting-gets-years/article_9b432862-5640-11e0 -ad3b-0017a4a78c22.html.

Picker, M., and C. Sun, dir. 2008. *The Price of Pleasure: Pornography, Sexuality & Relationships.* Open Lens Media.

Polaris Project. 2013. "Report Spotlights Human Trafficking Trends in the U.S." *Polaris,* November 21. http://www.polarisproject.org/media-center/news-and-press /press-releases/915-report-spotlights-human-trafficking-trends-in-the-us.

——. 2014a. "Sex Trafficking in the U.S." *Polaris.* http://www.polarisproject.org /human-trafficking/sex-trafficking-in-the-us.

——. 2014b. "National Human Trafficking Resource Center (NHTC) Annual Report 1/1/2014–12/31/2014." *Polaris.* http://www.traffickingresourcecenter.org/sites /default/files/2014%20NHTRC%20Annual%20Report_Final.pdf.

——. 2015a. "Current Federal Laws." *Polaris.* http://www.polarisproject.org/what-we -do/policy-advocacy/national-policy/current-federal-laws.

——. 2015b. "Sex Trafficking in the U.S.—A Closer Look at U.S. Citizen Victims." *Polaris.* https://polarisproject.org/resources/sex-trafficking-us-closer-look-us -citizen-victims.

———. 2015c. "State Ratings." *Polaris.* http://www.polarisproject.org/what-we-do /policy-advocacy/national-policy/state-ratings-on-human-trafficking -laws#categories.

Ponting, B. 2014. "24 San Diego Gang Members Indicted for Sex Trafficking." *Fox 5 San Diego,* January 8. Retrieved from http://fox5sandiego.com/2014/01/08 /24-san-diego-gang-members-indicted-for-sex-trafficking/.

Porter, D. M., C. Jackson, and B. Parrott. 2003. "P.I.M.P." http://www.metrolyrics. com/pimp-lyrics-50-cent.html.

Price, Lloyd. 2002. "Stagger Lee." *20th Century Masters: The Millennium Collection: Best of Lloyd Price.* Geffen Records.

Rader, D. 2013. "Inside the Actors Studio Host James Lipton on His Favorite Interview and Pimping in Paris." *Parade,* May 28. http://parade.com/17599 /dotsonrader/inside-the-actors-studio-host-james-lipton-on-his-favorite-inter- view-and-pimping-in-paris/.

Rand, A. 2010. "It Can't Happen in My Backyard: The Commercial Sexual Exploita- tion of Girls in the United States." *Child & Youth Services* 31, no. 3–4: 138–56. doi: 10.1080/0145935X.2009.524480.

Raphael, J., and B. Myers-Powell. 2010. "From Victims to Victimizers: Interviews with 25 Ex-Pimps in Chicago." Schiller DuCanto & Fleck Family Law Center of DePaul University College of Law. newsroom.depaul.edu/PDF/FAMILY_LAW_ CENTER_REPORT-final.pdf.

Raphael, J., J. Reichert, and M. Powers. 2010. "Pimp Control and Violence: Domestic Sex Trafficking of Chicago Women and Girls." *Women & Criminal Justice* 20: 89–104.

Ray, N. 2006. *Lesbian, Gay, Bisexual and Transgender Youth: An Epidemic of Home- lessness.* New York: National Gay and Lesbian Task Force Policy Institute and the National Coalition for the Homeless. http://www.thetaskforce.org/downloads /HomelessYouth.pdf.

Raymond, J. G. 2004. "Prostitution on Demand Legalizing the Buyers as Sex- ual Consumers." *Violence Against Women* 10, no. 10: 1156–86. doi:10.1177 /1077801204268609.

Raymond, J., D. Hughes, and C. Gomez. 2001. *Sex Trafficking of Women in the United States: Links Between International and Domestic Sex Industries.* North Amherst, Mass.: Coalition Against Trafficking in Women.

Reavy, P. 2014. "Man Forced Teen Boys into Sex and Drug Trafficking, Police Say." *Deseret News,* February 13. http://www.deseretnews.com/article/865596411/ man-forced-teen-boys-into-sex-and-drug-trafficking-police-say.html?pg=all.

Reid, J. A. 2010. "Doors Wide Shut: Barriers to the Successful Delivery of Victim Ser- vices for Domestically Trafficked Minors in a Southern U.S. Metropolitan Area." *Women & Criminal Justice* 20, no. 1–2: 147–66. doi:10.1080/08974451003641206.

———. 2011. "An Exploratory Model of Girl's Vulnerability to Commercial Sexual Exploitation in Prostitution." *Child Maltreatment* 16, no. 2: 146–57. doi:10.1177/1077559511404700.

———. 2014. "Entrapment and Enmeshment Schemes Used by Sex Traffickers." *Sexual Abuse: A Journal of Research and Treatment.*

———. 2015. "Sex Trafficking of Girls: How Sex Traffickers Exploit Youth and System Vulnerabilities." Presented at Washington University in St. Louis, Sex Trafficking Lecture Series, September 17, 2015.

Reid, J. A., and A. R. Piquero. 2013. "Age-Graded Risks for Commercial Sexual Exploitation of Male and Female Youth. *Journal of Interpersonal Violence* 29, no. 9: 1747–77. doi:10.1177/0886260513511535.

Renzetti, C., D. Curran, and S. L. Maier. 2012. *Women, Men, and Society*, 6th ed. Boston: Pearson Education.

Resnick, H. S., and M. K. Schnicke. 1992. "Cognitive Processing Therapy for Sexual Assault Victims." *Journal of Consulting and Clinical Psychology* 60: 748–56.

———. 1993. *Cognitive Processing Therapy for Rape Victims: A Treatment Manual*. Newbury Park, Calif.: Sage.

Resnick, P. A., P. Nishith, T. L. Weaver, M. C. Astin, and C. A. Feuer. 2002. "A Comparison of Cognitive-Processing Therapy with Prolonged Exposure and a Waiting Condition for the Treatment for Chronic Posttraumatic Stress Disorder in Female Rape Victims." *Journal of Consulting and Clinical Psychology* 70: 867–79.

Rew, L., T. A. Whittaker, M. A. Taylor-Seehafer, and L. R. Smith. 2005. "Sexual Health Risks and Protective Resources in Gay, Lesbian, Bisexual, and Heterosexual Homeless Youth." *Journal for Specialists in Pediatric Nursing* 10, no. 1: 11–19.

Rich, J. 2010. *Modern Feminist Theory: An Introduction*. Philosophy Insights series. 2nd ed. Penrith, U.K.: Humanities-Ebooks.

Richard, A. O. 2000. "International Trafficking in Women to the United States: A Contemporary Manifestation of Slavery and Organized Crime." Washington, D.C.: Central Intelligence Agency.

Rizvi, S., D. Vogt, and P. Resick. 2009. "Cognitive and Affective Predictors of Treatment Outcomes in Cognitive Processing Therapy and Prolonged Exposure for Posttraumatic Stress Disorder." *Behaviour Research and Therapy* 47, no. 9: 737–43.

Roe-Sepowitz, D. E. 2012. "Juvenile Entry into Prostitution: The Role of Emotional Abuse." *Violence Against Women* 18, no. 5: 562–79. doi:10.1177/1077801212453140.

Roe-Sepowitz, D. E., J. Gallagher, M. Risinger, and K. Hickle. 2014. "The Sexual Exploitation of Girls in the United States: The Role of Female Pimps." *Journal of Interpersonal Violence* 11, no. 39: 1–17. doi:10.1177/0886260514554292.

Romo, Z. 2013. "Cultural Effects of Pimp Culture in Popular Rap Music and Sex Trafficking." December. Sex Trafficking Education Culminating Experience Paper presented at Washington University, Saint Louis, Missouri.

Rose, T. 1994. *Black Noise: Rap Music and Black Culture in Contemporary America.* Middletown, Conn.: Wesleyan University Press.

Rosenblum, G. 2013. "Reasons for Female Sex Traffickers Are Complex." *Star-Tribune,* July 10, 2013. http://www.startribune.com/local/east/215007601.html.

Rothbaum, B. O., E. A. Meadows, P. Resick, and D.W. Foy. 2000. "Cognitive-Behavioral Therapy." In *Effective Treatments for PTSD: Practice Guidelines from the International Society for Traumatic Stress Studies,* ed. E. B. Foa, T. M. Keane, and M. J. Friedman, 60–83. New York: Guilford.

Rubin, G. 1975. "The Traffic in Women: Notes on the 'Political Economy' of Sex." In *Toward an Anthropology of Women,* ed. R. Reiter, 87–106. New York: Monthly Review Press.

Sanchez, L. 2001. "Gender Troubles: The Entanglement of Agency, Violence, and Law in the Lives of Women in Prostitution." In *Women Crime and Criminal Justice,* ed. C. Renzetti and L. Goodstein, 60–76. Los Angeles: Roxbury.

Schaeffer-Grabiel, F. 2010. "Sex Trafficking as the 'New Slave Trade'?" *Sexualities* 13, no. 2: 153–60. doi:10.1177/1363460709359234.

Schauer, E. J., and E. M. Wheaton. 2006. "Sex Trafficking into the United States: A Literature Review." *Criminal Justice Review* 31, no. 2: 146–69. doi:10.1177/0734016806290136.

Schisgall, D., and N. Alvarez, dir. 2008. *Very Young Girls.* Written by Jonsey. Swinging T Productions.

Schubert, S., and C. Lee. 2009. "Adult PTSD and Its Treatment with EMDR: A Review of Controversies, Evidence, and Theoretical Knowledge." *Journal of EMDR Practice and Research* 3 no. 3: 117–32.

Schulz, P., C. Huber, and P. Resick. 2006. "Practical Adaptations of Cognitive Processing Therapy with Bosnian Refugees: Implications for Adapting Practice to a Multicultural Clientele." *Cognitive and Behavioral Practice* 13, no. 4: 310–21.

Schulz, P., P. Resick, C. Huber, and M. Griffin. 2006. "The Effectiveness of Cognitive Processing Therapy for PTSD with Refugees in a Community Setting. *Cognitive and Behavioral Practice* 13, no. 4: 322–31.

Segrave, M. 2009. "Order at the Border: The Repatriation of Victims of Trafficking." *Women's Studies International Forum* 32: 251–60.

Seper, J. 2012. "Feds Team Up with Amtrak to Fight Human Trafficking." *Washington Times,* October 4. http://www.washingtontimes.com/news/2012/oct/4/feds-team-up-with-amtrak-to-fight-human-traffickin/.

Shaddox, R. 2015. "San Joaquin County Teen Relives Sex Trafficking Nightmare." *Fox 40,* July 30. http://fox40.com/2015/07/30/san-joaquin-county-teen-relives-sex-trafficking-nightmare/.

Shared Hope International (SHI). 2011. *DEMAND: A Comparative Examination of Sex Tourism and Trafficking in Jamaica, Japan, the Netherlands, and the United States.* http://sharedhope.org/wp-content/uploads/2012/09/DEMAND.pdf.

Shaver, F. M. 2005. "Sex Work Research: Methodological and Ethical Challenges." *Journal of Interpersonal Violence* 20, no. 3: 296–319. doi:10.1177/0886260504274340.

Shaw, P. 2015. "Jefferson High School Focuses on Injustices Facing Black Women." *Portland Occupier*, February 13. http://www.portlandoccupier.org/2015/02/13/jefferson-high-school-focuses-on-injustices-facing-black-women/.

Shay, J. 2002. *Odysseus in America: Combat Trauma and the Trials of Homecoming.* New York: Scribner.

Sheppard, H. 2015. "PSP Traffic Stop: Man Charged with Human Trafficking; Drug Possession." *Fox 43 News*, February 20. http://fox43.com/2015/02/20/psp-traffic-stop-man-charged-with-human-trafficking-drug-possession/.

Shively, M., K. Kliorys, K. Wheeler, and D. Hunt. 2012. *National Overview of Prostitution and Sex Trafficking Demand.* U.S. Department of Justice. https://www.ncjrs.gov/pdffiles1/nij/grants/238796.pdf.

Silvestrini, E. 2015. "Child Sex Trafficker Was Victim as a Teen." *Tampa Tribune*, January 11. http://www.tbo.com/news/crime/child-sex-trafficker-was-victim-as-a-teen-20150111/.

Singh, A. K. 2011. *Feminist Politics and Human Nature.* New Delhi: MD Publications.

Smith, H. A. 2014. *Walking Prey: How America's Youth Are Vulnerable to Sex Slavery.* New York: Palgrave Macmillan.

Smith, H. M. 2011. "Sex Trafficking: Trends, Challenges, and the Limitations of International Law." *Human Rights Review* 12, no. 3: 271–86. doi:10.1007/s12142-010-0185-4.

Smith, L., S. H. Vardaman, and M. Snow. 2009. *The National Report on Domestic Minor Sex Trafficking.* Vancouver, Wash.: Shared Hope International. http://sharedhope.org/wp-content/uploads/2012/09/SHI_National_Report_on_DMST_2009.pdf.

Smith, M. D., and C. Grov. 2011. *In the Company of Men: Inside the Lives of Male Prostitutes.* Santa Barbara, Calif.: Praeger.

Smith, T. W., P. V. Marsden, and M. Hout. 2011. "General Social Survey, 1972–2010." ICPSR 31521-v1. Storrs: Roper Center for Public Opinion Research, University of Connecticut/Ann Arbor, Mich.: Inter-university Consortium for Political and Social Research. doi:10.3886/ICPSR31521.v1.

Stoltenberg, J. 1999. *Refusing to Be a Man: Essays on Social Justice.* New York: Taylor & Francis.

Stolz, B. 2005. "Educating Policymakers and Setting the Criminal Justice Policy-making Agenda Interest Groups and the 'Victims of Trafficking and Violence Act of 2000.'" *Criminal Justice* 5, no. 4: 407–30. doi:10.1177/1466802505057718.

Stoltzfus, E., and K. Lynch. 2009. *Home Visitation for Families with Young Children*. Washington, D.C.: Congressional Research Service.

Sullivan, E., and W. Simon. 1998. "The Client: Asocial, Psychological, and Behavioral Look at the Unseen Patron of Prostitution." In *Prostitution: On Whores, Hustlers, and Johns*, ed. J. E. Elias, V. L. Bullough, V. Elias, and G. Brewer, 134–54. Amherst, N.Y.: Prometheus.

Sutherland, E. H., and D. R. Cressey. 2006. "A Theory of Differential Association (1960)." In *Criminological Theory: Past to Present*, ed. F. T. Cullin and R. Agnew, 122–25. Los Angeles: Roxbury Company.

Surtees, R. 2008. "Traffickers and Trafficking in Southern and Eastern Europe Considering the Other Side of Human Trafficking." *European Journal of Criminology* 5, no. 1: 39–68.

Sviridoff, M., D. Rottman, B. Ostrom, and R. Curtis. 2000. *Dispensing Justice Locally: The Implementation and Effects of the Midtown Community Court*. Amsterdam: Harwood Academic.

Tremaine, J., dir. 2013. *Jackass Presents: Bad Grandpa*. Dickhouse Productions, MTV Films.

Tucker, S. 1990. "Gender, Fucking, and Utopia: An Essay in Response to John Stoltenberg's *Refusing to Be a Man*." *Social Text* 27 (January): 3–34. doi:10.2307/466305.

Twill, S. E., D. M. Green, and A. Traylor. 2010. "A Descriptive Study on Sexually Exploited Children in Residential Treatment." *Child & Youth Care Forum* 39, no. 3: 187–99. doi:10.1007/s10566-010-9098-2.

Ugarte, M., L. Zarate, and M. Farley. 2003. "Prostitution and Trafficking of Women and Children from Mexico to the United States." *Journal of Trauma Practice* 2, no 3: 147–66.

U.S. Department of State. 2006. *Trafficking Victims Protection Reauthorization Act of 2005*. January 10. http://www.state.gov/j/tip/laws/61106.htm.

——. 2008. *Trafficking Victims Protection Reauthorization Act of 2008*. January 1. http://www.state.gov/j/tip/laws/113178.htm.

——. 2012. *Trafficking in Persons Report 2012*. http://www.state.gov/j/tip/rls/tiprpt/2012/index.htm.

——. 2013. *Trafficking in Persons Report 2013*. http://www.state.gov/j/tip/rls/tiprpt/2013/.

——. 2014. *Trafficking in Persons Report 2014*. http://www.state.gov/j/tip/rls/tiprpt/2014/index.htm.

United Nations Office on Drugs and Crime. 2004. *United Nations Convention Against Transnational Organized Crime and the Protocols Thereto*. http://www.unodc.org/documents/middleeastandnorthafrica/organised-crime/UNITED_NATIONS_CONVENTION_AGAINST_TRANSNATIONAL_ORGANIZED_CRIME_AND_THE_PROTOCOLS_THERETO.pdf.

———. 2009. *Global Report on Trafficking in Persons.* http://www.unodc.org/docu-ments/Global_Report_on_TIP.pdf.

Vickerman, K. A., and G. Margolin. 2009. "Rape Treatment Outcome Research: Empirical Findings and State of the Literature." *Clinical Psychology Review* 29: 431–48.

Vito, G., and J. Maahs, 2012. *Criminology Theory, Research, and Policy.* Burlington, Mass.: Jones & Bartlett Learning.

Wade, K. 2008. "Domestic Minor Sex Trafficking Assessment Report—Indepen-dence, Missouri." *Shared Hope International*, April. http://sharedhope.org/wp-content/uploads/2012/09/Independence_PrinterFriendly2.pdf.

Weiner, J. 2013. "Snoop Lion Opens up About His Pimp Past." *Rolling Stone*, May 8. http://www.rollingstone.com.

Weisburd, D., L. A. Wyckoff, J. Ready, J. E. Eck, J. C. Hinkle, and F. Gajewski, F. 2006. "Does Crime Just Move Around the Corner? A Controlled Study of Special Displacement and Diffusion of Crime Control Benefits." *Criminology* 44, no. 3: 549–91.

Weitzer, R. 2007. "Prostitution: Facts and Fictions." *Contexts* 6, no. 4: 28–33. doi:10.1525/ctx.2007.6.4.28.

———. 2010. "The Movement to Criminalize Sex Work in the United States." *Journal of Law and Society* 37, no. 1 (March): 61–84. doi:10.1111/j.1467-6478.2010.00495.x.

———. 2011. "Pornography's Effects: The Need for Solid Evidence." *Violence Against Women* 17, no. 5 (May): 666–75. SSRN Scholarly Paper ID 1877985. Rochester, N.Y.: Social Science Research Network. http://papers.ssrn.com/abstract=1877985.

Wells, M., and K. J. Mitchell. 2007. "Youth Sexual Exploitation on the Internet: DSM-IV Diagnoses and Gender Differences in Co-Occurring Mental Health Issues. *Child and Adolescent Social Work Journal* 24, no. 3: 235–60. doi:10.1007/s10560-007-0083-z.

Wheeler, K. 2013. "Truckers Fighting Back Against Human Trafficking." *WKYC-TV*, July 26. http://www.wkyc.com/story/local/2013/07/24/3268529/.

Williamson, C., and M. Prior. 2009. "Domestic Minor Sex Trafficking: A Network of Underground Players in the Midwest." *Journal of Child & Adolescent Trauma* 2, no. 1: 46–61. doi:10.1080/19361520802702191.

Williamson, E., N. Dutch, and H. Clawson. 2008. *National Symposium on the Health Needs of Human Trafficking Victims: Post-Symposium Brief.* Washington, D.C.: Office of the Assistant Secretary for Planning and Evaluation, U.S. Department of Health and Human Services.

Wilson, D. G., W. F. Walsh, and S. Klueber. 2006. "Trafficking in Human Beings: Training and Services Among U.S. Law Enforcement Agencies." *Police Practice and Research* 7: 149–60.

Wilson, J. M., and E. Dalton. 2008. "Human Trafficking in the Heartland: Variation in Law Enforcement Awareness and Response." *Journal of Contemporary Criminal Justice* 2, no. 3: 296–313. doi:10.1177/1043986208318227.

Wissink, I. B., E. van Vugt, X. Moonen, J. M. Stams, and J. Hendriks. 2015. "Sexual Abuse Involving Children with an Intellectual Disability (ID): A Narrative Review." *Research in Developmental Disabilities* 36: 20–35. doi:10.1016/j.ridd.2014.09.007.

Xiong, Chao. 2014. "St. Paul Man Gets Record 40-Year Sentence for Sex-Trafficking." *Star Tribune*, January 9. http://www.startribune.com/local/east/239444671.html?page=1&c=y.

Zillmann, D. 1989. "Effects of Prolonged Consumption of Pornography." In *Pornography: Research Advances and Policy Considerations*, ed. D. Zillmann and J. Bryant, 127–58. Hillsdale, N.J.: Lawrence Erlbaum.

Zillmann, D., and J. Bryant. 1982. "Pornography, Sexual Callousness, and the Trivialization of Rape." *Journal of Communication* 32: 10–21.

Zimmerman, M. 2012. "The Pimp Culture." *VAST*, October 2. http://thevast.org/?p=863.

Zweig, J., and M. Burt. 2007. "Predicting Women's Perceptions of Domestic Violence and Sexual Assault Agency Helpfulness: What Matters to Program Clients?" *Violence Against Women* 13: 1149–78.

Index

mail-order bride schemes, 106
Maksimenko, Aleksandr, 93–94
Manian, Sabita, 146
Mann Act, 12
Marcus, Anthony, 116
Martin, E., 159
Martin, Lauren, 102–3, 112, 157, 199
Martinez-Rojas, Severiano, 146–47, 150
Masters, R. E. L., 159
McCabe, Kimberly A., 146
McCullouch, Timothy, Jr., 99
McDevitt, Jack, 200, 201
McKee, A., 46
McPeak, Patty, 260
McPhatter, Veronica S., 224
McPherson, Deanna, 112–13
media, 116, 136; and antitrafficking movement, 21, 261–62
Mendez-Hernandez, Joaquin "El Flaco," 122
Meneses, Christina, 277
Metro Transit, 258–59
Mexico, 122, 146, 147
Middlebrook, Robert, 193
migration, 6–7, 196. See also undocumented immigrants
military personnel, 147–48, 158
Millas, Andrew, 39
Miller, Linda, 251
Miller, William, 242
Milrod, Christine, 159
Minichiello, Victor, 89
Minneapolis, MN, 102–3
misreporting, 197–99
Mixon, Bionca Elizabethelen, 113
Monto, Martin A., 159
motivational interviewing (MI), 242–44
MSNBC Undercover, 261

music lyrics, 131–33
Myers-Powell, Brenda, 10, 112–13, 119, 123
My Life, My Choice, 36, 252

Naar-King, Sylvie, 243–44
Nabokov, Vladimir, 52
Nashville Model, 239
National Human Trafficking Resource Center (NHTRC), 11; hotline of, 15, 257, 140, 175–76, 212, 260
National Institute of Justice, 112
National Network for Youth, 87
National Report on Domestic Minor Sex Trafficking, 113
National School Climate Survey, 88
National Survivor Network (NSN), 262, 264, 265–66
Nelly, 131, 136
neoliberals, 30–31, 157; and liberal feminism, 32, 33; on pornography, 42–43, 45–46, 54; on sex trafficking, 31–32, 68, 79, 89
Netherlands, 69, 71
Neumayer, E., 71
New York City, 67, 87–88, 252–53
New York Human Trafficking Intervention Initiative, 206
New York State, 205
New York Times, 262
New Zealand, 70, 71
Nguyen, Trina, 149
Nichols, Andrea J., 34, 94, 193, 225; on LGBTQ* youth, 87, 105; on sex traffickers, 119, 143, 254; on survivor services, 178, 219, 221, 222, 227, 235, 238, 240
No Child Left Behind, 101, 188

CPSIA information can be obtained
at www.ICGtesting.com
Printed in the USA
LVOW03s1101271217
560929LV00004B/23/P